A Day at the Beach

Other Books by Jim Toomey

Sherman's Lagoon: Ate That, What's Next?

Poodle: The Other White Meat

An Illustrated Guide to Shark Etiquette

Another Day in Paradise

Greetings from Sherman's Lagoon

Surf's Up!

The Shark Diaries

Catch of the Day

Treasury

Sherman's Lagoon 1991 to 2001:
Greatest Hits and Near Misses

A Day AT THE Beach

The Ninth SHERMAN'S LAGOON Collection
by Jim Toomey

Andrews McMeel Publishing

Kansas City

Sherman's Lagoon is distributed internationally by King Features Syndicate, Inc. For information, write King Features Syndicate, Inc., 888 Seventh Avenue, New York, New York 10019.

05 06 07 08 09 BBG 10 9 8 7 6 5 4 3 2 1

ISBN: 0-7407-5130-1

Library of Congress Control Number: 2004114458

Sherman's Lagoon may be viewed on the Internet at
www.shermanslagoon.com.

To William

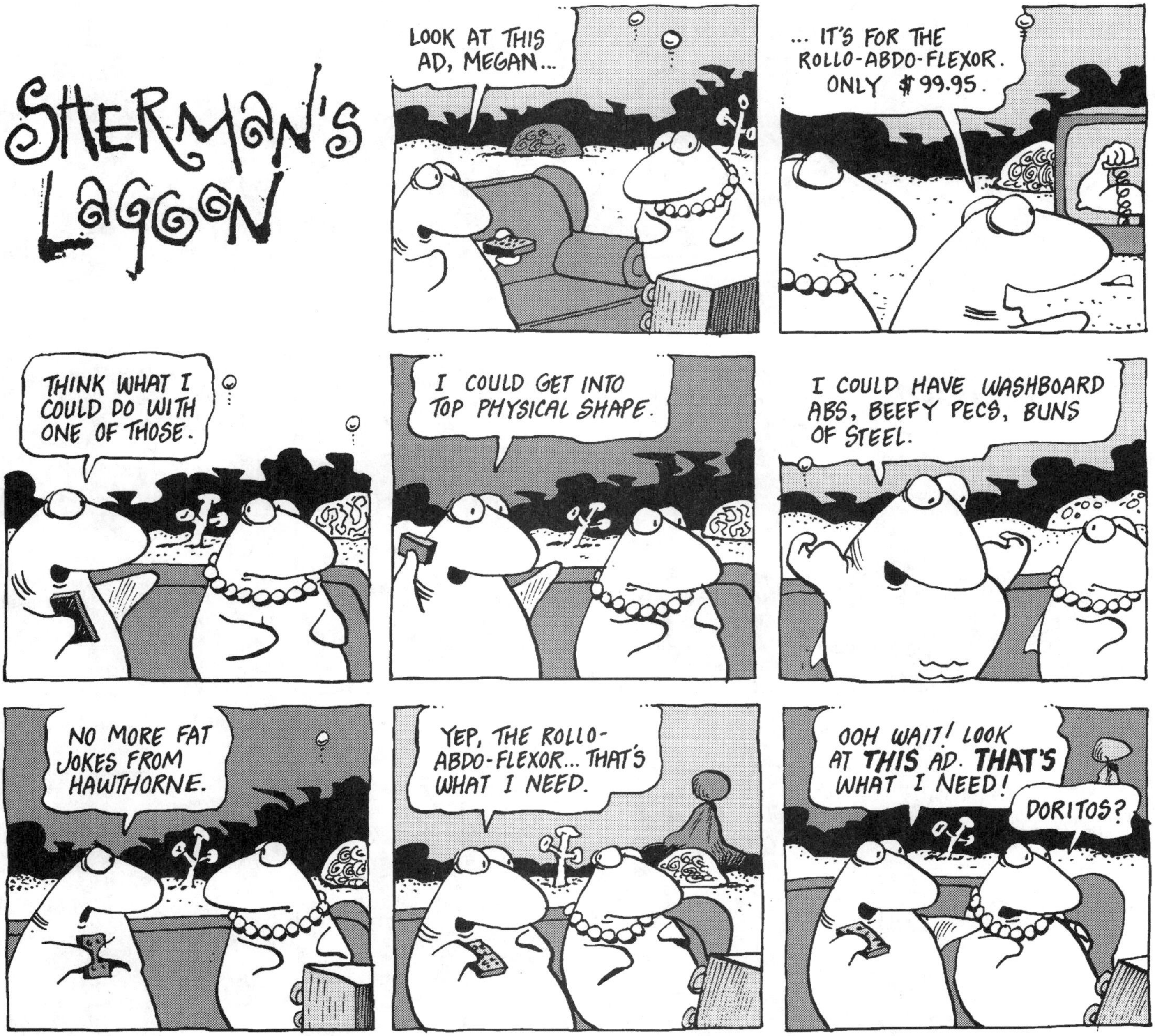
SHERMAN'S LAGOON
LOOK AT THIS AD, MEGAN...
... IT'S FOR THE ROLLO-ABDO-FLEXOR. ONLY $99.95.
THINK WHAT I COULD DO WITH ONE OF THOSE.
I COULD GET INTO TOP PHYSICAL SHAPE.
I COULD HAVE WASHBOARD ABS, BEEFY PECS, BUNS OF STEEL.
NO MORE FAT JOKES FROM HAWTHORNE.
YEP, THE ROLLO-ABDO-FLEXOR... THAT'S WHAT I NEED.
OOH WAIT! LOOK AT THIS AD. THAT'S WHAT I NEED!
DORITOS?

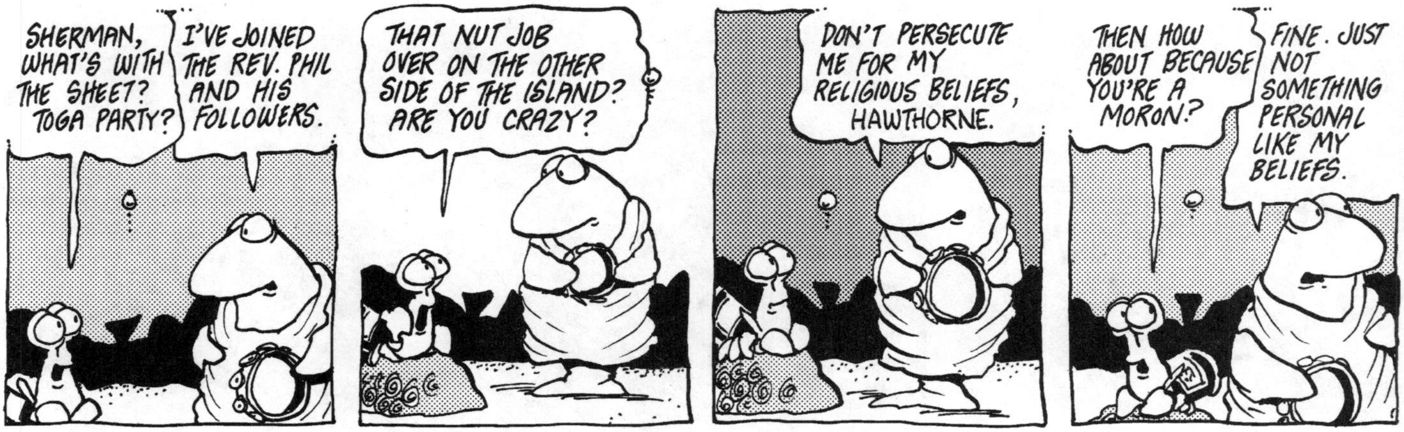
SHERMAN, WHAT'S WITH THE SHEET? TOGA PARTY?
I'VE JOINED THE REV. PHIL AND HIS FOLLOWERS.
THAT NUT JOB OVER ON THE OTHER SIDE OF THE ISLAND? ARE YOU CRAZY?
DON'T PERSECUTE ME FOR MY RELIGIOUS BELIEFS, HAWTHORNE.
THEN HOW ABOUT BECAUSE YOU'RE A MORON?
FINE. JUST NOT SOMETHING PERSONAL LIKE MY BELIEFS.

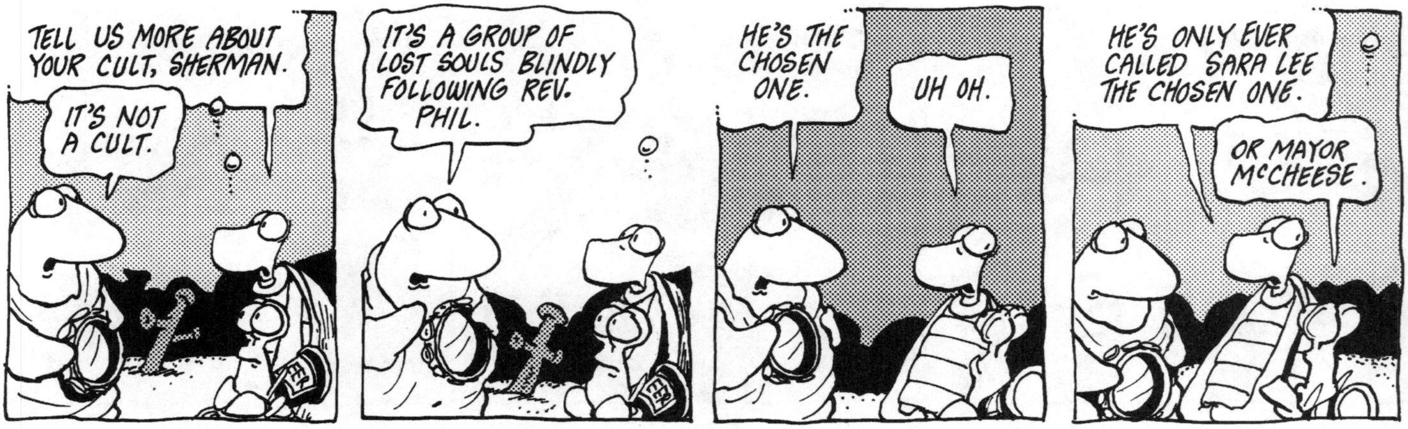
TELL US MORE ABOUT YOUR CULT, SHERMAN.
IT'S NOT A CULT.
IT'S A GROUP OF LOST SOULS BLINDLY FOLLOWING REV. PHIL.
HE'S THE CHOSEN ONE.
UH OH.
HE'S ONLY EVER CALLED SARA LEE THE CHOSEN ONE.
OR MAYOR McCHEESE.

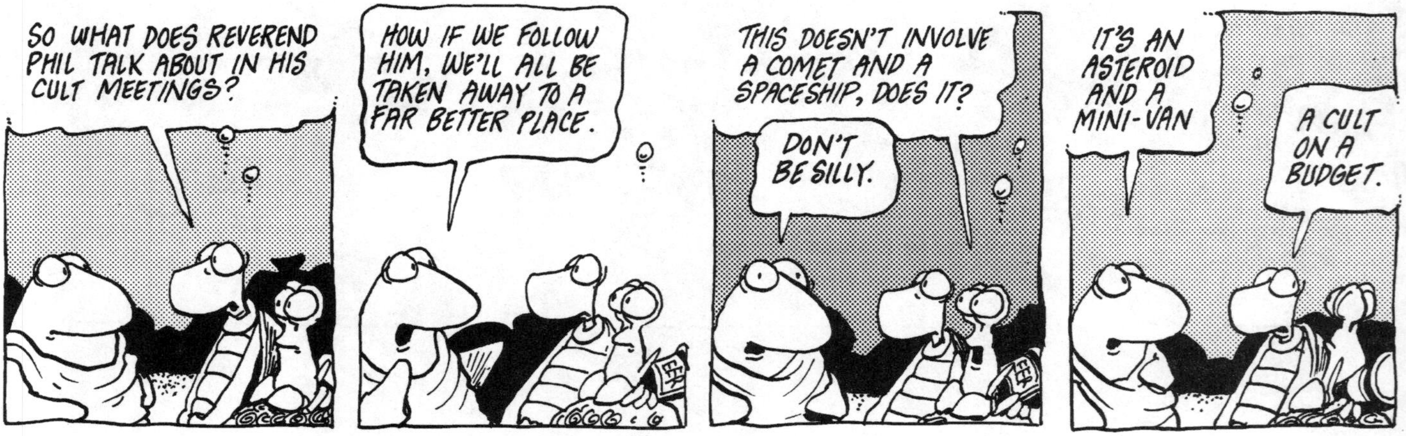
SO WHAT DOES REVEREND PHIL TALK ABOUT IN HIS CULT MEETINGS?
HOW IF WE FOLLOW HIM, WE'LL ALL BE TAKEN AWAY TO A FAR BETTER PLACE.
THIS DOESN'T INVOLVE A COMET AND A SPACESHIP, DOES IT?
DON'T BE SILLY.
IT'S AN ASTEROID AND A MINI-VAN
A CULT ON A BUDGET.

Panel 1: SO, ERNEST, DID YOU FIND ANYTHING OUT ON SHERMAN'S CULT?

YEAH, I DID.

Panel 2: WOW. IF THEY HAVE THEIR OWN WEBSITE THEY MUST BE POWERFUL.

THEY DON'T.

Panel 3: BUT, YOU CAN HOTLINK TO THEM OFF OF A MORE POWERFUL CULT LEADER'S WEB SITE. LOOK.

Panel 4: MARTHA STEWART?

DON'T BE SO NAIVE, FILLMORE.

Panel 5: SO, SHERMAN, WHAT'S THE APPEAL OF THIS CULT?

Panel 6: REVEREND PHIL CARES DEEPLY ABOUT EACH MEMBER OF THE GROUP.

UH-HUH.

Panel 7: HE TREATS YOU WITH RESPECT. HE MAKES YOU WANT TO CARRY OUT HIS WORD.

Panel 8: SO, WHAT EXACTLY ARE YOU CARRYING OUT THERE?

HIS DRY CLEANING.

Panel 9: SHERMAN, WHERE'S YOUR CULT OUTFIT?

I'VE LEFT THE REV. PHIL.

Panel 10: THEY WANTED ME TO DO SOMETHING THAT GOES AGAINST EVERYTHING I BELIEVE IN.

Panel 11: WHAT? LIE? STEAL? CHEAT?

WORSE.

Panel 12: GO ON A FAST.

THERE'S A DEAL BREAKER.

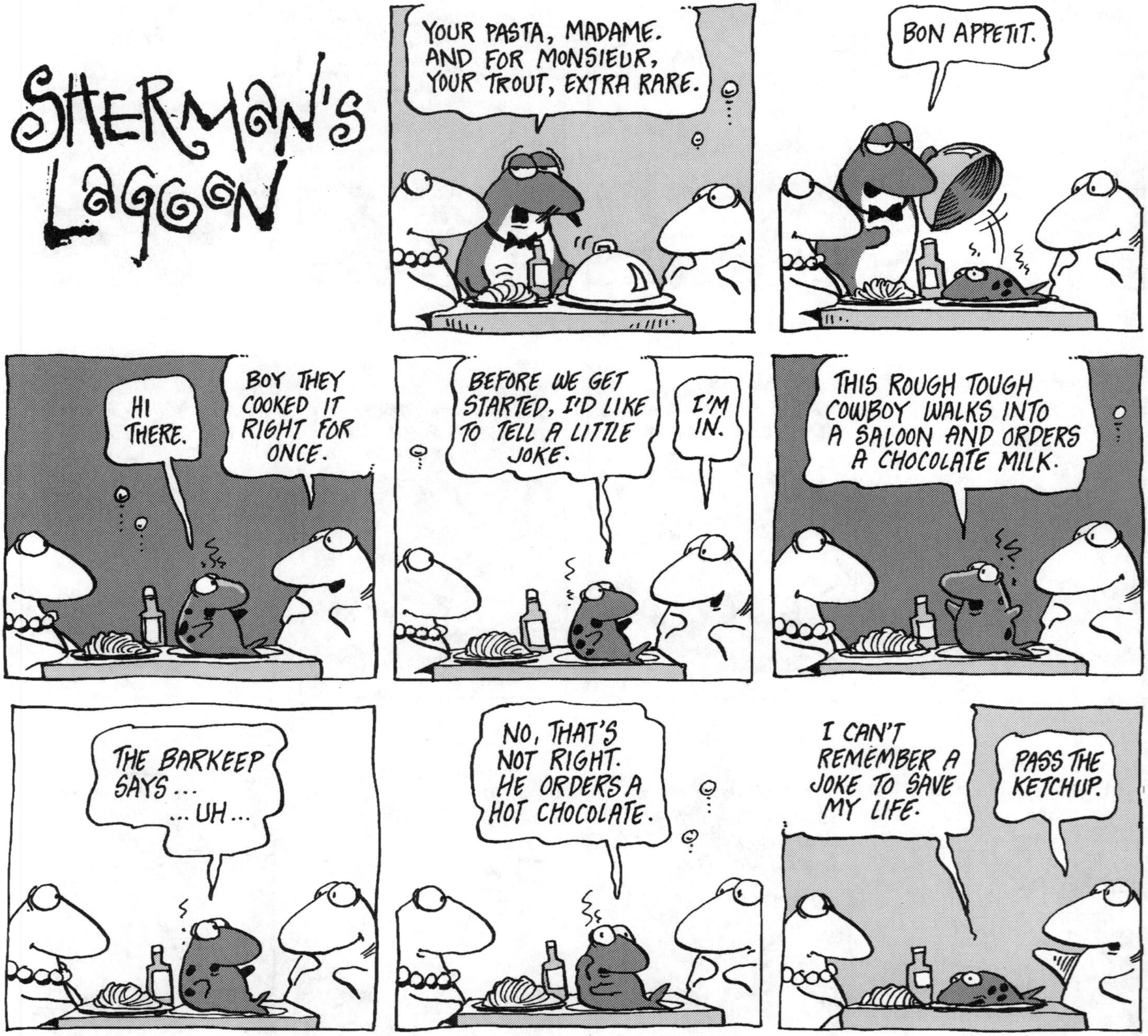
SHERMAN'S LAGOON
YOUR PASTA, MADAME. AND FOR MONSIEUR, YOUR TROUT, EXTRA RARE.
BON APPETIT.
HI THERE.
BOY THEY COOKED IT RIGHT FOR ONCE.
BEFORE WE GET STARTED, I'D LIKE TO TELL A LITTLE JOKE.
I'M IN.
THIS ROUGH TOUGH COWBOY WALKS INTO A SALOON AND ORDERS A CHOCOLATE MILK.
THE BARKEEP SAYS... ...UH...
NO, THAT'S NOT RIGHT. HE ORDERS A HOT CHOCOLATE.
I CAN'T REMEMBER A JOKE TO SAVE MY LIFE.
PASS THE KETCHUP.

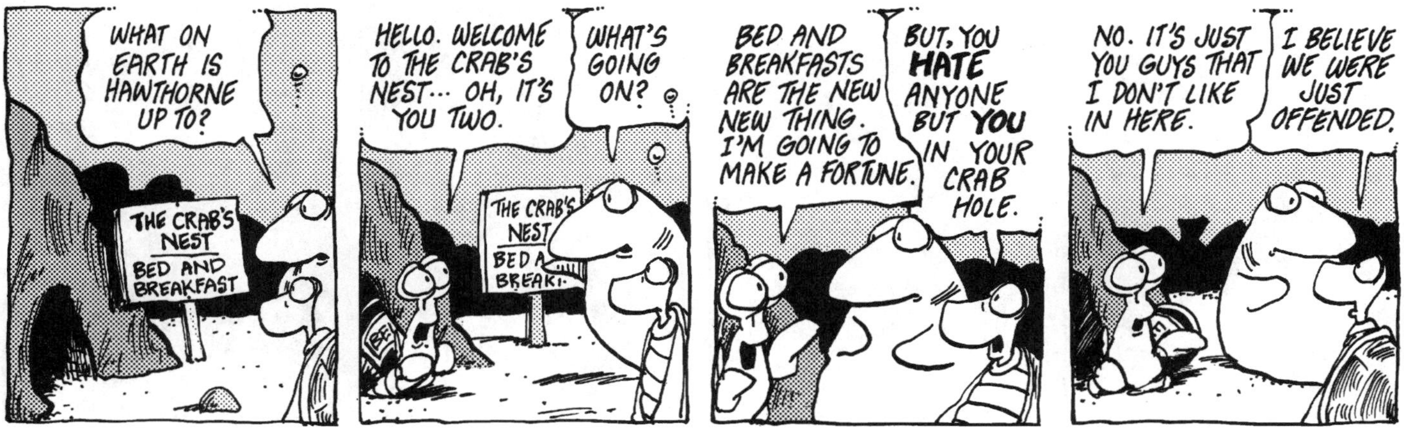
WHAT ON EARTH IS HAWTHORNE UP TO?
THE CRAB'S NEST
BED AND BREAKFAST
HELLO. WELCOME TO THE CRAB'S NEST... OH, IT'S YOU TWO.
WHAT'S GOING ON?
THE CRAB'S NEST
BED A
BREAK
BED AND BREAKFASTS ARE THE NEW NEW THING. I'M GOING TO MAKE A FORTUNE.
BUT, YOU **HATE** ANYONE BUT **YOU** IN YOUR CRAB HOLE.
NO. IT'S JUST YOU GUYS THAT I DON'T LIKE IN HERE.
I BELIEVE WE WERE JUST OFFENDED.

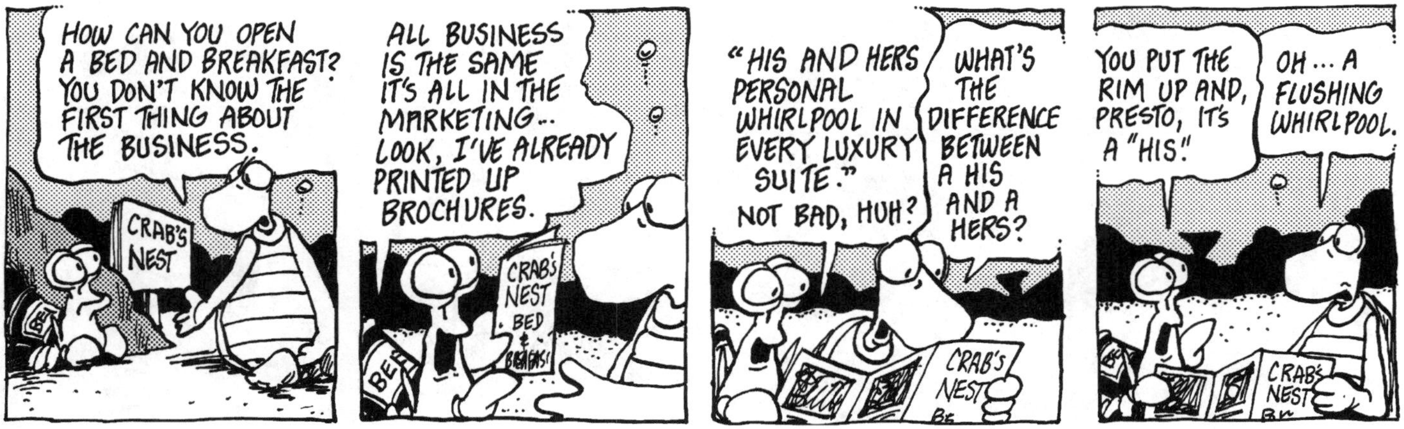
HOW CAN YOU OPEN A BED AND BREAKFAST? YOU DON'T KNOW THE FIRST THING ABOUT THE BUSINESS.
CRAB'S NEST
ALL BUSINESS IS THE SAME IT'S ALL IN THE MARKETING... LOOK, I'VE ALREADY PRINTED UP BROCHURES.
CRAB'S NEST BED & BREAKFAST
"HIS AND HERS PERSONAL WHIRLPOOL IN EVERY LUXURY SUITE." NOT BAD, HUH?
WHAT'S THE DIFFERENCE BETWEEN A HIS AND A HERS?
CRAB'S NEST
YOU PUT THE RIM UP AND, PRESTO, IT'S A "HIS."
OH... A FLUSHING WHIRLPOOL.
CRAB'S NEST

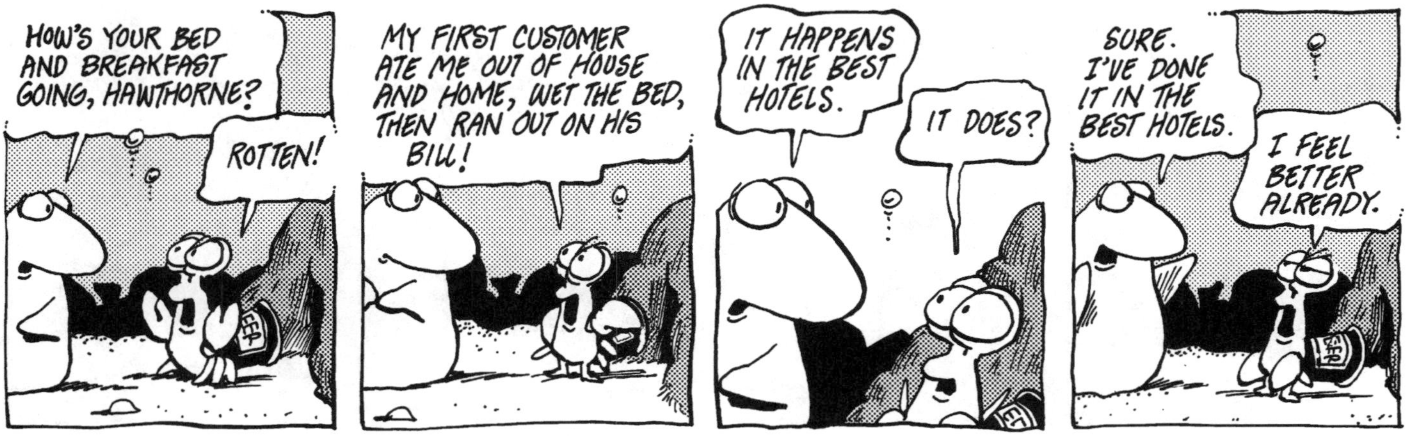
HOW'S YOUR BED AND BREAKFAST GOING, HAWTHORNE?
ROTTEN!
MY FIRST CUSTOMER ATE ME OUT OF HOUSE AND HOME, WET THE BED, THEN RAN OUT ON HIS BILL!
IT HAPPENS IN THE BEST HOTELS.
IT DOES?
SURE. I'VE DONE IT IN THE BEST HOTELS.
I FEEL BETTER ALREADY.

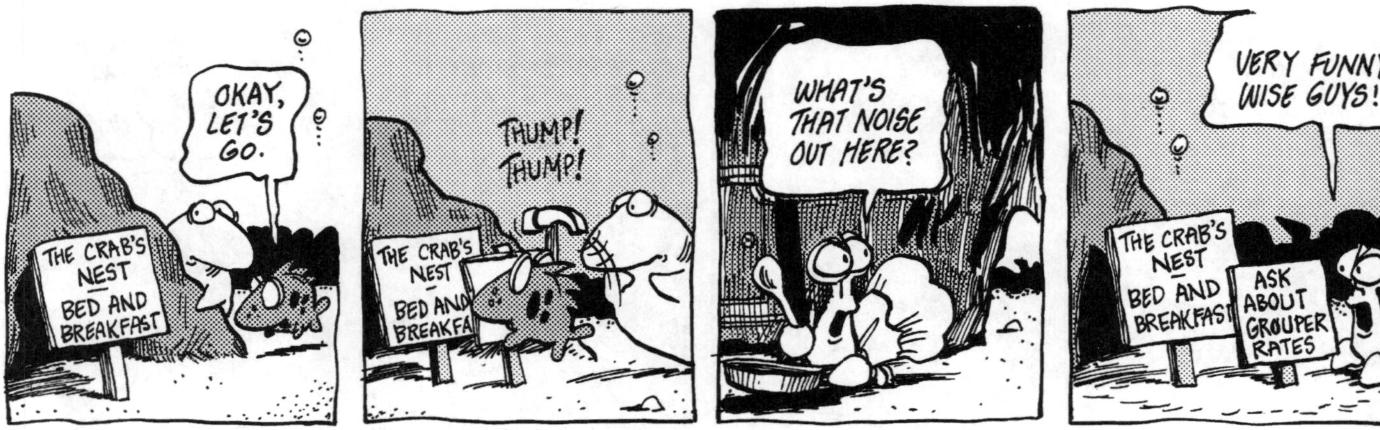
OKAY, LET'S GO.
THE CRAB'S NEST — BED AND BREAKFAST
THUMP! THUMP!
WHAT'S THAT NOISE OUT HERE?
VERY FUNNY, WISE GUYS!
ASK ABOUT GROUPER RATES

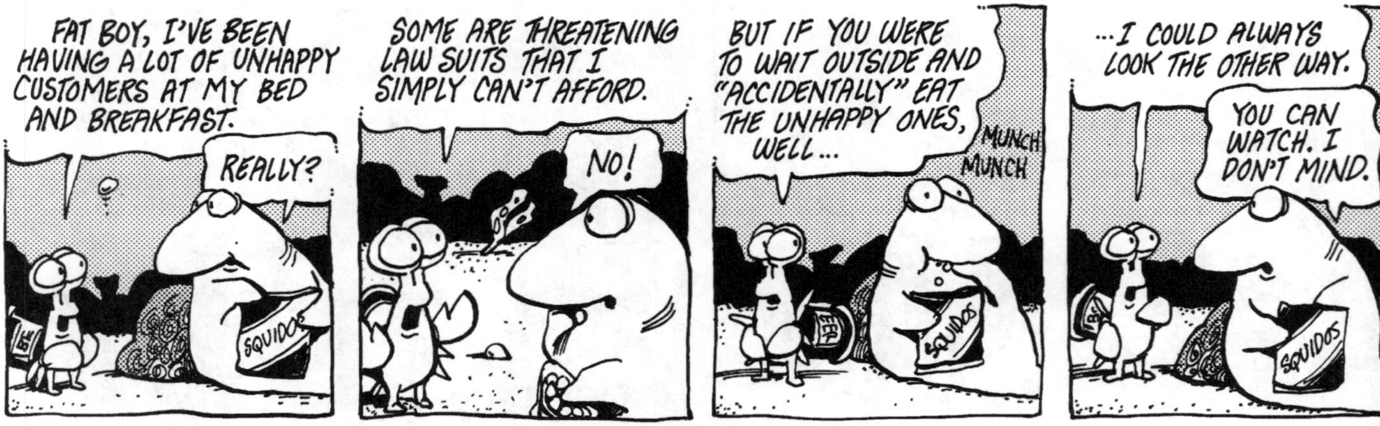
FAT BOY, I'VE BEEN HAVING A LOT OF UNHAPPY CUSTOMERS AT MY BED AND BREAKFAST.
REALLY?
SQUIDOS
SOME ARE THREATENING LAW SUITS THAT I SIMPLY CAN'T AFFORD.
NO!
BUT IF YOU WERE TO WAIT OUTSIDE AND "ACCIDENTALLY" EAT THE UNHAPPY ONES, WELL...
MUNCH MUNCH
...I COULD ALWAYS LOOK THE OTHER WAY.
YOU CAN WATCH. I DON'T MIND.

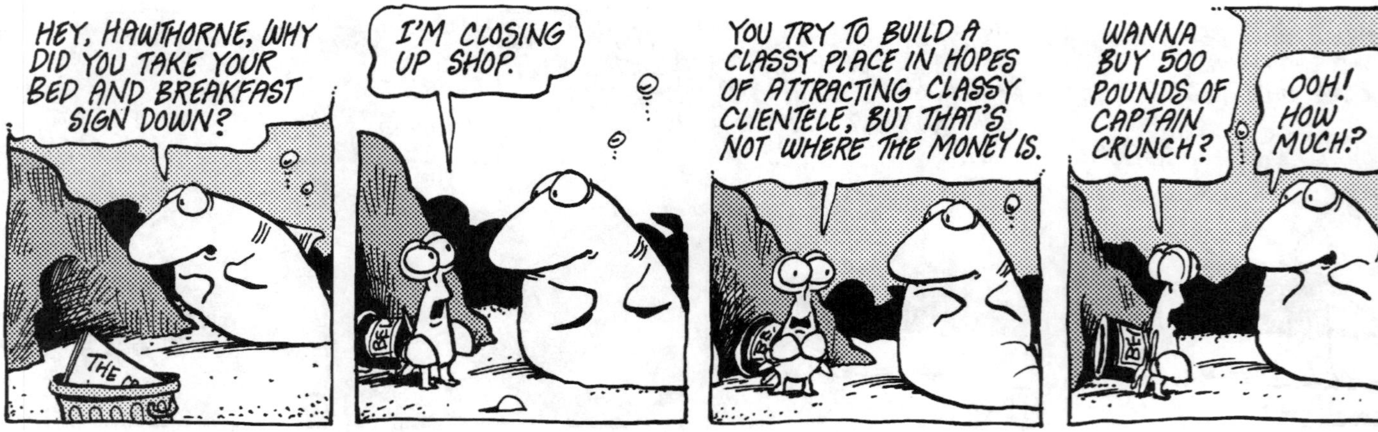
HEY, HAWTHORNE, WHY DID YOU TAKE YOUR BED AND BREAKFAST SIGN DOWN?
I'M CLOSING UP SHOP.
YOU TRY TO BUILD A CLASSY PLACE IN HOPES OF ATTRACTING CLASSY CLIENTELE, BUT THAT'S NOT WHERE THE MONEY IS.
WANNA BUY 500 POUNDS OF CAPTAIN CRUNCH?
OOH! HOW MUCH?

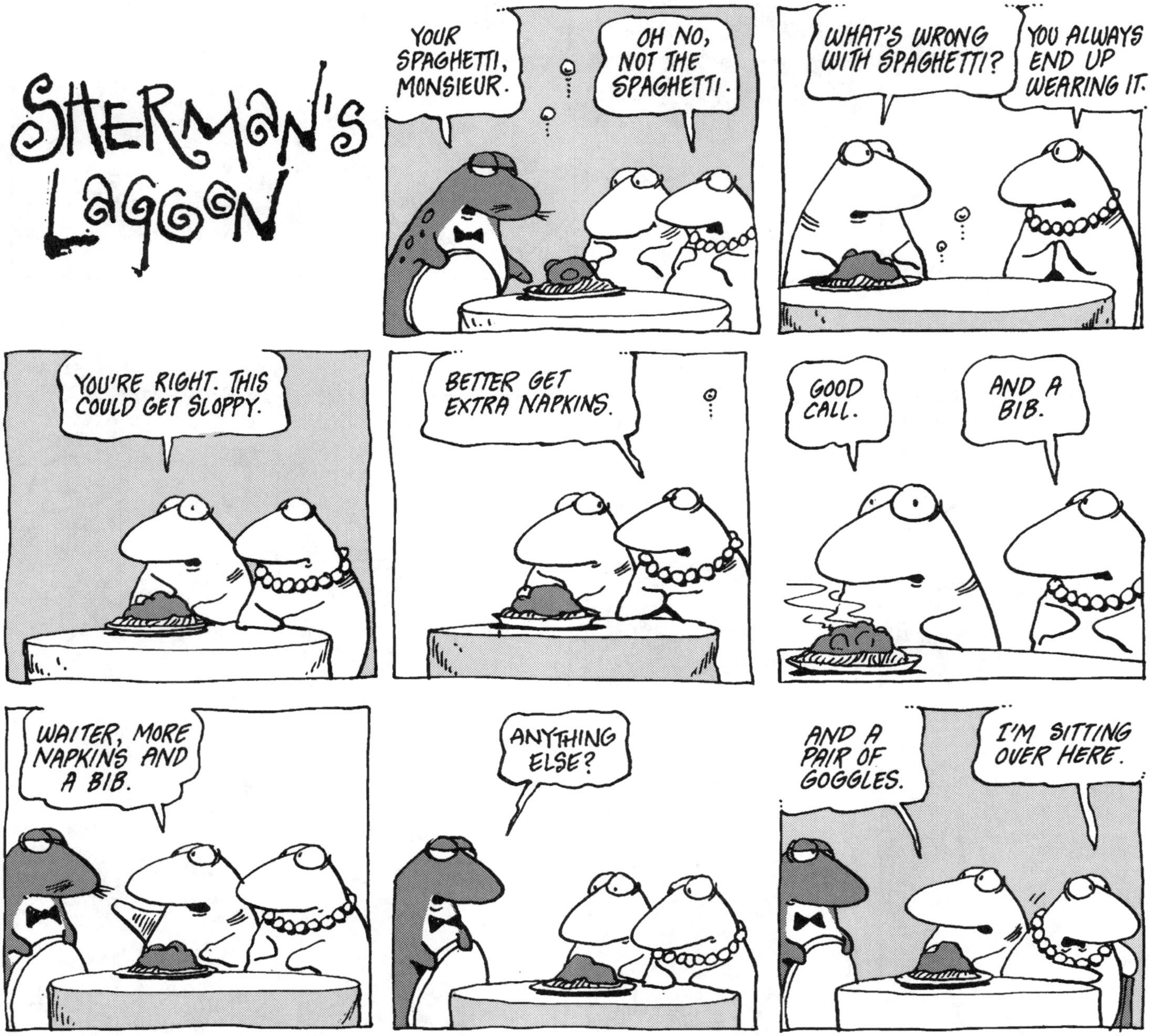
SHERMAN'S LAGOON
YOUR SPAGHETTI, MONSIEUR.
OH NO, NOT THE SPAGHETTI.
WHAT'S WRONG WITH SPAGHETTI?
YOU ALWAYS END UP WEARING IT.
YOU'RE RIGHT. THIS COULD GET SLOPPY.
BETTER GET EXTRA NAPKINS.
GOOD CALL.
AND A BIB.
WAITER, MORE NAPKINS AND A BIB.
ANYTHING ELSE?
AND A PAIR OF GOGGLES.
I'M SITTING OVER HERE.

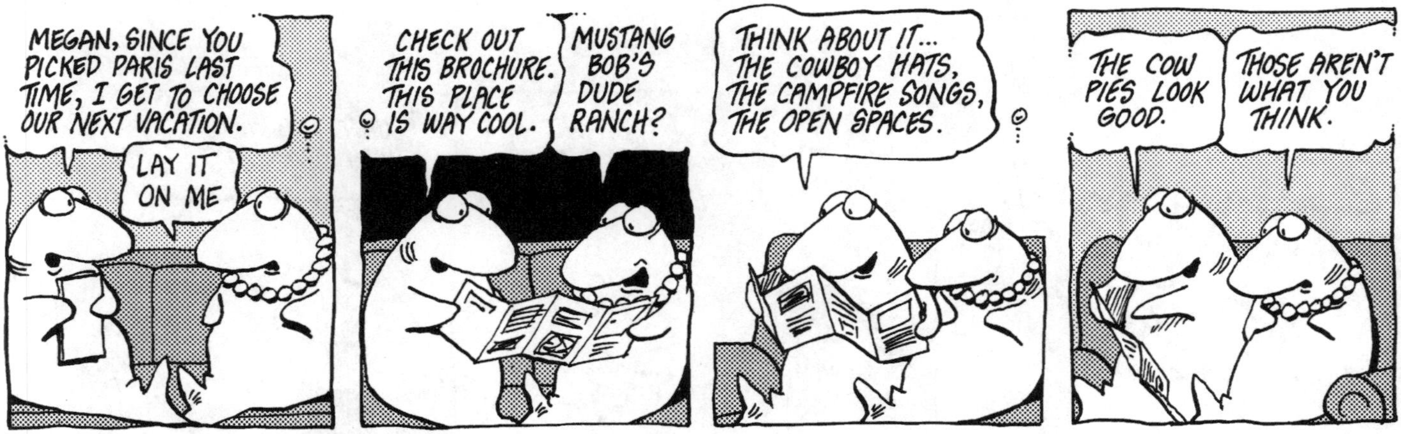
MEGAN, SINCE YOU PICKED PARIS LAST TIME, I GET TO CHOOSE OUR NEXT VACATION.
LAY IT ON ME
CHECK OUT THIS BROCHURE. THIS PLACE IS WAY COOL.
MUSTANG BOB'S DUDE RANCH?
THINK ABOUT IT... THE COWBOY HATS, THE CAMPFIRE SONGS, THE OPEN SPACES.
THE COW PIES LOOK GOOD.
THOSE AREN'T WHAT YOU THINK.

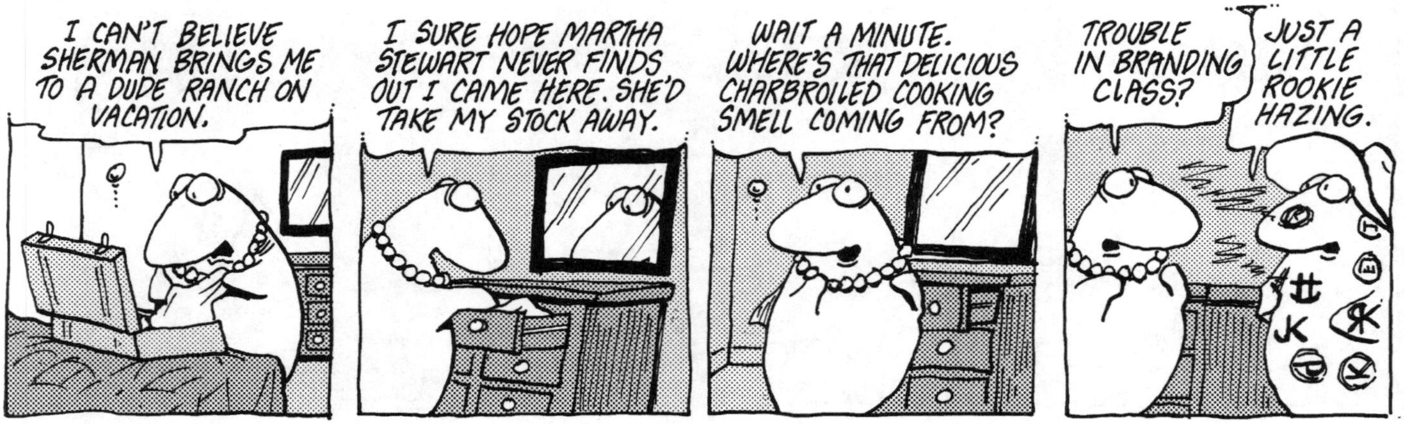
I CAN'T BELIEVE SHERMAN BRINGS ME TO A DUDE RANCH ON VACATION.
I SURE HOPE MARTHA STEWART NEVER FINDS OUT I CAME HERE. SHE'D TAKE MY STOCK AWAY.
WAIT A MINUTE. WHERE'S THAT DELICIOUS CHARBROILED COOKING SMELL COMING FROM?
TROUBLE IN BRANDING CLASS?
JUST A LITTLE ROOKIE HAZING.

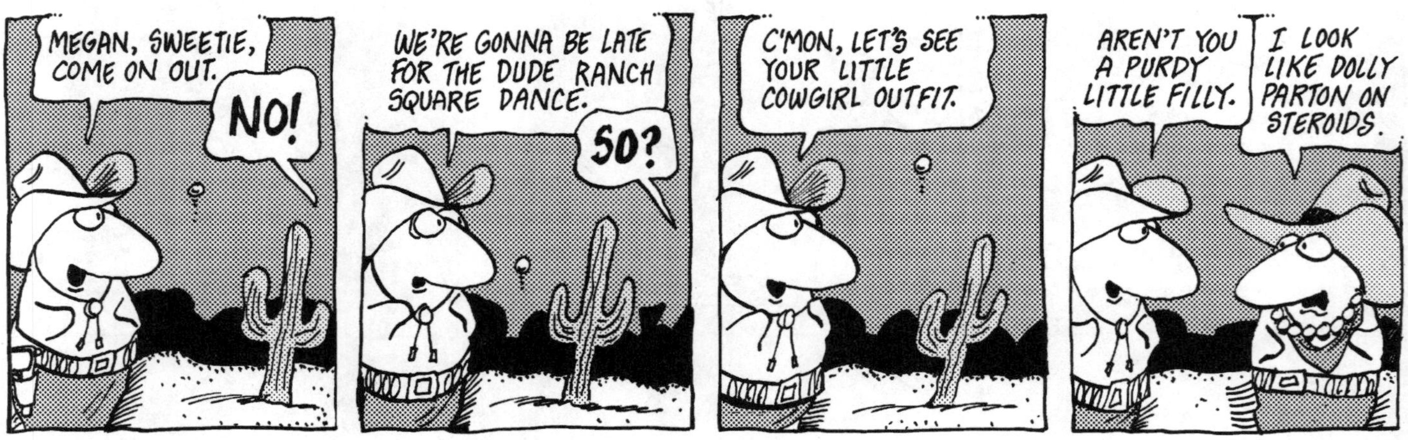
MEGAN, SWEETIE, COME ON OUT.
NO!
WE'RE GONNA BE LATE FOR THE DUDE RANCH SQUARE DANCE.
SO?
C'MON, LET'S SEE YOUR LITTLE COWGIRL OUTFIT.
AREN'T YOU A PURDY LITTLE FILLY.
I LOOK LIKE DOLLY PARTON ON STEROIDS.

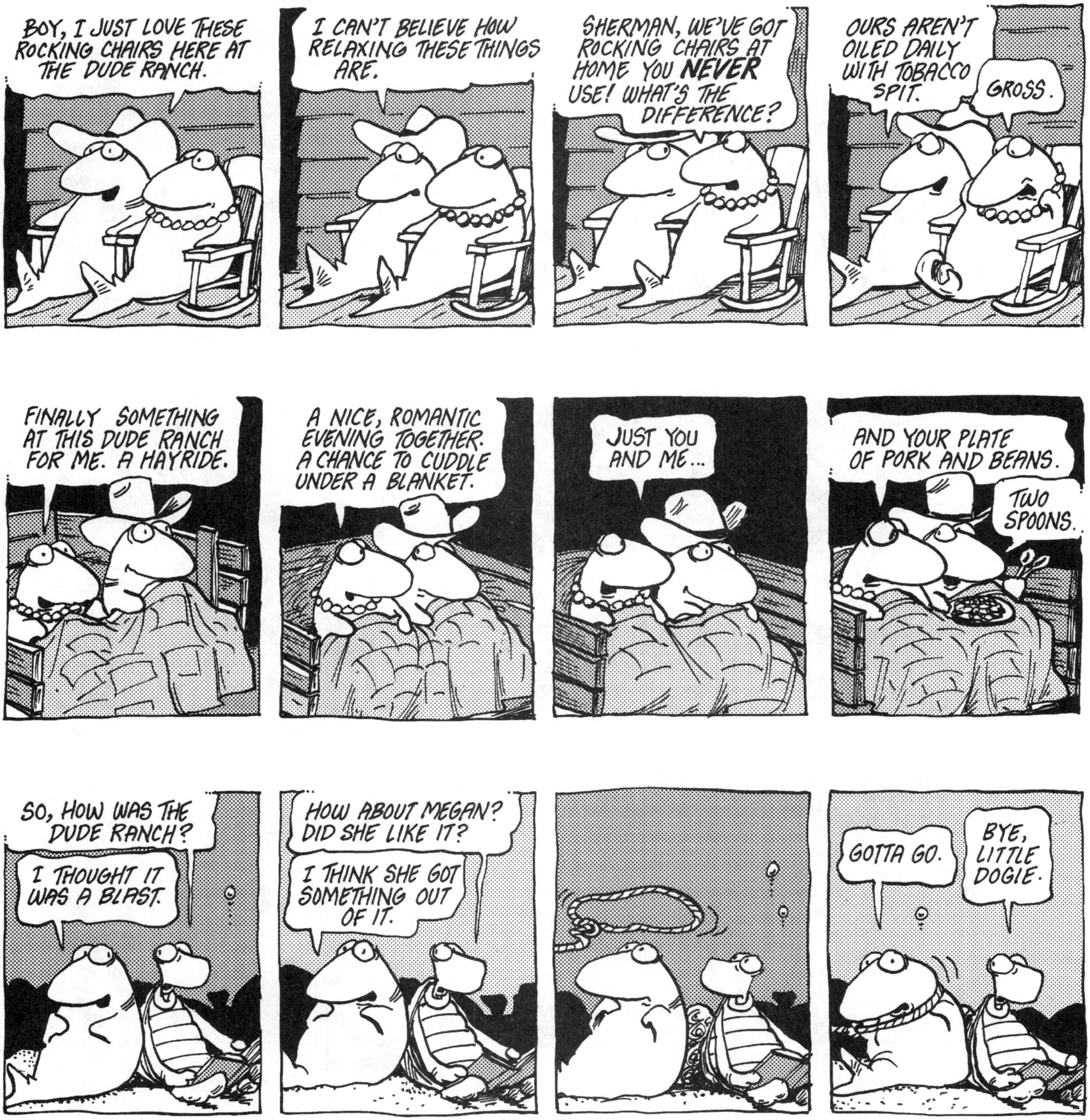
BOY, I JUST LOVE THESE ROCKING CHAIRS HERE AT THE DUDE RANCH.
I CAN'T BELIEVE HOW RELAXING THESE THINGS ARE.
SHERMAN, WE'VE GOT ROCKING CHAIRS AT HOME YOU **NEVER** USE! WHAT'S THE DIFFERENCE?
OURS AREN'T OILED DAILY WITH TOBACCO SPIT.
GROSS.
FINALLY SOMETHING AT THIS DUDE RANCH FOR ME. A HAYRIDE.
A NICE, ROMANTIC EVENING TOGETHER. A CHANCE TO CUDDLE UNDER A BLANKET.
JUST YOU AND ME...
AND YOUR PLATE OF PORK AND BEANS.
TWO SPOONS.
SO, HOW WAS THE DUDE RANCH?
I THOUGHT IT WAS A BLAST.
HOW ABOUT MEGAN? DID SHE LIKE IT?
I THINK SHE GOT SOMETHING OUT OF IT.
GOTTA GO.
BYE, LITTLE DOGIE.

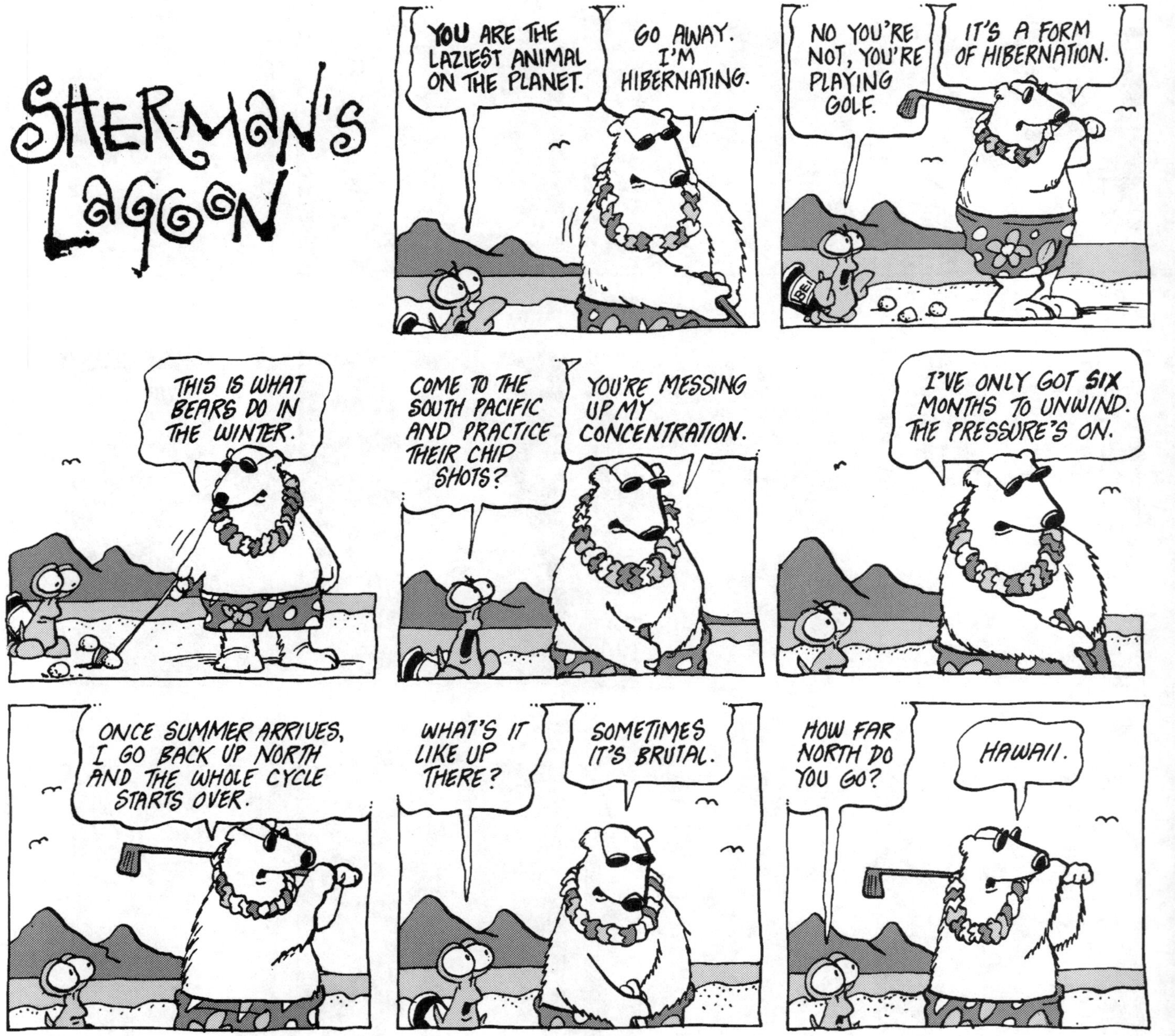
SHERMAN'S LAGOON
YOU ARE THE LAZIEST ANIMAL ON THE PLANET.
GO AWAY. I'M HIBERNATING.
NO YOU'RE NOT, YOU'RE PLAYING GOLF.
IT'S A FORM OF HIBERNATION.
THIS IS WHAT BEARS DO IN THE WINTER.
COME TO THE SOUTH PACIFIC AND PRACTICE THEIR CHIP SHOTS?
YOU'RE MESSING UP MY CONCENTRATION.
I'VE ONLY GOT SIX MONTHS TO UNWIND. THE PRESSURE'S ON.
ONCE SUMMER ARRIVES, I GO BACK UP NORTH AND THE WHOLE CYCLE STARTS OVER.
WHAT'S IT LIKE UP THERE?
SOMETIMES IT'S BRUTAL.
HOW FAR NORTH DO YOU GO?
HAWAII.

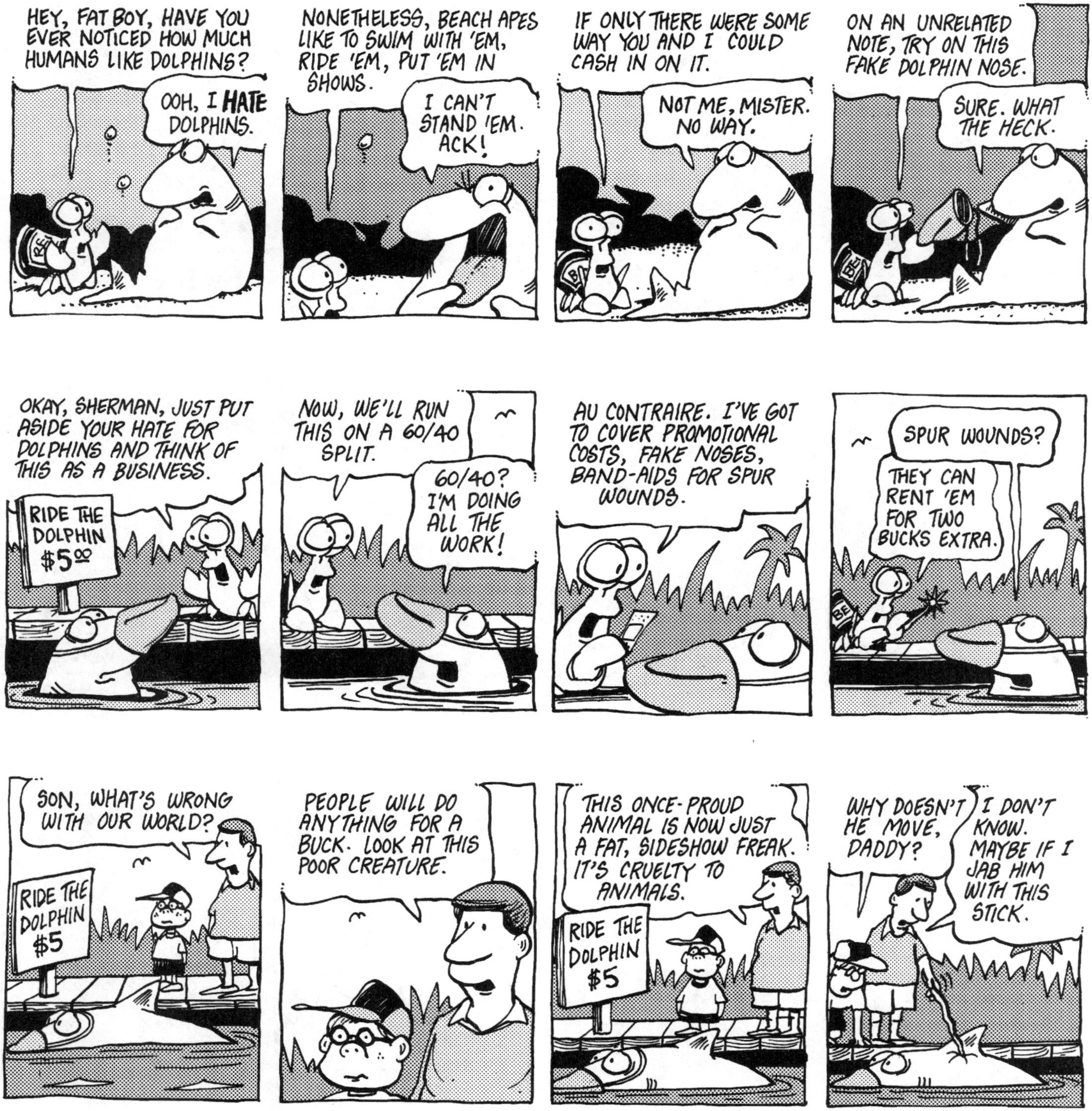
HEY, FAT BOY, HAVE YOU EVER NOTICED HOW MUCH HUMANS LIKE DOLPHINS?
OOH, I HATE DOLPHINS.
NONETHELESS, BEACH APES LIKE TO SWIM WITH 'EM, RIDE 'EM, PUT 'EM IN SHOWS.
I CAN'T STAND 'EM. ACK!
IF ONLY THERE WERE SOME WAY YOU AND I COULD CASH IN ON IT.
NOT ME, MISTER. NO WAY.
ON AN UNRELATED NOTE, TRY ON THIS FAKE DOLPHIN NOSE.
SURE. WHAT THE HECK.
OKAY, SHERMAN, JUST PUT ASIDE YOUR HATE FOR DOLPHINS AND THINK OF THIS AS A BUSINESS.
RIDE THE DOLPHIN $5.00
NOW, WE'LL RUN THIS ON A 60/40 SPLIT.
60/40? I'M DOING ALL THE WORK!
AU CONTRAIRE. I'VE GOT TO COVER PROMOTIONAL COSTS, FAKE NOSES, BAND-AIDS FOR SPUR WOUNDS.
SPUR WOUNDS?
THEY CAN RENT 'EM FOR TWO BUCKS EXTRA.
SON, WHAT'S WRONG WITH OUR WORLD?
RIDE THE DOLPHIN $5
PEOPLE WILL DO ANYTHING FOR A BUCK. LOOK AT THIS POOR CREATURE.
THIS ONCE-PROUD ANIMAL IS NOW JUST A FAT, SIDESHOW FREAK. IT'S CRUELTY TO ANIMALS.
RIDE THE DOLPHIN $5
WHY DOESN'T HE MOVE, DADDY?
I DON'T KNOW. MAYBE IF I JAB HIM WITH THIS STICK.

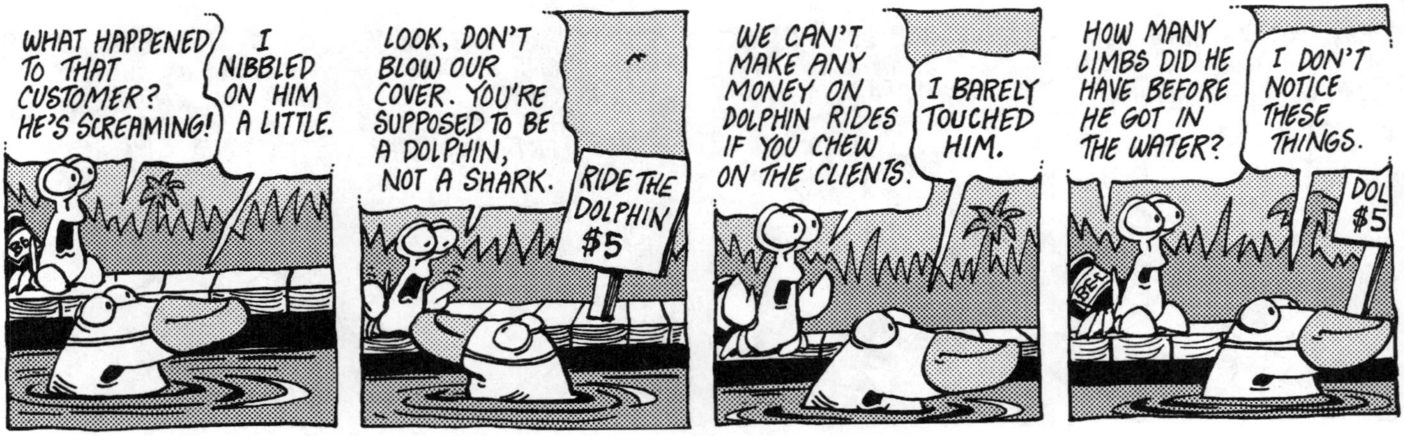
WHAT HAPPENED TO THAT CUSTOMER? HE'S SCREAMING!
I NIBBLED ON HIM A LITTLE.
LOOK, DON'T BLOW OUR COVER. YOU'RE SUPPOSED TO BE A DOLPHIN, NOT A SHARK.
RIDE THE DOLPHIN $5
WE CAN'T MAKE ANY MONEY ON DOLPHIN RIDES IF YOU CHEW ON THE CLIENTS.
I BARELY TOUCHED HIM.
HOW MANY LIMBS DID HE HAVE BEFORE HE GOT IN THE WATER?
I DON'T NOTICE THESE THINGS.
DOL $5

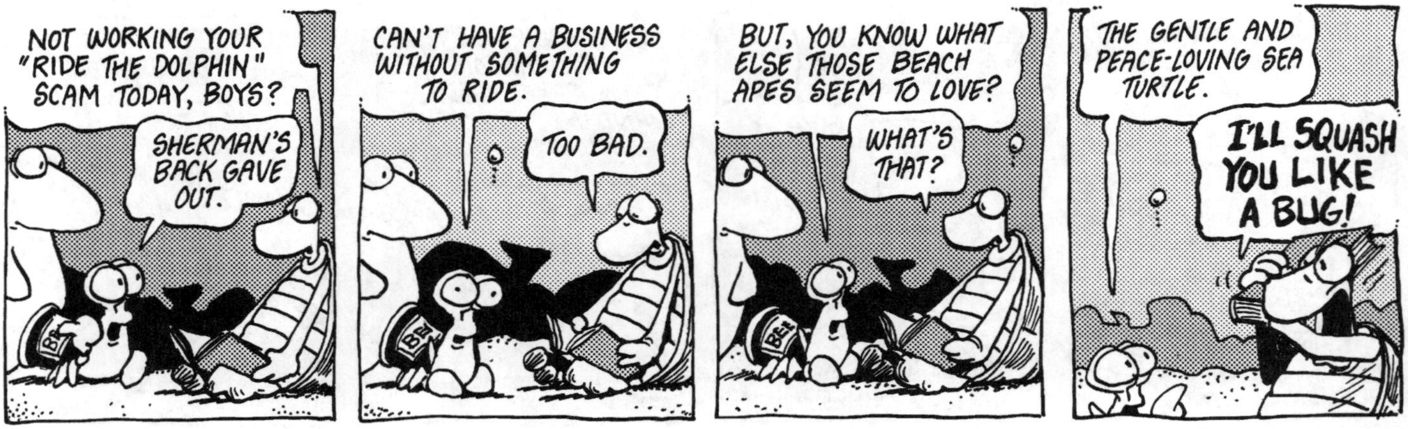
NOT WORKING YOUR "RIDE THE DOLPHIN" SCAM TODAY, BOYS?
SHERMAN'S BACK GAVE OUT.
CAN'T HAVE A BUSINESS WITHOUT SOMETHING TO RIDE.
TOO BAD.
BUT, YOU KNOW WHAT ELSE THOSE BEACH APES SEEM TO LOVE?
WHAT'S THAT?
THE GENTLE AND PEACE-LOVING SEA TURTLE.
I'LL SQUASH YOU LIKE A BUG!

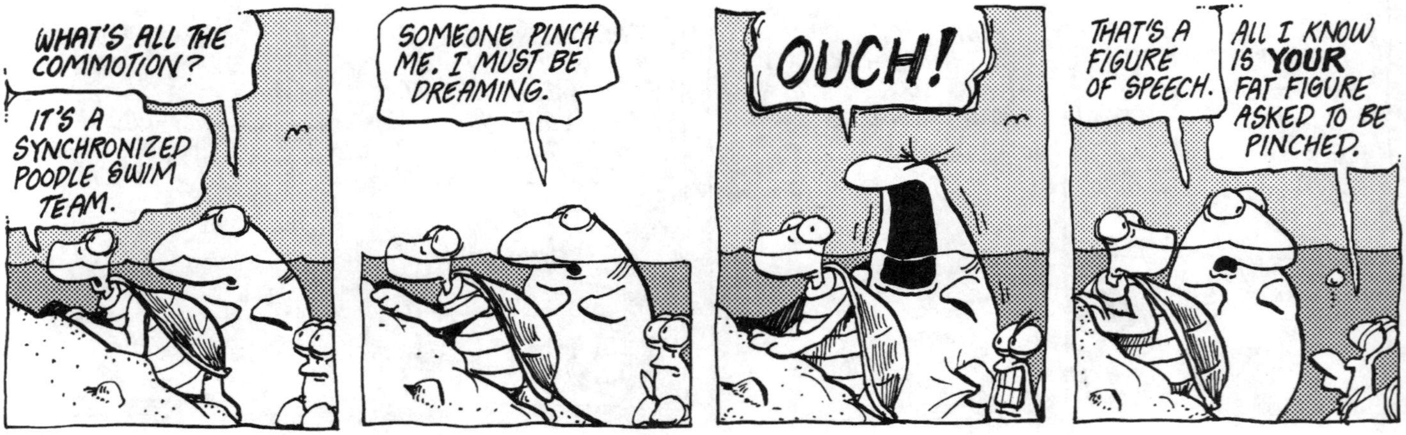
WHAT'S ALL THE COMMOTION?
IT'S A SYNCHRONIZED POODLE SWIM TEAM.
SOMEONE PINCH ME. I MUST BE DREAMING.
OUCH!
THAT'S A FIGURE OF SPEECH.
ALL I KNOW IS YOUR FAT FIGURE ASKED TO BE PINCHED.

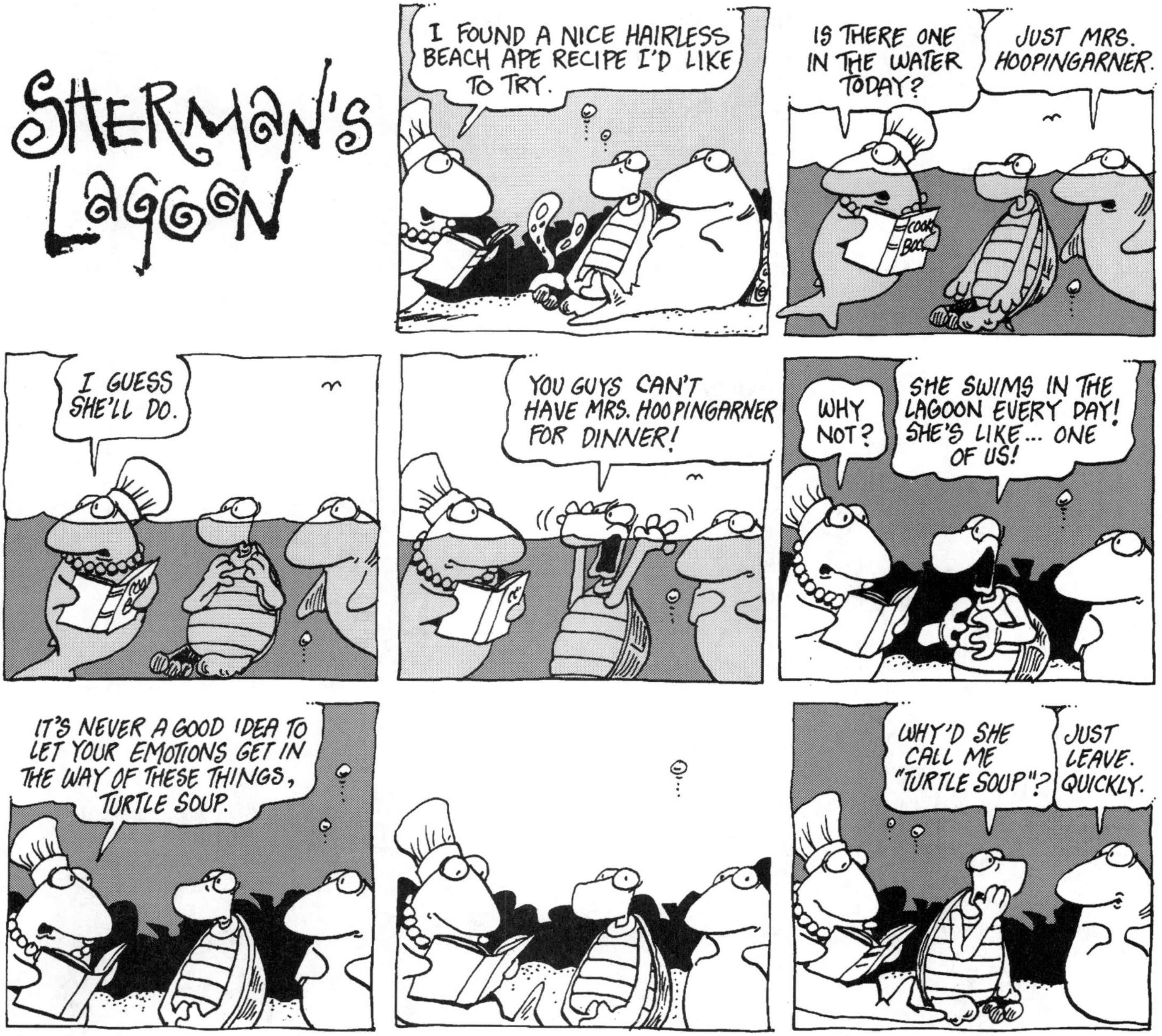
SHERMAN'S LAGOON
I FOUND A NICE HAIRLESS BEACH APE RECIPE I'D LIKE TO TRY.
IS THERE ONE IN THE WATER TODAY?
JUST MRS. HOOPINGARNER.
I GUESS SHE'LL DO.
YOU GUYS CAN'T HAVE MRS. HOOPINGARNER FOR DINNER!
WHY NOT?
SHE SWIMS IN THE LAGOON EVERY DAY! SHE'S LIKE... ONE OF US!
IT'S NEVER A GOOD IDEA TO LET YOUR EMOTIONS GET IN THE WAY OF THESE THINGS, TURTLE SOUP.
WHY'D SHE CALL ME "TURTLE SOUP"?
JUST LEAVE. QUICKLY.

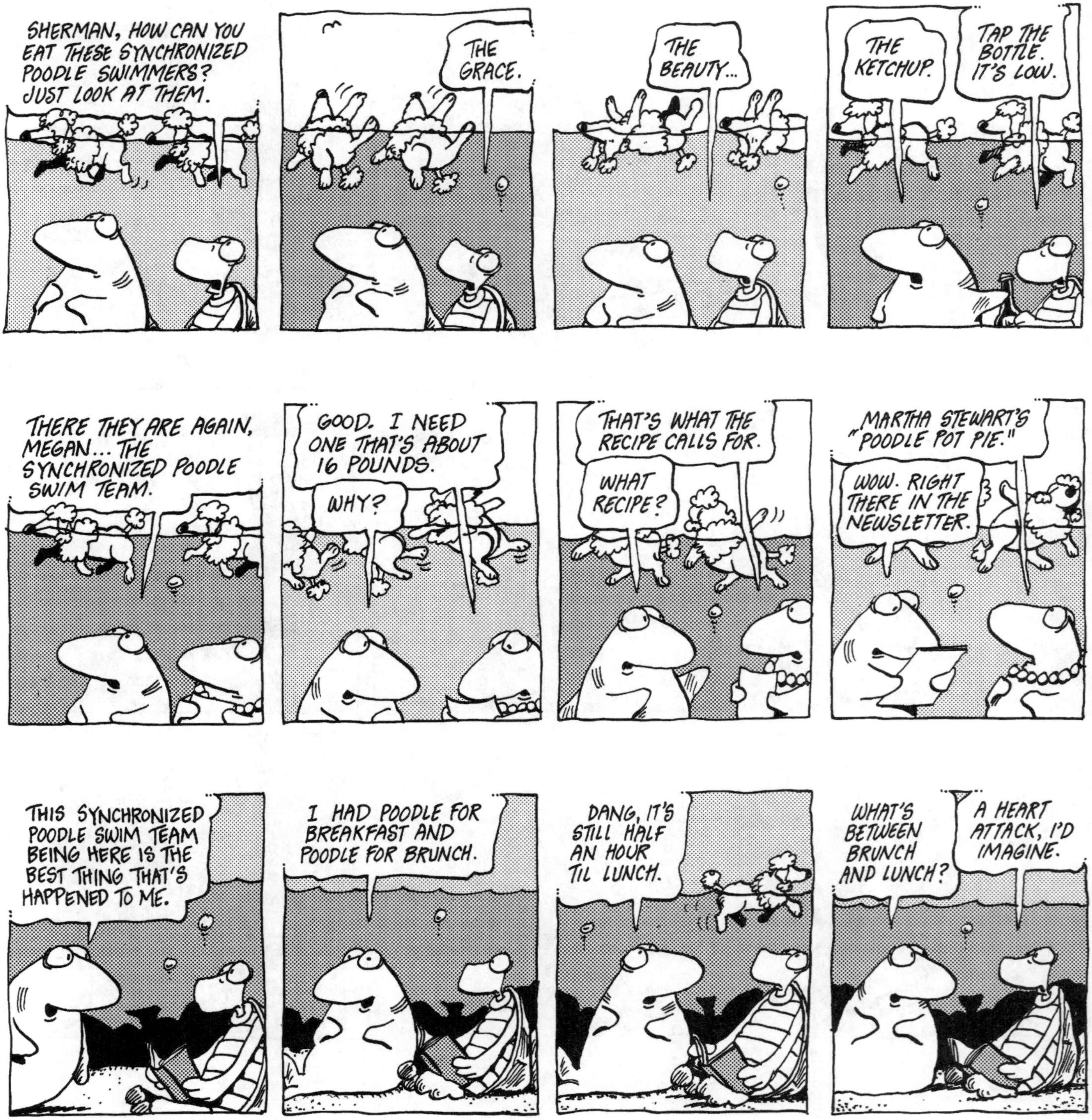
SHERMAN, HOW CAN YOU EAT THESE SYNCHRONIZED POODLE SWIMMERS? JUST LOOK AT THEM.
THE GRACE.
THE BEAUTY...
THE KETCHUP.
TAP THE BOTTLE. IT'S LOW.
THERE THEY ARE AGAIN, MEGAN... THE SYNCHRONIZED POODLE SWIM TEAM.
GOOD. I NEED ONE THAT'S ABOUT 16 POUNDS.
WHY?
THAT'S WHAT THE RECIPE CALLS FOR.
WHAT RECIPE?
"MARTHA STEWART'S "POODLE POT PIE."
WOW. RIGHT THERE IN THE NEWSLETTER.
THIS SYNCHRONIZED POODLE SWIM TEAM BEING HERE IS THE BEST THING THAT'S HAPPENED TO ME.
I HAD POODLE FOR BREAKFAST AND POODLE FOR BRUNCH.
DANG, IT'S STILL HALF AN HOUR TIL LUNCH.
WHAT'S BETWEEN BRUNCH AND LUNCH?
A HEART ATTACK, I'D IMAGINE.

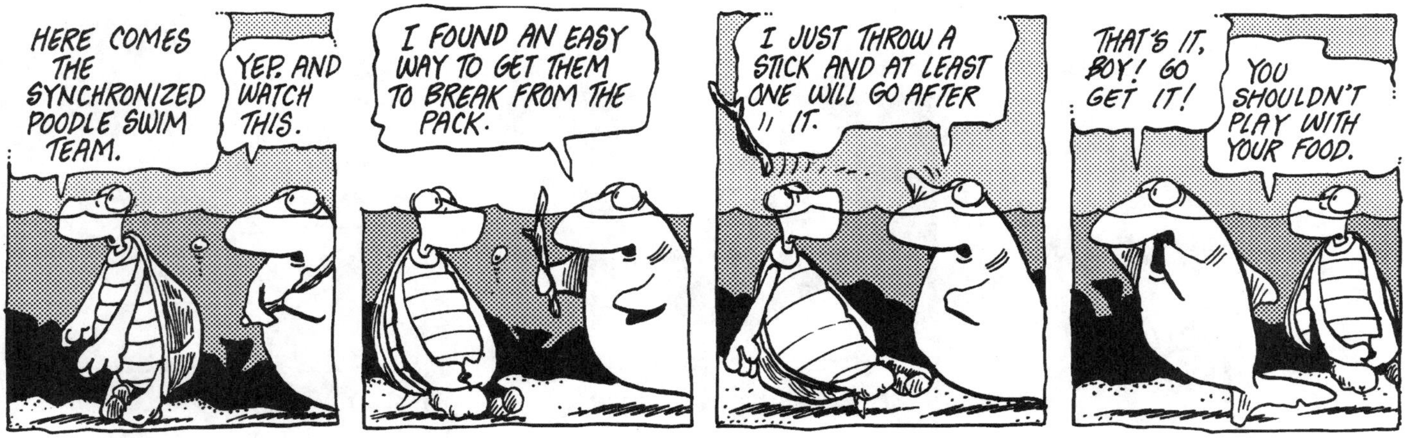
HERE COMES THE SYNCHRONIZED POODLE SWIM TEAM.
YEP. AND WATCH THIS.
I FOUND AN EASY WAY TO GET THEM TO BREAK FROM THE PACK.
I JUST THROW A STICK AND AT LEAST ONE WILL GO AFTER IT.
THAT'S IT, BOY! GO GET IT!
YOU SHOULDN'T PLAY WITH YOUR FOOD.

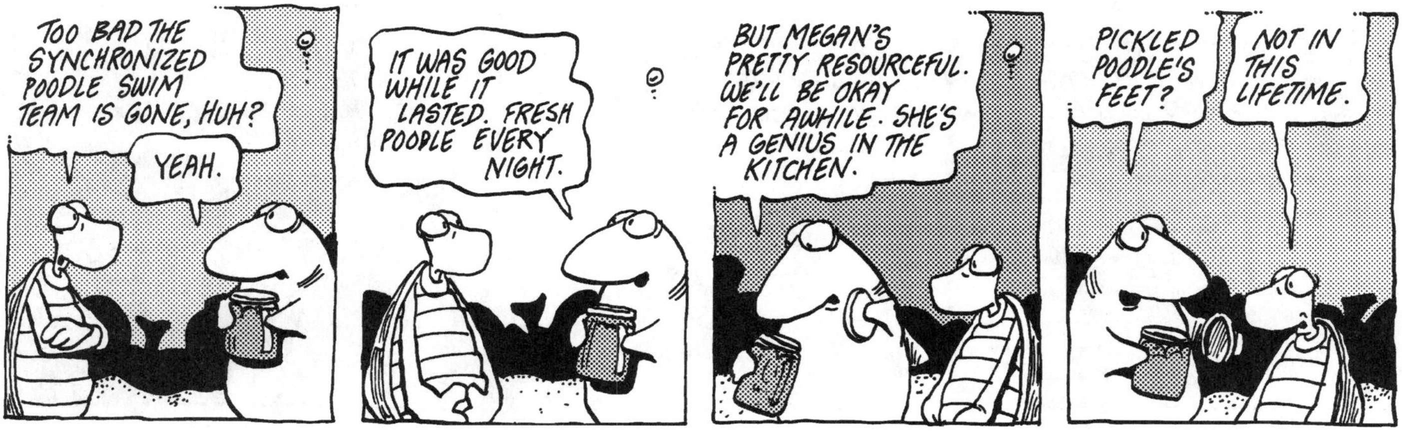
TOO BAD THE SYNCHRONIZED POODLE SWIM TEAM IS GONE, HUH?
YEAH.
IT WAS GOOD WHILE IT LASTED. FRESH POODLE EVERY NIGHT.
BUT MEGAN'S PRETTY RESOURCEFUL. WE'LL BE OKAY FOR AWHILE. SHE'S A GENIUS IN THE KITCHEN.
PICKLED POODLE'S FEET?
NOT IN THIS LIFETIME.

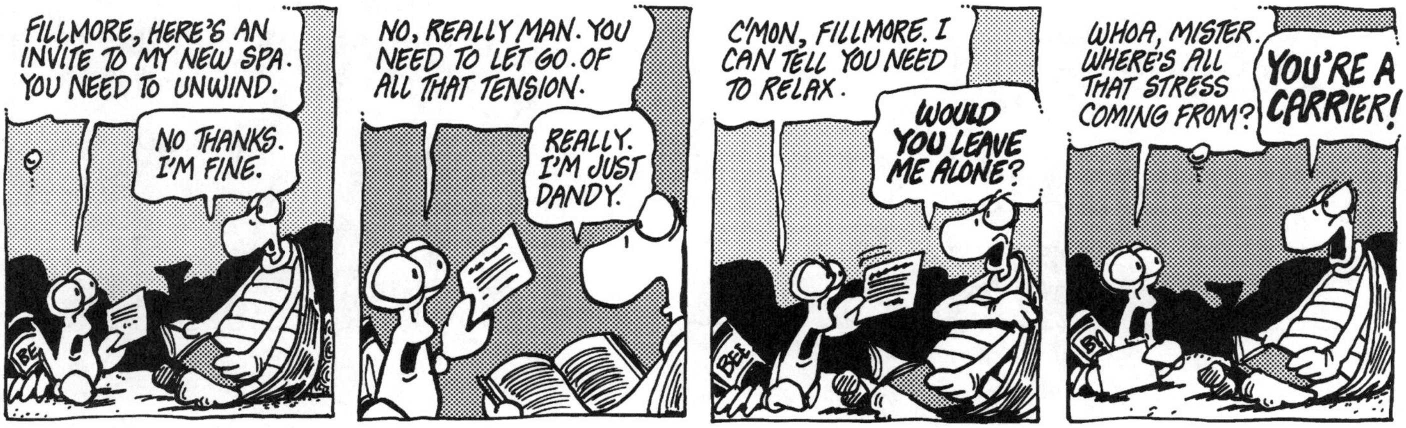
FILLMORE, HERE'S AN INVITE TO MY NEW SPA. YOU NEED TO UNWIND.
NO THANKS. I'M FINE.
NO, REALLY MAN. YOU NEED TO LET GO OF ALL THAT TENSION.
REALLY. I'M JUST DANDY.
C'MON, FILLMORE. I CAN TELL YOU NEED TO RELAX.
WOULD YOU LEAVE ME ALONE?
WHOA, MISTER. WHERE'S ALL THAT STRESS COMING FROM?
YOU'RE A CARRIER!

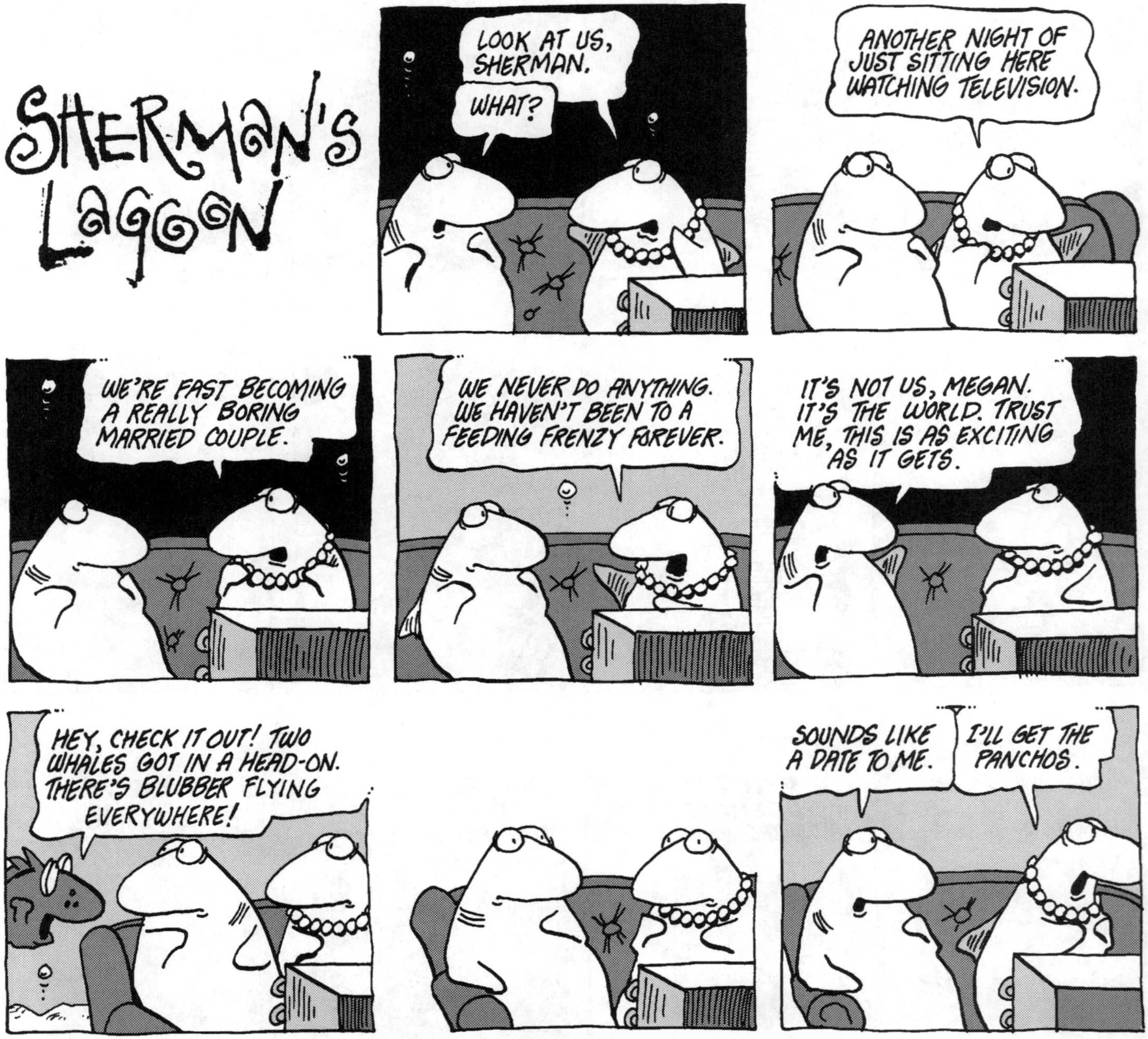
SHERMAN'S LAGOON
LOOK AT US, SHERMAN.
WHAT?
ANOTHER NIGHT OF JUST SITTING HERE WATCHING TELEVISION.
WE'RE FAST BECOMING A REALLY BORING MARRIED COUPLE.
WE NEVER DO ANYTHING. WE HAVEN'T BEEN TO A FEEDING FRENZY FOREVER.
IT'S NOT US, MEGAN. IT'S THE WORLD. TRUST ME, THIS IS AS EXCITING AS IT GETS.
HEY, CHECK IT OUT! TWO WHALES GOT IN A HEAD-ON. THERE'S BLUBBER FLYING EVERYWHERE!
SOUNDS LIKE A DATE TO ME.
I'LL GET THE PANCHOS.

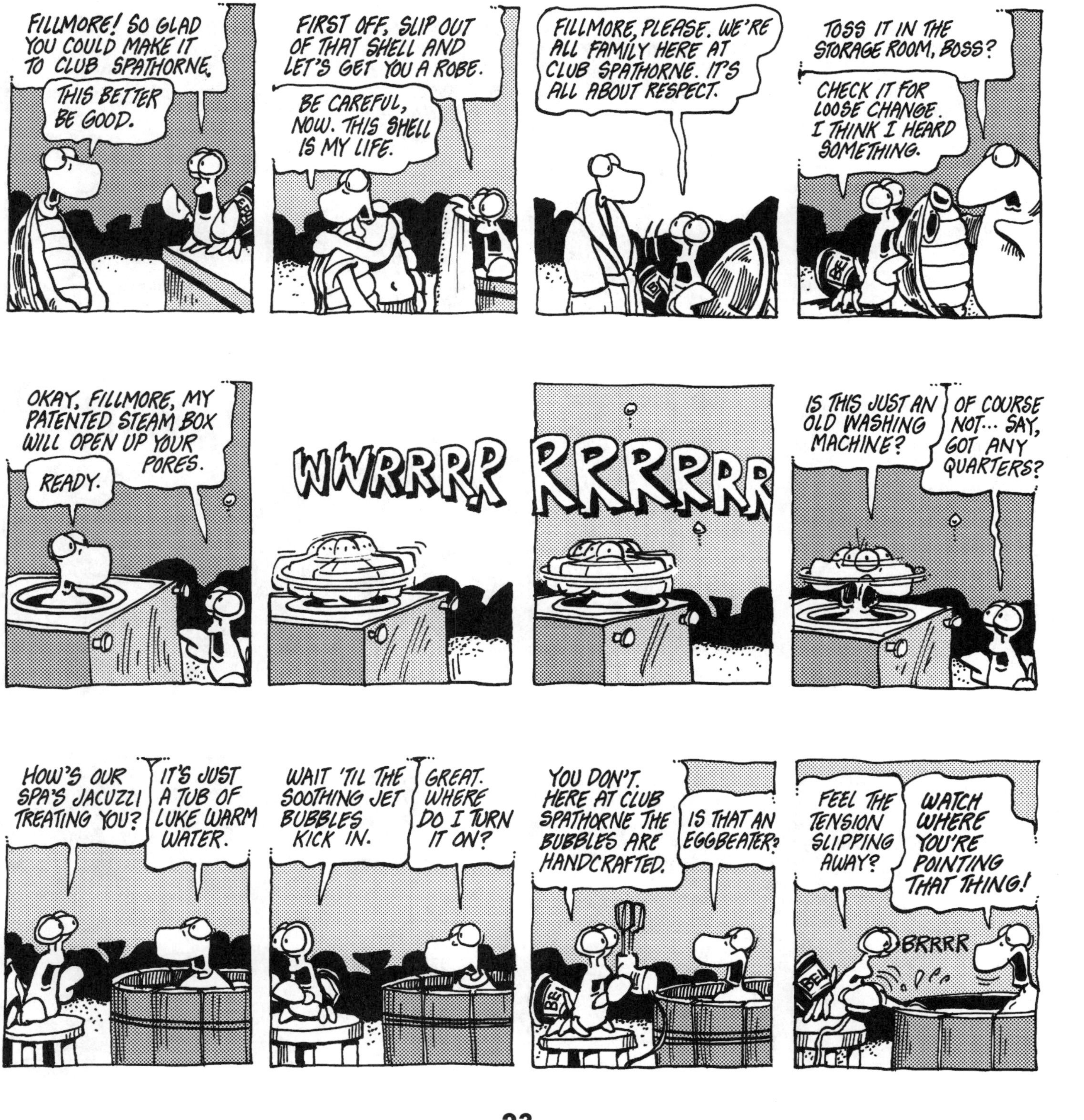
FILLMORE! SO GLAD YOU COULD MAKE IT TO CLUB SPATHORNE.
THIS BETTER BE GOOD.
FIRST OFF, SLIP OUT OF THAT SHELL AND LET'S GET YOU A ROBE.
BE CAREFUL, NOW. THIS SHELL IS MY LIFE.
FILLMORE, PLEASE. WE'RE ALL FAMILY HERE AT CLUB SPATHORNE. IT'S ALL ABOUT RESPECT.
TOSS IT IN THE STORAGE ROOM, BOSS?
CHECK IT FOR LOOSE CHANGE. I THINK I HEARD SOMETHING.
OKAY, FILLMORE, MY PATENTED STEAM BOX WILL OPEN UP YOUR PORES.
READY.
WWRRRRR RRRRRRR
IS THIS JUST AN OLD WASHING MACHINE?
OF COURSE NOT... SAY, GOT ANY QUARTERS?
HOW'S OUR SPA'S JACUZZI TREATING YOU?
IT'S JUST A TUB OF LUKE WARM WATER.
WAIT 'TIL THE SOOTHING JET BUBBLES KICK IN.
GREAT. WHERE DO I TURN IT ON?
YOU DON'T. HERE AT CLUB SPATHORNE THE BUBBLES ARE HANDCRAFTED.
IS THAT AN EGGBEATER?
FEEL THE TENSION SLIPPING AWAY?
WATCH WHERE YOU'RE POINTING THAT THING!
BRRRR

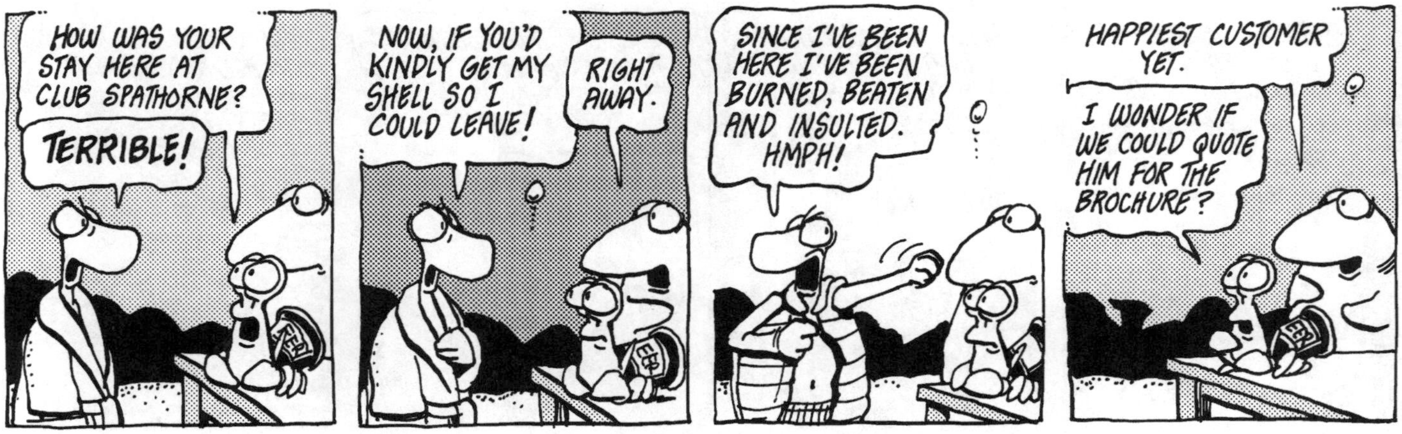
HOW WAS YOUR STAY HERE AT CLUB SPATHORNE?
TERRIBLE!
NOW, IF YOU'D KINDLY GET MY SHELL SO I COULD LEAVE!
RIGHT AWAY.
SINCE I'VE BEEN HERE I'VE BEEN BURNED, BEATEN AND INSULTED. HMPH!
HAPPIEST CUSTOMER YET.
I WONDER IF WE COULD QUOTE HIM FOR THE BROCHURE?

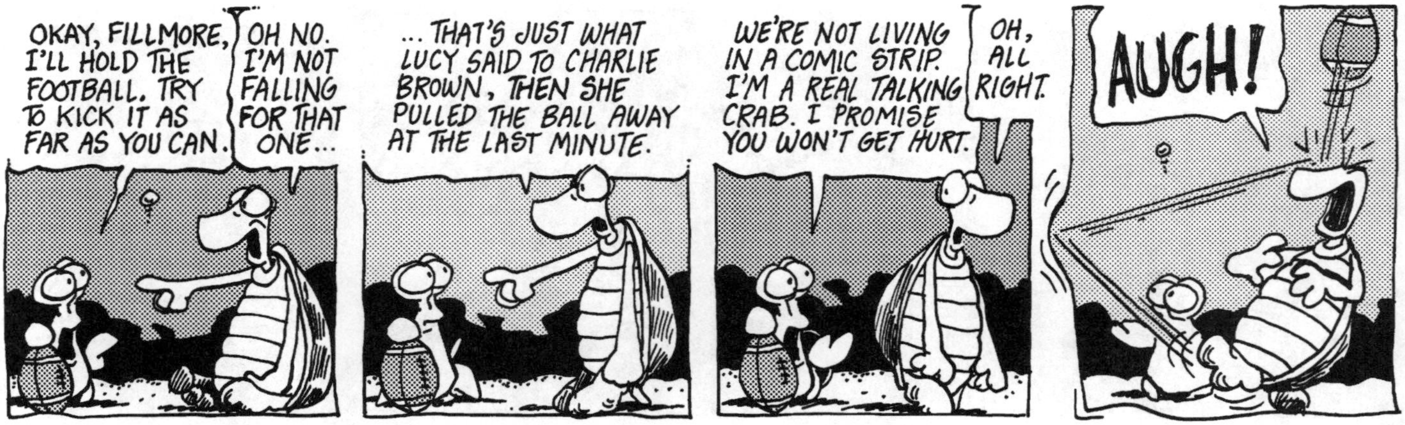
OKAY, FILLMORE, I'LL HOLD THE FOOTBALL. TRY TO KICK IT AS FAR AS YOU CAN.
OH NO. I'M NOT FALLING FOR THAT ONE...
... THAT'S JUST WHAT LUCY SAID TO CHARLIE BROWN, THEN SHE PULLED THE BALL AWAY AT THE LAST MINUTE.
WE'RE NOT LIVING IN A COMIC STRIP. I'M A REAL TALKING CRAB. I PROMISE YOU WON'T GET HURT.
OH, ALL RIGHT.
AUGH!

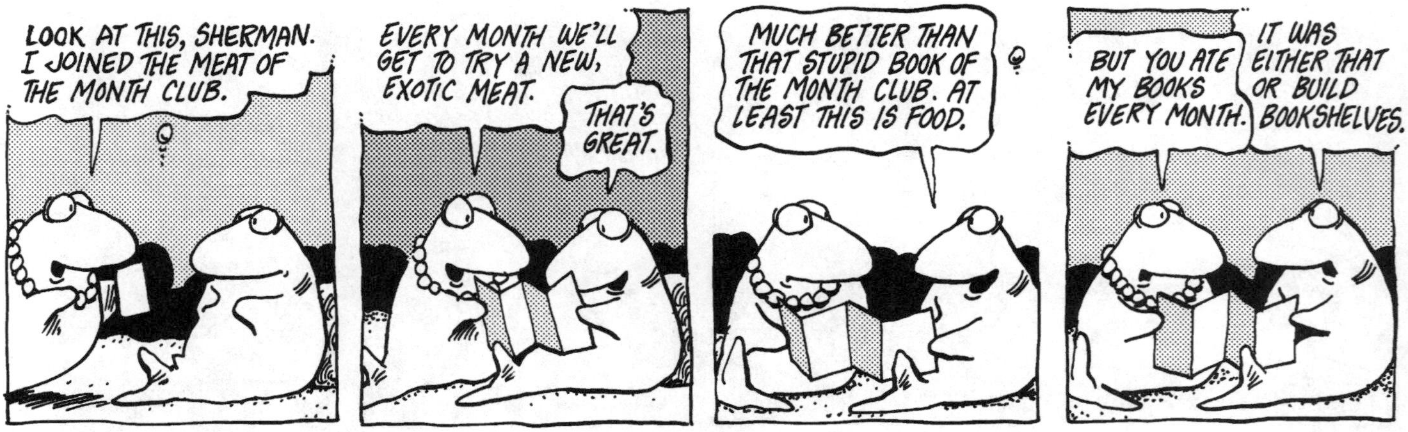
LOOK AT THIS, SHERMAN. I JOINED THE MEAT OF THE MONTH CLUB.
EVERY MONTH WE'LL GET TO TRY A NEW, EXOTIC MEAT.
THAT'S GREAT.
MUCH BETTER THAN THAT STUPID BOOK OF THE MONTH CLUB. AT LEAST THIS IS FOOD.
BUT YOU ATE MY BOOKS EVERY MONTH.
IT WAS EITHER THAT OR BUILD BOOKSHELVES.

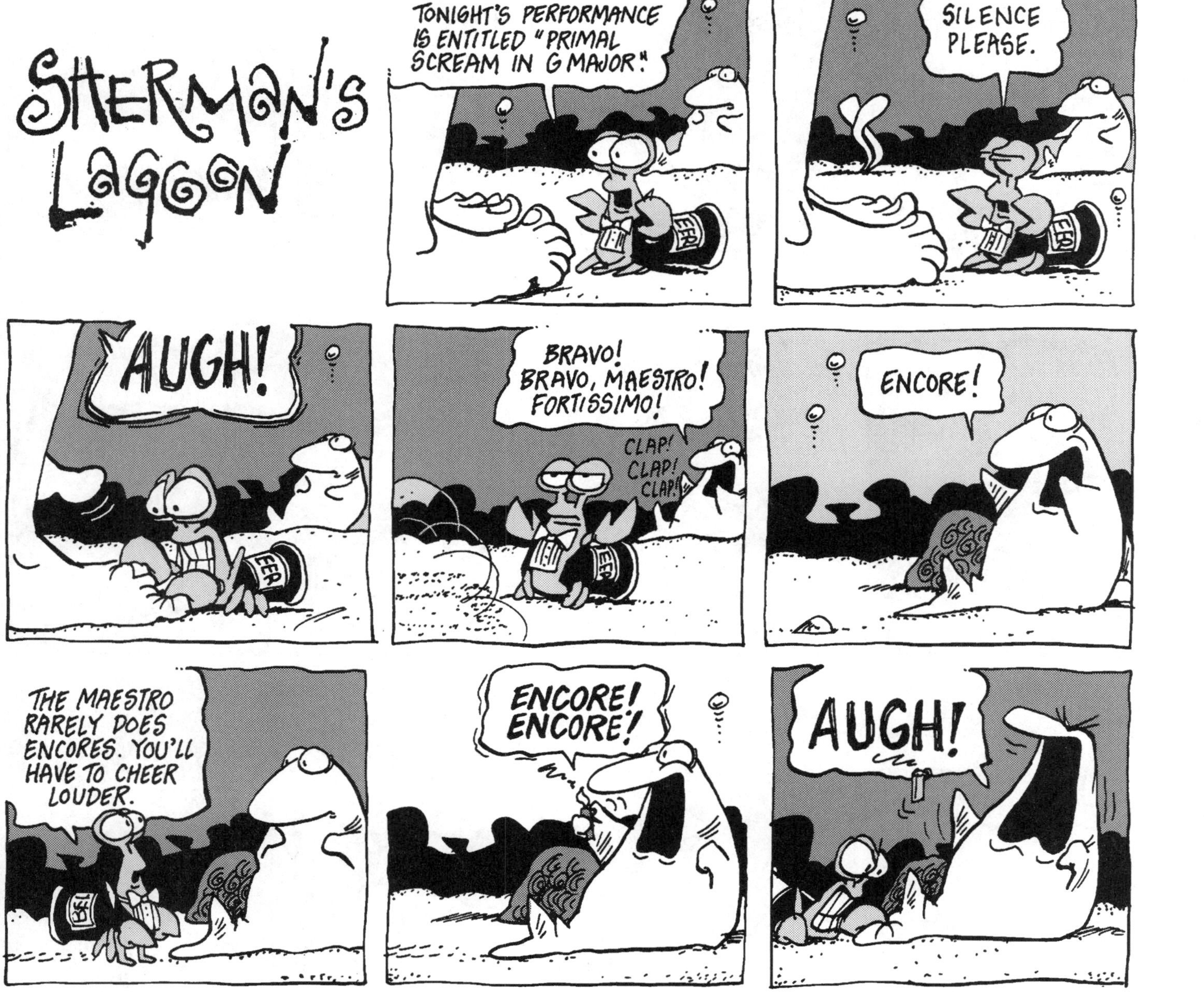
SHERMAN'S LAGOON
TONIGHT'S PERFORMANCE IS ENTITLED "PRIMAL SCREAM IN G MAJOR."
SILENCE PLEASE.
AUGH!
BRAVO! BRAVO, MAESTRO! FORTISSIMO!
CLAP! CLAP! CLAP!
ENCORE!
THE MAESTRO RARELY DOES ENCORES. YOU'LL HAVE TO CHEER LOUDER.
ENCORE! ENCORE!
AUGH!

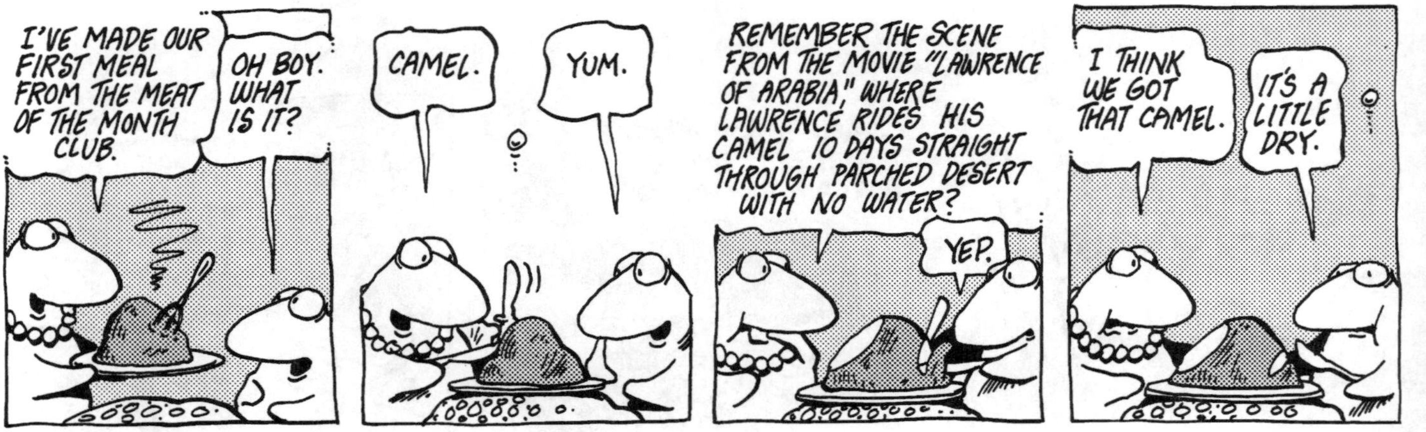
I'VE MADE OUR FIRST MEAL FROM THE MEAT OF THE MONTH CLUB.
OH BOY. WHAT IS IT?
CAMEL.
YUM.
REMEMBER THE SCENE FROM THE MOVIE "LAWRENCE OF ARABIA," WHERE LAWRENCE RIDES HIS CAMEL 10 DAYS STRAIGHT THROUGH PARCHED DESERT WITH NO WATER?
YEP.
I THINK WE GOT THAT CAMEL.
IT'S A LITTLE DRY.

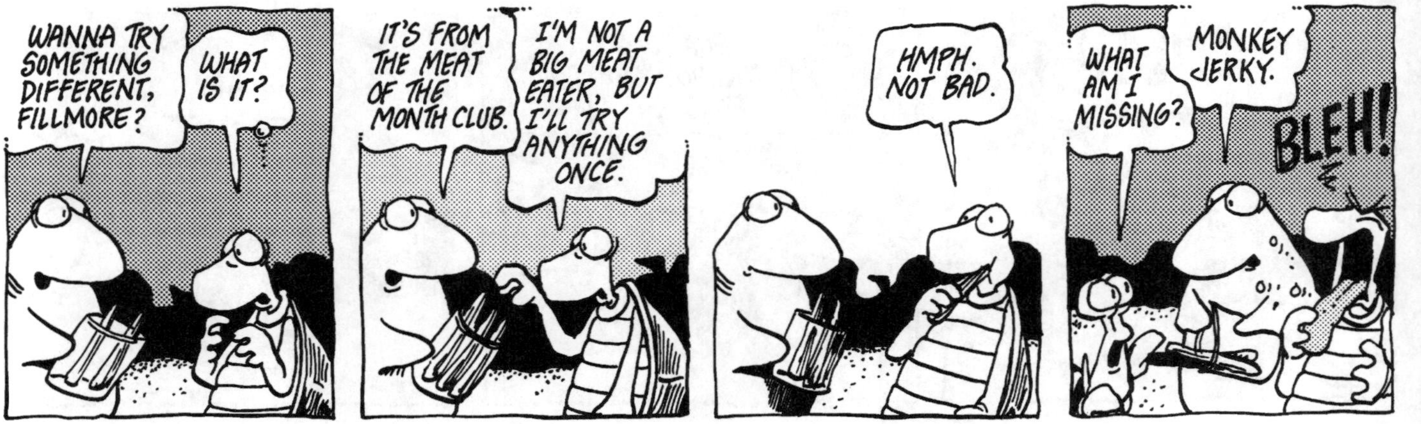
WANNA TRY SOMETHING DIFFERENT, FILLMORE?
WHAT IS IT?
IT'S FROM THE MEAT OF THE MONTH CLUB.
I'M NOT A BIG MEAT EATER, BUT I'LL TRY ANYTHING ONCE.
HMPH. NOT BAD.
WHAT AM I MISSING?
MONKEY JERKY.
BLEH!

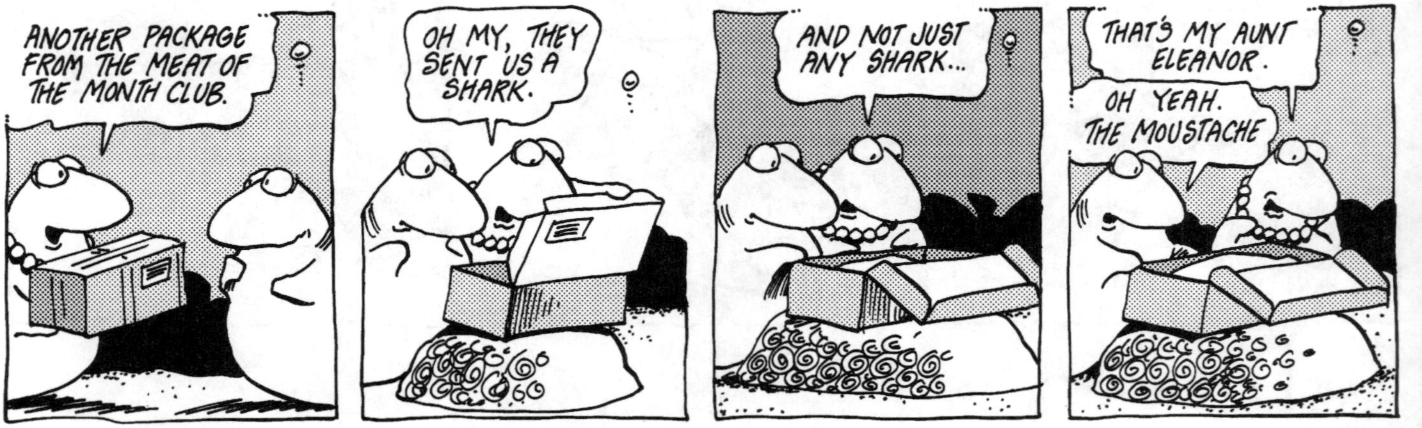
ANOTHER PACKAGE FROM THE MEAT OF THE MONTH CLUB.
OH MY, THEY SENT US A SHARK.
AND NOT JUST ANY SHARK...
THAT'S MY AUNT ELEANOR.
OH YEAH. THE MOUSTACHE

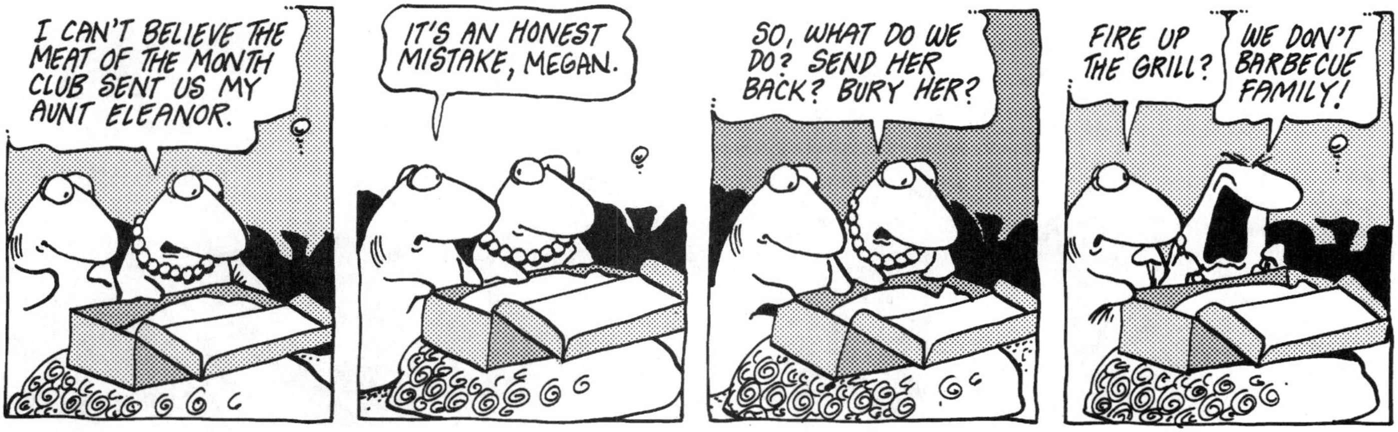
I CAN'T BELIEVE THE MEAT OF THE MONTH CLUB SENT US MY AUNT ELEANOR.
IT'S AN HONEST MISTAKE, MEGAN.
SO, WHAT DO WE DO? SEND HER BACK? BURY HER?
FIRE UP THE GRILL?
WE DON'T BARBECUE FAMILY!

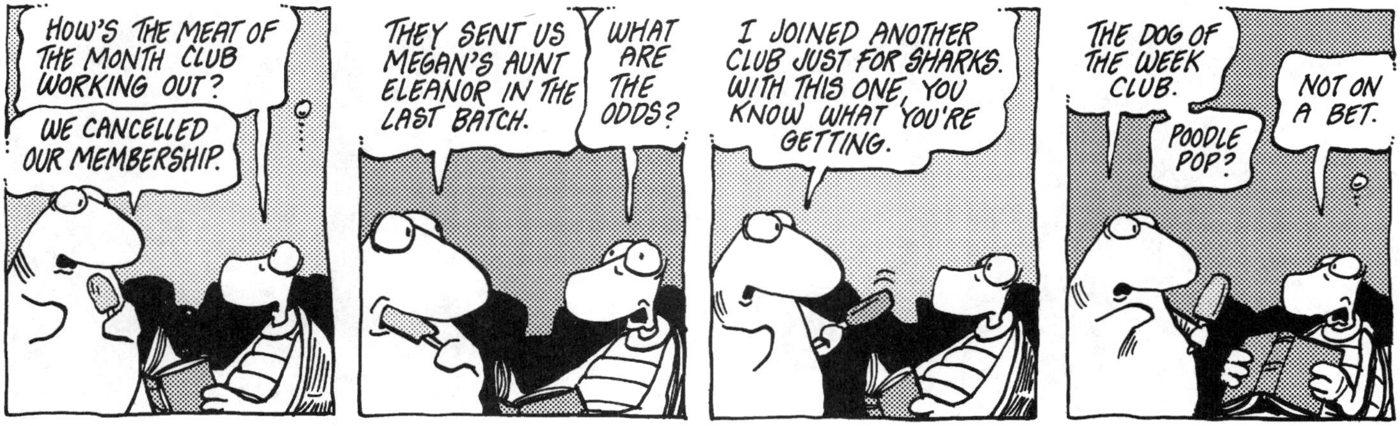
HOW'S THE MEAT OF THE MONTH CLUB WORKING OUT?
WE CANCELLED OUR MEMBERSHIP.
THEY SENT US MEGAN'S AUNT ELEANOR IN THE LAST BATCH.
WHAT ARE THE ODDS?
I JOINED ANOTHER CLUB JUST FOR SHARKS. WITH THIS ONE, YOU KNOW WHAT YOU'RE GETTING.
THE DOG OF THE WEEK CLUB.
POODLE POP?
NOT ON A BET.

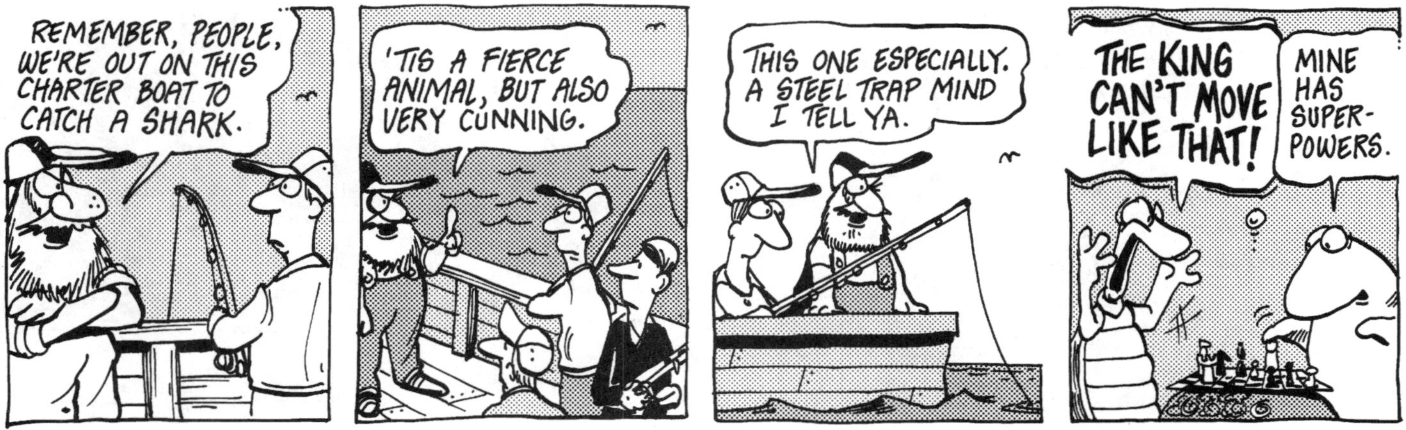
REMEMBER, PEOPLE, WE'RE OUT ON THIS CHARTER BOAT TO CATCH A SHARK.
'TIS A FIERCE ANIMAL, BUT ALSO VERY CUNNING.
THIS ONE ESPECIALLY. A STEEL TRAP MIND I TELL YA.
THE KING CAN'T MOVE LIKE THAT!
MINE HAS SUPER-POWERS.

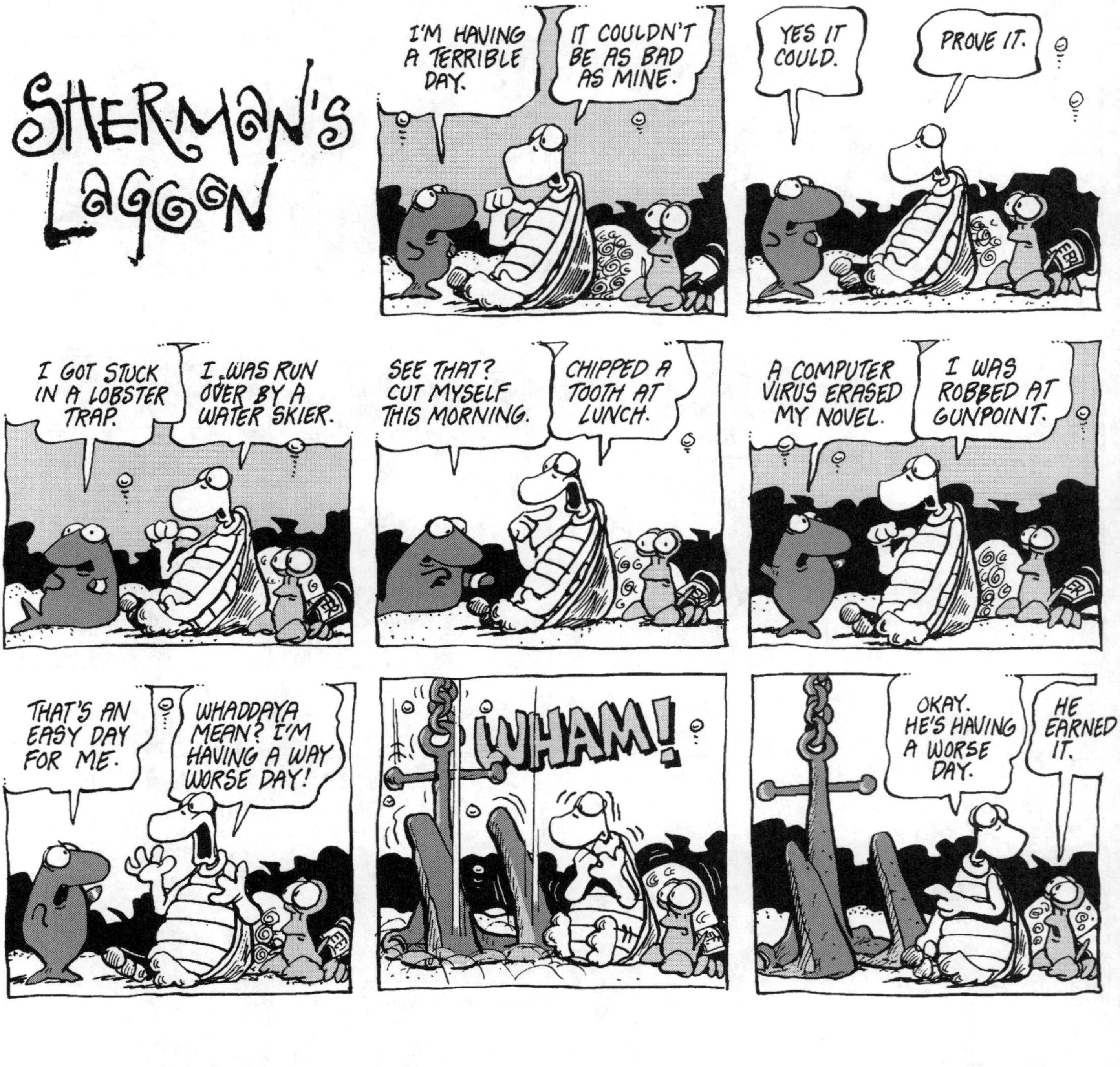
Sherman's Lagoon
I'M HAVING A TERRIBLE DAY.
IT COULDN'T BE AS BAD AS MINE.
YES IT COULD.
PROVE IT.
I GOT STUCK IN A LOBSTER TRAP.
I WAS RUN OVER BY A WATER SKIER.
SEE THAT? CUT MYSELF THIS MORNING.
CHIPPED A TOOTH AT LUNCH.
A COMPUTER VIRUS ERASED MY NOVEL.
I WAS ROBBED AT GUNPOINT.
THAT'S AN EASY DAY FOR ME.
WHADDAYA MEAN? I'M HAVING A WAY WORSE DAY!
WHAM!
OKAY. HE'S HAVING A WORSE DAY.
HE EARNED IT.

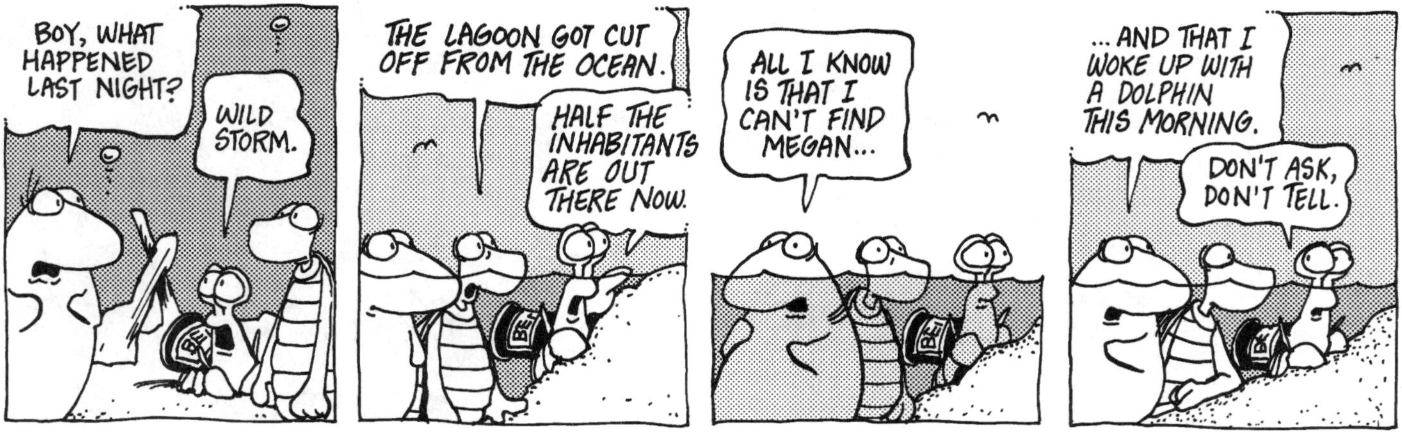
BOY, WHAT HAPPENED LAST NIGHT?
WILD STORM.
THE LAGOON GOT CUT OFF FROM THE OCEAN.
HALF THE INHABITANTS ARE OUT THERE NOW.
ALL I KNOW IS THAT I CAN'T FIND MEGAN...
...AND THAT I WOKE UP WITH A DOLPHIN THIS MORNING.
DON'T ASK, DON'T TELL.

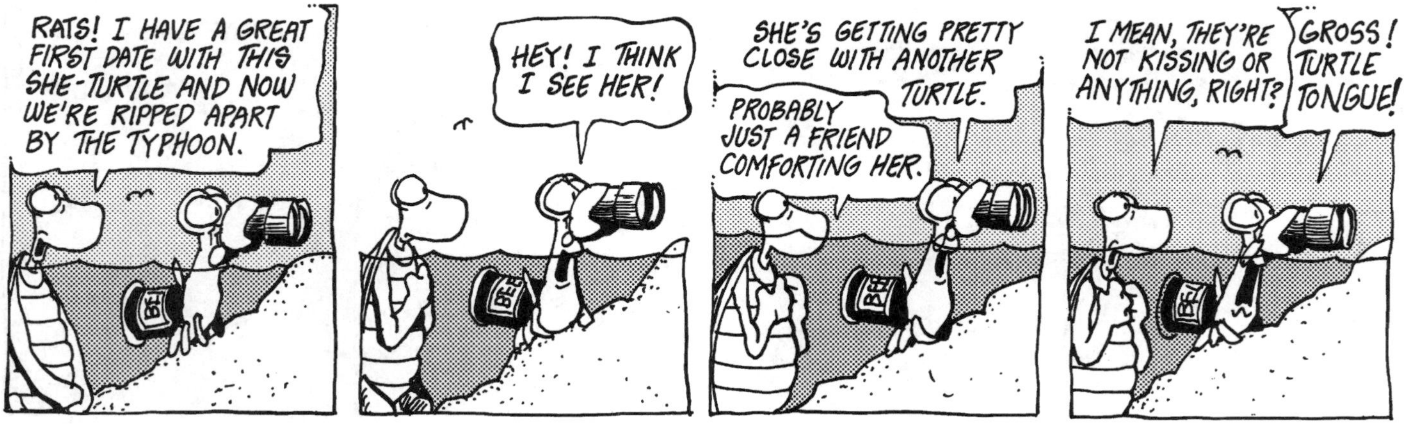
RATS! I HAVE A GREAT FIRST DATE WITH THIS SHE-TURTLE AND NOW WE'RE RIPPED APART BY THE TYPHOON.
HEY! I THINK I SEE HER!
SHE'S GETTING PRETTY CLOSE WITH ANOTHER TURTLE.
PROBABLY JUST A FRIEND COMFORTING HER.
I MEAN, THEY'RE NOT KISSING OR ANYTHING, RIGHT?
GROSS! TURTLE TONGUE!

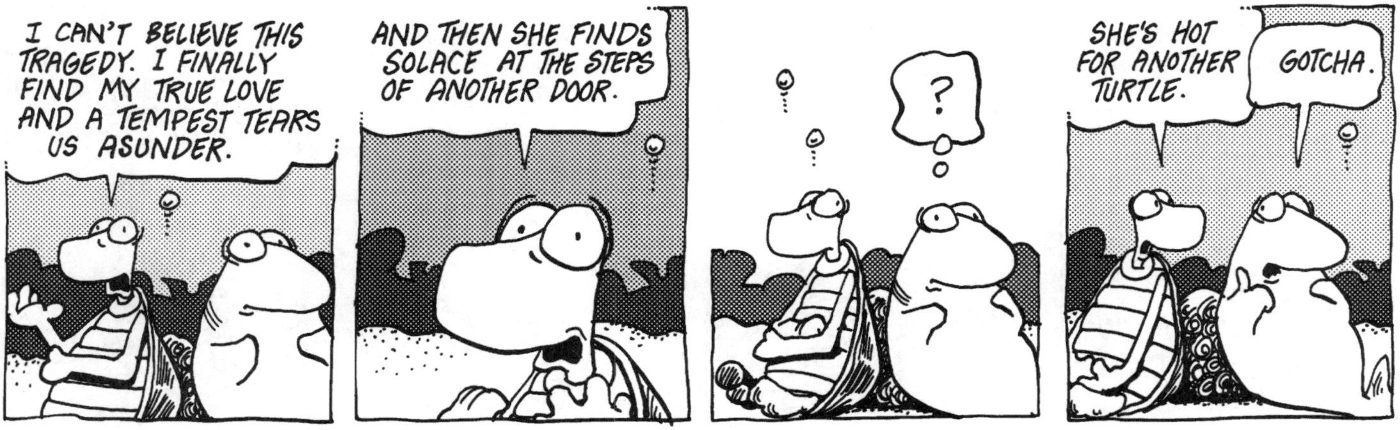
I CAN'T BELIEVE THIS TRAGEDY. I FINALLY FIND MY TRUE LOVE AND A TEMPEST TEARS US ASUNDER.
AND THEN SHE FINDS SOLACE AT THE STEPS OF ANOTHER DOOR.
?
SHE'S HOT FOR ANOTHER TURTLE.
GOTCHA.

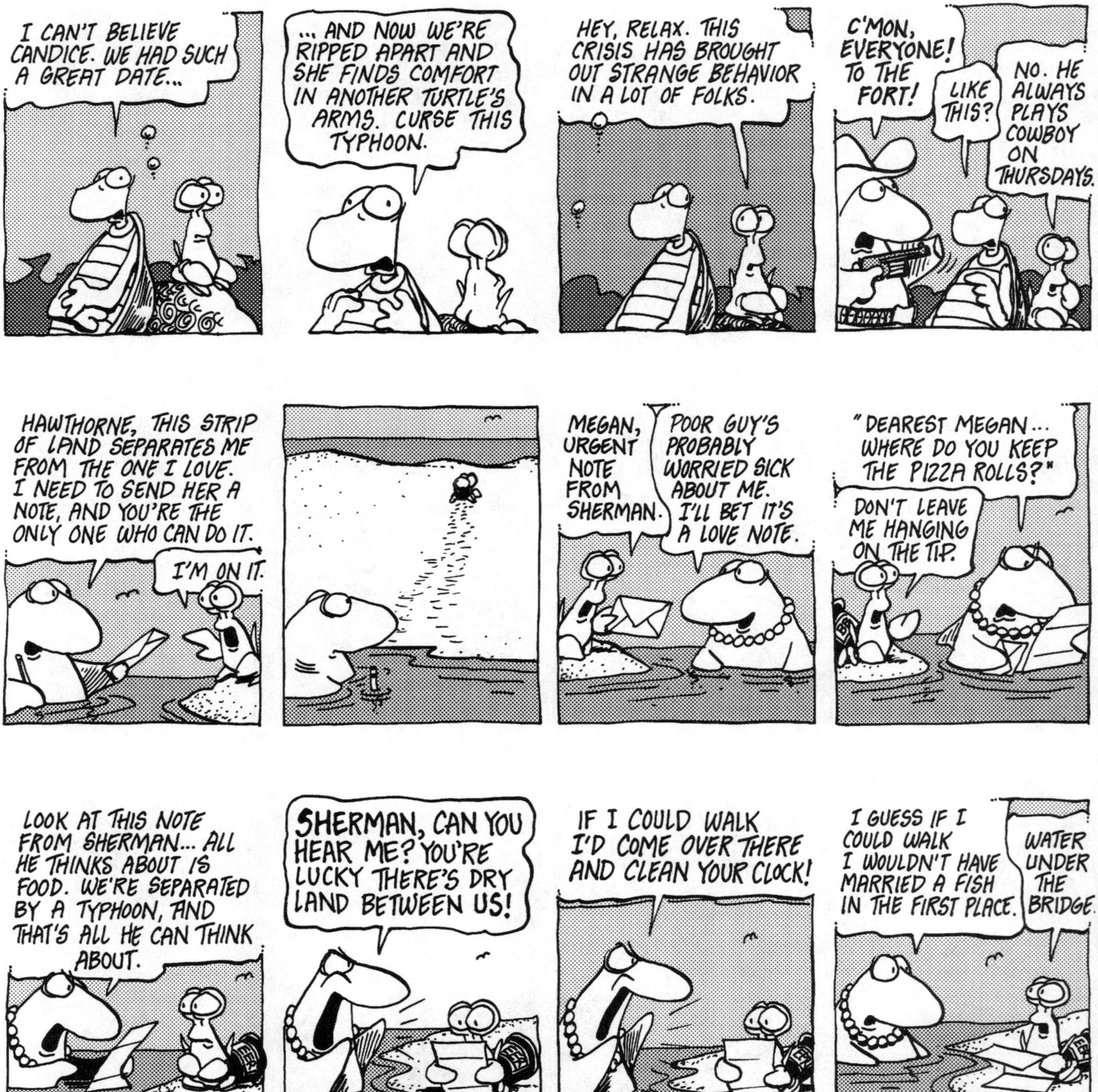

I CAN'T BELIEVE CANDICE. WE HAD SUCH A GREAT DATE...
... AND NOW WE'RE RIPPED APART AND SHE FINDS COMFORT IN ANOTHER TURTLE'S ARMS. CURSE THIS TYPHOON.
HEY, RELAX. THIS CRISIS HAS BROUGHT OUT STRANGE BEHAVIOR IN A LOT OF FOLKS.
C'MON, EVERYONE! TO THE FORT!
LIKE THIS?
NO. HE ALWAYS PLAYS COWBOY ON THURSDAYS.
HAWTHORNE, THIS STRIP OF LAND SEPARATES ME FROM THE ONE I LOVE. I NEED TO SEND HER A NOTE, AND YOU'RE THE ONLY ONE WHO CAN DO IT.
I'M ON IT.
MEGAN, URGENT NOTE FROM SHERMAN.
POOR GUY'S PROBABLY WORRIED SICK ABOUT ME. I'LL BET IT'S A LOVE NOTE.
"DEAREST MEGAN... WHERE DO YOU KEEP THE PIZZA ROLLS?"
DON'T LEAVE ME HANGING ON THE TIP.
LOOK AT THIS NOTE FROM SHERMAN... ALL HE THINKS ABOUT IS FOOD. WE'RE SEPARATED BY A TYPHOON, AND THAT'S ALL HE CAN THINK ABOUT.
SHERMAN, CAN YOU HEAR ME? YOU'RE LUCKY THERE'S DRY LAND BETWEEN US!
IF I COULD WALK I'D COME OVER THERE AND CLEAN YOUR CLOCK!
I GUESS IF I COULD WALK I WOULDN'T HAVE MARRIED A FISH IN THE FIRST PLACE.
WATER UNDER THE BRIDGE.

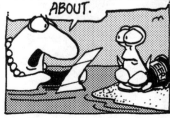

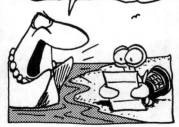

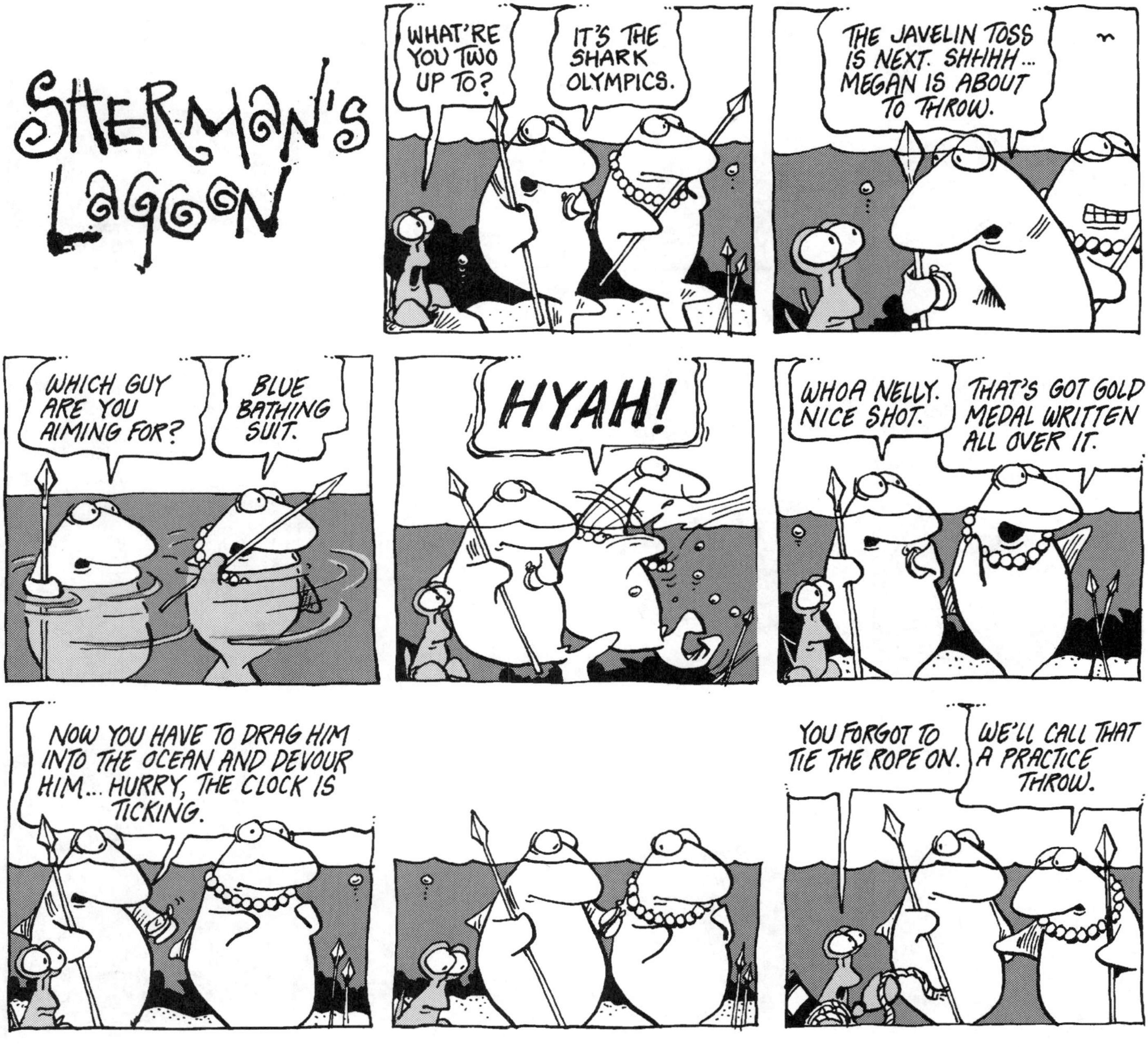
SHERMAN'S LAGOON
WHAT'RE YOU TWO UP TO?
IT'S THE SHARK OLYMPICS.
THE JAVELIN TOSS IS NEXT. SHHHH... MEGAN IS ABOUT TO THROW.
WHICH GUY ARE YOU AIMING FOR?
BLUE BATHING SUIT.
HYAH!
WHOA NELLY. NICE SHOT.
THAT'S GOT GOLD MEDAL WRITTEN ALL OVER IT.
NOW YOU HAVE TO DRAG HIM INTO THE OCEAN AND DEVOUR HIM... HURRY, THE CLOCK IS TICKING.
YOU FORGOT TO TIE THE ROPE ON.
WE'LL CALL THAT A PRACTICE THROW.

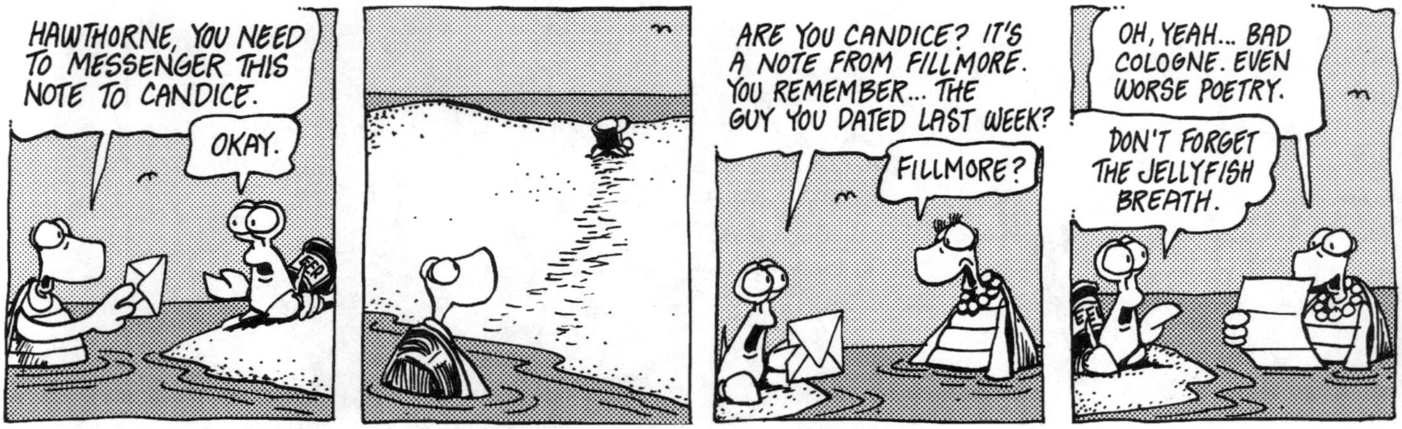
HAWTHORNE, YOU NEED TO MESSENGER THIS NOTE TO CANDICE.
OKAY.
ARE YOU CANDICE? IT'S A NOTE FROM FILLMORE. YOU REMEMBER... THE GUY YOU DATED LAST WEEK?
FILLMORE?
OH, YEAH... BAD COLOGNE. EVEN WORSE POETRY.
DON'T FORGET THE JELLYFISH BREATH.

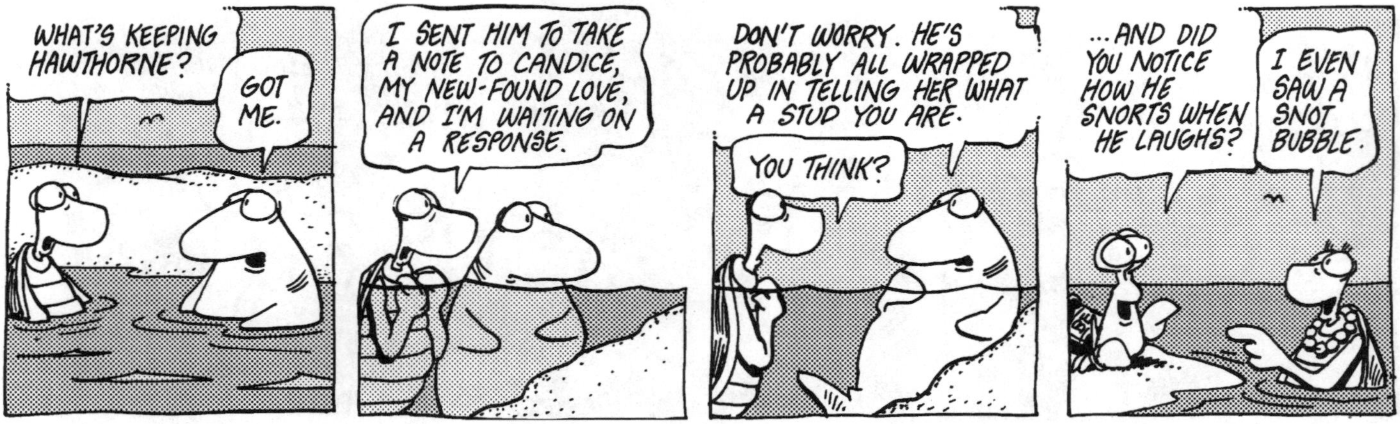
WHAT'S KEEPING HAWTHORNE?
GOT ME.
I SENT HIM TO TAKE A NOTE TO CANDICE, MY NEW-FOUND LOVE, AND I'M WAITING ON A RESPONSE.
DON'T WORRY. HE'S PROBABLY ALL WRAPPED UP IN TELLING HER WHAT A STUD YOU ARE.
YOU THINK?
...AND DID YOU NOTICE HOW HE SNORTS WHEN HE LAUGHS?
I EVEN SAW A SNOT BUBBLE.

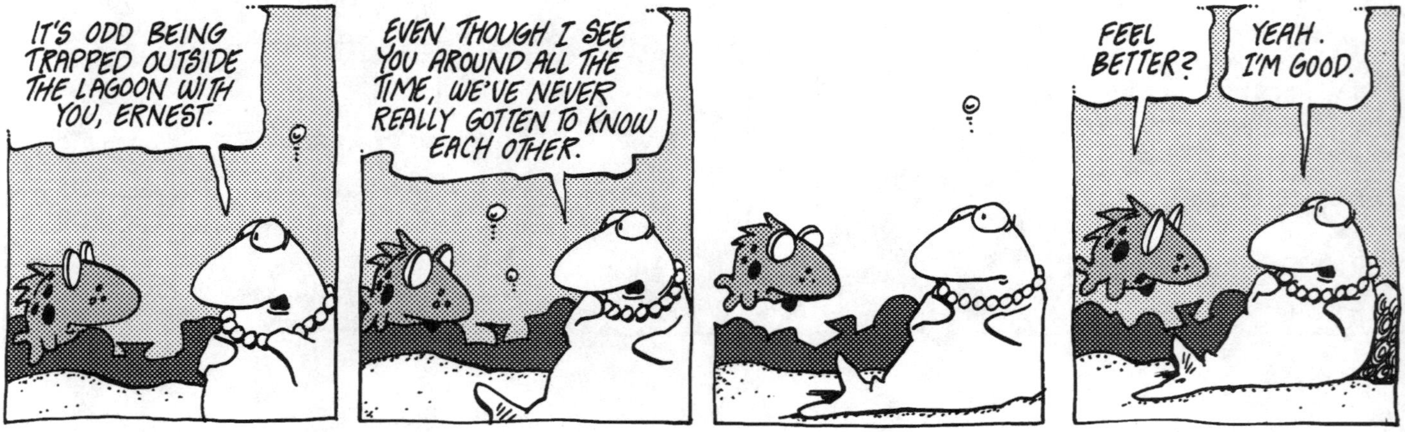
IT'S ODD BEING TRAPPED OUTSIDE THE LAGOON WITH YOU, ERNEST.
EVEN THOUGH I SEE YOU AROUND ALL THE TIME, WE'VE NEVER REALLY GOTTEN TO KNOW EACH OTHER.
FEEL BETTER?
YEAH. I'M GOOD.

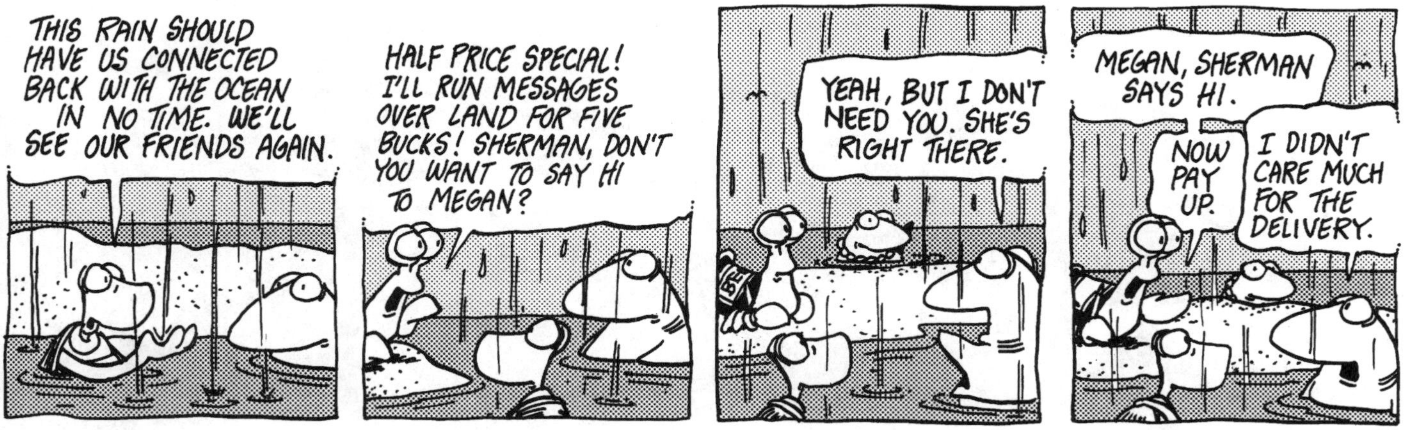
THIS RAIN SHOULD HAVE US CONNECTED BACK WITH THE OCEAN IN NO TIME. WE'LL SEE OUR FRIENDS AGAIN.
HALF PRICE SPECIAL! I'LL RUN MESSAGES OVER LAND FOR FIVE BUCKS! SHERMAN, DON'T YOU WANT TO SAY HI TO MEGAN?
YEAH, BUT I DON'T NEED YOU. SHE'S RIGHT THERE.
MEGAN, SHERMAN SAYS HI.
NOW PAY UP.
I DIDN'T CARE MUCH FOR THE DELIVERY.

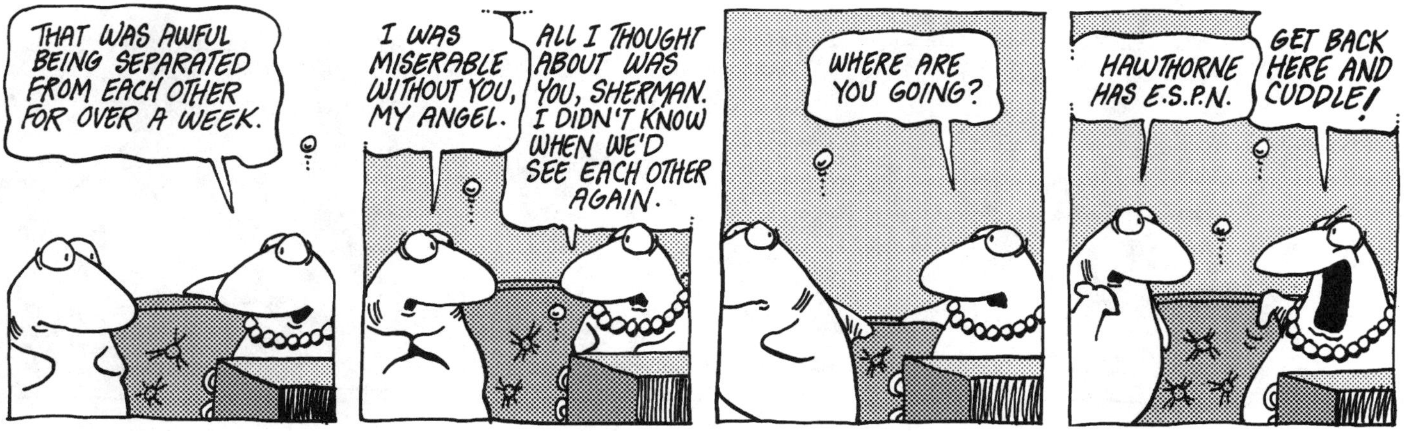
THAT WAS AWFUL BEING SEPARATED FROM EACH OTHER FOR OVER A WEEK.
I WAS MISERABLE WITHOUT YOU, MY ANGEL.
ALL I THOUGHT ABOUT WAS YOU, SHERMAN. I DIDN'T KNOW WHEN WE'D SEE EACH OTHER AGAIN.
WHERE ARE YOU GOING?
HAWTHORNE HAS E.S.P.N.
GET BACK HERE AND CUDDLE!

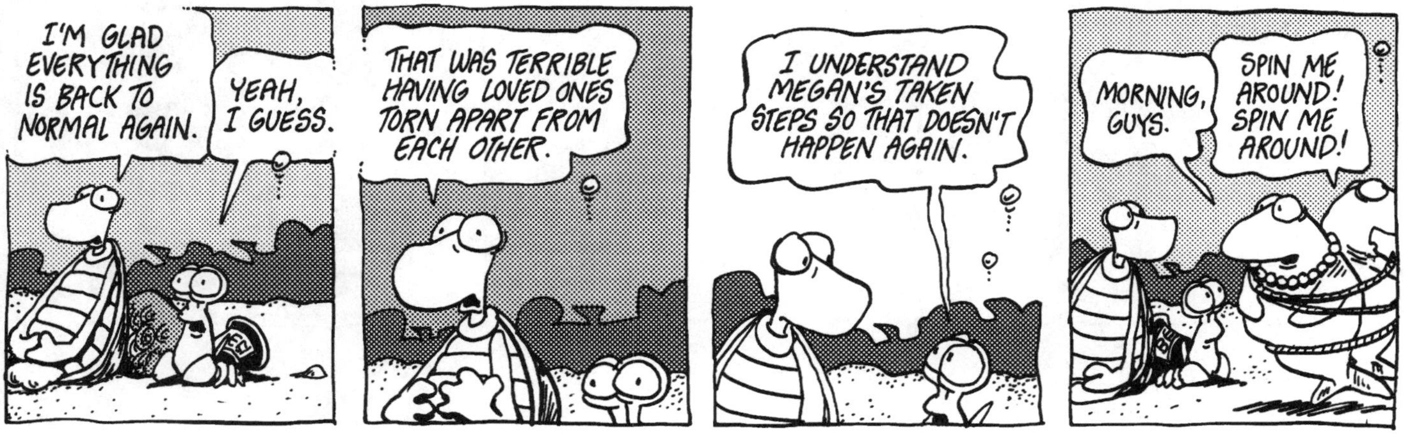
I'M GLAD EVERYTHING IS BACK TO NORMAL AGAIN.
YEAH, I GUESS.
THAT WAS TERRIBLE HAVING LOVED ONES TORN APART FROM EACH OTHER.
I UNDERSTAND MEGAN'S TAKEN STEPS SO THAT DOESN'T HAPPEN AGAIN.
MORNING, GUYS.
SPIN ME AROUND! SPIN ME AROUND!

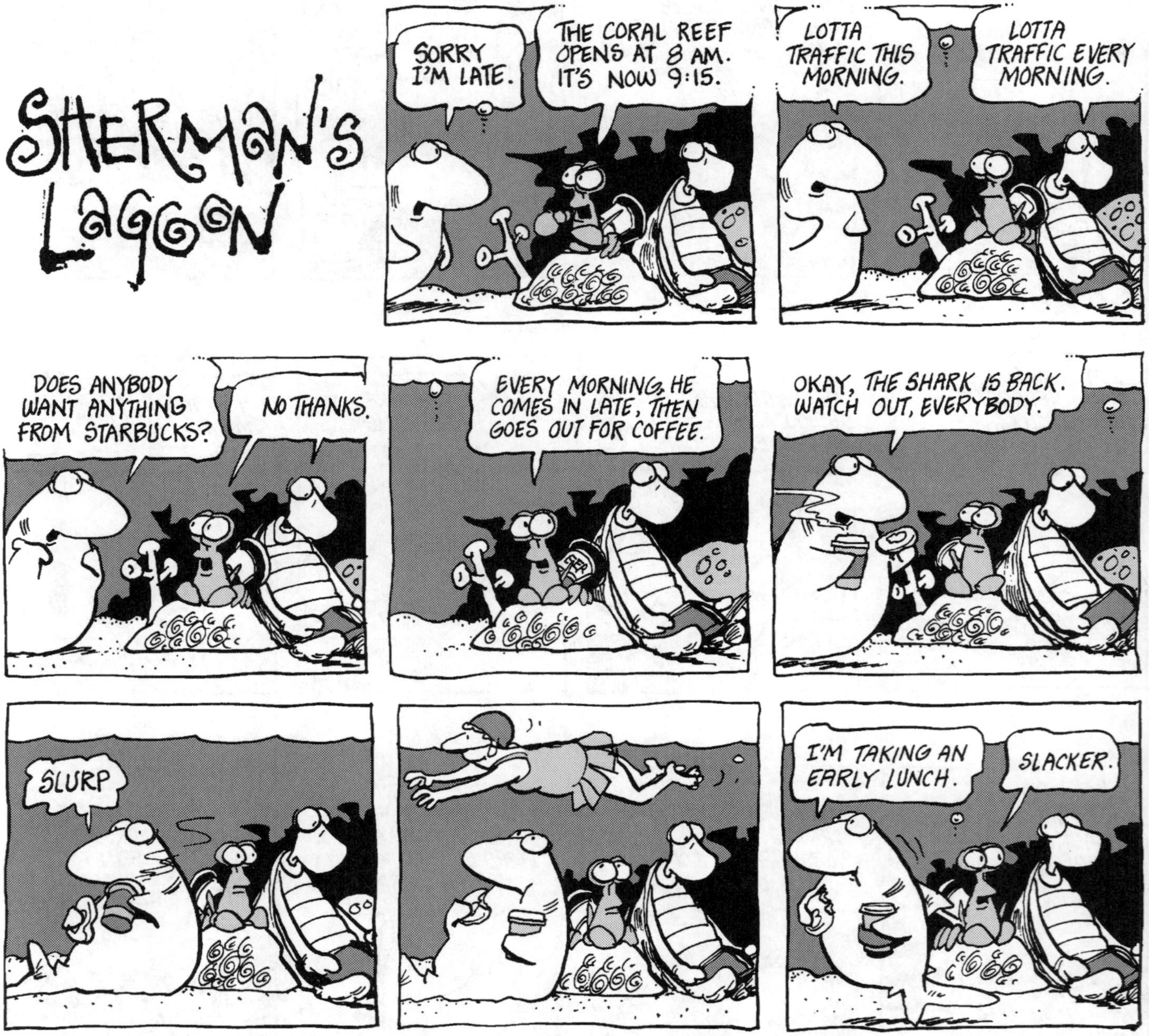
SHERMAN'S LAGOON
SORRY I'M LATE.
THE CORAL REEF OPENS AT 8 AM. IT'S NOW 9:15.
LOTTA TRAFFIC THIS MORNING.
LOTTA TRAFFIC EVERY MORNING.
DOES ANYBODY WANT ANYTHING FROM STARBUCKS?
NO THANKS.
EVERY MORNING HE COMES IN LATE, THEN GOES OUT FOR COFFEE.
OKAY, THE SHARK IS BACK. WATCH OUT, EVERYBODY.
SLURP
I'M TAKING AN EARLY LUNCH.
SLACKER.

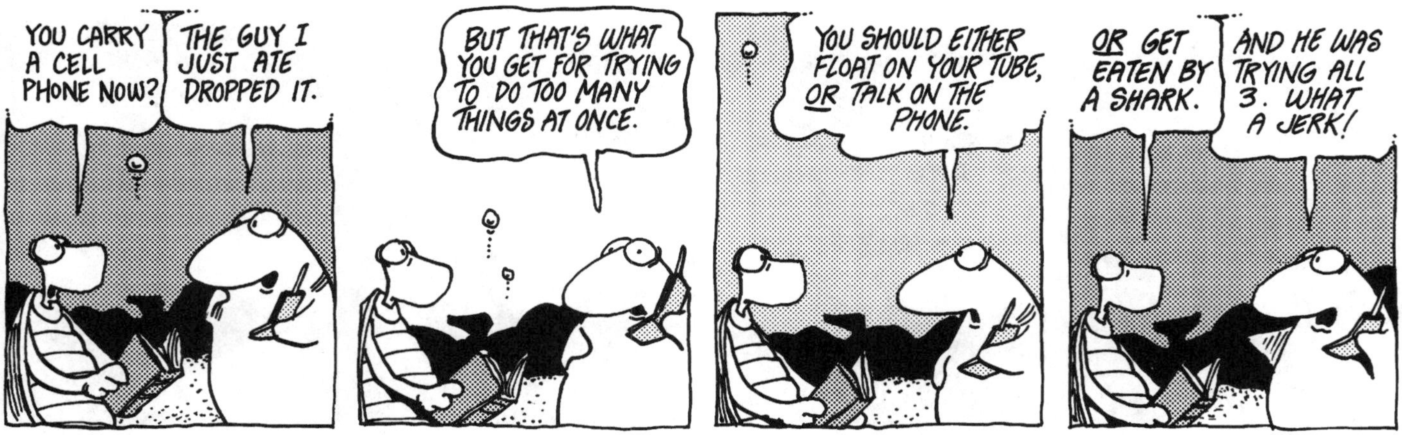
YOU CARRY A CELL PHONE NOW?
THE GUY I JUST ATE DROPPED IT.
BUT THAT'S WHAT YOU GET FOR TRYING TO DO TOO MANY THINGS AT ONCE.
YOU SHOULD EITHER FLOAT ON YOUR TUBE, OR TALK ON THE PHONE.
OR GET EATEN BY A SHARK.
AND HE WAS TRYING ALL 3. WHAT A JERK!

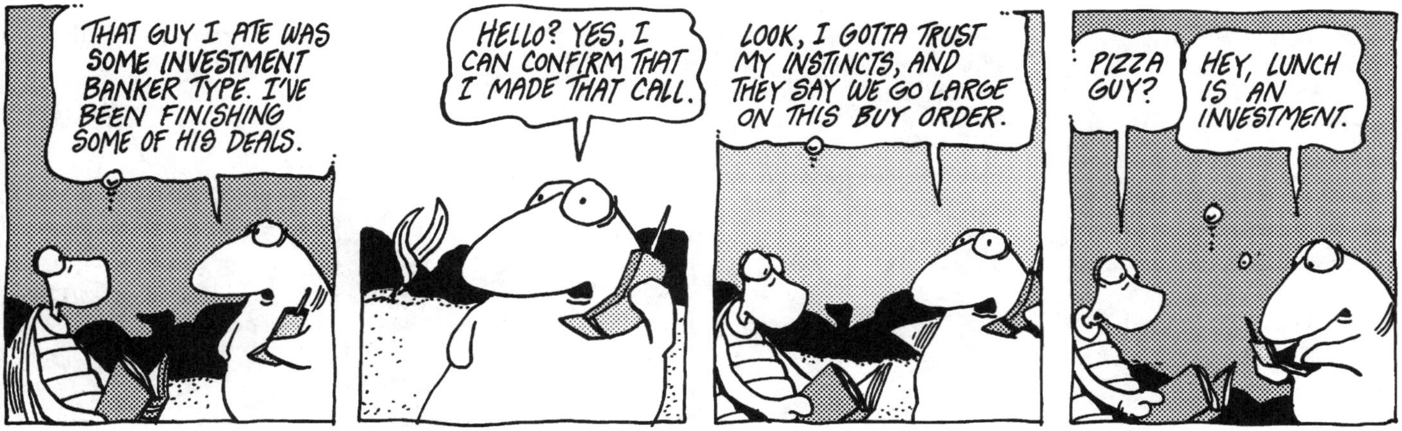
THAT GUY I ATE WAS SOME INVESTMENT BANKER TYPE. I'VE BEEN FINISHING SOME OF HIS DEALS.
HELLO? YES, I CAN CONFIRM THAT I MADE THAT CALL.
LOOK, I GOTTA TRUST MY INSTINCTS, AND THEY SAY WE GO LARGE ON THIS BUY ORDER.
PIZZA GUY?
HEY, LUNCH IS AN INVESTMENT.

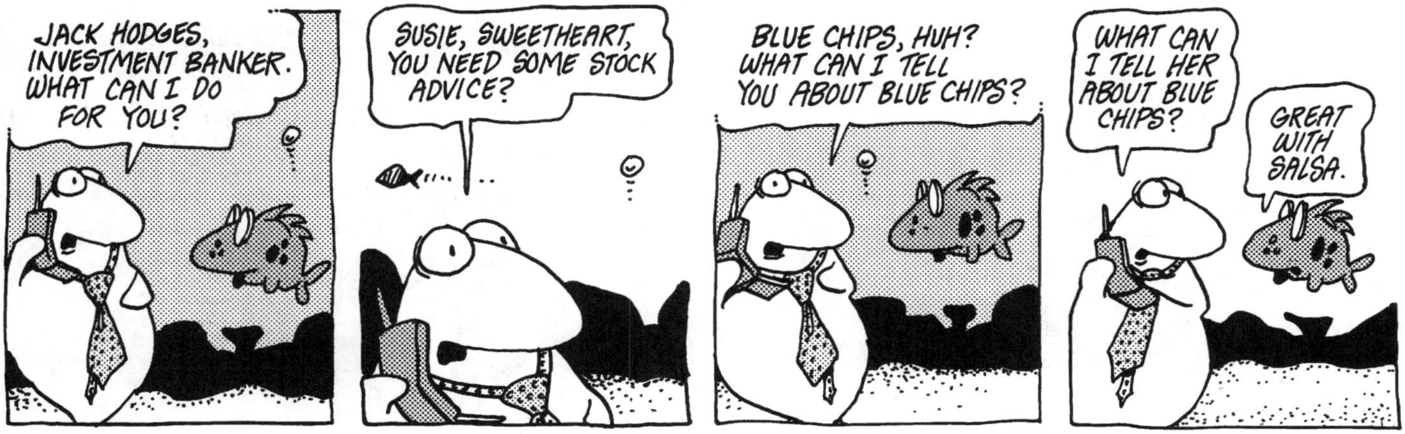
JACK HODGES, INVESTMENT BANKER. WHAT CAN I DO FOR YOU?
SUSIE, SWEETHEART, YOU NEED SOME STOCK ADVICE?
BLUE CHIPS, HUH? WHAT CAN I TELL YOU ABOUT BLUE CHIPS?
WHAT CAN I TELL HER ABOUT BLUE CHIPS?
GREAT WITH SALSA.

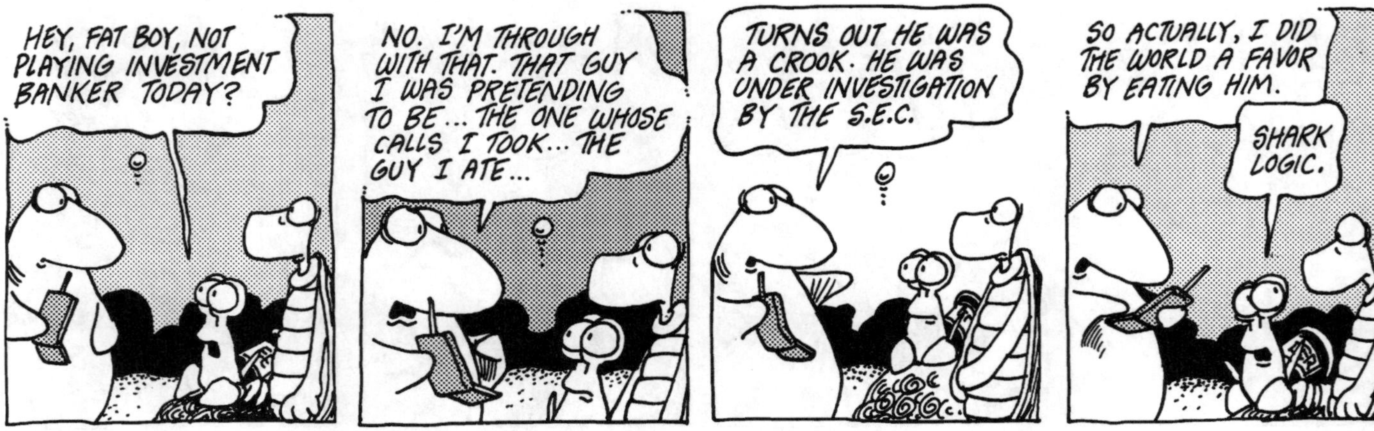
HEY, FAT BOY, NOT PLAYING INVESTMENT BANKER TODAY?
NO. I'M THROUGH WITH THAT. THAT GUY I WAS PRETENDING TO BE... THE ONE WHOSE CALLS I TOOK... THE GUY I ATE...
TURNS OUT HE WAS A CROOK. HE WAS UNDER INVESTIGATION BY THE S.E.C.
SO ACTUALLY, I DID THE WORLD A FAVOR BY EATING HIM.
SHARK LOGIC.

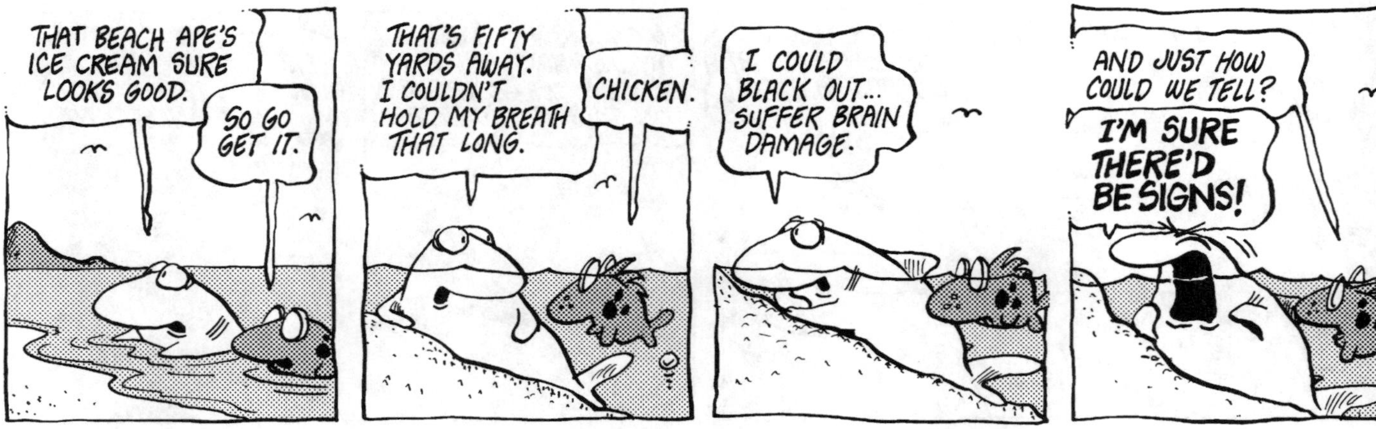
THAT BEACH APE'S ICE CREAM SURE LOOKS GOOD.
SO GO GET IT.
THAT'S FIFTY YARDS AWAY. I COULDN'T HOLD MY BREATH THAT LONG.
CHICKEN.
I COULD BLACK OUT... SUFFER BRAIN DAMAGE.
AND JUST HOW COULD WE TELL?
I'M SURE THERE'D BE SIGNS!

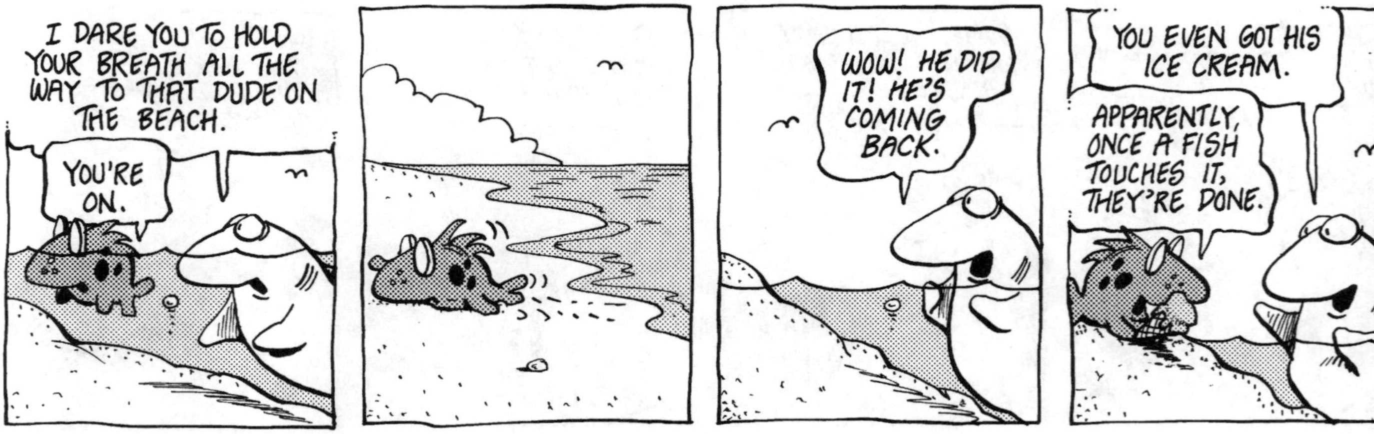
I DARE YOU TO HOLD YOUR BREATH ALL THE WAY TO THAT DUDE ON THE BEACH.
YOU'RE ON.
WOW! HE DID IT! HE'S COMING BACK.
YOU EVEN GOT HIS ICE CREAM.
APPARENTLY, ONCE A FISH TOUCHES IT, THEY'RE DONE.

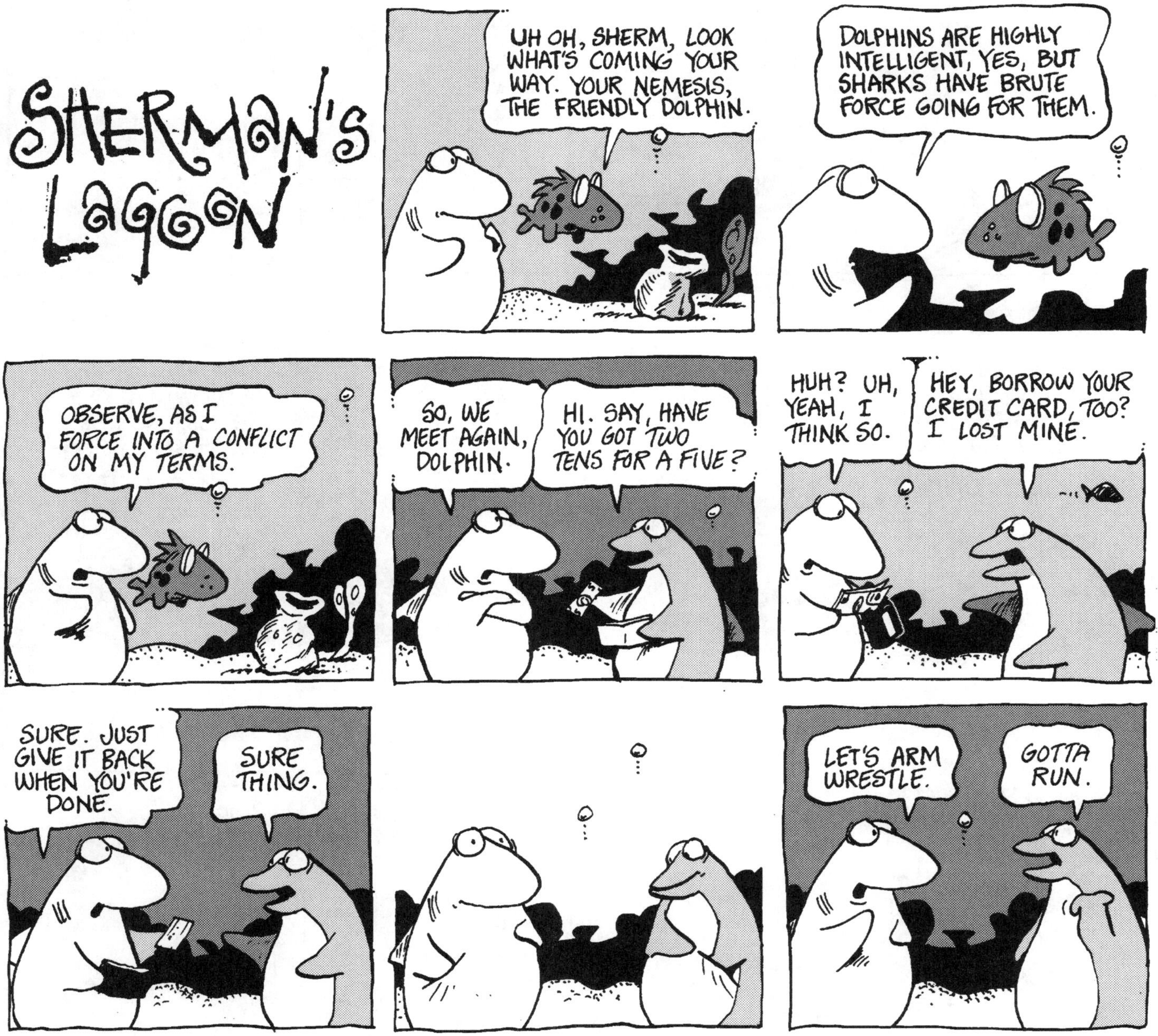
SHERMAN'S LAGOON
UH OH, SHERM, LOOK WHAT'S COMING YOUR WAY. YOUR NEMESIS, THE FRIENDLY DOLPHIN.
DOLPHINS ARE HIGHLY INTELLIGENT, YES, BUT SHARKS HAVE BRUTE FORCE GOING FOR THEM.
OBSERVE, AS I FORCE INTO A CONFLICT ON MY TERMS.
SO, WE MEET AGAIN, DOLPHIN.
HI. SAY, HAVE YOU GOT TWO TENS FOR A FIVE?
HUH? UH, YEAH, I THINK SO.
HEY, BORROW YOUR CREDIT CARD, TOO? I LOST MINE.
SURE. JUST GIVE IT BACK WHEN YOU'RE DONE.
SURE THING.
LET'S ARM WRESTLE.
GOTTA RUN.

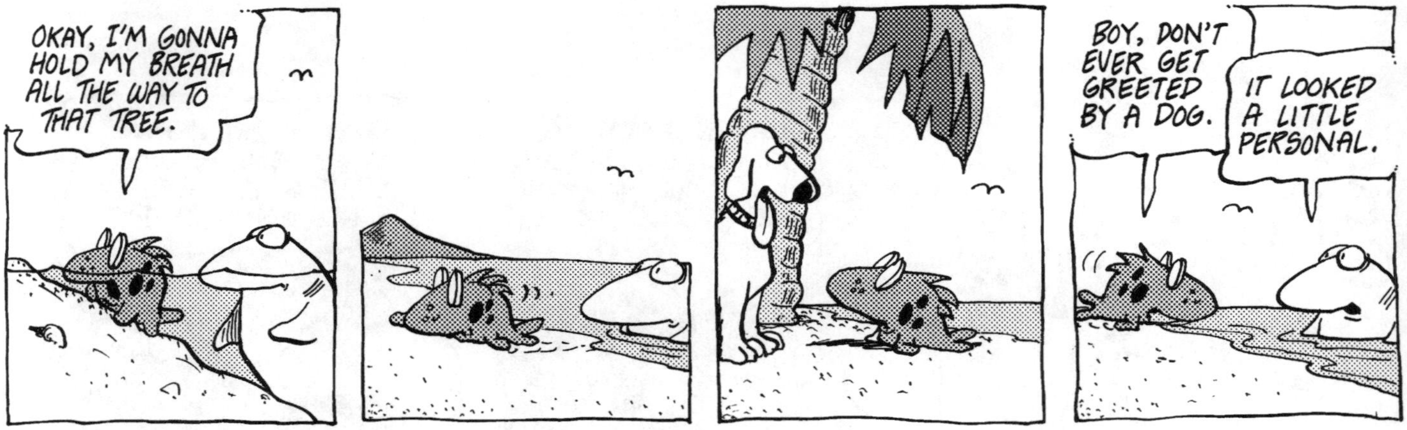
OKAY, I'M GONNA HOLD MY BREATH ALL THE WAY TO THAT TREE.
BOY, DON'T EVER GET GREETED BY A DOG.
IT LOOKED A LITTLE PERSONAL.

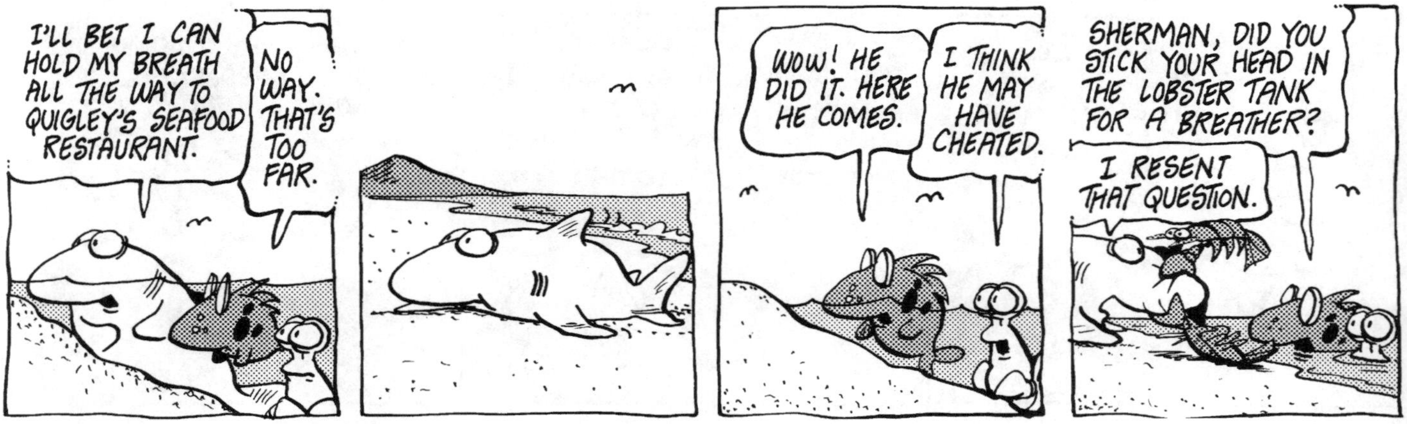
I'LL BET I CAN HOLD MY BREATH ALL THE WAY TO QUIGLEY'S SEAFOOD RESTAURANT.
NO WAY. THAT'S TOO FAR.
WOW! HE DID IT. HERE HE COMES.
I THINK HE MAY HAVE CHEATED.
SHERMAN, DID YOU STICK YOUR HEAD IN THE LOBSTER TANK FOR A BREATHER?
I RESENT THAT QUESTION.

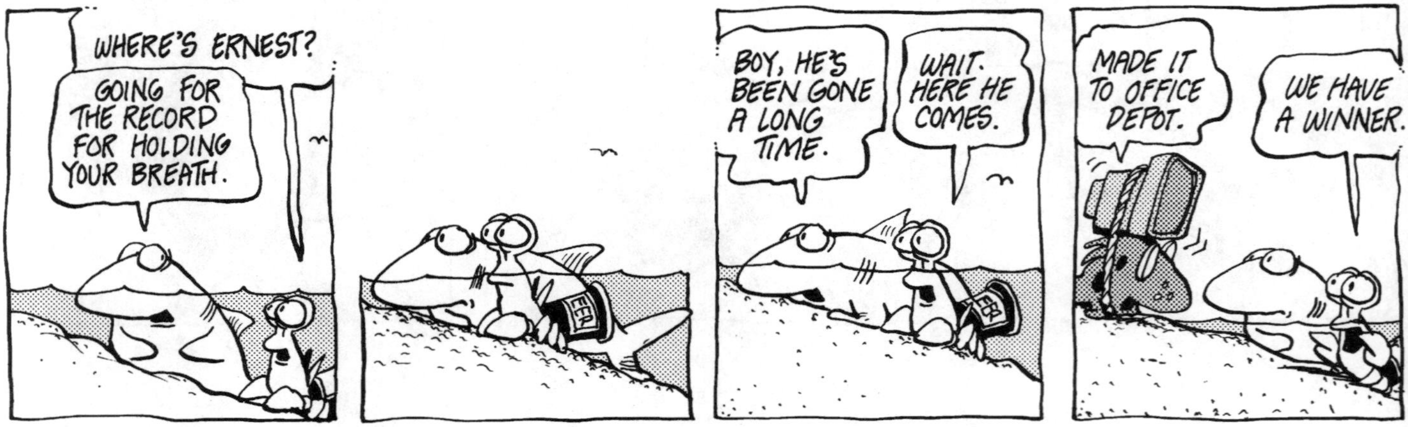
WHERE'S ERNEST?
GOING FOR THE RECORD FOR HOLDING YOUR BREATH.
BOY, HE'S BEEN GONE A LONG TIME.
WAIT. HERE HE COMES.
MADE IT TO OFFICE DEPOT.
WE HAVE A WINNER.

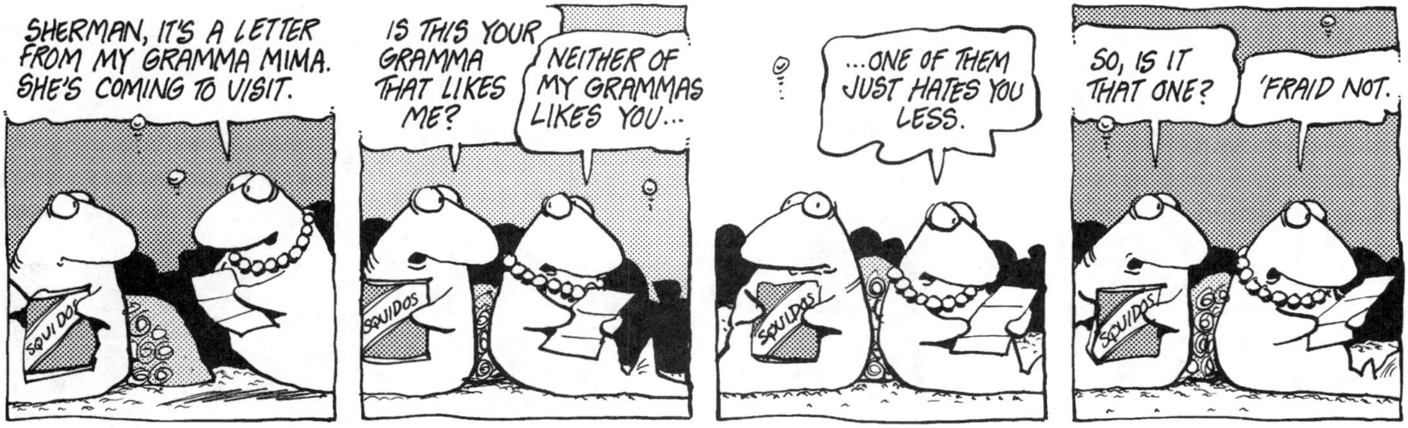
SHERMAN, IT'S A LETTER FROM MY GRAMMA MIMA. SHE'S COMING TO VISIT.
IS THIS YOUR GRAMMA THAT LIKES ME?
NEITHER OF MY GRAMMAS LIKES YOU...
...ONE OF THEM JUST HATES YOU LESS.
SO, IS IT THAT ONE?
'FRAID NOT.
SQUIDOS

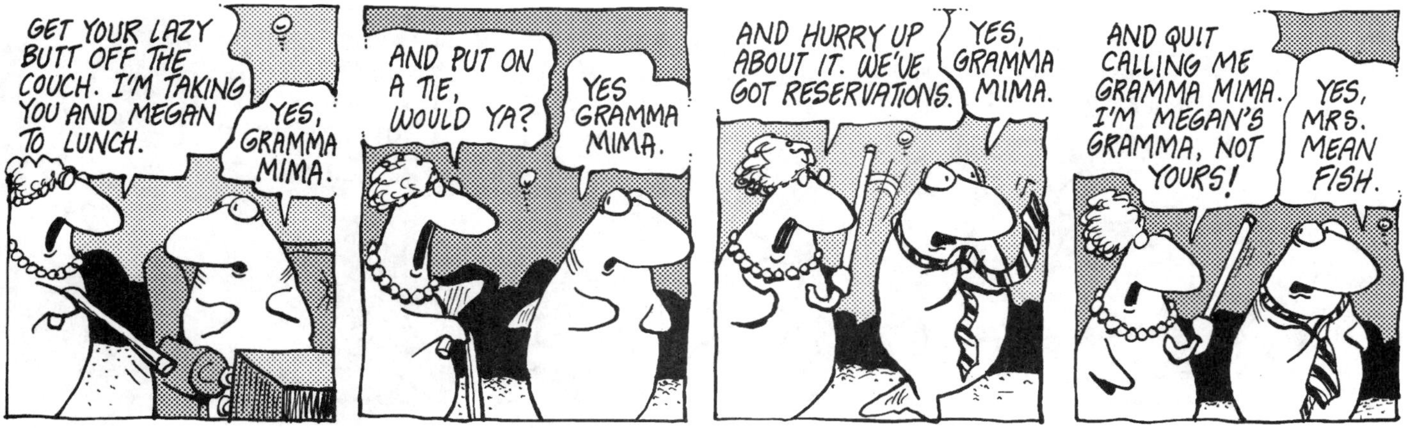
GET YOUR LAZY BUTT OFF THE COUCH. I'M TAKING YOU AND MEGAN TO LUNCH.
YES, GRAMMA MIMA.
AND PUT ON A TIE, WOULD YA?
YES GRAMMA MIMA.
AND HURRY UP ABOUT IT. WE'VE GOT RESERVATIONS.
YES, GRAMMA MIMA.
AND QUIT CALLING ME GRAMMA MIMA. I'M MEGAN'S GRAMMA, NOT YOURS!
YES, MRS. MEAN FISH.

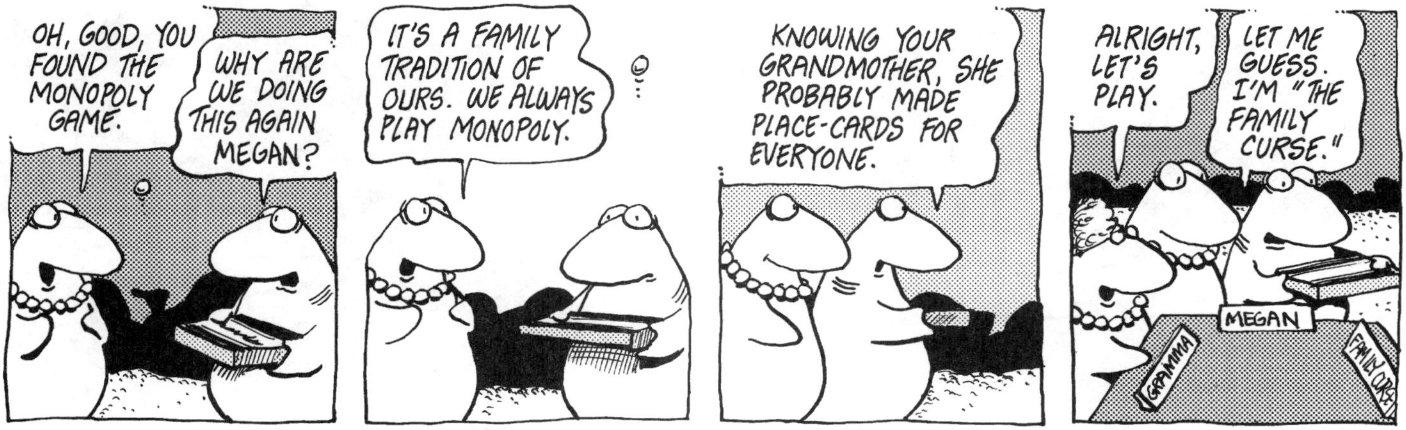
OH, GOOD, YOU FOUND THE MONOPOLY GAME.
WHY ARE WE DOING THIS AGAIN MEGAN?
IT'S A FAMILY TRADITION OF OURS. WE ALWAYS PLAY MONOPOLY.
KNOWING YOUR GRANDMOTHER, SHE PROBABLY MADE PLACE-CARDS FOR EVERYONE.
ALRIGHT, LET'S PLAY.
LET ME GUESS. I'M "THE FAMILY CURSE."
MEGAN
GRAMMA
FAMILY CURSE

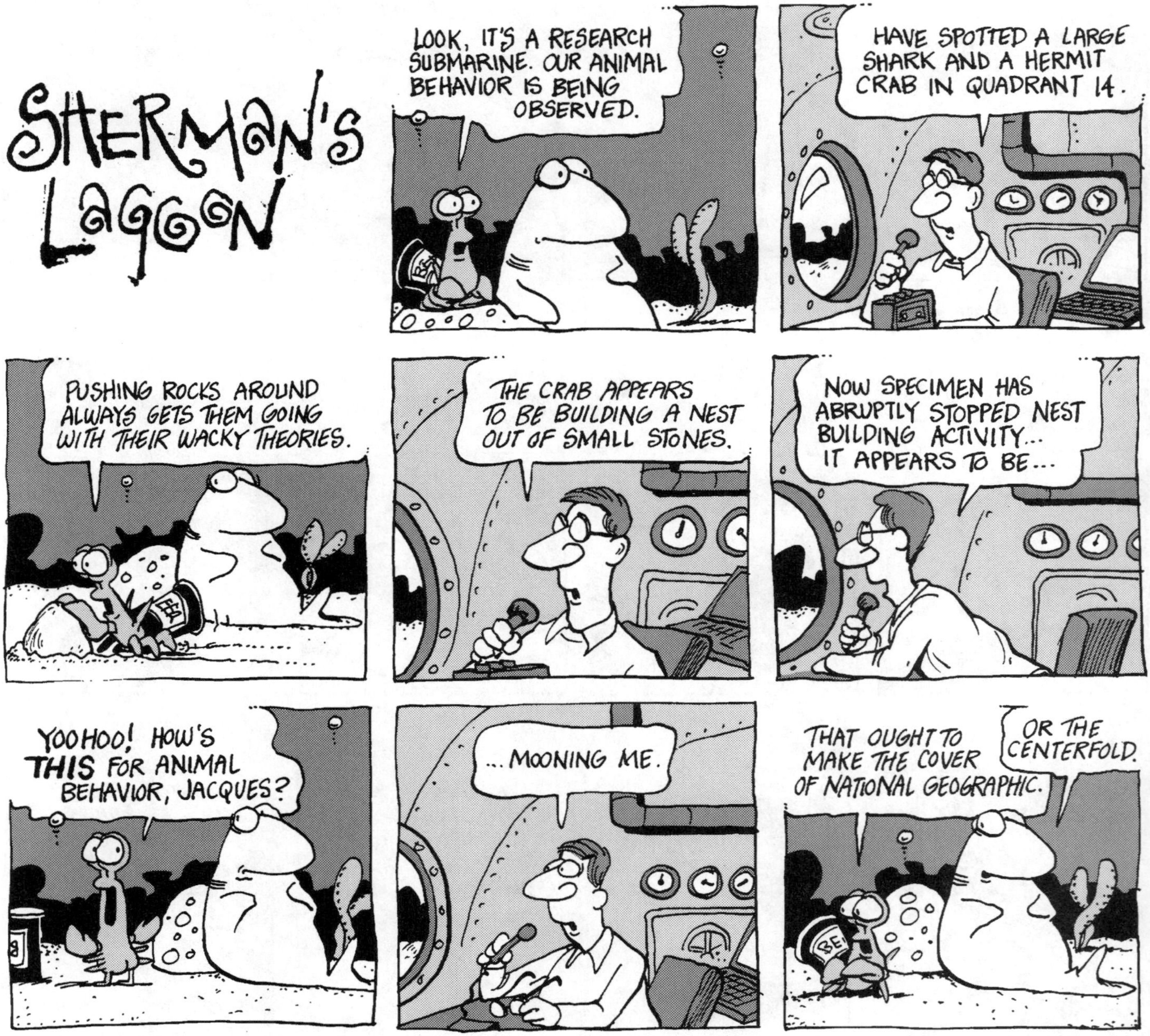
SHERMAN'S LAGOON
LOOK, IT'S A RESEARCH SUBMARINE. OUR ANIMAL BEHAVIOR IS BEING OBSERVED.
HAVE SPOTTED A LARGE SHARK AND A HERMIT CRAB IN QUADRANT 14.
PUSHING ROCKS AROUND ALWAYS GETS THEM GOING WITH THEIR WACKY THEORIES.
THE CRAB APPEARS TO BE BUILDING A NEST OUT OF SMALL STONES.
NOW SPECIMEN HAS ABRUPTLY STOPPED NEST BUILDING ACTIVITY... IT APPEARS TO BE...
YOOHOO! HOW'S **THIS** FOR ANIMAL BEHAVIOR, JACQUES?
...MOONING ME.
THAT OUGHT TO MAKE THE COVER OF NATIONAL GEOGRAPHIC.
OR THE CENTERFOLD.

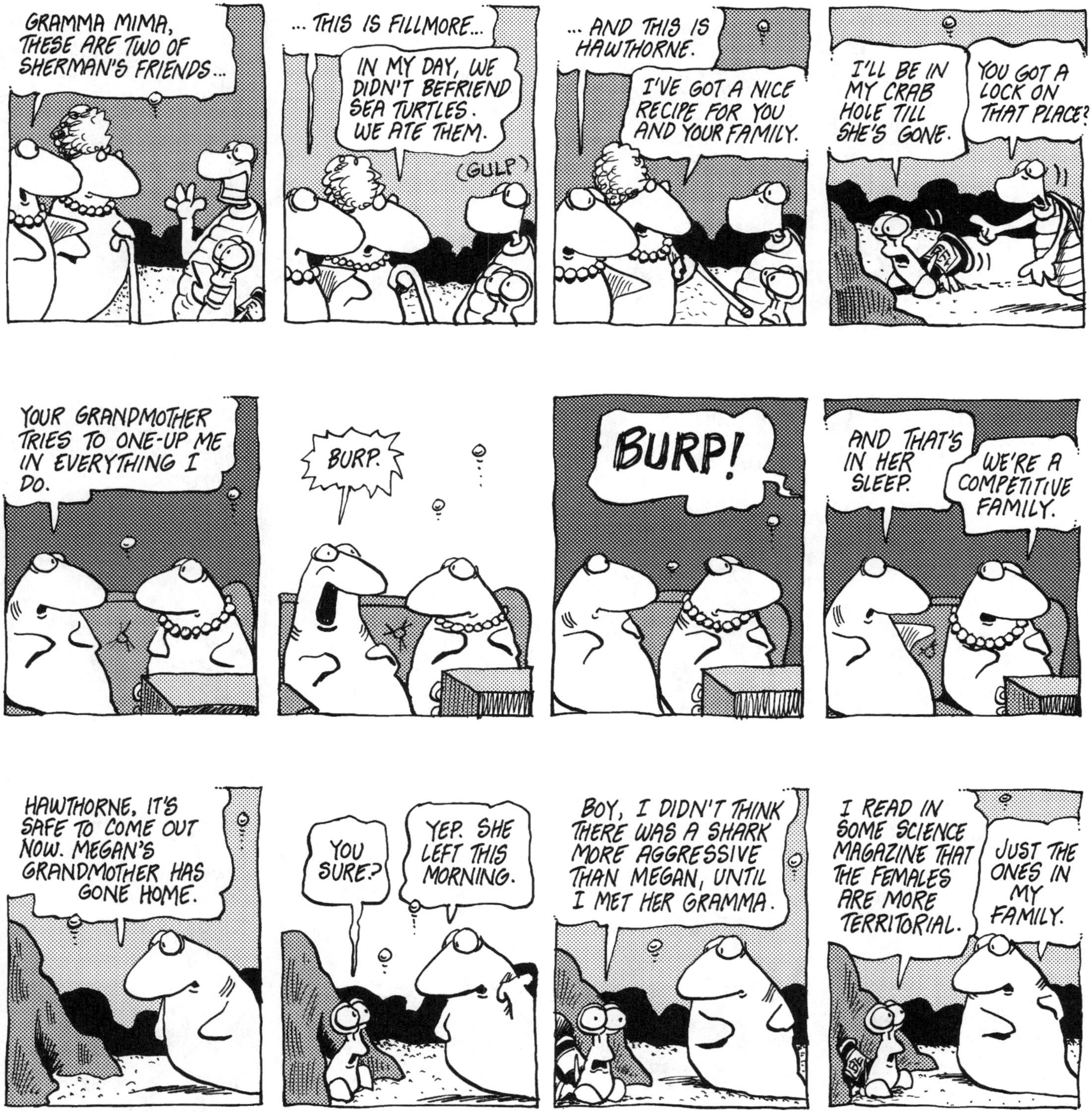
GRAMMA MIMA, THESE ARE TWO OF SHERMAN'S FRIENDS...
... THIS IS FILLMORE...
IN MY DAY, WE DIDN'T BEFRIEND SEA TURTLES. WE ATE THEM.
(GULP)
... AND THIS IS HAWTHORNE.
I'VE GOT A NICE RECIPE FOR YOU AND YOUR FAMILY.
I'LL BE IN MY CRAB HOLE TILL SHE'S GONE.
YOU GOT A LOCK ON THAT PLACE?
YOUR GRANDMOTHER TRIES TO ONE-UP ME IN EVERYTHING I DO.
BURP.
BURP!
AND THAT'S IN HER SLEEP.
WE'RE A COMPETITIVE FAMILY.
HAWTHORNE, IT'S SAFE TO COME OUT NOW. MEGAN'S GRANDMOTHER HAS GONE HOME.
YOU SURE?
YEP. SHE LEFT THIS MORNING.
BOY, I DIDN'T THINK THERE WAS A SHARK MORE AGGRESSIVE THAN MEGAN, UNTIL I MET HER GRAMMA.
I READ IN SOME SCIENCE MAGAZINE THAT THE FEMALES ARE MORE TERRITORIAL.
JUST THE ONES IN MY FAMILY.

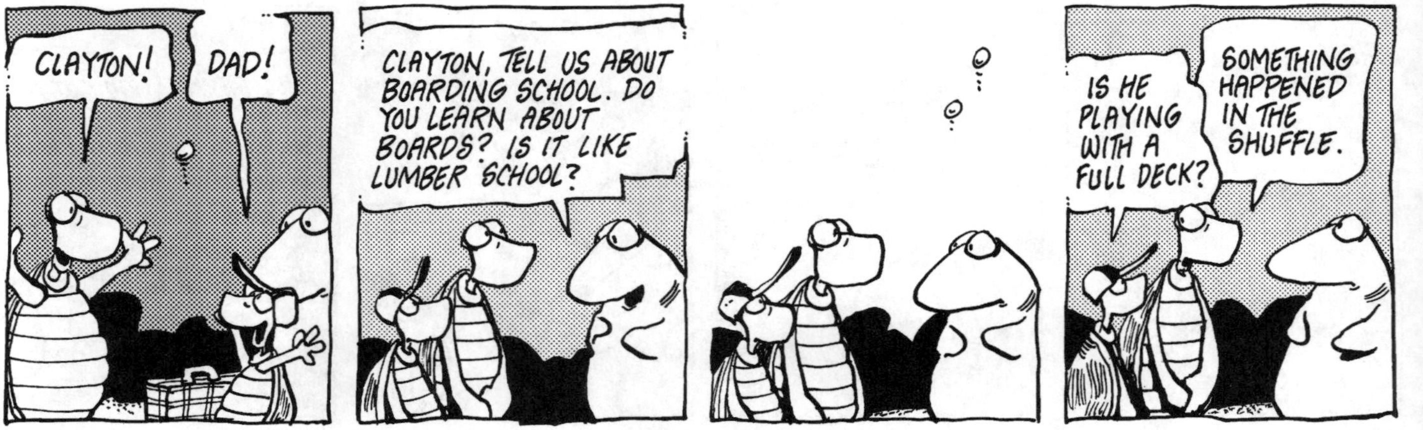
CLAYTON!
DAD!
CLAYTON, TELL US ABOUT BOARDING SCHOOL. DO YOU LEARN ABOUT BOARDS? IS IT LIKE LUMBER SCHOOL?
IS HE PLAYING WITH A FULL DECK?
SOMETHING HAPPENED IN THE SHUFFLE.

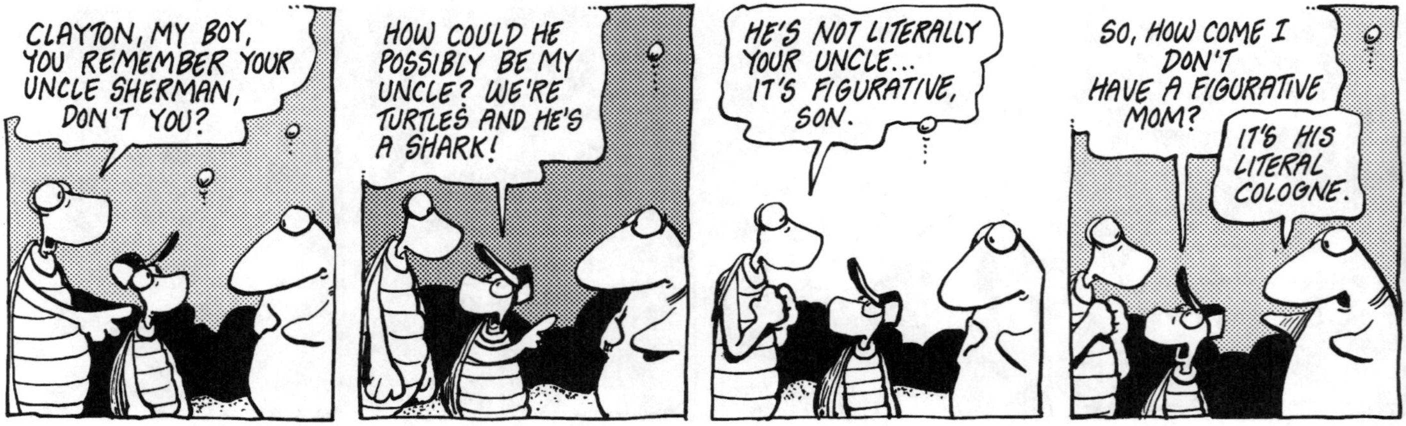
CLAYTON, MY BOY, YOU REMEMBER YOUR UNCLE SHERMAN, DON'T YOU?
HOW COULD HE POSSIBLY BE MY UNCLE? WE'RE TURTLES AND HE'S A SHARK!
HE'S NOT LITERALLY YOUR UNCLE... IT'S FIGURATIVE, SON.
SO, HOW COME I DON'T HAVE A FIGURATIVE MOM?
IT'S HIS LITERAL COLOGNE.

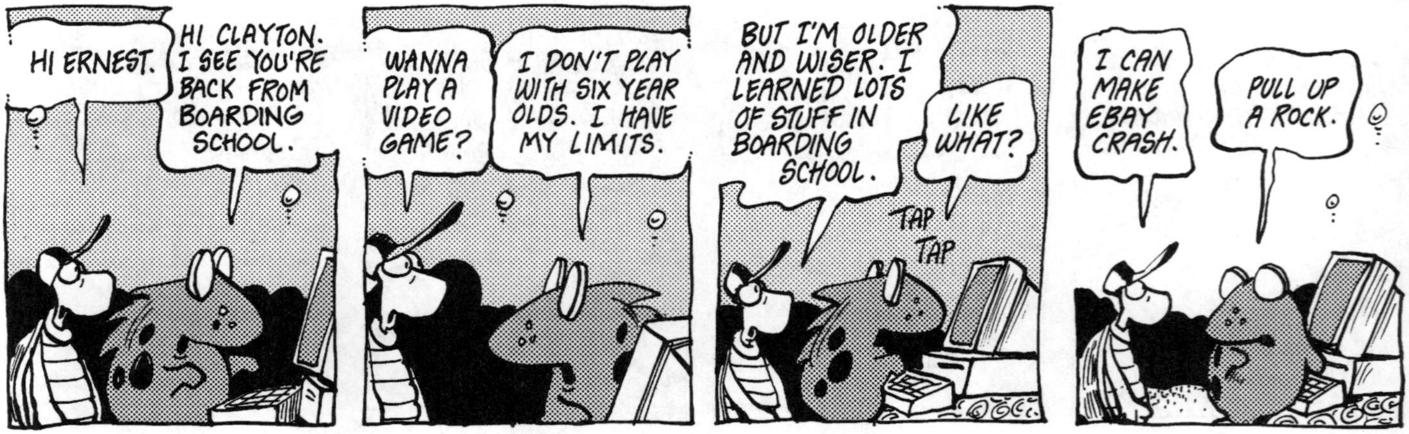
HI ERNEST.
HI CLAYTON. I SEE YOU'RE BACK FROM BOARDING SCHOOL.
WANNA PLAY A VIDEO GAME?
I DON'T PLAY WITH SIX YEAR OLDS. I HAVE MY LIMITS.
BUT I'M OLDER AND WISER. I LEARNED LOTS OF STUFF IN BOARDING SCHOOL.
LIKE WHAT?
TAP TAP
I CAN MAKE EBAY CRASH.
PULL UP A ROCK.

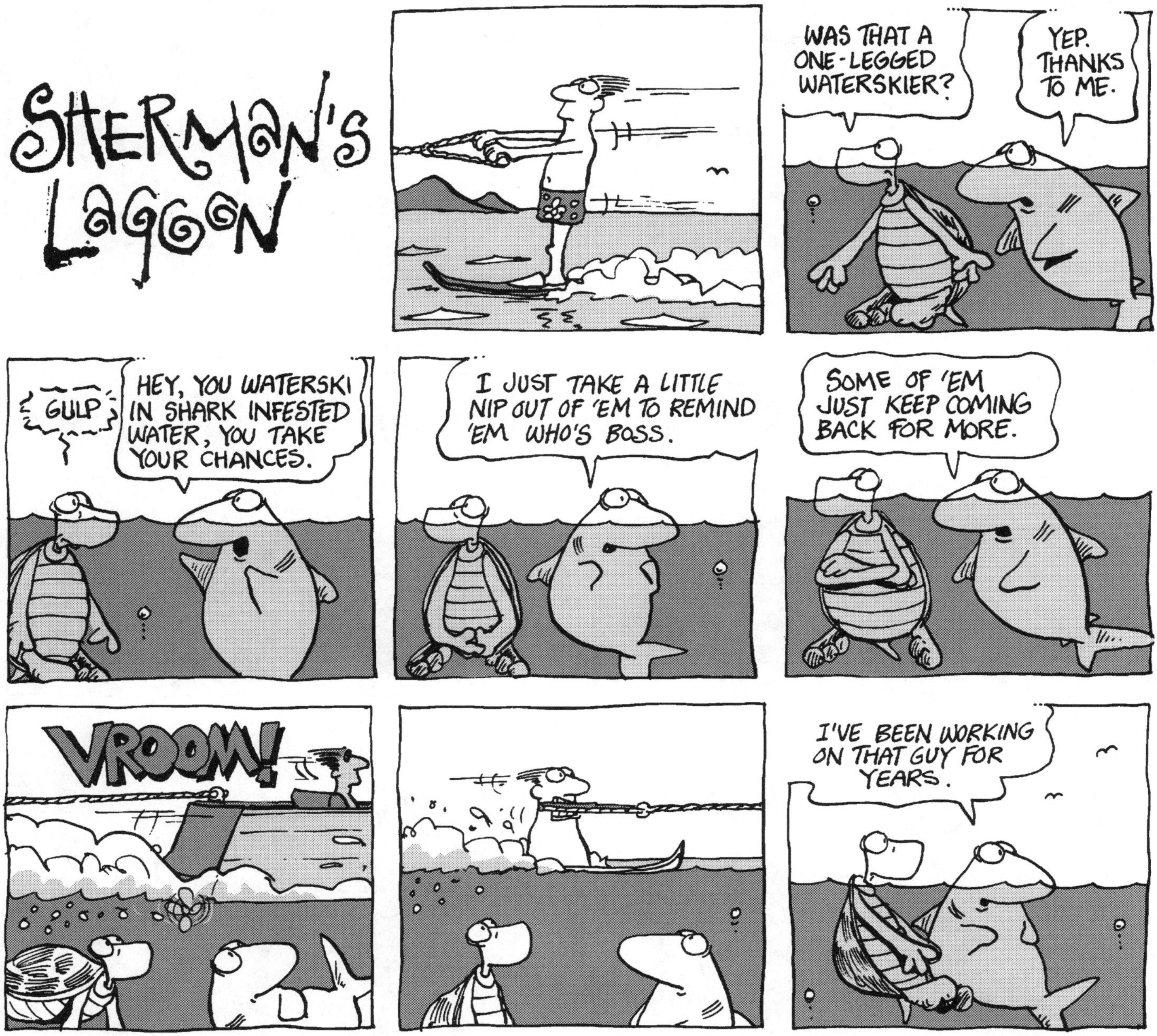
SHERMAN'S LAGOON
WAS THAT A ONE-LEGGED WATERSKIER?
YEP. THANKS TO ME.
GULP
HEY, YOU WATERSKI IN SHARK INFESTED WATER, YOU TAKE YOUR CHANCES.
I JUST TAKE A LITTLE NIP OUT OF 'EM TO REMIND 'EM WHO'S BOSS.
SOME OF 'EM JUST KEEP COMING BACK FOR MORE.
VROOM!
I'VE BEEN WORKING ON THAT GUY FOR YEARS.

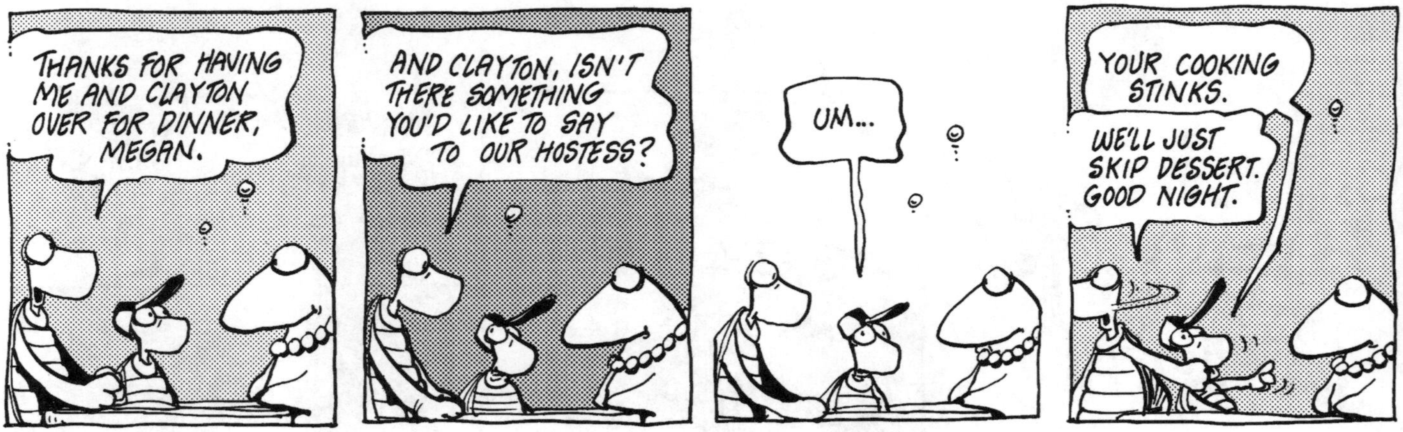
THANKS FOR HAVING ME AND CLAYTON OVER FOR DINNER, MEGAN.
AND CLAYTON, ISN'T THERE SOMETHING YOU'D LIKE TO SAY TO OUR HOSTESS?
UM...
YOUR COOKING STINKS.
WE'LL JUST SKIP DESSERT. GOOD NIGHT.

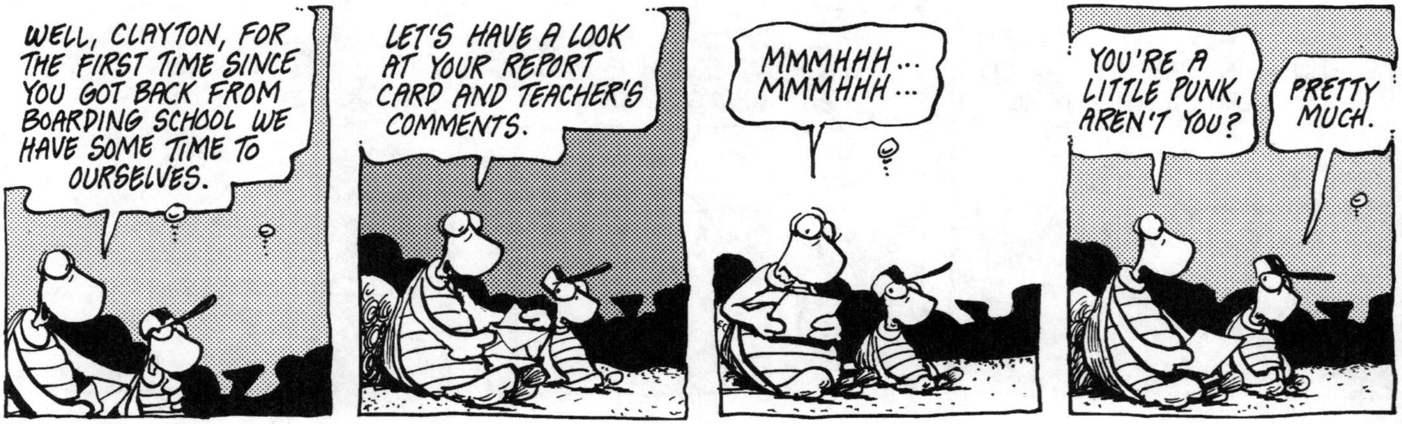
WELL, CLAYTON, FOR THE FIRST TIME SINCE YOU GOT BACK FROM BOARDING SCHOOL WE HAVE SOME TIME TO OURSELVES.
LET'S HAVE A LOOK AT YOUR REPORT CARD AND TEACHER'S COMMENTS.
MMMHHH... MMMHHH...
YOU'RE A LITTLE PUNK, AREN'T YOU?
PRETTY MUCH.

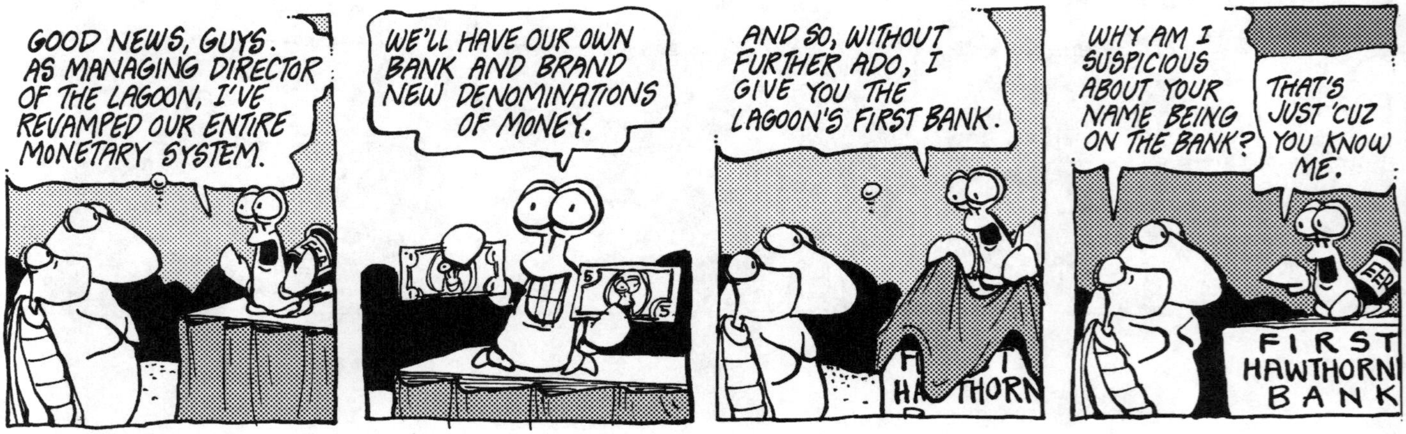
GOOD NEWS, GUYS. AS MANAGING DIRECTOR OF THE LAGOON, I'VE REVAMPED OUR ENTIRE MONETARY SYSTEM.
WE'LL HAVE OUR OWN BANK AND BRAND NEW DENOMINATIONS OF MONEY.
AND SO, WITHOUT FURTHER ADO, I GIVE YOU THE LAGOON'S FIRST BANK.
HA THORN
WHY AM I SUSPICIOUS ABOUT YOUR NAME BEING ON THE BANK?
THAT'S JUST 'CUZ YOU KNOW ME.
FIRST HAWTHORN BANK

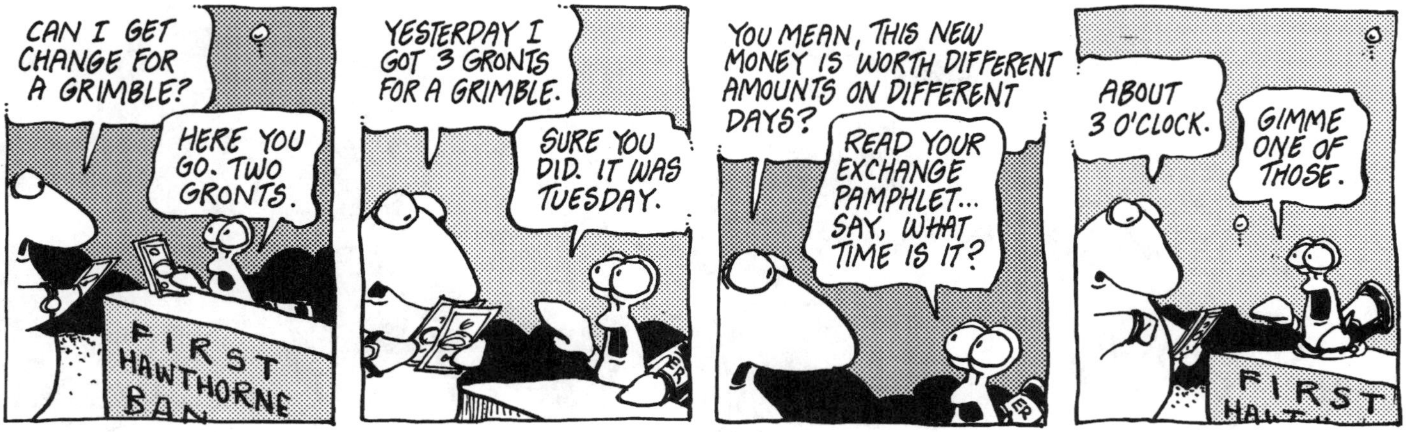
CAN I GET CHANGE FOR A GRIMBLE?
HERE YOU GO. TWO GRONTS.
YESTERDAY I GOT 3 GRONTS FOR A GRIMBLE.
SURE YOU DID. IT WAS TUESDAY.
YOU MEAN, THIS NEW MONEY IS WORTH DIFFERENT AMOUNTS ON DIFFERENT DAYS?
READ YOUR EXCHANGE PAMPHLET... SAY, WHAT TIME IS IT?
ABOUT 3 O'CLOCK.
GIMME ONE OF THOSE.

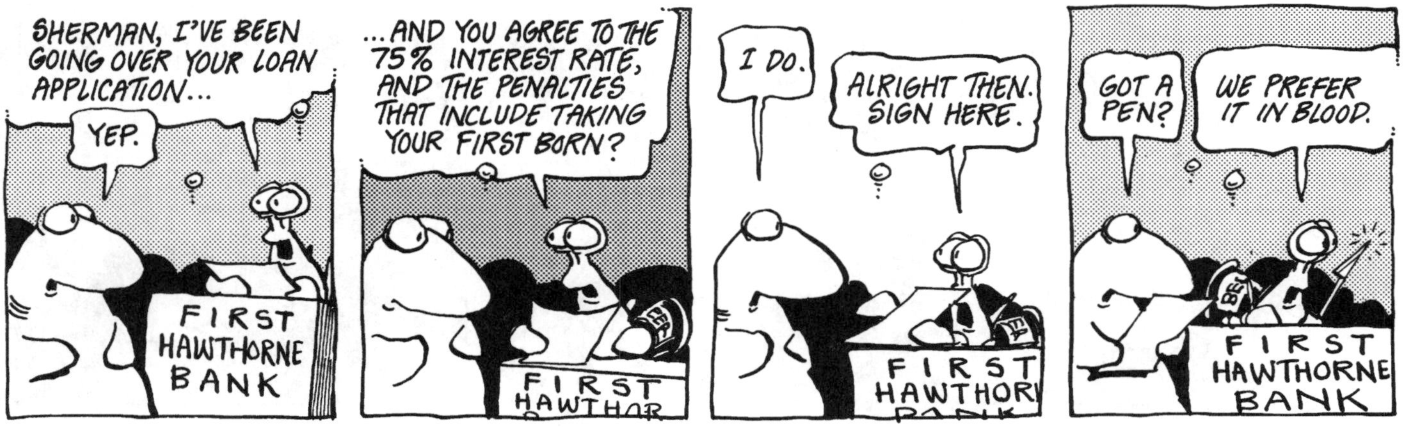
SHERMAN, I'VE BEEN GOING OVER YOUR LOAN APPLICATION...
YEP.
FIRST HAWTHORNE BANK
...AND YOU AGREE TO THE 75% INTEREST RATE, AND THE PENALTIES THAT INCLUDE TAKING YOUR FIRST BORN?
I DO.
ALRIGHT THEN. SIGN HERE.
GOT A PEN?
WE PREFER IT IN BLOOD.
FIRST HAWTHORNE BANK

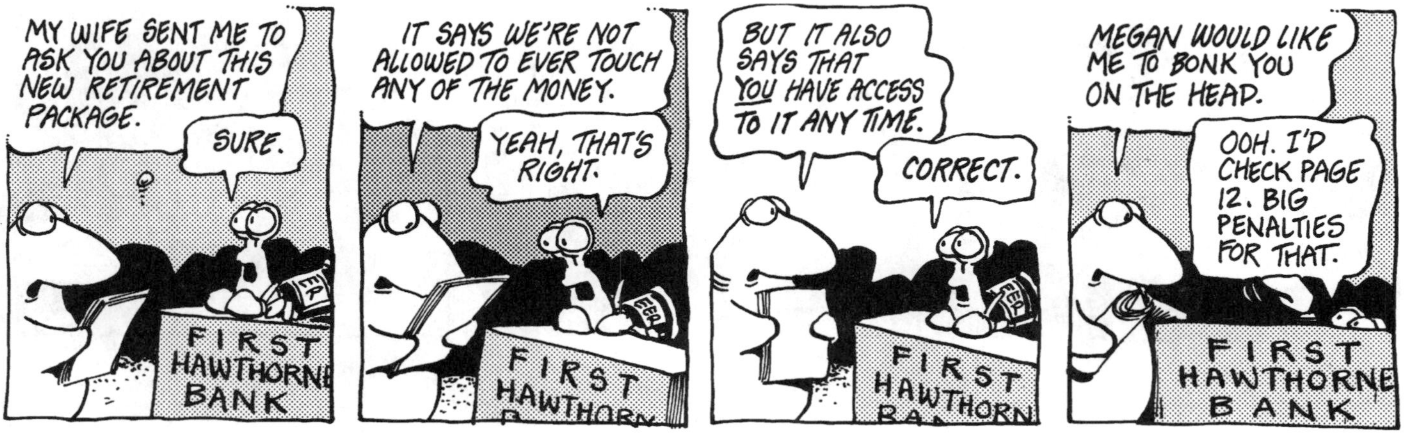
MY WIFE SENT ME TO ASK YOU ABOUT THIS NEW RETIREMENT PACKAGE.
SURE.
FIRST HAWTHORNE BANK
IT SAYS WE'RE NOT ALLOWED TO EVER TOUCH ANY OF THE MONEY.
YEAH, THAT'S RIGHT.
BUT IT ALSO SAYS THAT YOU HAVE ACCESS TO IT ANY TIME.
CORRECT.
MEGAN WOULD LIKE ME TO BONK YOU ON THE HEAD.
OOH. I'D CHECK PAGE 12. BIG PENALTIES FOR THAT.
FIRST HAWTHORNE BANK

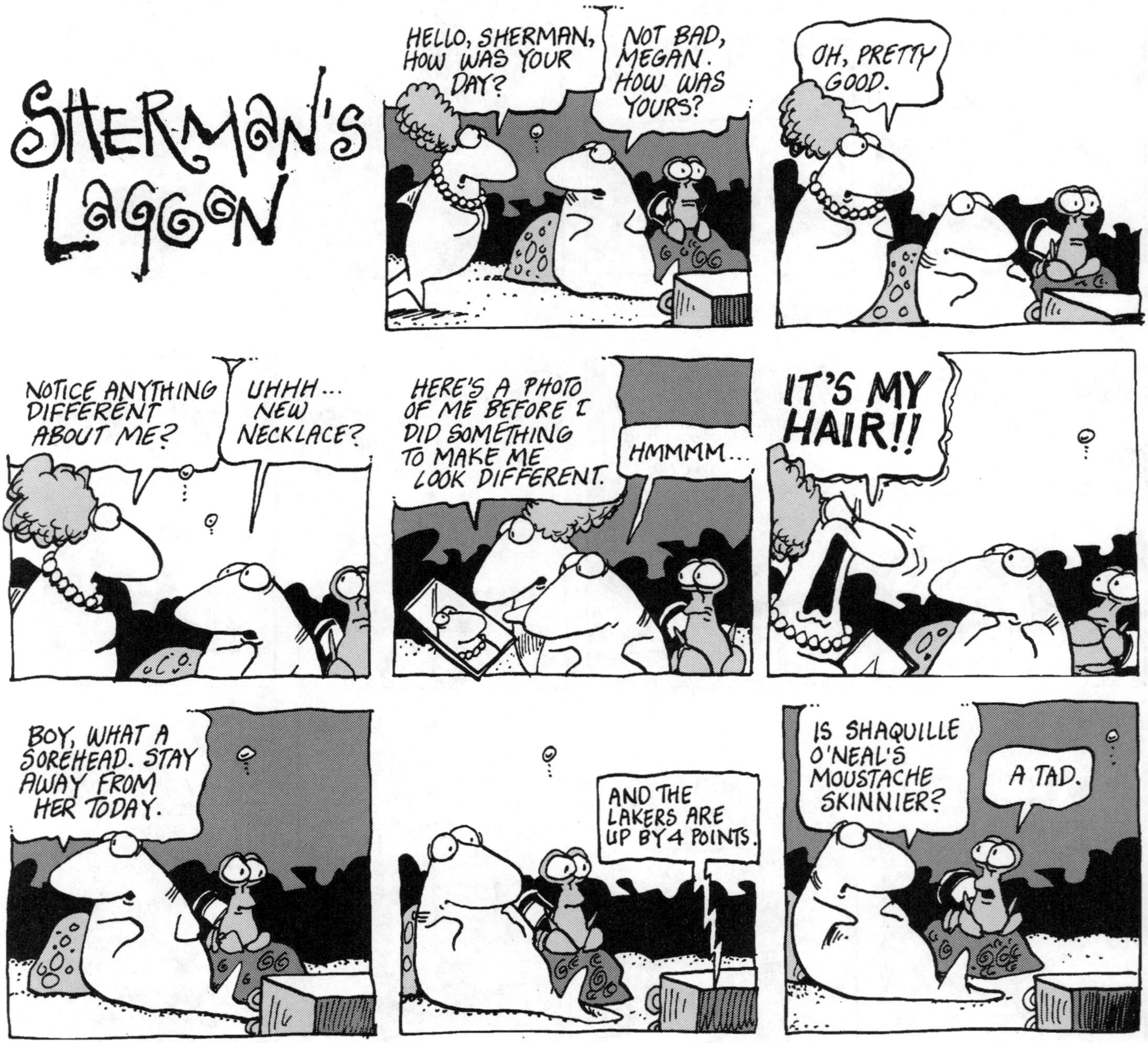
SHERMAN'S LAGOON
HELLO, SHERMAN, HOW WAS YOUR DAY?
NOT BAD, MEGAN. HOW WAS YOURS?
OH, PRETTY GOOD.
NOTICE ANYTHING DIFFERENT ABOUT ME?
UHHH... NEW NECKLACE?
HERE'S A PHOTO OF ME BEFORE I DID SOMETHING TO MAKE ME LOOK DIFFERENT.
HMMMM...
IT'S MY HAIR!!
BOY, WHAT A SOREHEAD. STAY AWAY FROM HER TODAY.
AND THE LAKERS ARE UP BY 4 POINTS.
IS SHAQUILLE O'NEAL'S MOUSTACHE SKINNIER?
A TAD.

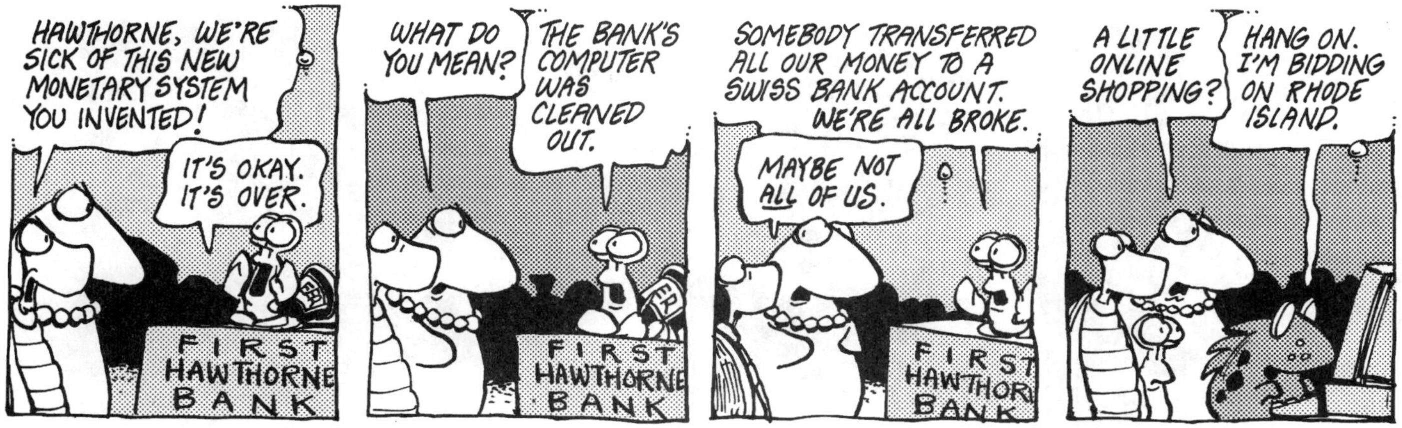
HAWTHORNE, WE'RE SICK OF THIS NEW MONETARY SYSTEM YOU INVENTED!
IT'S OKAY. IT'S OVER.
FIRST HAWTHORNE BANK
WHAT DO YOU MEAN?
THE BANK'S COMPUTER WAS CLEANED OUT.
FIRST HAWTHORNE BANK
SOMEBODY TRANSFERRED ALL OUR MONEY TO A SWISS BANK ACCOUNT. WE'RE ALL BROKE.
MAYBE NOT ALL OF US.
FIRST HAWTHOR BANK
A LITTLE ONLINE SHOPPING?
HANG ON. I'M BIDDING ON RHODE ISLAND.

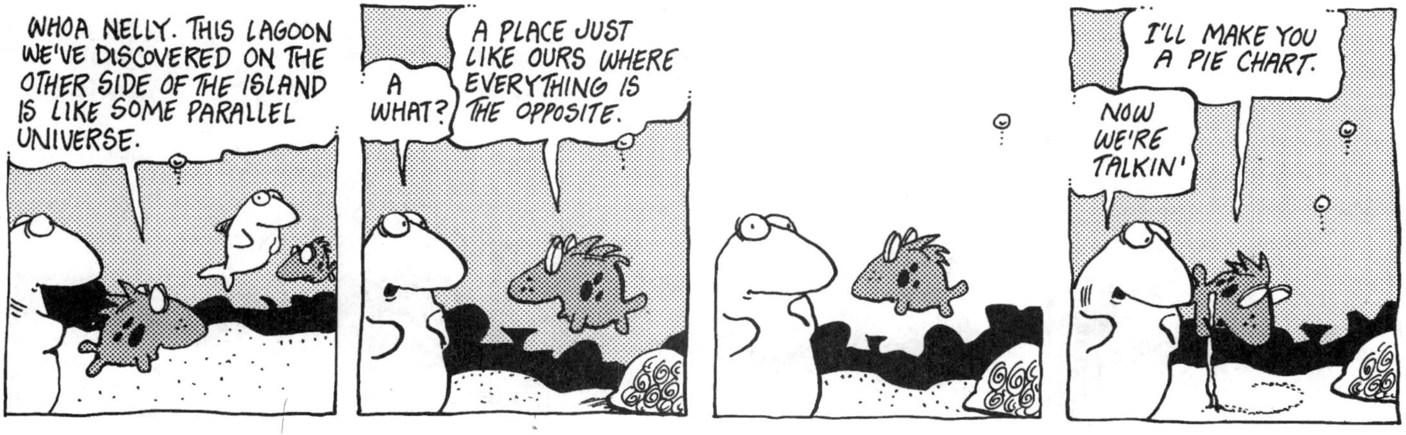
WHOA NELLY. THIS LAGOON WE'VE DISCOVERED ON THE OTHER SIDE OF THE ISLAND IS LIKE SOME PARALLEL UNIVERSE.
A WHAT?
A PLACE JUST LIKE OURS WHERE EVERYTHING IS THE OPPOSITE.
I'LL MAKE YOU A PIE CHART.
NOW WE'RE TALKIN'

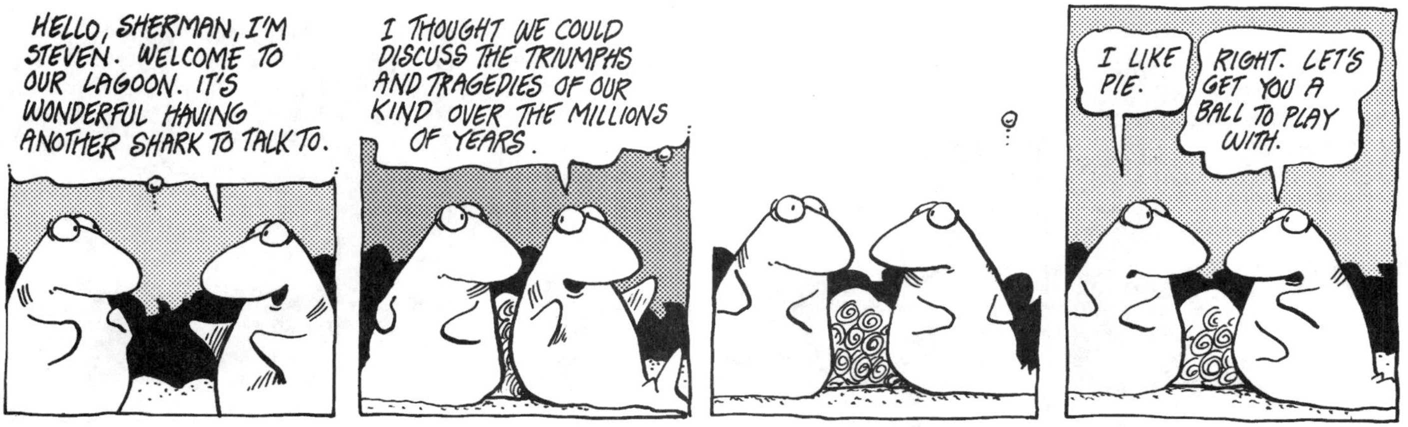
HELLO, SHERMAN, I'M STEVEN. WELCOME TO OUR LAGOON. IT'S WONDERFUL HAVING ANOTHER SHARK TO TALK TO.
I THOUGHT WE COULD DISCUSS THE TRIUMPHS AND TRAGEDIES OF OUR KIND OVER THE MILLIONS OF YEARS.
I LIKE PIE.
RIGHT. LET'S GET YOU A BALL TO PLAY WITH.

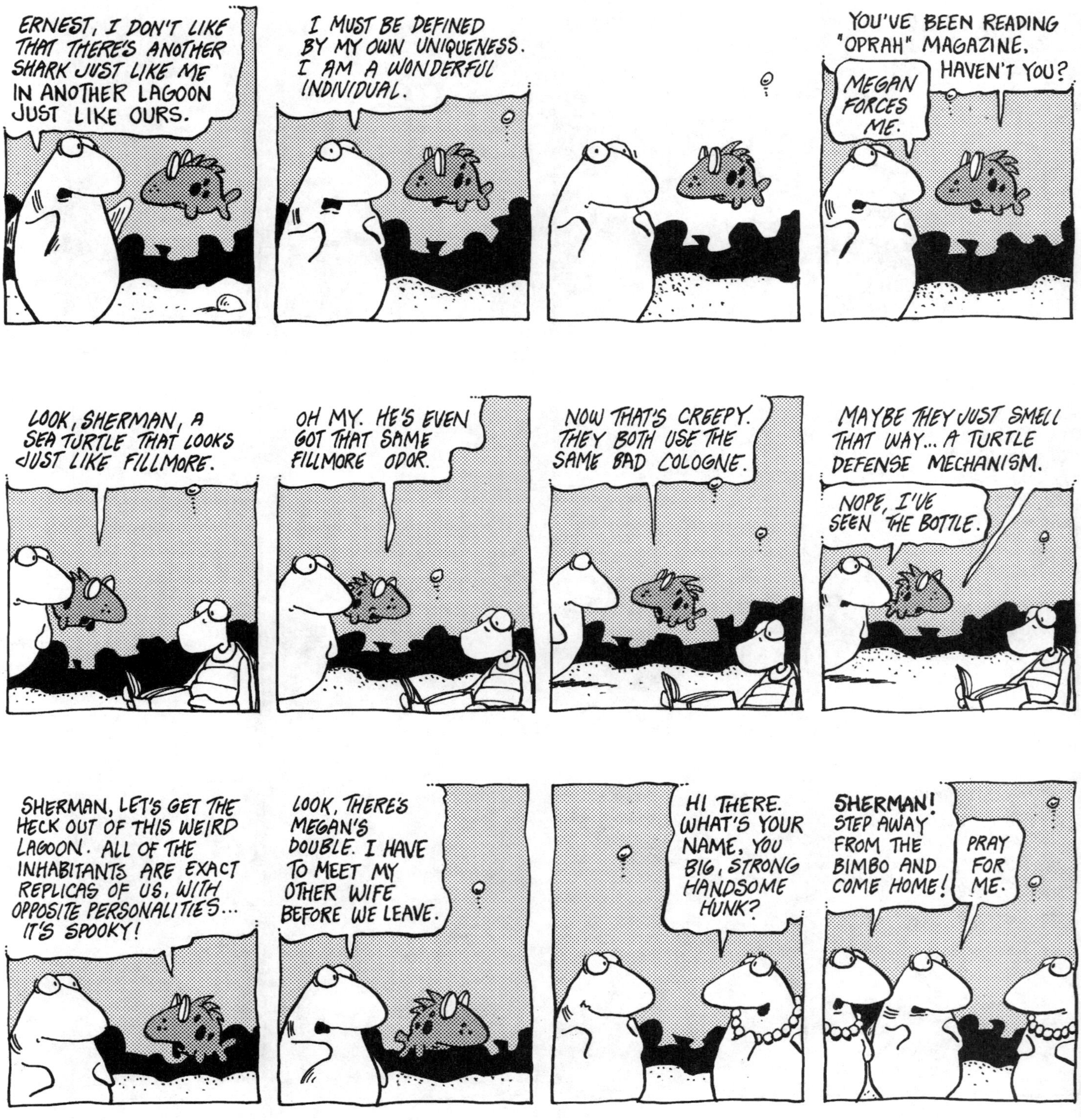
ERNEST, I DON'T LIKE THAT THERE'S ANOTHER SHARK JUST LIKE ME IN ANOTHER LAGOON JUST LIKE OURS.
I MUST BE DEFINED BY MY OWN UNIQUENESS. I AM A WONDERFUL INDIVIDUAL.
YOU'VE BEEN READING "OPRAH" MAGAZINE, HAVEN'T YOU?
MEGAN FORCES ME.
LOOK, SHERMAN, A SEA TURTLE THAT LOOKS JUST LIKE FILLMORE.
OH MY. HE'S EVEN GOT THAT SAME FILLMORE ODOR.
NOW THAT'S CREEPY. THEY BOTH USE THE SAME BAD COLOGNE.
MAYBE THEY JUST SMELL THAT WAY... A TURTLE DEFENSE MECHANISM.
NOPE, I'VE SEEN THE BOTTLE.
SHERMAN, LET'S GET THE HECK OUT OF THIS WEIRD LAGOON. ALL OF THE INHABITANTS ARE EXACT REPLICAS OF US, WITH OPPOSITE PERSONALITIES... IT'S SPOOKY!
LOOK, THERE'S MEGAN'S DOUBLE. I HAVE TO MEET MY OTHER WIFE BEFORE WE LEAVE.
HI THERE. WHAT'S YOUR NAME, YOU BIG, STRONG HANDSOME HUNK?
SHERMAN! STEP AWAY FROM THE BIMBO AND COME HOME!
PRAY FOR ME.

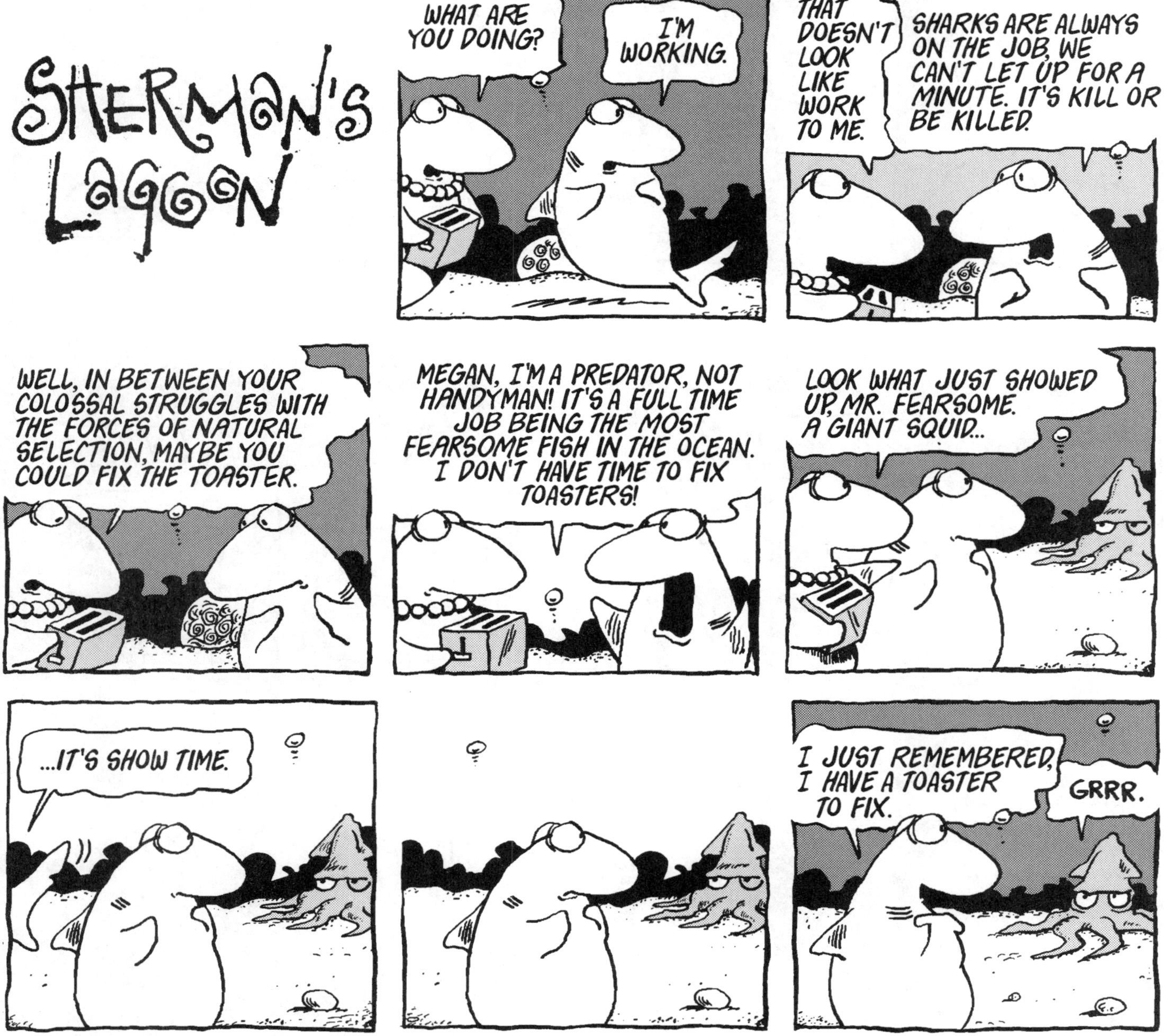
SHERMAN'S LAGOON
WHAT ARE YOU DOING?
I'M WORKING.
THAT DOESN'T LOOK LIKE WORK TO ME.
SHARKS ARE ALWAYS ON THE JOB, WE CAN'T LET UP FOR A MINUTE. IT'S KILL OR BE KILLED.
WELL, IN BETWEEN YOUR COLOSSAL STRUGGLES WITH THE FORCES OF NATURAL SELECTION, MAYBE YOU COULD FIX THE TOASTER.
MEGAN, I'M A PREDATOR, NOT HANDYMAN! IT'S A FULL TIME JOB BEING THE MOST FEARSOME FISH IN THE OCEAN. I DON'T HAVE TIME TO FIX TOASTERS!
LOOK WHAT JUST SHOWED UP, MR. FEARSOME. A GIANT SQUID...
...IT'S SHOW TIME.
I JUST REMEMBERED, I HAVE A TOASTER TO FIX.
GRRR.

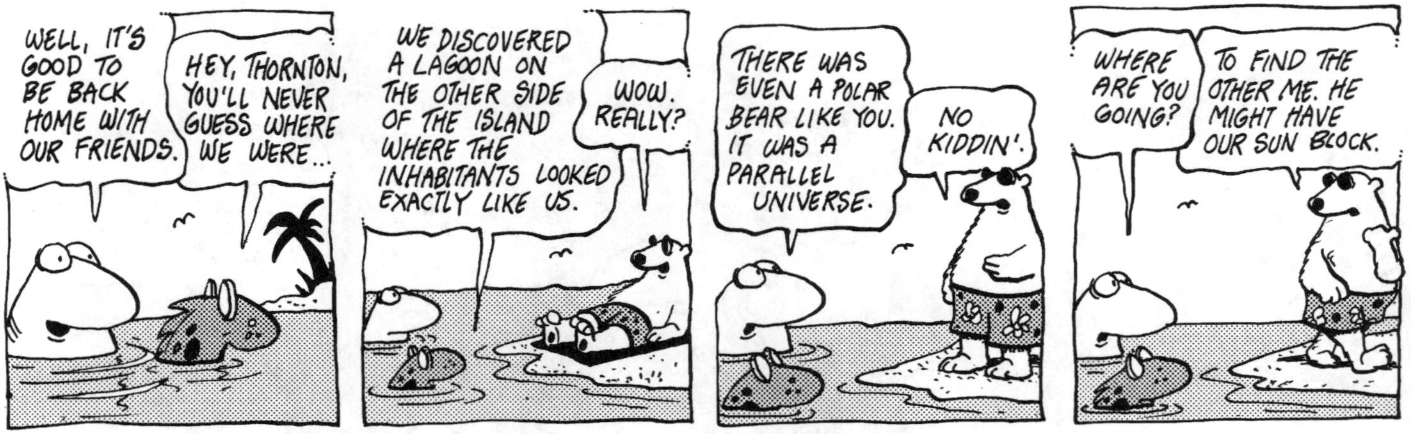
WELL, IT'S GOOD TO BE BACK HOME WITH OUR FRIENDS.
HEY, THORNTON, YOU'LL NEVER GUESS WHERE WE WERE...
WE DISCOVERED A LAGOON ON THE OTHER SIDE OF THE ISLAND WHERE THE INHABITANTS LOOKED EXACTLY LIKE US.
WOW. REALLY?
THERE WAS EVEN A POLAR BEAR LIKE YOU. IT WAS A PARALLEL UNIVERSE.
NO KIDDIN'.
WHERE ARE YOU GOING?
TO FIND THE OTHER ME. HE MIGHT HAVE OUR SUN BLOCK.

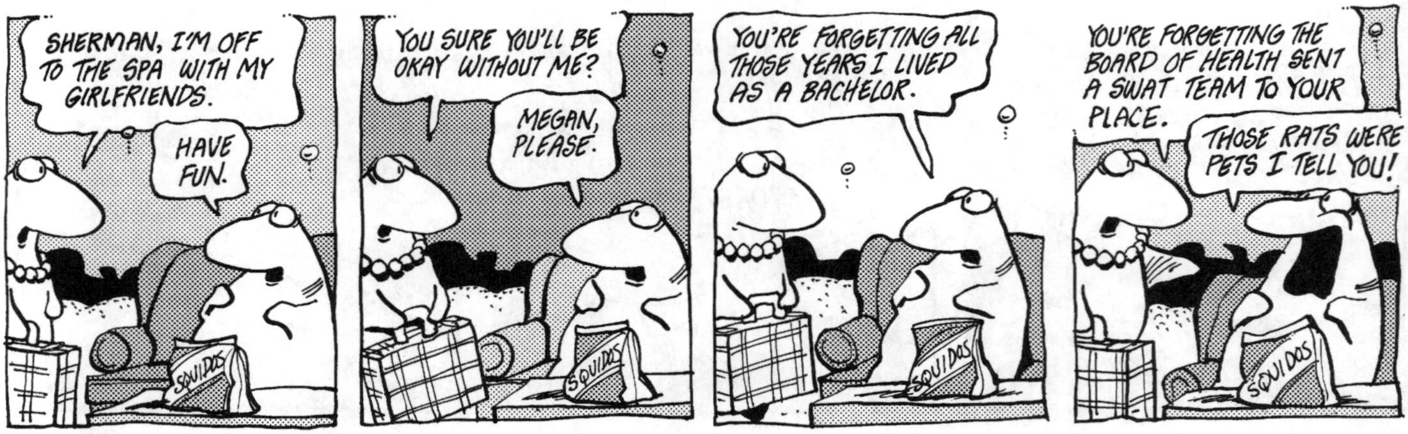
SHERMAN, I'M OFF TO THE SPA WITH MY GIRLFRIENDS.
HAVE FUN.
SQUIDOS
YOU SURE YOU'LL BE OKAY WITHOUT ME?
MEGAN, PLEASE.
SQUIDOS
YOU'RE FORGETTING ALL THOSE YEARS I LIVED AS A BACHELOR.
SQUIDOS
YOU'RE FORGETTING THE BOARD OF HEALTH SENT A SWAT TEAM TO YOUR PLACE.
THOSE RATS WERE PETS I TELL YOU!
SQUIDOS

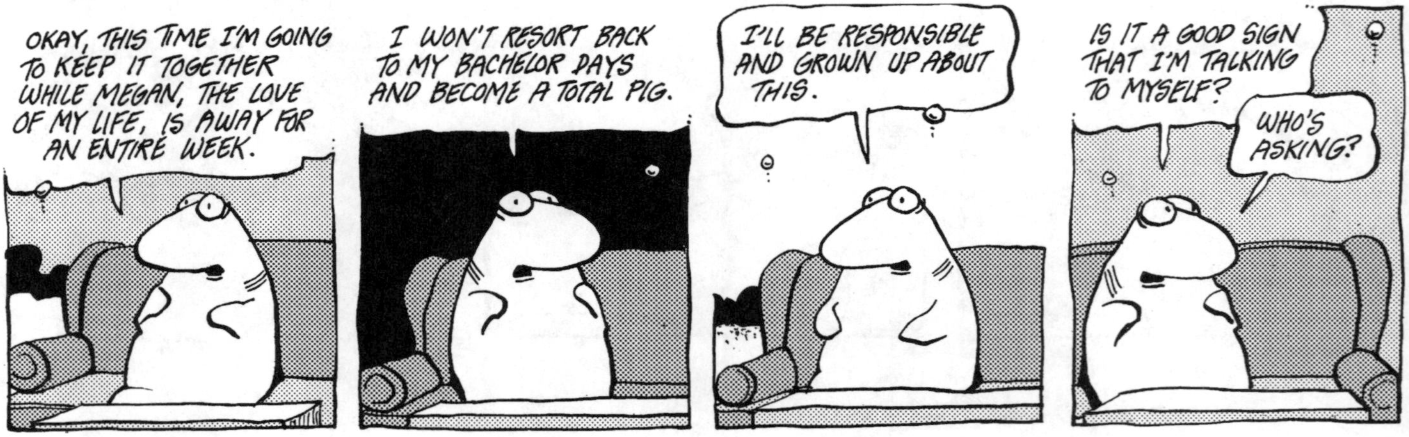
OKAY, THIS TIME I'M GOING TO KEEP IT TOGETHER WHILE MEGAN, THE LOVE OF MY LIFE, IS AWAY FOR AN ENTIRE WEEK.
I WON'T RESORT BACK TO MY BACHELOR DAYS AND BECOME A TOTAL PIG.
I'LL BE RESPONSIBLE AND GROWN UP ABOUT THIS.
IS IT A GOOD SIGN THAT I'M TALKING TO MYSELF?
WHO'S ASKING?

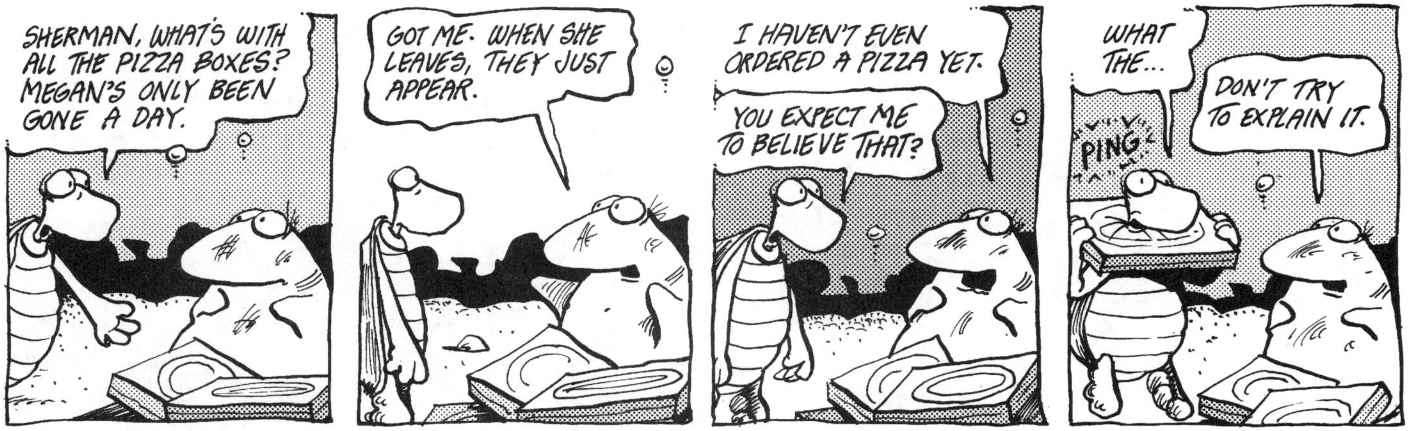
SHERMAN, WHAT'S WITH ALL THE PIZZA BOXES? MEGAN'S ONLY BEEN GONE A DAY.
GOT ME. WHEN SHE LEAVES, THEY JUST APPEAR.
I HAVEN'T EVEN ORDERED A PIZZA YET.
YOU EXPECT ME TO BELIEVE THAT?
WHAT THE...
PING
DON'T TRY TO EXPLAIN IT.

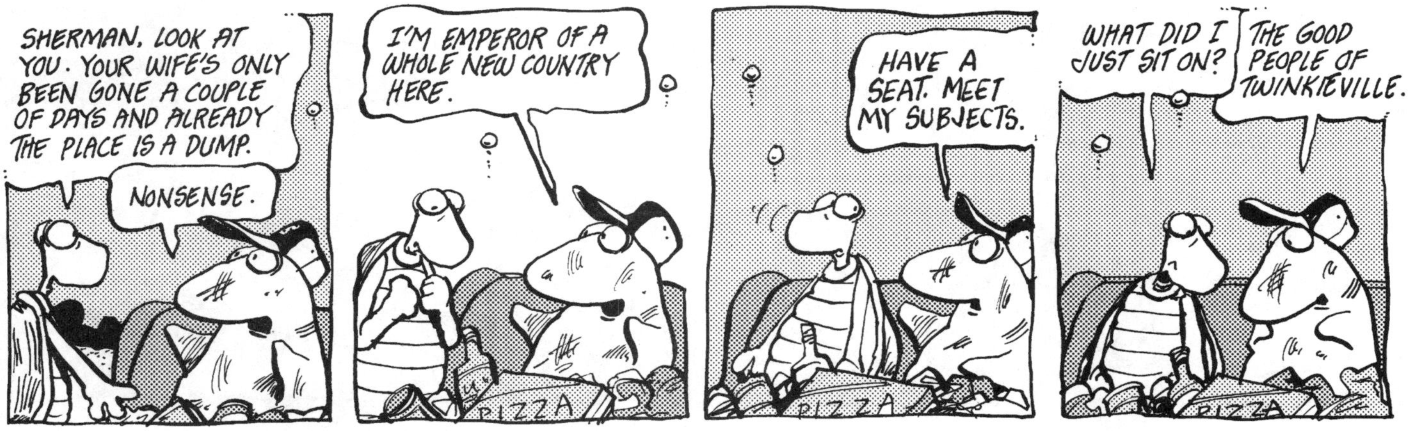
SHERMAN, LOOK AT YOU. YOUR WIFE'S ONLY BEEN GONE A COUPLE OF DAYS AND ALREADY THE PLACE IS A DUMP.
NONSENSE.
I'M EMPEROR OF A WHOLE NEW COUNTRY HERE.
HAVE A SEAT. MEET MY SUBJECTS.
WHAT DID I JUST SIT ON?
THE GOOD PEOPLE OF TWINKIEVILLE.

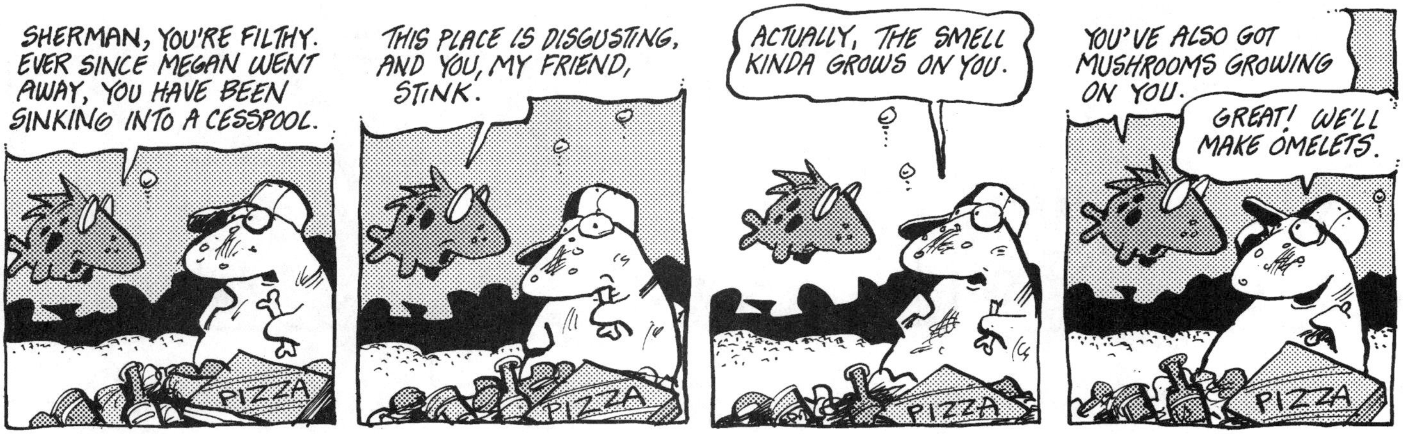
SHERMAN, YOU'RE FILTHY. EVER SINCE MEGAN WENT AWAY, YOU HAVE BEEN SINKING INTO A CESSPOOL.
THIS PLACE IS DISGUSTING, AND YOU, MY FRIEND, STINK.
ACTUALLY, THE SMELL KINDA GROWS ON YOU.
YOU'VE ALSO GOT MUSHROOMS GROWING ON YOU.
GREAT! WE'LL MAKE OMELETS.

SHERMAN'S LAGOON
WHAT A NICE, PEACEFUL SUNDAY.
YEP.
MAN BITES SHARK
JUST TAKIN' 'ER EASY.
YEP.
JUST ME AND MY GOOD FRIEND FILLMORE.
MAN BITES SHARK
I THINK IT'S GREAT HOW WE CAN JUST CHILL OUT AND DO ANYTHING.
WITH YOU I CAN JUST RELAX AND BE MYSELF.
HELP!!
MAN BITES SHARK
FOR CRYING OUT LOUD, GET IT OFF ME!!
BUT OTHERS JUST CRAVE THAT ATTENTION.
IT'S A SICKNESS.
MAN BITES SHARK

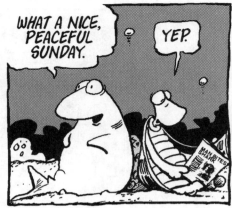

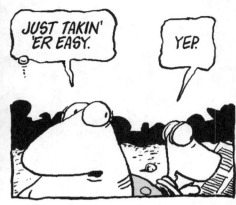

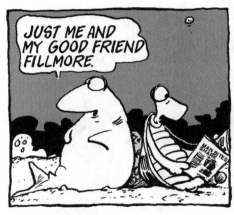

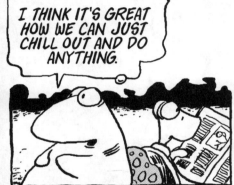

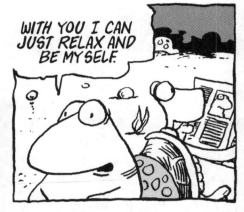

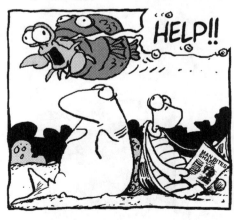

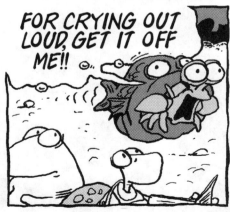

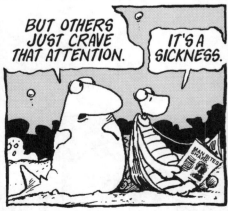

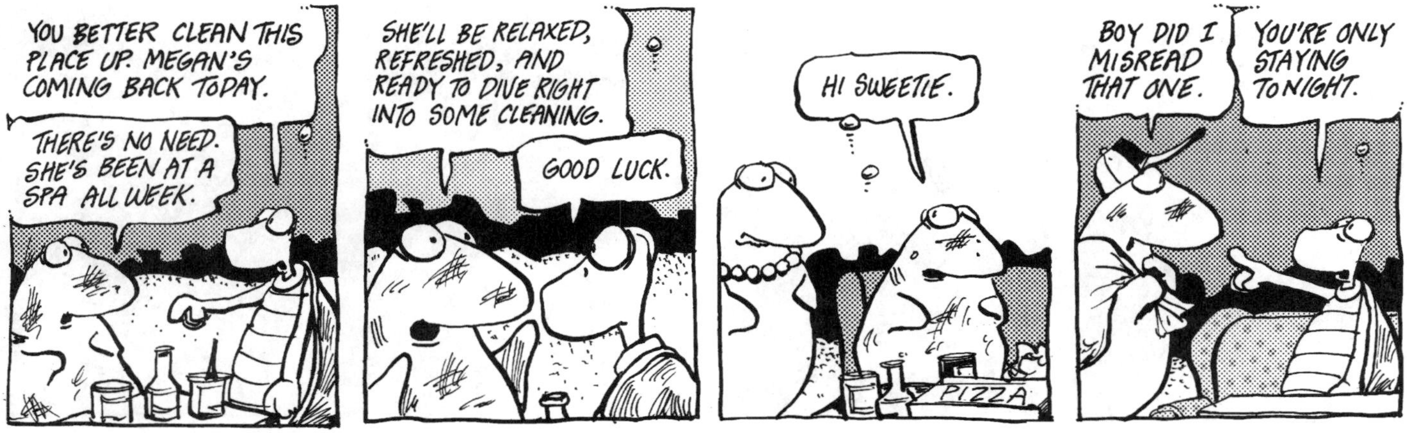
YOU BETTER CLEAN THIS PLACE UP. MEGAN'S COMING BACK TODAY.
THERE'S NO NEED. SHE'S BEEN AT A SPA ALL WEEK.
SHE'LL BE RELAXED, REFRESHED, AND READY TO DIVE RIGHT INTO SOME CLEANING.
GOOD LUCK.
HI SWEETIE.
PIZZA
BOY DID I MISREAD THAT ONE.
YOU'RE ONLY STAYING TONIGHT.

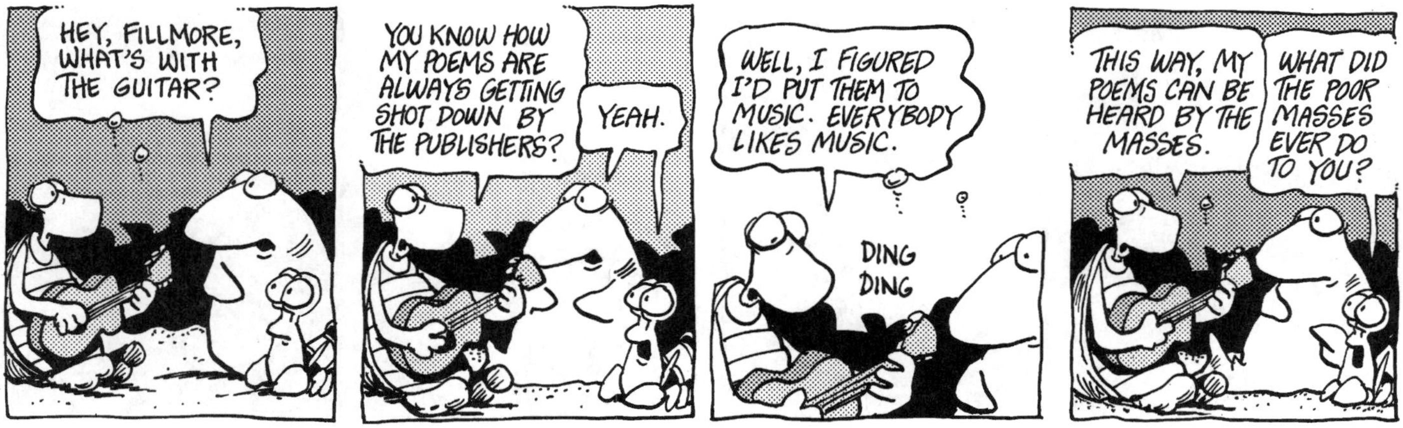
HEY, FILLMORE, WHAT'S WITH THE GUITAR?
YOU KNOW HOW MY POEMS ARE ALWAYS GETTING SHOT DOWN BY THE PUBLISHERS?
YEAH.
WELL, I FIGURED I'D PUT THEM TO MUSIC. EVERYBODY LIKES MUSIC.
DING DING
THIS WAY, MY POEMS CAN BE HEARD BY THE MASSES.
WHAT DID THE POOR MASSES EVER DO TO YOU?

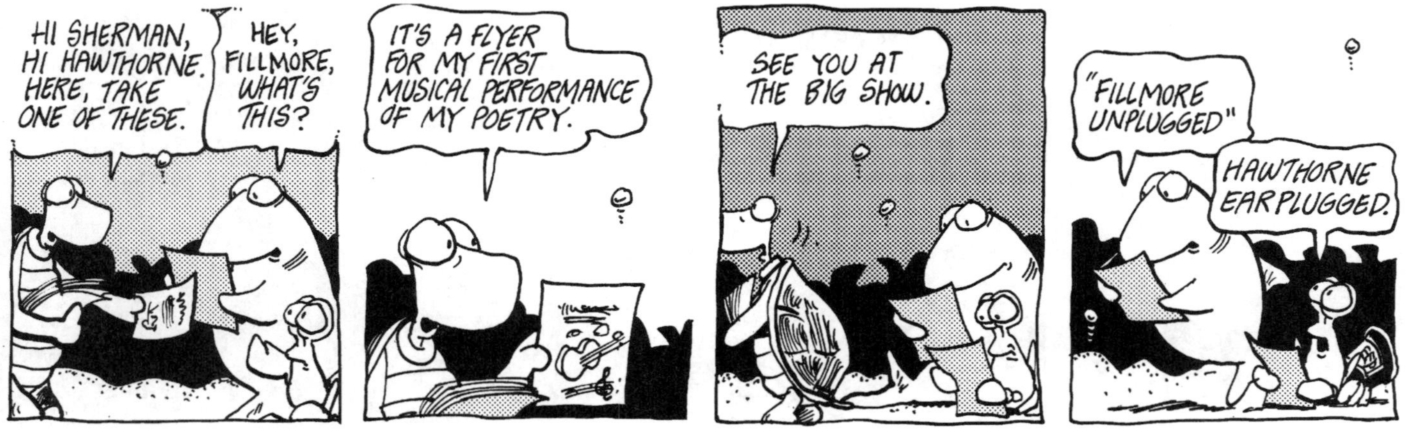
HI SHERMAN, HI HAWTHORNE. HERE, TAKE ONE OF THESE.
HEY, FILLMORE, WHAT'S THIS?
IT'S A FLYER FOR MY FIRST MUSICAL PERFORMANCE OF MY POETRY.
SEE YOU AT THE BIG SHOW.
"FILLMORE UNPLUGGED"
HAWTHORNE EARPLUGGED.

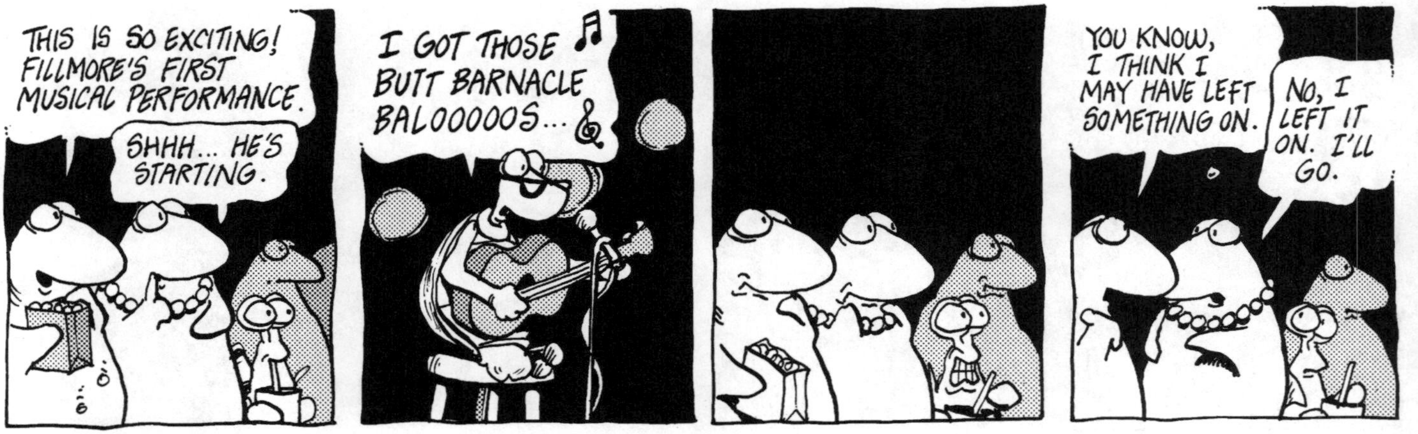
THIS IS SO EXCITING! FILLMORE'S FIRST MUSICAL PERFORMANCE.
SHHH... HE'S STARTING.
I GOT THOSE BUTT BARNACLE BALOOOOOS...
YOU KNOW, I THINK I MAY HAVE LEFT SOMETHING ON.
NO, I LEFT IT ON. I'LL GO.

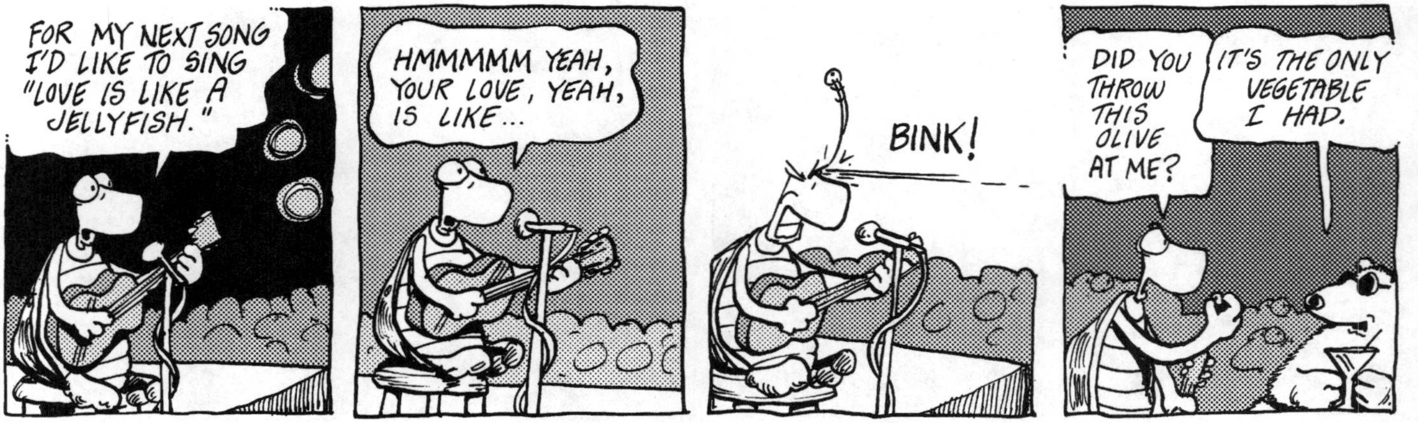
FOR MY NEXT SONG I'D LIKE TO SING "LOVE IS LIKE A JELLYFISH."
HMMMMM YEAH, YOUR LOVE, YEAH, IS LIKE...
BINK!
DID YOU THROW THIS OLIVE AT ME?
IT'S THE ONLY VEGETABLE I HAD.

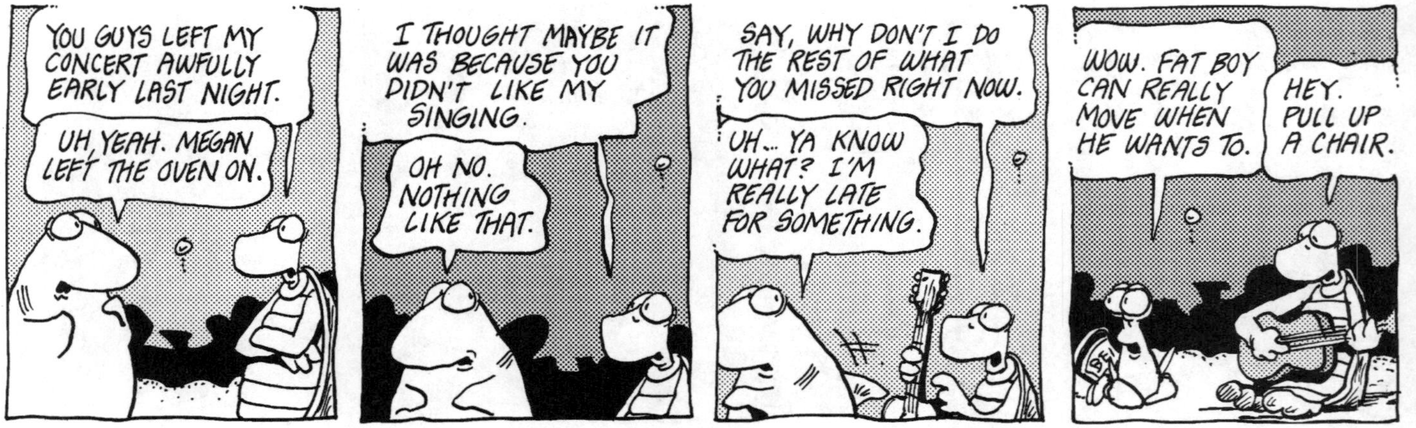
YOU GUYS LEFT MY CONCERT AWFULLY EARLY LAST NIGHT.
UH, YEAH. MEGAN LEFT THE OVEN ON.
I THOUGHT MAYBE IT WAS BECAUSE YOU DIDN'T LIKE MY SINGING.
OH NO. NOTHING LIKE THAT.
SAY, WHY DON'T I DO THE REST OF WHAT YOU MISSED RIGHT NOW.
UH... YA KNOW WHAT? I'M REALLY LATE FOR SOMETHING.
WOW. FAT BOY CAN REALLY MOVE WHEN HE WANTS TO.
HEY. PULL UP A CHAIR.

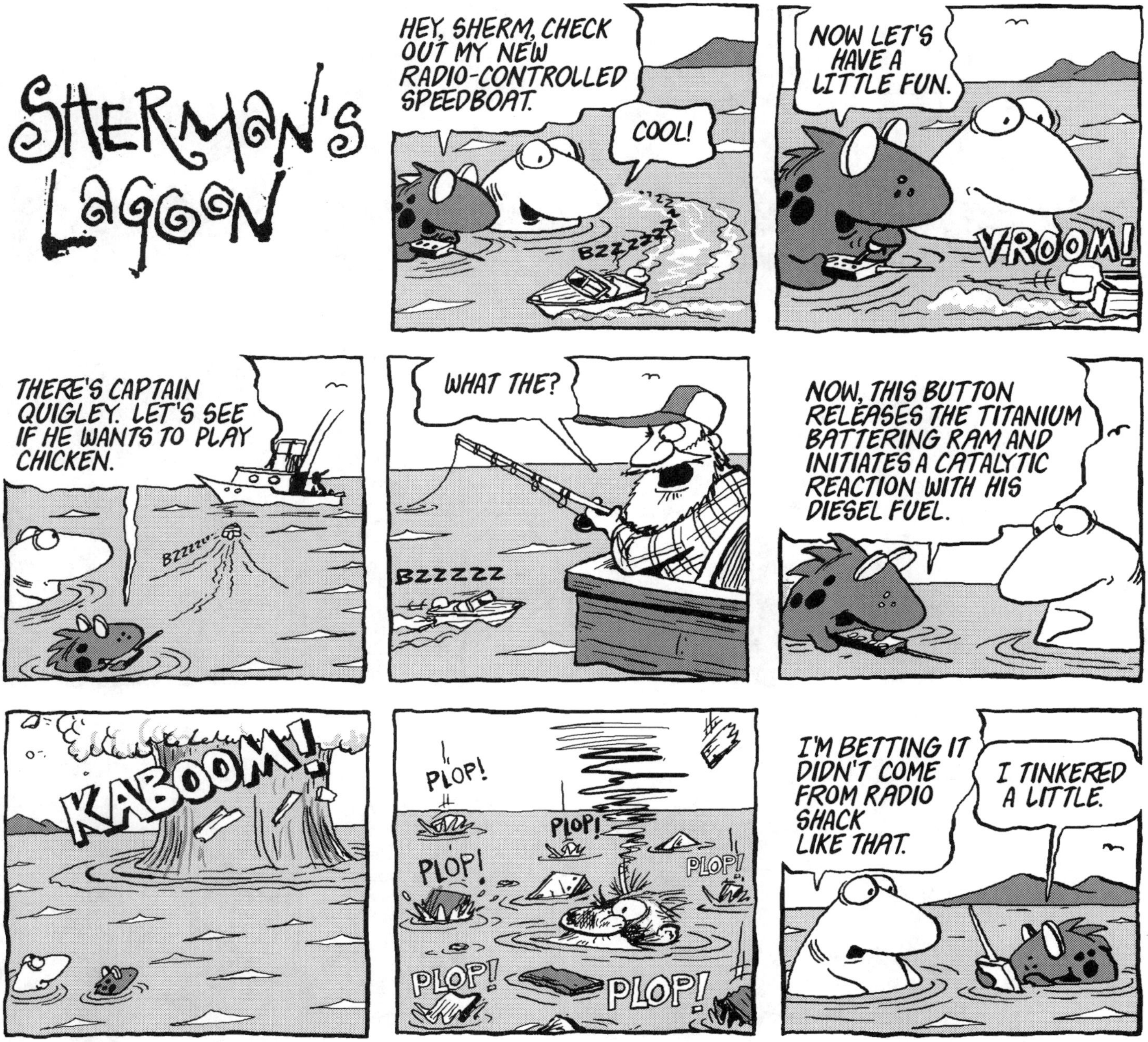
SHERMAN'S LAGOON
HEY, SHERM, CHECK OUT MY NEW RADIO-CONTROLLED SPEEDBOAT.
COOL!
BZZZZZZ
NOW LET'S HAVE A LITTLE FUN.
VROOM!
THERE'S CAPTAIN QUIGLEY. LET'S SEE IF HE WANTS TO PLAY CHICKEN.
BZZZZZ
WHAT THE?
BZZZZZ
NOW, THIS BUTTON RELEASES THE TITANIUM BATTERING RAM AND INITIATES A CATALYTIC REACTION WITH HIS DIESEL FUEL.
KABOOM!
PLOP!
PLOP!
PLOP!
PLOP!
PLOP!
PLOP!
I'M BETTING IT DIDN'T COME FROM RADIO SHACK LIKE THAT.
I TINKERED A LITTLE.

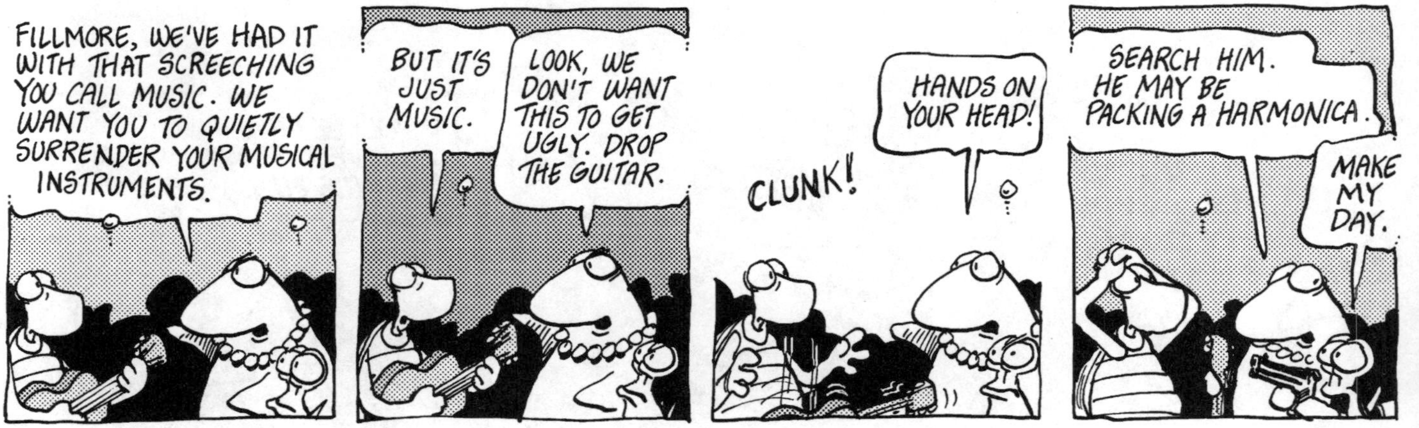
FILLMORE, WE'VE HAD IT WITH THAT SCREECHING YOU CALL MUSIC. WE WANT YOU TO QUIETLY SURRENDER YOUR MUSICAL INSTRUMENTS.
BUT IT'S JUST MUSIC.
LOOK, WE DON'T WANT THIS TO GET UGLY. DROP THE GUITAR.
CLUNK!
HANDS ON YOUR HEAD!
SEARCH HIM. HE MAY BE PACKING A HARMONICA.
MAKE MY DAY.

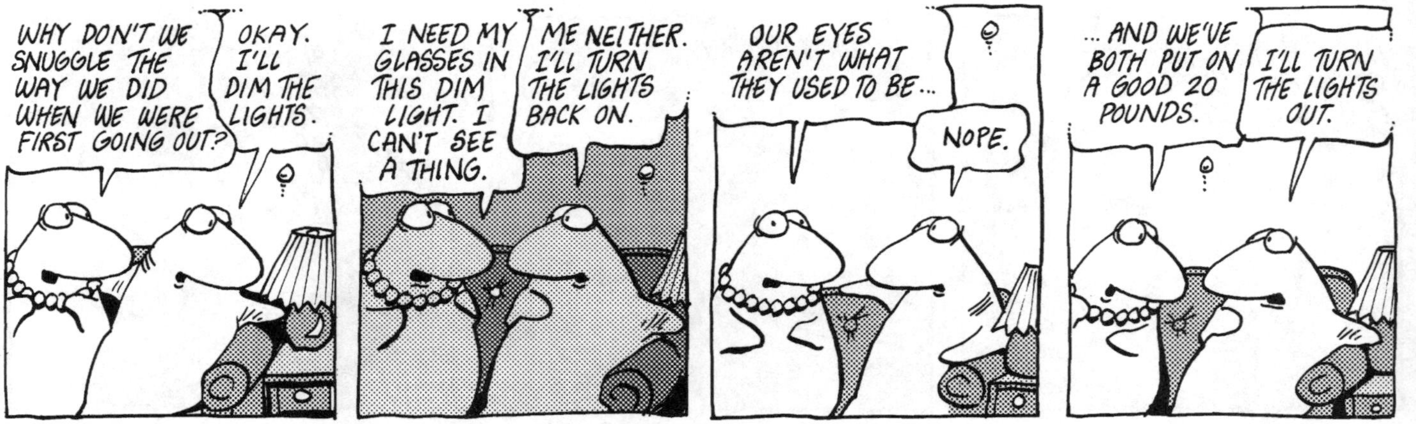
WHY DON'T WE SNUGGLE THE WAY WE DID WHEN WE WERE FIRST GOING OUT?
OKAY. I'LL DIM THE LIGHTS.
I NEED MY GLASSES IN THIS DIM LIGHT. I CAN'T SEE A THING.
ME NEITHER. I'LL TURN THE LIGHTS BACK ON.
OUR EYES AREN'T WHAT THEY USED TO BE...
NOPE.
...AND WE'VE BOTH PUT ON A GOOD 20 POUNDS.
I'LL TURN THE LIGHTS OUT.

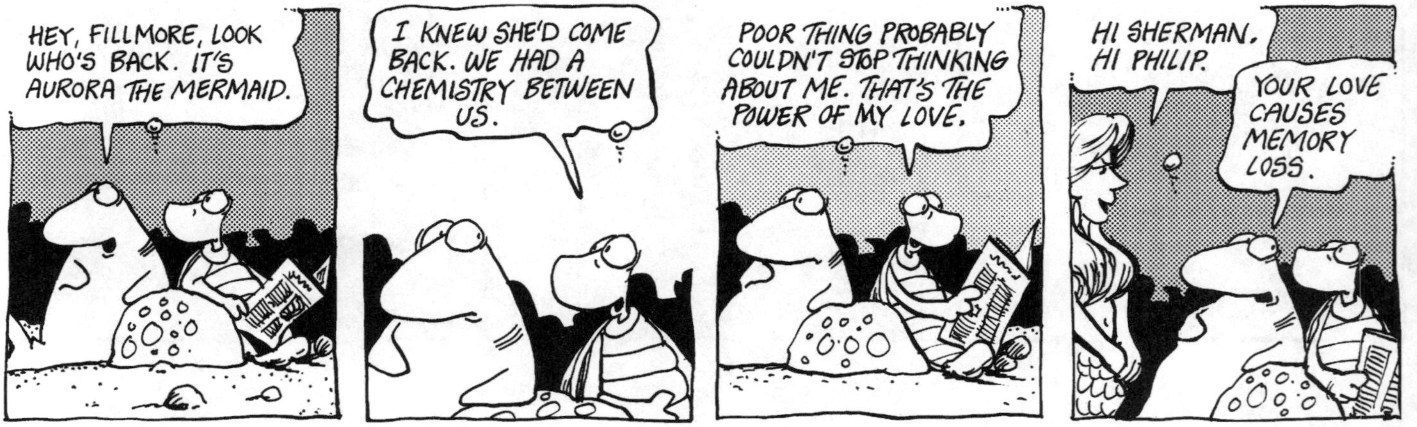
HEY, FILLMORE, LOOK WHO'S BACK. IT'S AURORA THE MERMAID.
I KNEW SHE'D COME BACK. WE HAD A CHEMISTRY BETWEEN US.
POOR THING PROBABLY COULDN'T STOP THINKING ABOUT ME. THAT'S THE POWER OF MY LOVE.
HI SHERMAN. HI PHILIP.
YOUR LOVE CAUSES MEMORY LOSS.

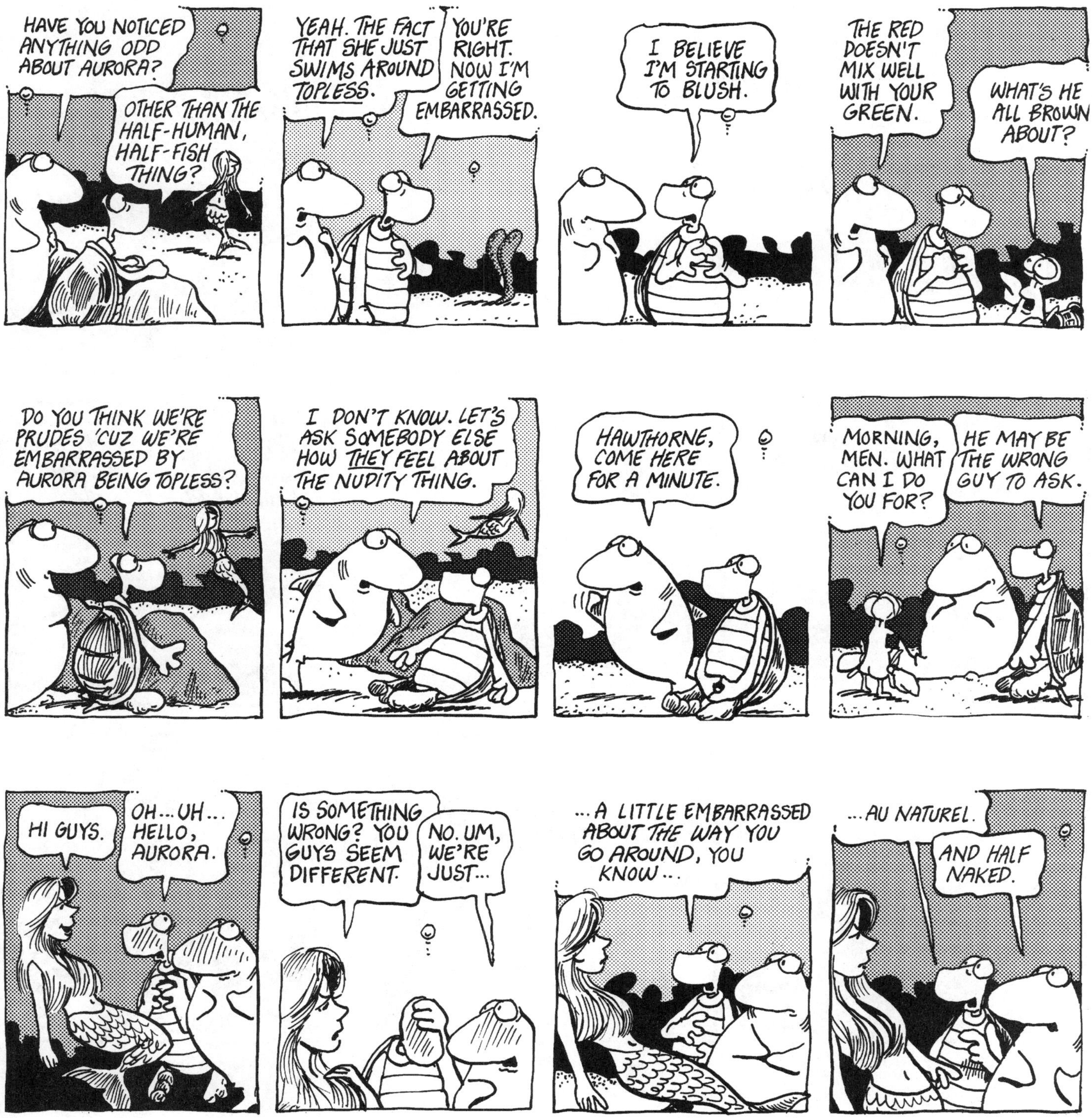
HAVE YOU NOTICED ANYTHING ODD ABOUT AURORA?
OTHER THAN THE HALF-HUMAN, HALF-FISH THING?
YEAH. THE FACT THAT SHE JUST SWIMS AROUND TOPLESS.
YOU'RE RIGHT. NOW I'M GETTING EMBARRASSED.
I BELIEVE I'M STARTING TO BLUSH.
THE RED DOESN'T MIX WELL WITH YOUR GREEN.
WHAT'S HE ALL BROWN ABOUT?
DO YOU THINK WE'RE PRUDES 'CUZ WE'RE EMBARRASSED BY AURORA BEING TOPLESS?
I DON'T KNOW. LET'S ASK SOMEBODY ELSE HOW THEY FEEL ABOUT THE NUDITY THING.
HAWTHORNE, COME HERE FOR A MINUTE.
MORNING, MEN. WHAT CAN I DO YOU FOR?
HE MAY BE THE WRONG GUY TO ASK.
HI GUYS.
OH... UH... HELLO, AURORA.
IS SOMETHING WRONG? YOU GUYS SEEM DIFFERENT.
NO. UM, WE'RE JUST...
...A LITTLE EMBARRASSED ABOUT THE WAY YOU GO AROUND, YOU KNOW...
...AU NATUREL.
AND HALF NAKED.

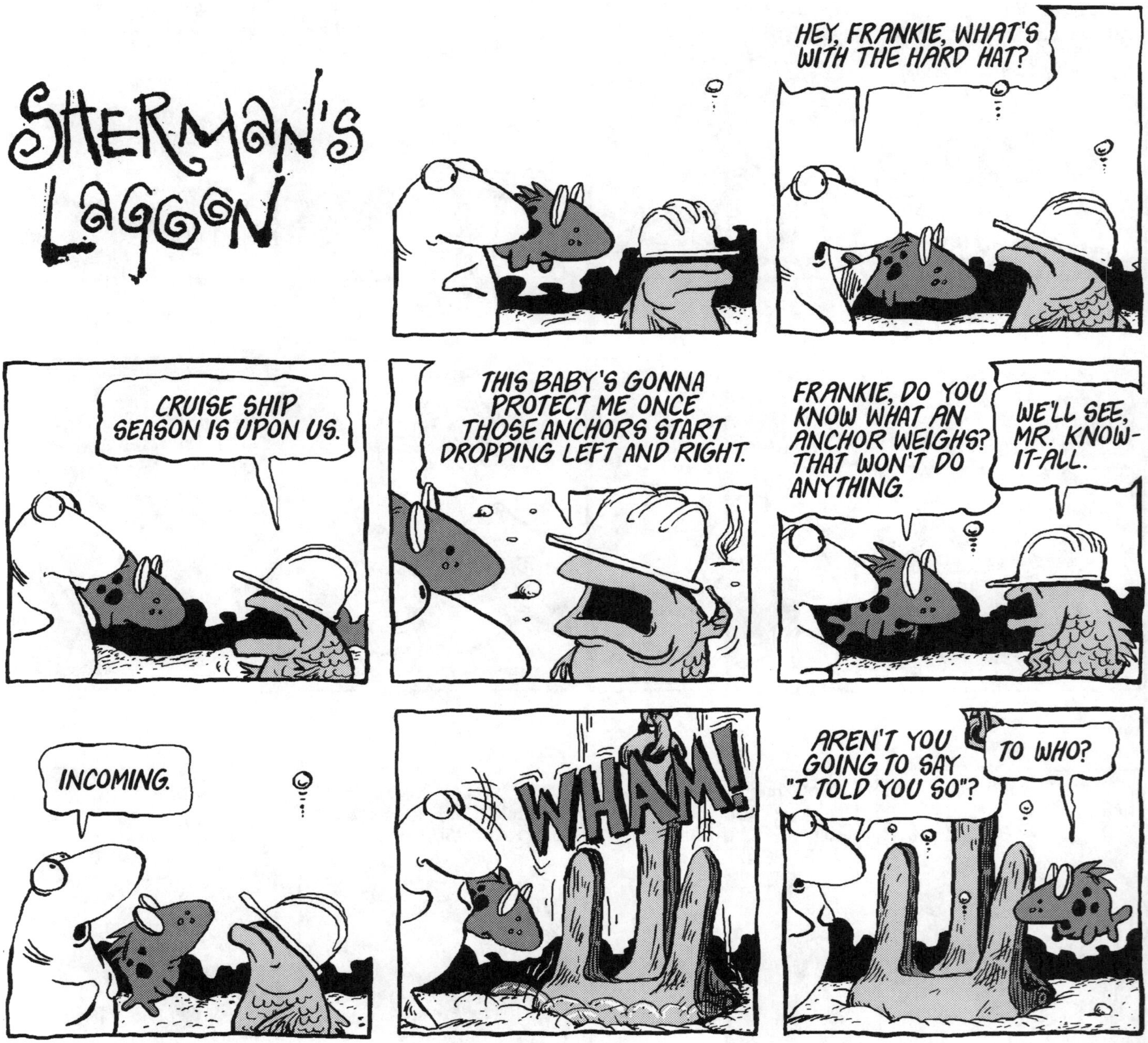
SHERMAN'S LAGOON
HEY, FRANKIE, WHAT'S WITH THE HARD HAT?
CRUISE SHIP SEASON IS UPON US.
THIS BABY'S GONNA PROTECT ME ONCE THOSE ANCHORS START DROPPING LEFT AND RIGHT.
FRANKIE, DO YOU KNOW WHAT AN ANCHOR WEIGHS? THAT WON'T DO ANYTHING.
WE'LL SEE, MR. KNOW-IT-ALL.
INCOMING.
WHAM!
AREN'T YOU GOING TO SAY "I TOLD YOU SO"?
TO WHO?

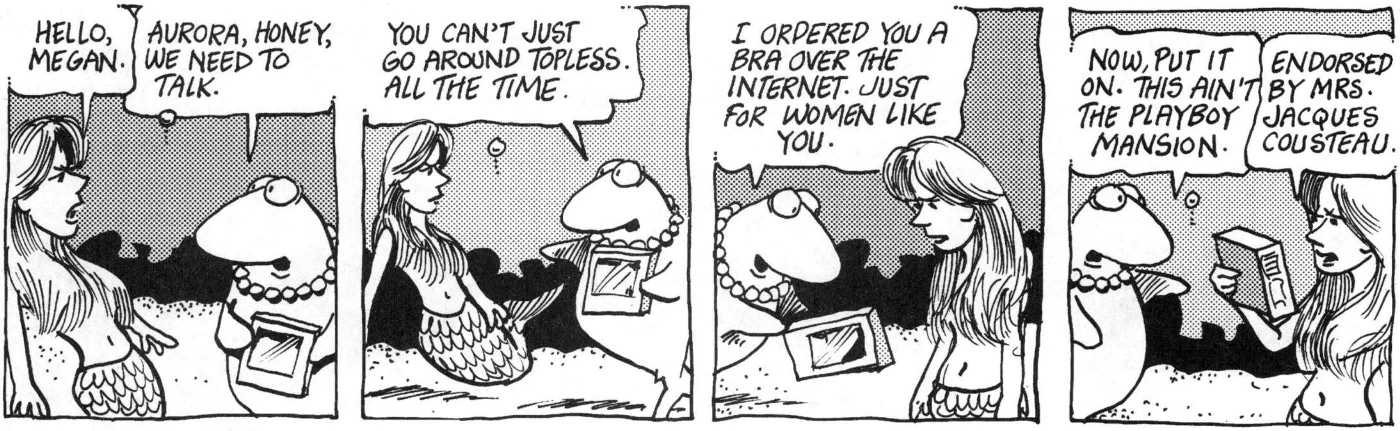
HELLO, MEGAN.
AURORA, HONEY, WE NEED TO TALK.
YOU CAN'T JUST GO AROUND TOPLESS. ALL THE TIME.
I ORDERED YOU A BRA OVER THE INTERNET. JUST FOR WOMEN LIKE YOU.
NOW, PUT IT ON. THIS AIN'T THE PLAYBOY MANSION.
ENDORSED BY MRS. JACQUES COUSTEAU.

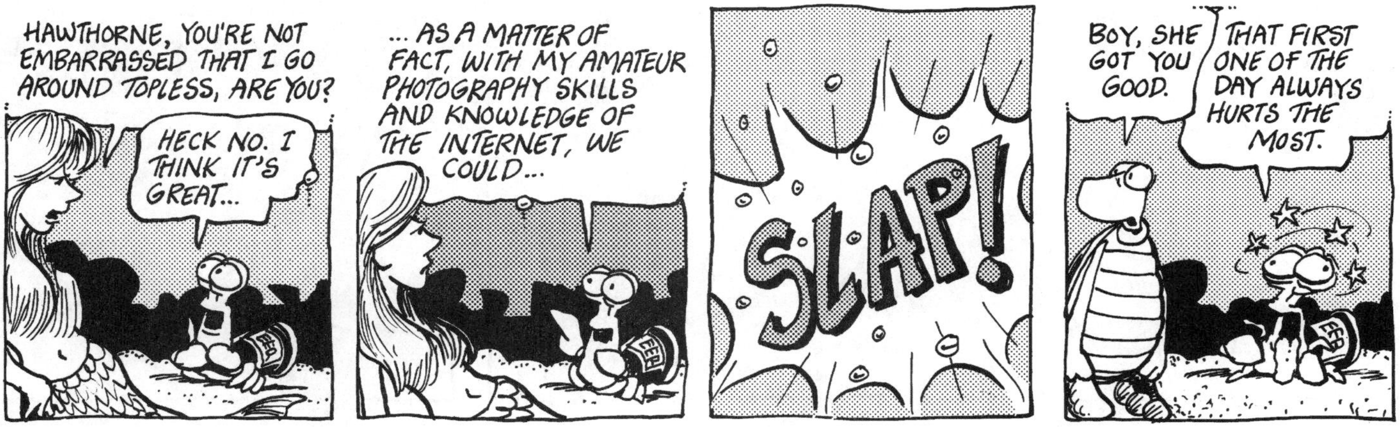
HAWTHORNE, YOU'RE NOT EMBARRASSED THAT I GO AROUND TOPLESS, ARE YOU?
HECK NO. I THINK IT'S GREAT...
... AS A MATTER OF FACT, WITH MY AMATEUR PHOTOGRAPHY SKILLS AND KNOWLEDGE OF THE INTERNET, WE COULD...
SLAP!
BOY, SHE GOT YOU GOOD.
THAT FIRST ONE OF THE DAY ALWAYS HURTS THE MOST.

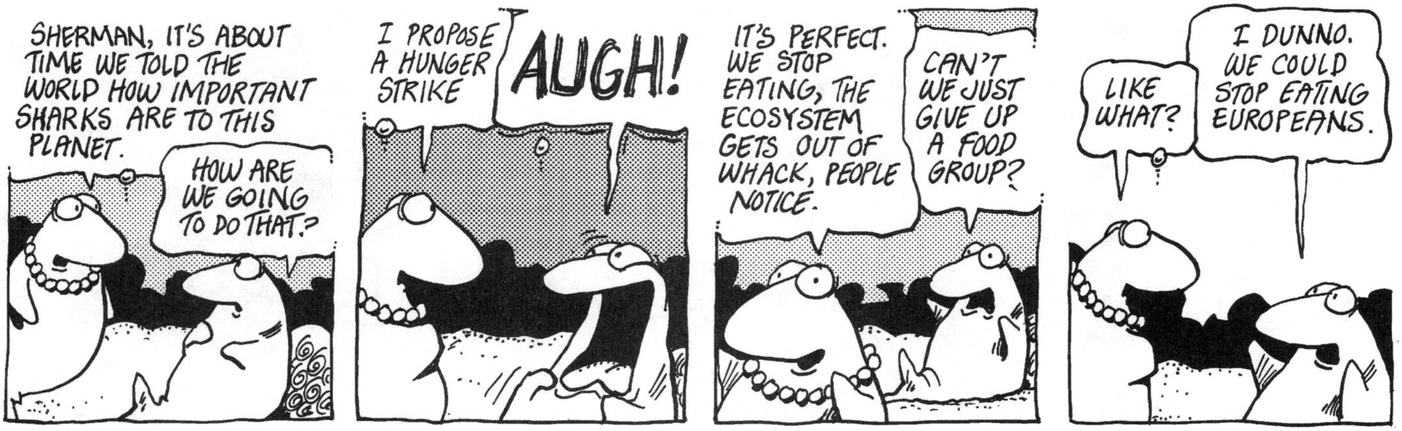
SHERMAN, IT'S ABOUT TIME WE TOLD THE WORLD HOW IMPORTANT SHARKS ARE TO THIS PLANET.
HOW ARE WE GOING TO DO THAT?
I PROPOSE A HUNGER STRIKE
AUGH!
IT'S PERFECT. WE STOP EATING, THE ECOSYSTEM GETS OUT OF WHACK, PEOPLE NOTICE.
CAN'T WE JUST GIVE UP A FOOD GROUP?
LIKE WHAT?
I DUNNO. WE COULD STOP EATING EUROPEANS.

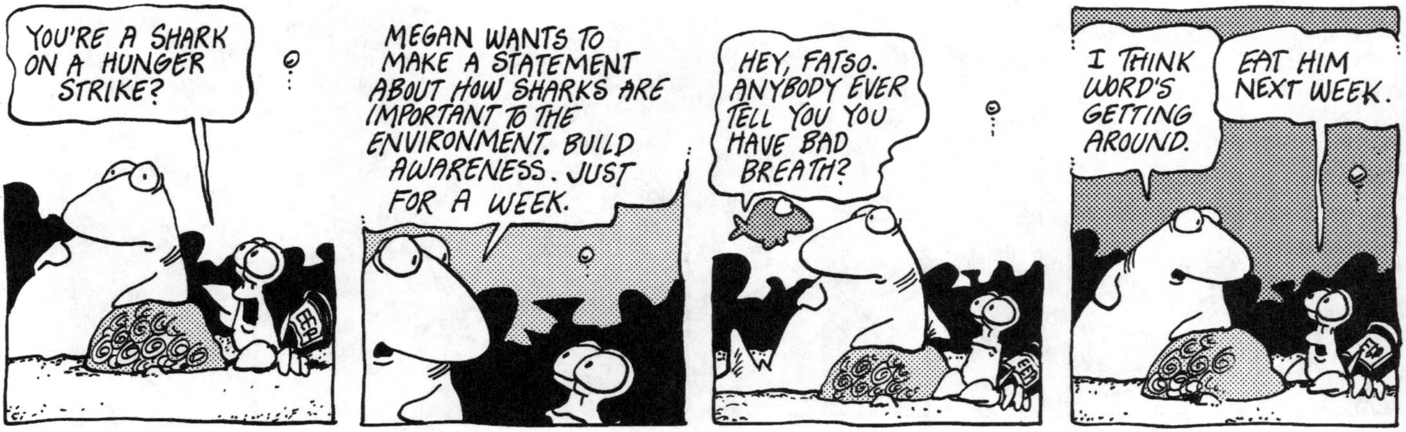
YOU'RE A SHARK ON A HUNGER STRIKE?
MEGAN WANTS TO MAKE A STATEMENT ABOUT HOW SHARKS ARE IMPORTANT TO THE ENVIRONMENT. BUILD AWARENESS. JUST FOR A WEEK.
HEY, FATSO. ANYBODY EVER TELL YOU YOU HAVE BAD BREATH?
I THINK WORD'S GETTING AROUND.
EAT HIM NEXT WEEK.

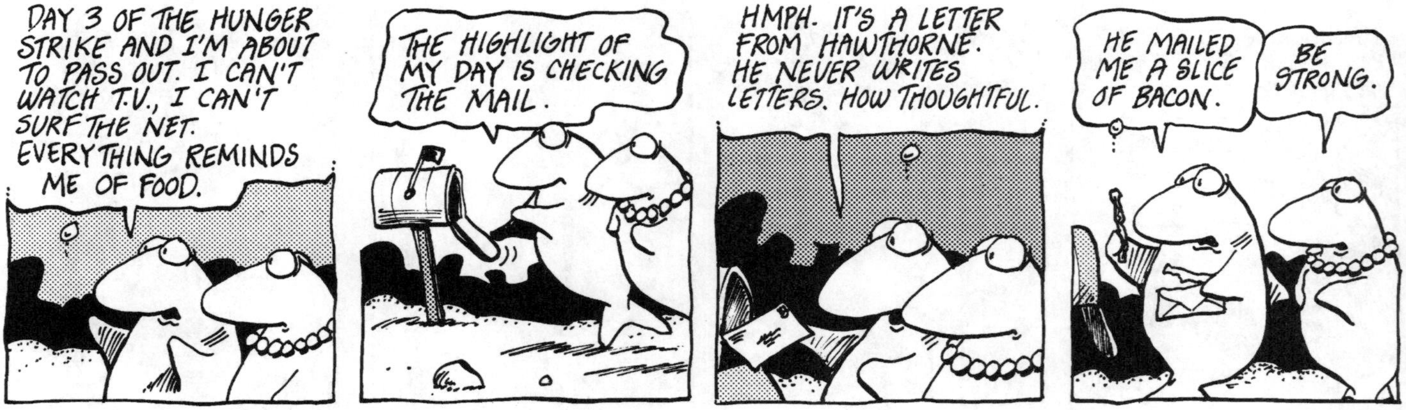
DAY 3 OF THE HUNGER STRIKE AND I'M ABOUT TO PASS OUT. I CAN'T WATCH T.V., I CAN'T SURF THE NET. EVERYTHING REMINDS ME OF FOOD.
THE HIGHLIGHT OF MY DAY IS CHECKING THE MAIL.
HMPH. IT'S A LETTER FROM HAWTHORNE. HE NEVER WRITES LETTERS. HOW THOUGHTFUL.
HE MAILED ME A SLICE OF BACON.
BE STRONG.

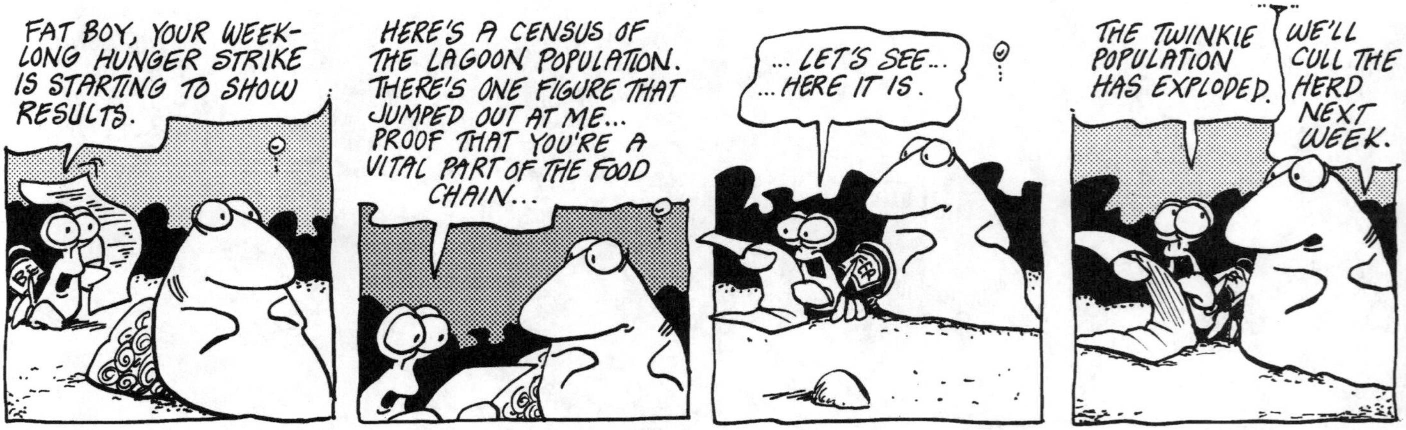
FAT BOY, YOUR WEEK-LONG HUNGER STRIKE IS STARTING TO SHOW RESULTS.
HERE'S A CENSUS OF THE LAGOON POPULATION. THERE'S ONE FIGURE THAT JUMPED OUT AT ME... PROOF THAT YOU'RE A VITAL PART OF THE FOOD CHAIN...
...LET'S SEE... ...HERE IT IS.
THE TWINKIE POPULATION HAS EXPLODED.
WE'LL CULL THE HERD NEXT WEEK.

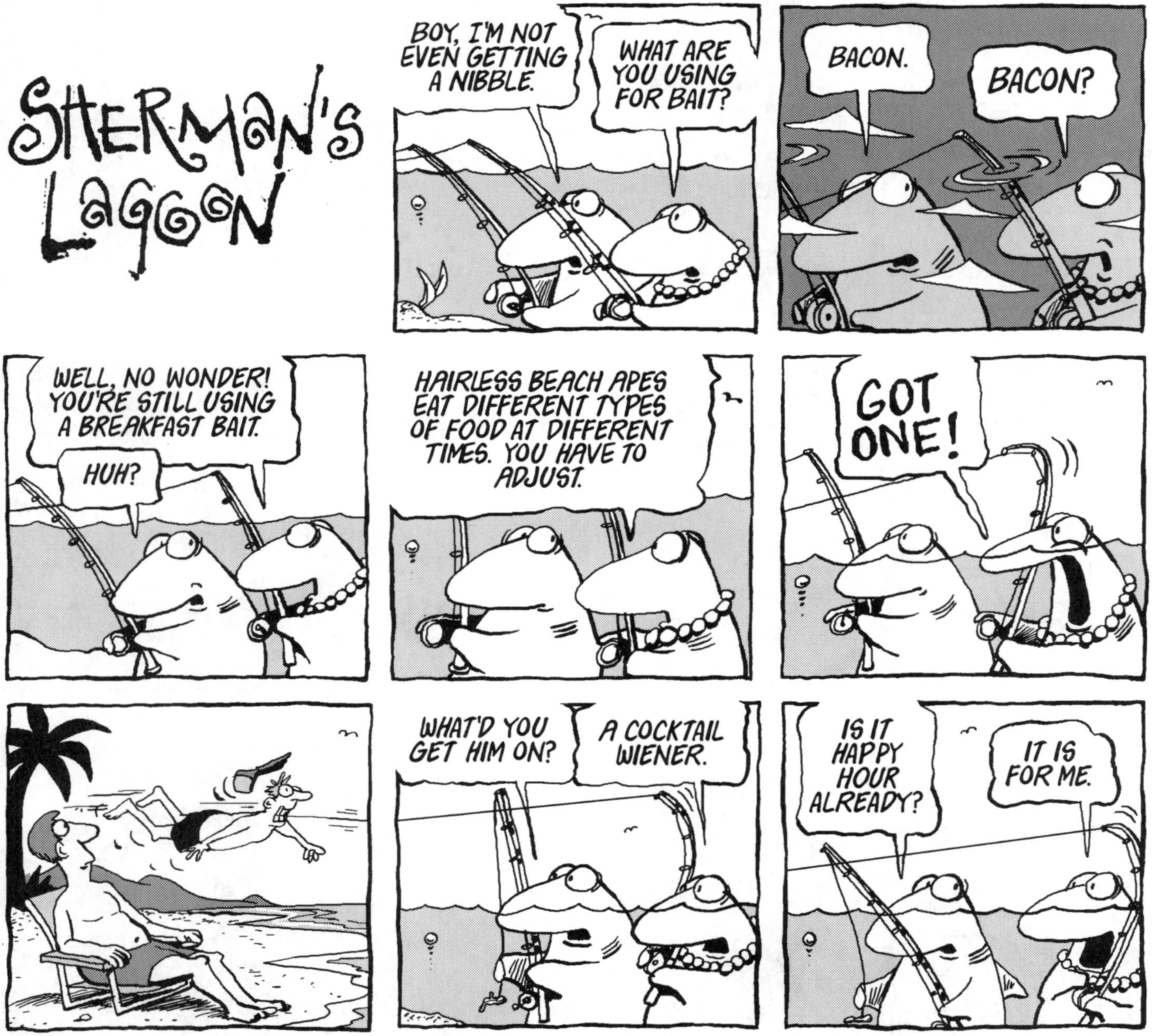
SHERMAN'S LAGOON
BOY, I'M NOT EVEN GETTING A NIBBLE.
WHAT ARE YOU USING FOR BAIT?
BACON.
BACON?
WELL, NO WONDER! YOU'RE STILL USING A BREAKFAST BAIT.
HUH?
HAIRLESS BEACH APES EAT DIFFERENT TYPES OF FOOD AT DIFFERENT TIMES. YOU HAVE TO ADJUST.
GOT ONE!
WHAT'D YOU GET HIM ON?
A COCKTAIL WIENER.
IS IT HAPPY HOUR ALREADY?
IT IS FOR ME.

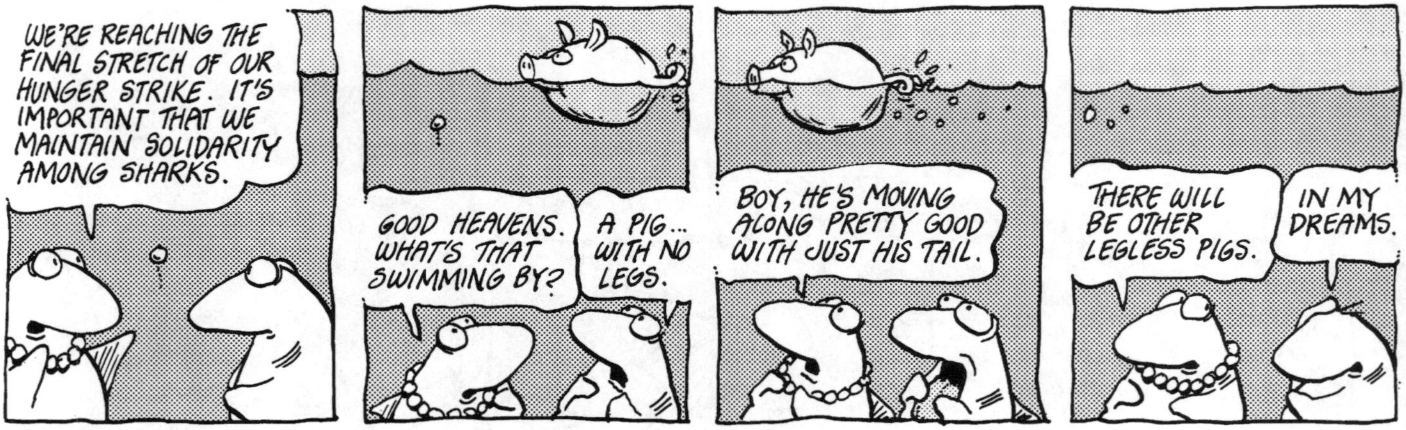
WE'RE REACHING THE FINAL STRETCH OF OUR HUNGER STRIKE. IT'S IMPORTANT THAT WE MAINTAIN SOLIDARITY AMONG SHARKS.
GOOD HEAVENS. WHAT'S THAT SWIMMING BY?
A PIG... WITH NO LEGS.
BOY, HE'S MOVING ALONG PRETTY GOOD WITH JUST HIS TAIL.
THERE WILL BE OTHER LEGLESS PIGS.
IN MY DREAMS.

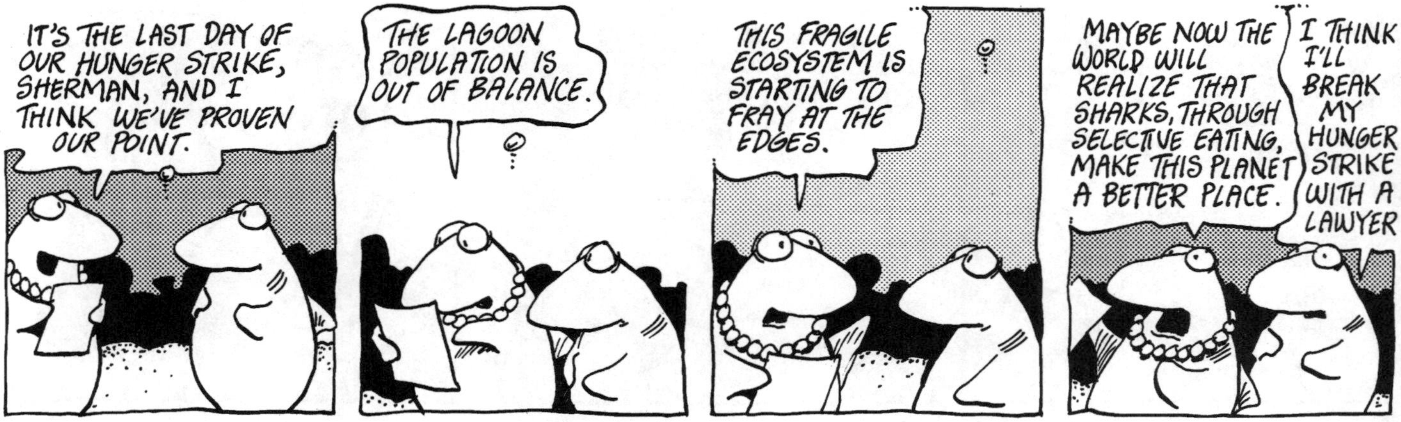
IT'S THE LAST DAY OF OUR HUNGER STRIKE, SHERMAN, AND I THINK WE'VE PROVEN OUR POINT.
THE LAGOON POPULATION IS OUT OF BALANCE.
THIS FRAGILE ECOSYSTEM IS STARTING TO FRAY AT THE EDGES.
MAYBE NOW THE WORLD WILL REALIZE THAT SHARKS, THROUGH SELECTIVE EATING, MAKE THIS PLANET A BETTER PLACE.
I THINK I'LL BREAK MY HUNGER STRIKE WITH A LAWYER

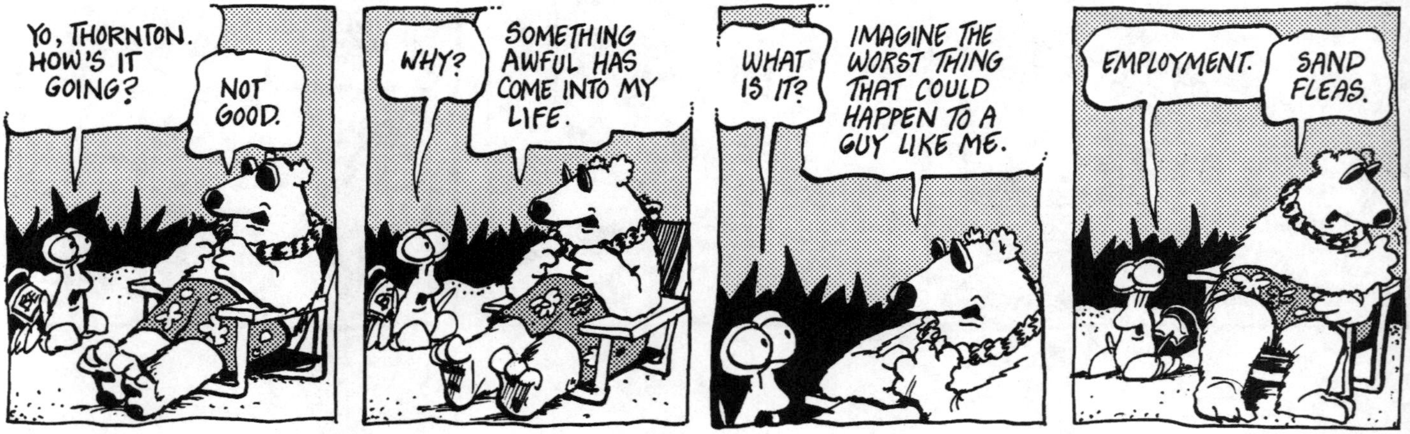
YO, THORNTON. HOW'S IT GOING?
NOT GOOD.
WHY?
SOMETHING AWFUL HAS COME INTO MY LIFE.
WHAT IS IT?
IMAGINE THE WORST THING THAT COULD HAPPEN TO A GUY LIKE ME.
EMPLOYMENT.
SAND FLEAS.

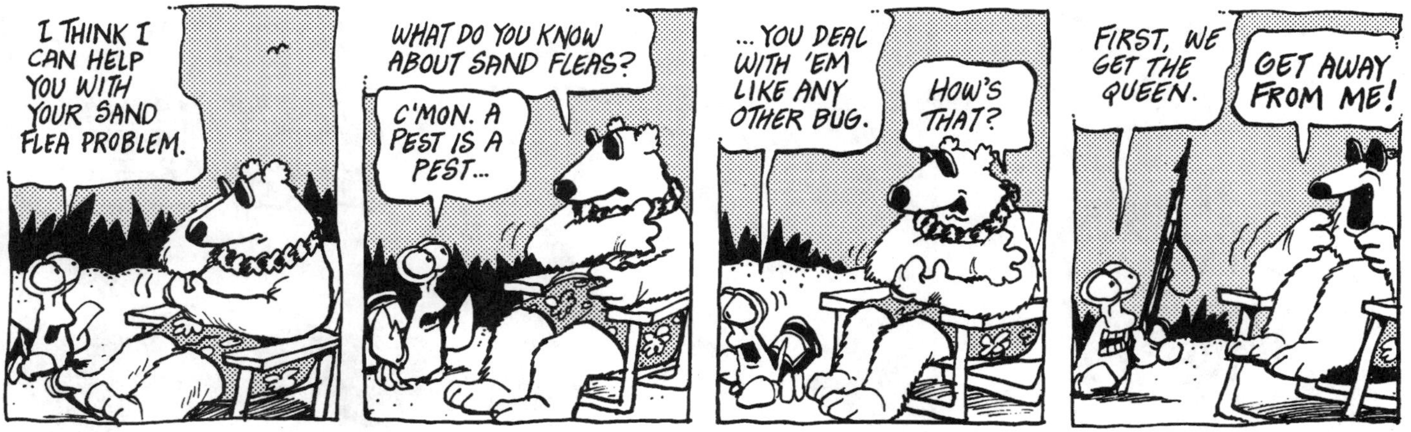
I THINK I CAN HELP YOU WITH YOUR SAND FLEA PROBLEM.
WHAT DO YOU KNOW ABOUT SAND FLEAS?
C'MON. A PEST IS A PEST...
...YOU DEAL WITH 'EM LIKE ANY OTHER BUG.
HOW'S THAT?
FIRST, WE GET THE QUEEN.
GET AWAY FROM ME!

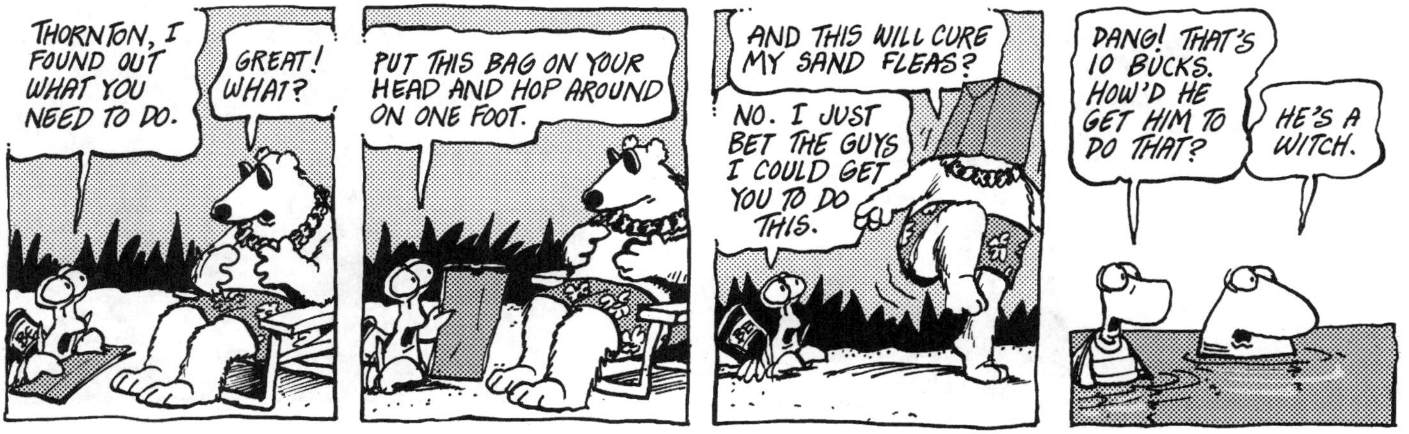
THORNTON, I FOUND OUT WHAT YOU NEED TO DO.
GREAT! WHAT?
PUT THIS BAG ON YOUR HEAD AND HOP AROUND ON ONE FOOT.
AND THIS WILL CURE MY SAND FLEAS?
NO. I JUST BET THE GUYS I COULD GET YOU TO DO THIS.
DANG! THAT'S 10 BUCKS. HOW'D HE GET HIM TO DO THAT?
HE'S A WITCH.

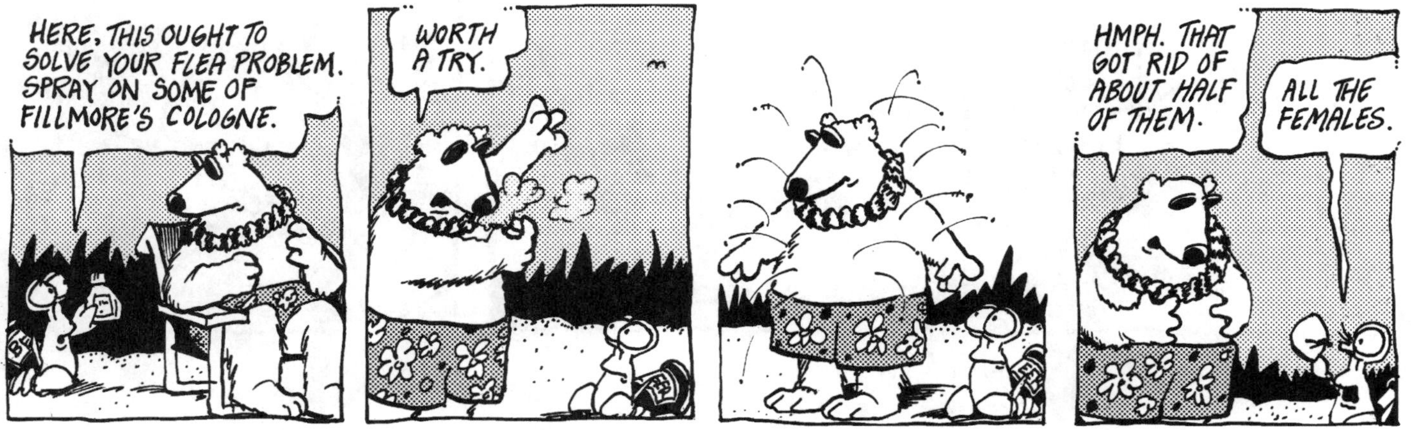
HERE, THIS OUGHT TO SOLVE YOUR FLEA PROBLEM. SPRAY ON SOME OF FILLMORE'S COLOGNE.
WORTH A TRY.
HMPH. THAT GOT RID OF ABOUT HALF OF THEM.
ALL THE FEMALES.

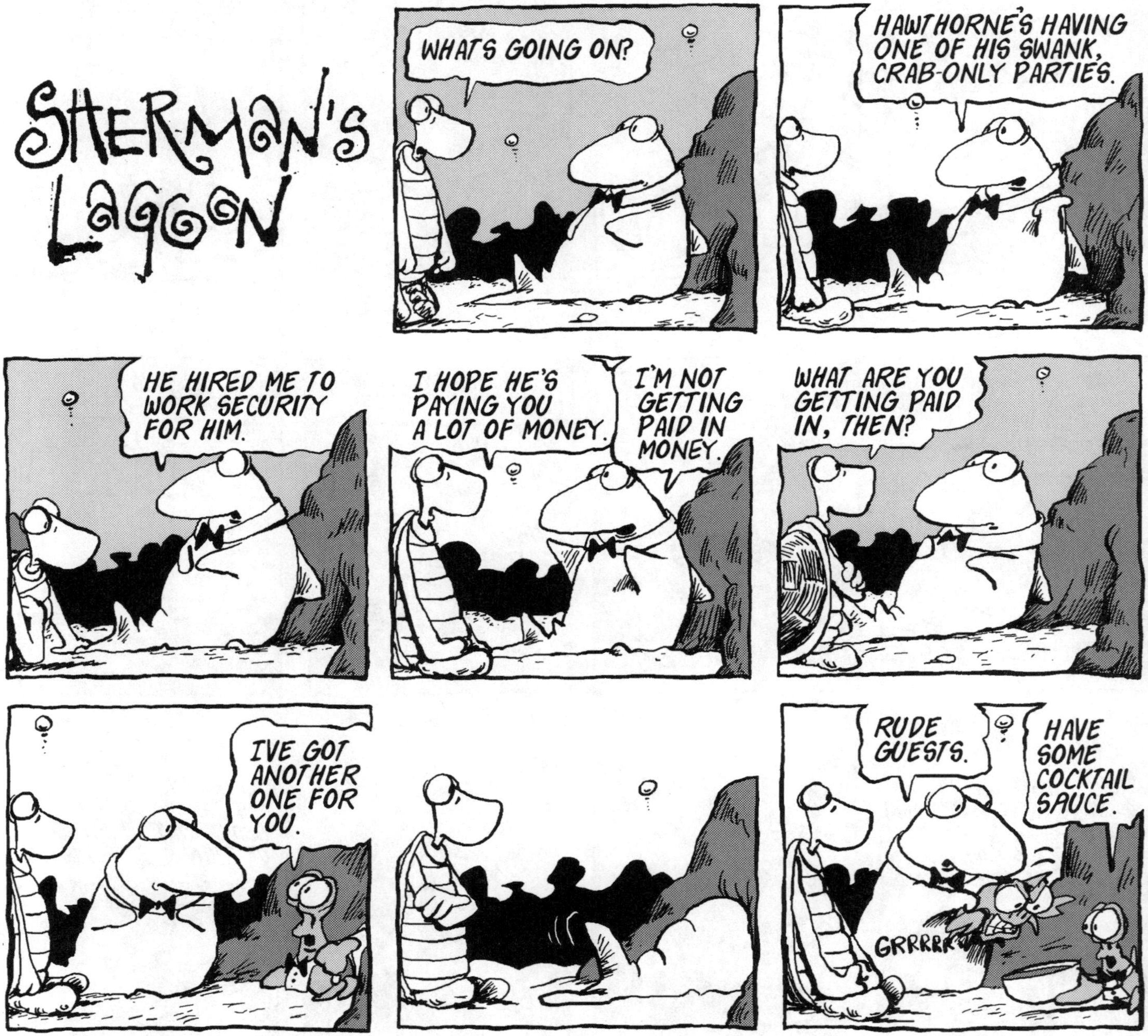
SHERMAN'S LAGOON
WHAT'S GOING ON?
HAWTHORNE'S HAVING ONE OF HIS SWANK, CRAB-ONLY PARTIES.
HE HIRED ME TO WORK SECURITY FOR HIM.
I HOPE HE'S PAYING YOU A LOT OF MONEY.
I'M NOT GETTING PAID IN MONEY.
WHAT ARE YOU GETTING PAID IN, THEN?
I'VE GOT ANOTHER ONE FOR YOU.
RUDE GUESTS.
HAVE SOME COCKTAIL SAUCE.
GRRRRR

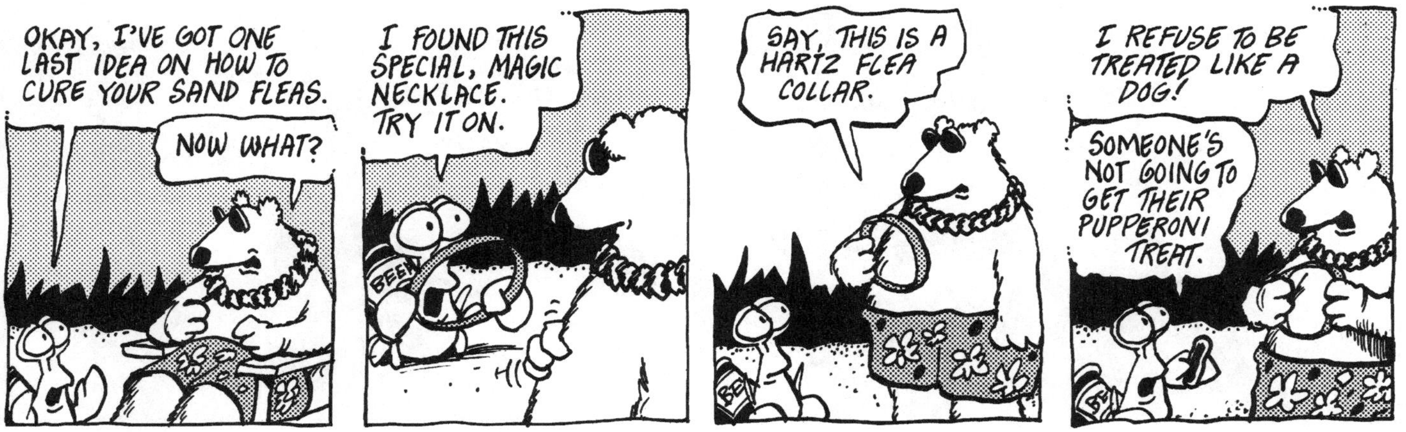
OKAY, I'VE GOT ONE LAST IDEA ON HOW TO CURE YOUR SAND FLEAS.
NOW WHAT?
I FOUND THIS SPECIAL, MAGIC NECKLACE. TRY IT ON.
SAY, THIS IS A HARTZ FLEA COLLAR.
I REFUSE TO BE TREATED LIKE A DOG!
SOMEONE'S NOT GOING TO GET THEIR PUPPERONI TREAT.

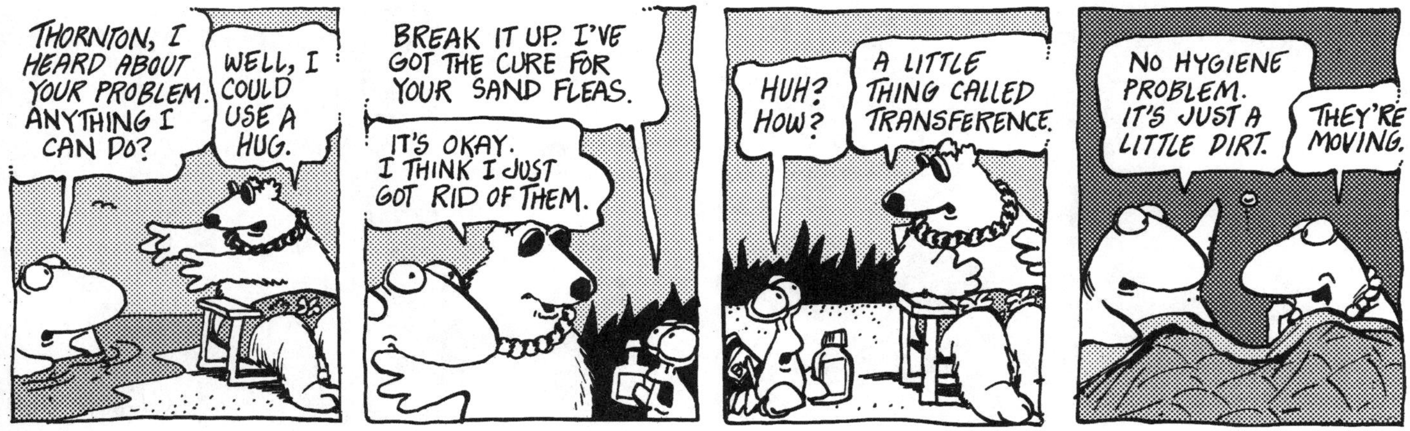
THORNTON, I HEARD ABOUT YOUR PROBLEM. ANYTHING I CAN DO?
WELL, I COULD USE A HUG.
BREAK IT UP. I'VE GOT THE CURE FOR YOUR SAND FLEAS.
IT'S OKAY. I THINK I JUST GOT RID OF THEM.
HUH? HOW?
A LITTLE THING CALLED TRANSFERENCE.
NO HYGIENE PROBLEM. IT'S JUST A LITTLE DIRT.
THEY'RE MOVING.

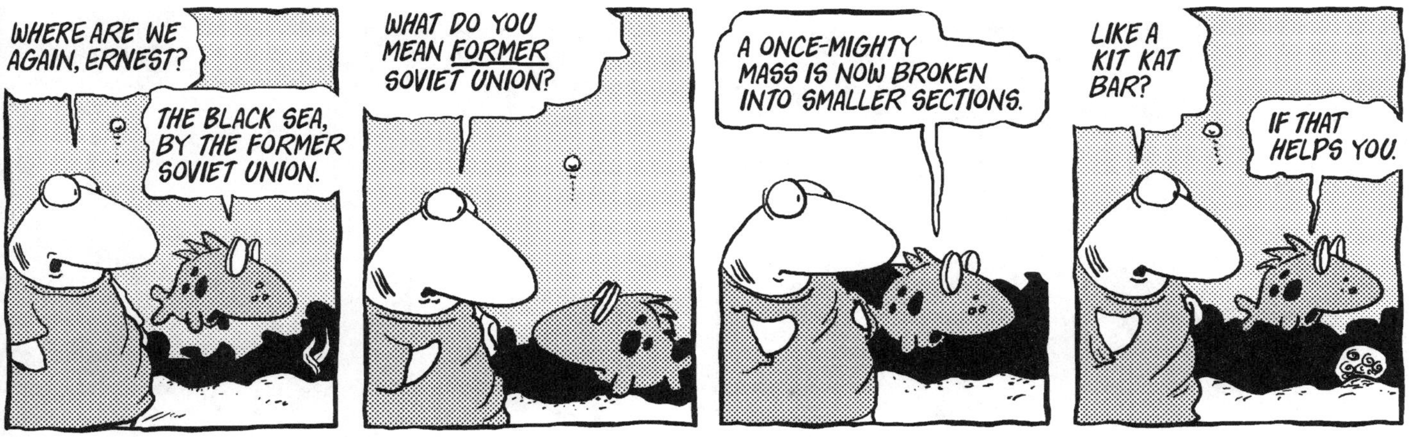
WHERE ARE WE AGAIN, ERNEST?
THE BLACK SEA, BY THE FORMER SOVIET UNION.
WHAT DO YOU MEAN FORMER SOVIET UNION?
A ONCE-MIGHTY MASS IS NOW BROKEN INTO SMALLER SECTIONS.
LIKE A KIT KAT BAR?
IF THAT HELPS YOU.

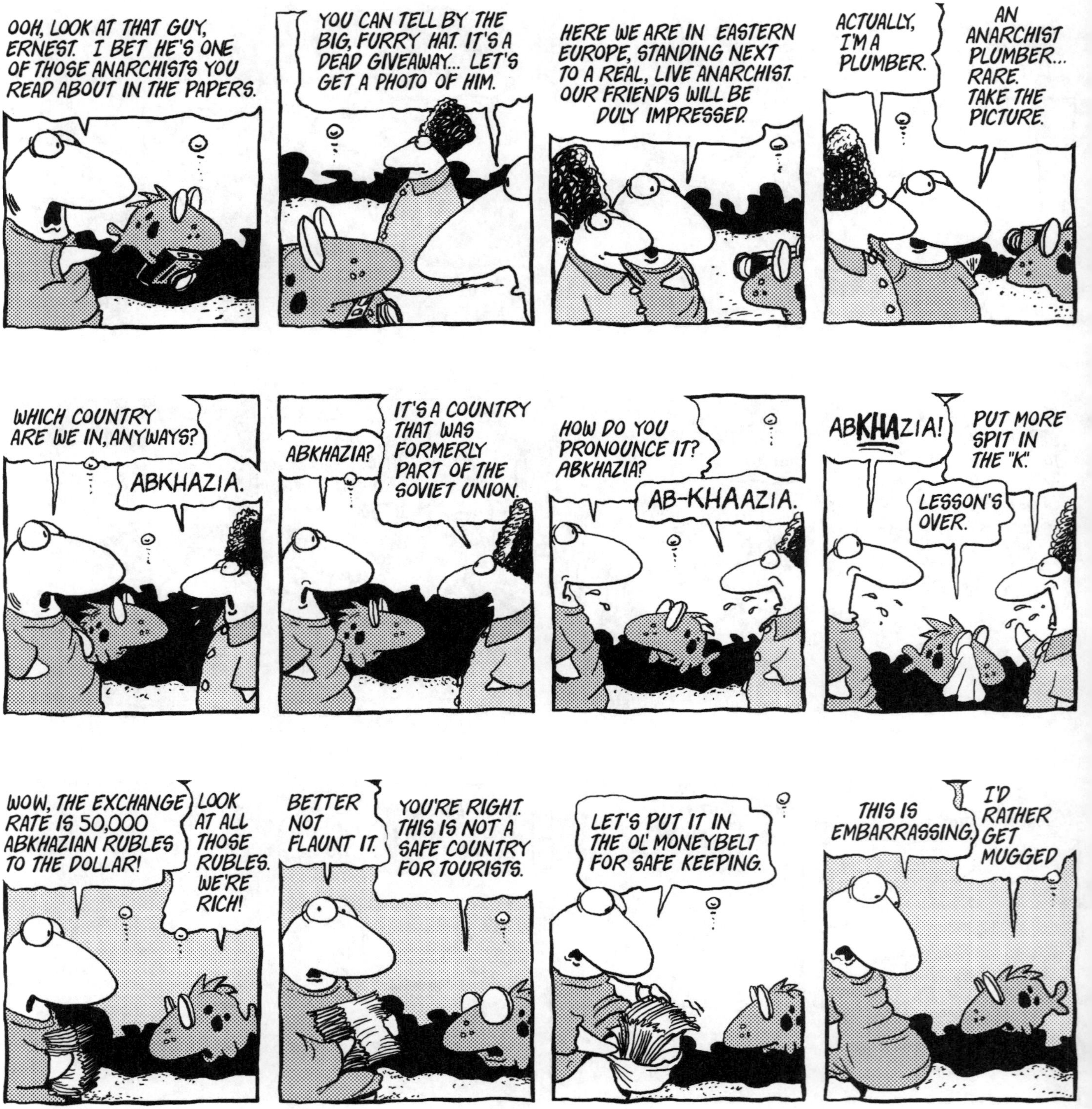
OOH, LOOK AT THAT GUY, ERNEST. I BET HE'S ONE OF THOSE ANARCHISTS YOU READ ABOUT IN THE PAPERS.
YOU CAN TELL BY THE BIG, FURRY HAT. IT'S A DEAD GIVEAWAY... LET'S GET A PHOTO OF HIM.
HERE WE ARE IN EASTERN EUROPE, STANDING NEXT TO A REAL, LIVE ANARCHIST. OUR FRIENDS WILL BE DULY IMPRESSED.
ACTUALLY, I'M A PLUMBER.
AN ANARCHIST PLUMBER... RARE. TAKE THE PICTURE.
WHICH COUNTRY ARE WE IN, ANYWAYS?
ABKHAZIA.
ABKHAZIA?
IT'S A COUNTRY THAT WAS FORMERLY PART OF THE SOVIET UNION.
HOW DO YOU PRONOUNCE IT? ABKHAZIA?
AB-KHAAZIA.
ABKHAZIA!
PUT MORE SPIT IN THE "K".
LESSON'S OVER.
WOW, THE EXCHANGE RATE IS 50,000 ABKHAZIAN RUBLES TO THE DOLLAR!
LOOK AT ALL THOSE RUBLES. WE'RE RICH!
BETTER NOT FLAUNT IT.
YOU'RE RIGHT. THIS IS NOT A SAFE COUNTRY FOR TOURISTS.
LET'S PUT IT IN THE OL' MONEYBELT FOR SAFE KEEPING.
THIS IS EMBARRASSING.
I'D RATHER GET MUGGED.

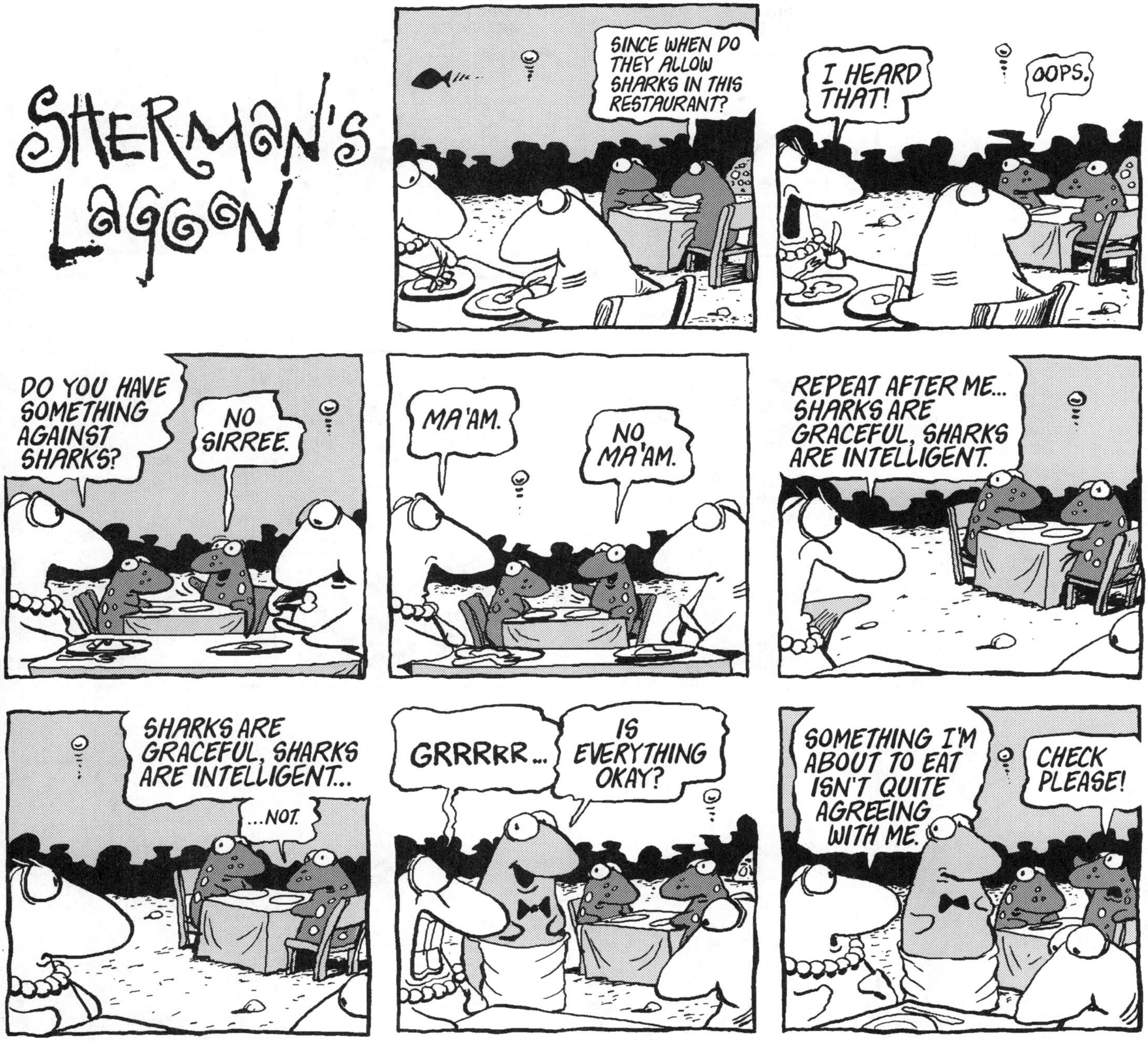
SHERMAN'S LAGOON
SINCE WHEN DO THEY ALLOW SHARKS IN THIS RESTAURANT?
I HEARD THAT!
OOPS.
DO YOU HAVE SOMETHING AGAINST SHARKS?
NO SIRREE.
MA'AM.
NO MA'AM.
REPEAT AFTER ME... SHARKS ARE GRACEFUL, SHARKS ARE INTELLIGENT.
SHARKS ARE GRACEFUL, SHARKS ARE INTELLIGENT...
...NOT.
GRRRRR...
IS EVERYTHING OKAY?
SOMETHING I'M ABOUT TO EAT ISN'T QUITE AGREEING WITH ME.
CHECK PLEASE!

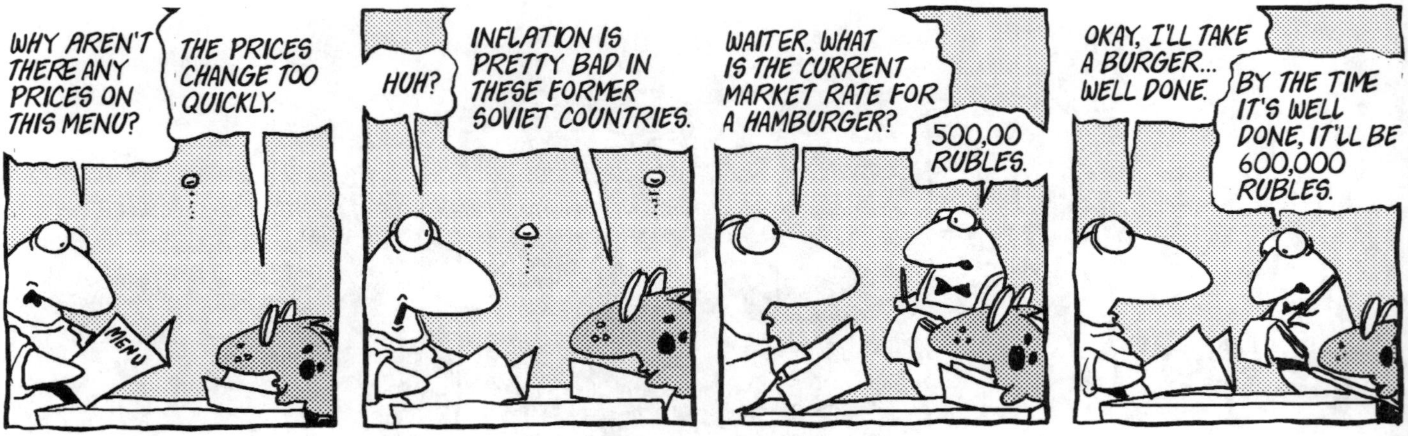
WHY AREN'T THERE ANY PRICES ON THIS MENU?
THE PRICES CHANGE TOO QUICKLY.
MENU
HUH?
INFLATION IS PRETTY BAD IN THESE FORMER SOVIET COUNTRIES.
WAITER, WHAT IS THE CURRENT MARKET RATE FOR A HAMBURGER?
500,00 RUBLES.
OKAY, I'LL TAKE A BURGER... WELL DONE.
BY THE TIME IT'S WELL DONE, IT'LL BE 600,000 RUBLES.

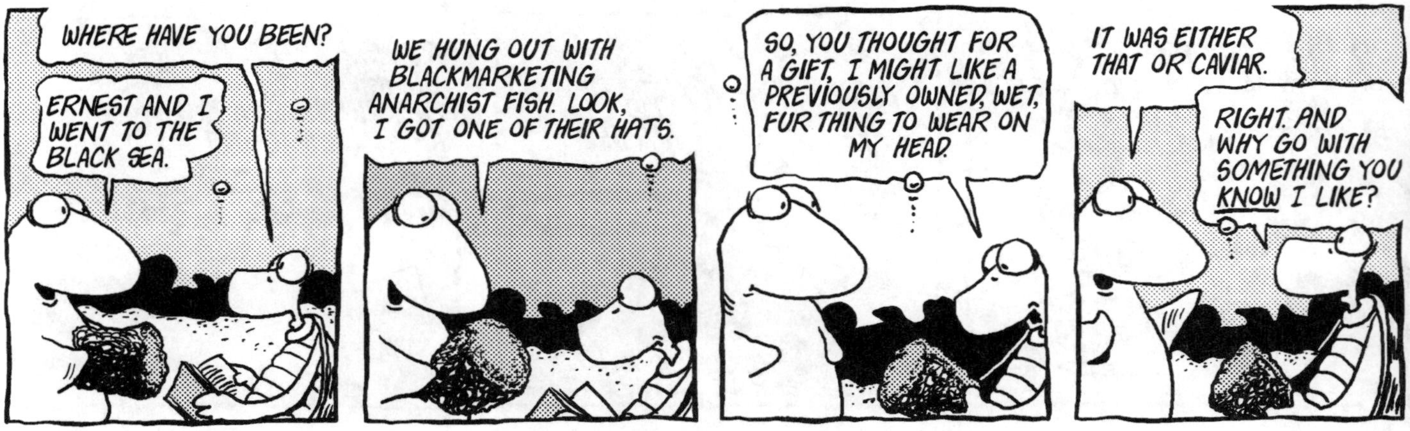
WHERE HAVE YOU BEEN?
ERNEST AND I WENT TO THE BLACK SEA.
WE HUNG OUT WITH BLACKMARKETING ANARCHIST FISH. LOOK, I GOT ONE OF THEIR HATS.
SO, YOU THOUGHT FOR A GIFT, I MIGHT LIKE A PREVIOUSLY OWNED, WET, FUR THING TO WEAR ON MY HEAD.
IT WAS EITHER THAT OR CAVIAR.
RIGHT. AND WHY GO WITH SOMETHING YOU KNOW I LIKE?

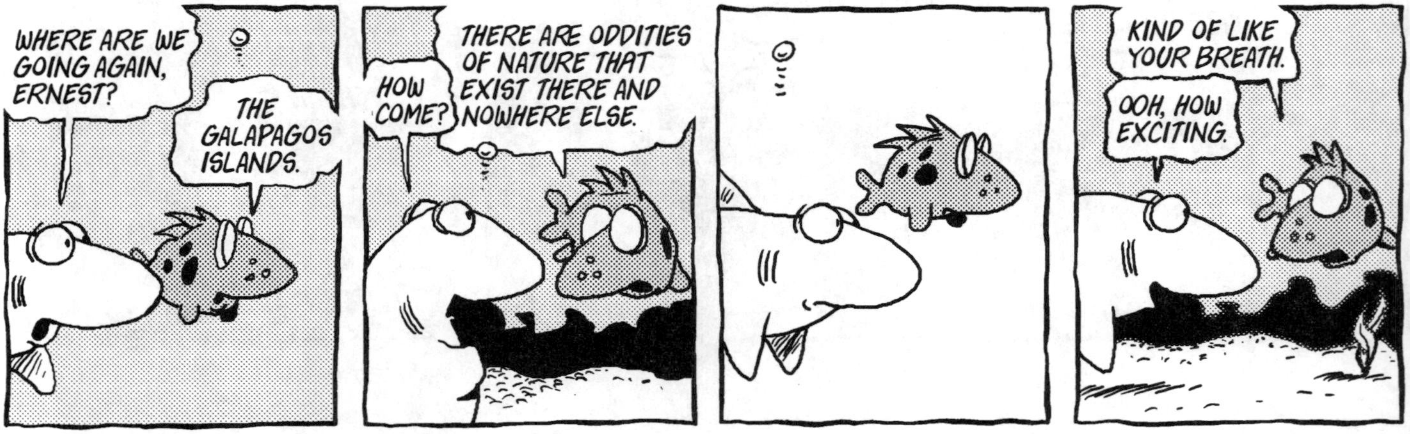
WHERE ARE WE GOING AGAIN, ERNEST?
THE GALAPAGOS ISLANDS.
HOW COME?
THERE ARE ODDITIES OF NATURE THAT EXIST THERE AND NOWHERE ELSE.
KIND OF LIKE YOUR BREATH.
OOH, HOW EXCITING.

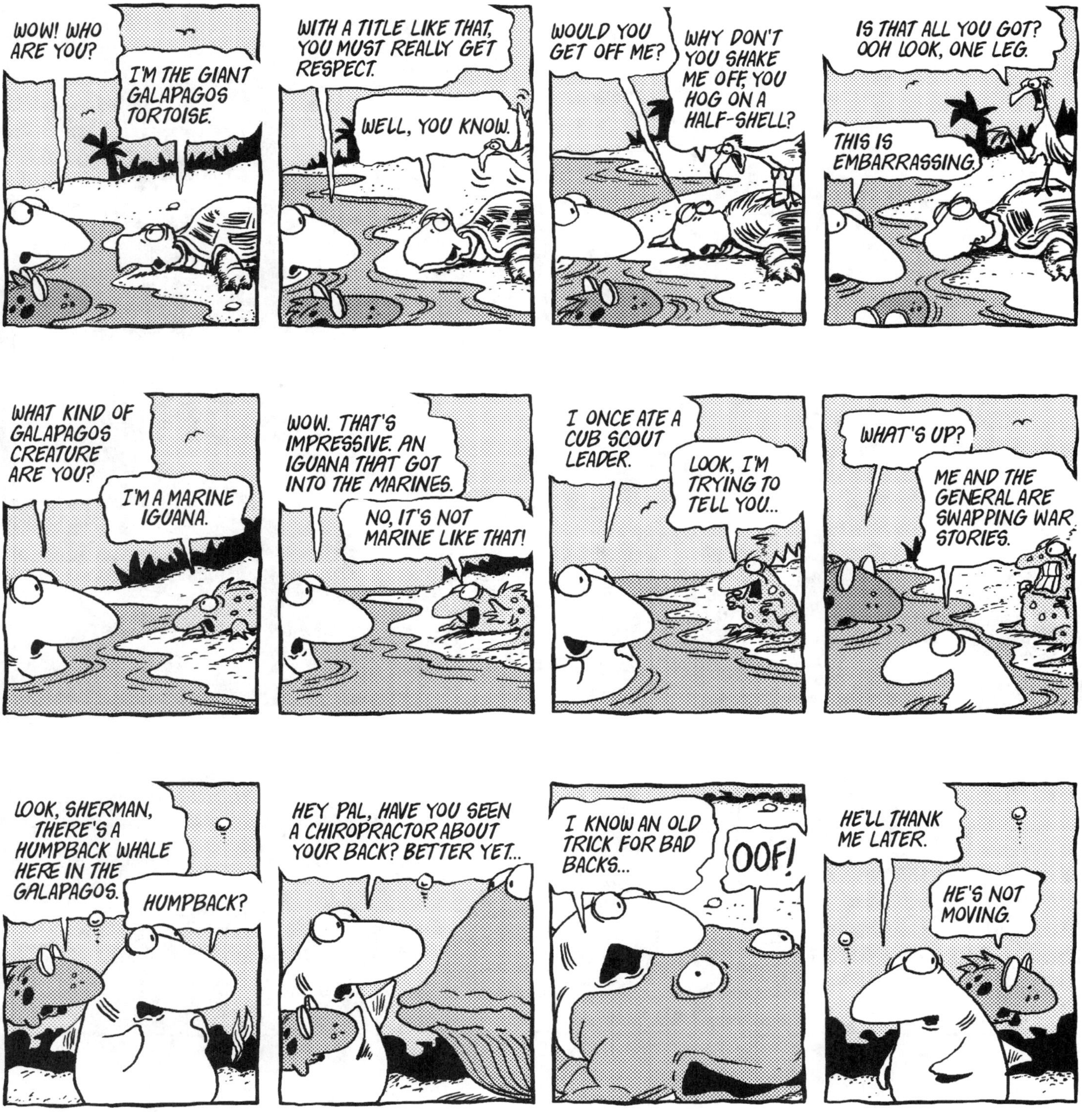
WOW! WHO ARE YOU?
I'M THE GIANT GALAPAGOS TORTOISE.
WITH A TITLE LIKE THAT, YOU MUST REALLY GET RESPECT.
WELL, YOU KNOW.
WOULD YOU GET OFF ME?
WHY DON'T YOU SHAKE ME OFF, YOU HOG ON A HALF-SHELL?
IS THAT ALL YOU GOT? OOH LOOK, ONE LEG.
THIS IS EMBARRASSING.
WHAT KIND OF GALAPAGOS CREATURE ARE YOU?
I'M A MARINE IGUANA.
WOW. THAT'S IMPRESSIVE. AN IGUANA THAT GOT INTO THE MARINES.
NO, IT'S NOT MARINE LIKE THAT!
I ONCE ATE A CUB SCOUT LEADER.
LOOK, I'M TRYING TO TELL YOU...
WHAT'S UP?
ME AND THE GENERAL ARE SWAPPING WAR STORIES.
LOOK, SHERMAN, THERE'S A HUMPBACK WHALE HERE IN THE GALAPAGOS.
HUMPBACK?
HEY PAL, HAVE YOU SEEN A CHIROPRACTOR ABOUT YOUR BACK? BETTER YET...
I KNOW AN OLD TRICK FOR BAD BACKS...
OOF!
HE'LL THANK ME LATER.
HE'S NOT MOVING.

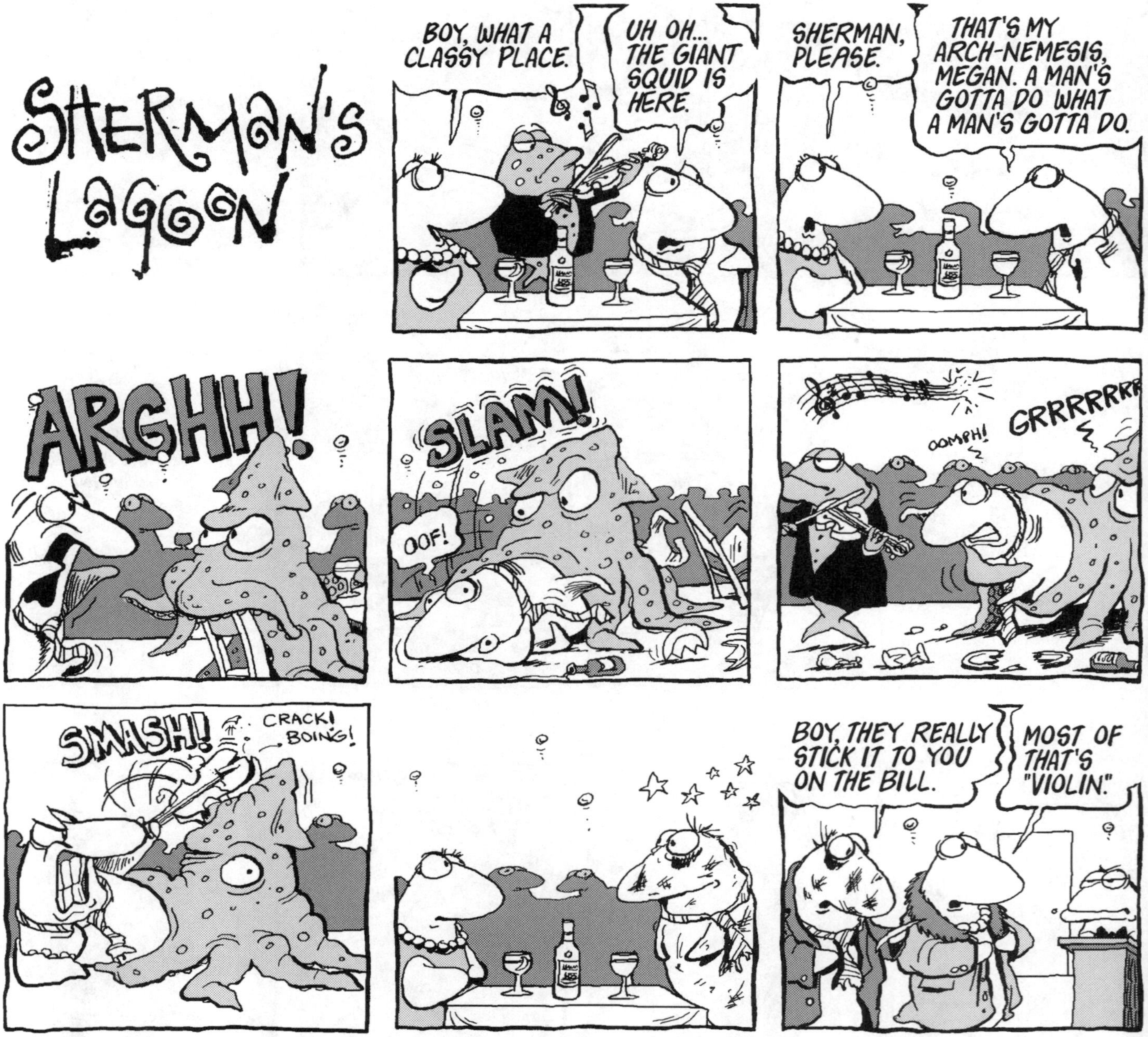
SHERMAN'S LAGOON
BOY, WHAT A CLASSY PLACE.
UH OH... THE GIANT SQUID IS HERE.
SHERMAN, PLEASE.
THAT'S MY ARCH-NEMESIS, MEGAN. A MAN'S GOTTA DO WHAT A MAN'S GOTTA DO.
ARGHH!
SLAM!
OOF!
OOMPH!
GRRRRRRR
SMASH!
CRACK!
BOING!
BOY, THEY REALLY STICK IT TO YOU ON THE BILL.
MOST OF THAT'S "VIOLIN."

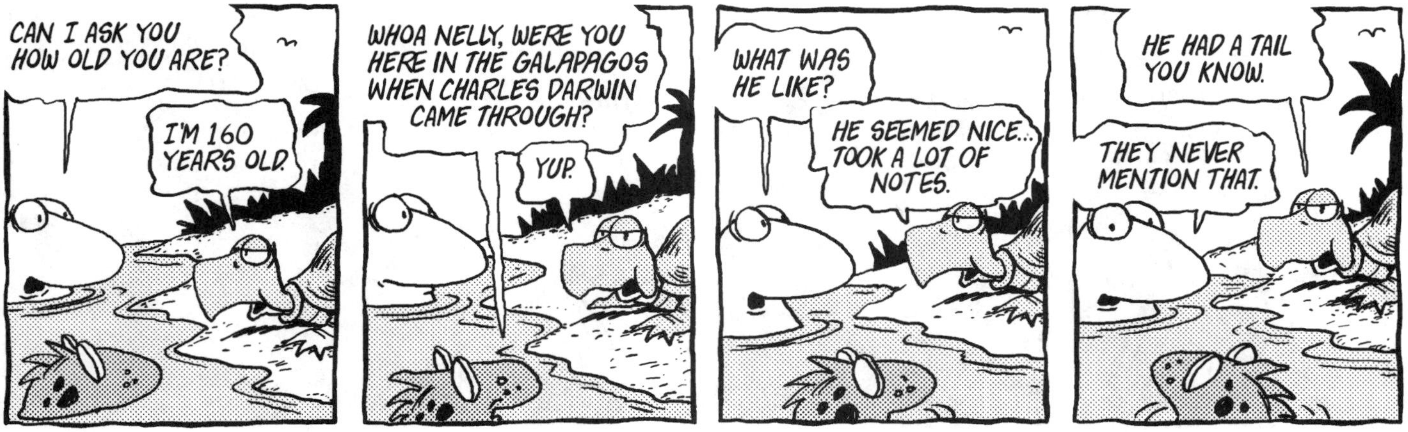
CAN I ASK YOU HOW OLD YOU ARE?
I'M 160 YEARS OLD.
WHOA NELLY, WERE YOU HERE IN THE GALAPAGOS WHEN CHARLES DARWIN CAME THROUGH?
YUP.
WHAT WAS HE LIKE?
HE SEEMED NICE... TOOK A LOT OF NOTES.
HE HAD A TAIL YOU KNOW.
THEY NEVER MENTION THAT.

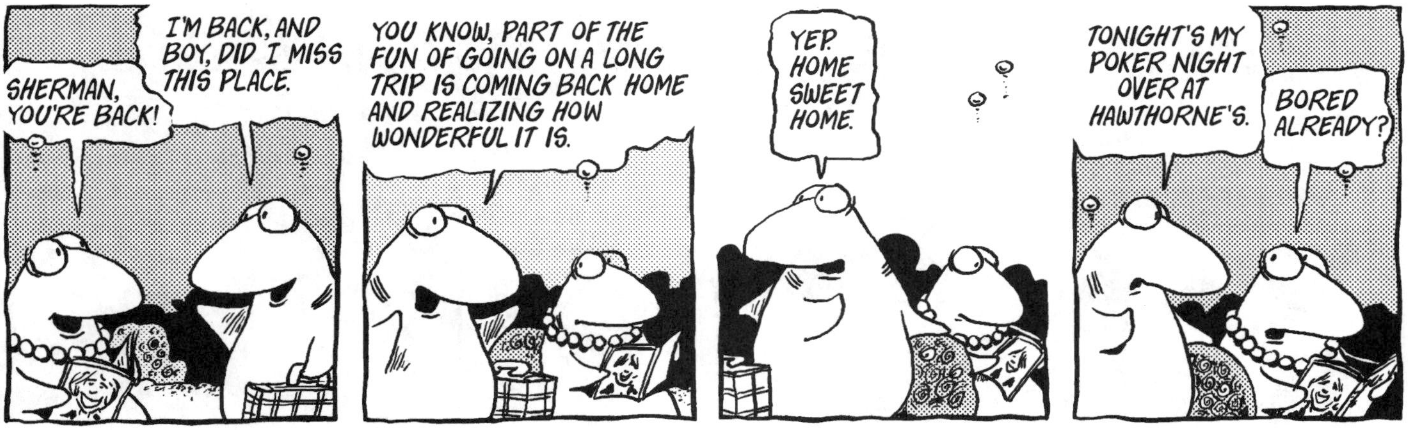
SHERMAN, YOU'RE BACK!
I'M BACK, AND BOY, DID I MISS THIS PLACE.
YOU KNOW, PART OF THE FUN OF GOING ON A LONG TRIP IS COMING BACK HOME AND REALIZING HOW WONDERFUL IT IS.
YEP. HOME SWEET HOME.
TONIGHT'S MY POKER NIGHT OVER AT HAWTHORNE'S.
BORED ALREADY?

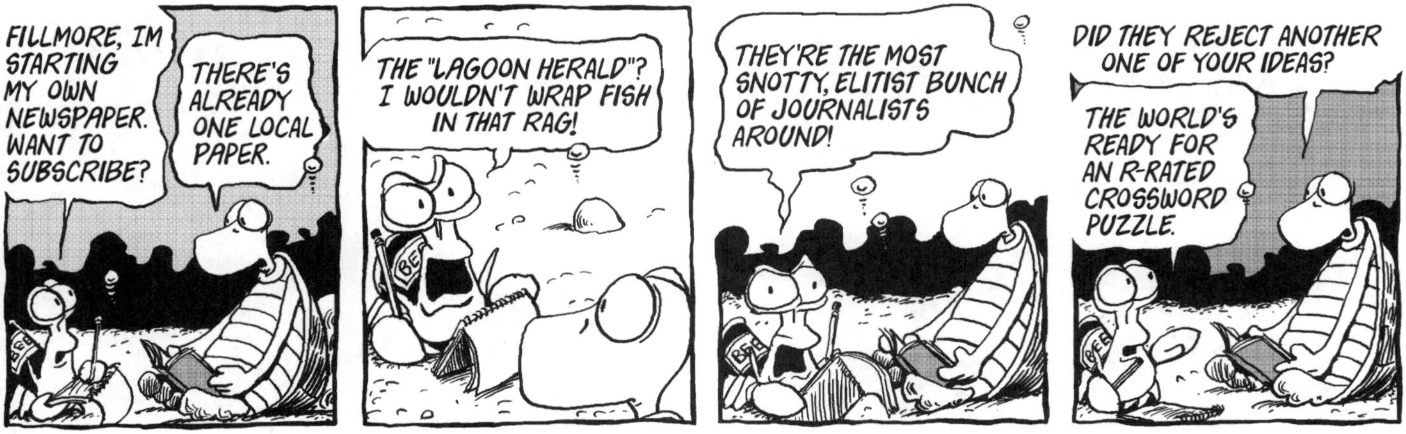
FILLMORE, I'M STARTING MY OWN NEWSPAPER. WANT TO SUBSCRIBE?
THERE'S ALREADY ONE LOCAL PAPER.
THE "LAGOON HERALD"? I WOULDN'T WRAP FISH IN THAT RAG!
THEY'RE THE MOST SNOTTY, ELITIST BUNCH OF JOURNALISTS AROUND!
DID THEY REJECT ANOTHER ONE OF YOUR IDEAS?
THE WORLD'S READY FOR AN R-RATED CROSSWORD PUZZLE.

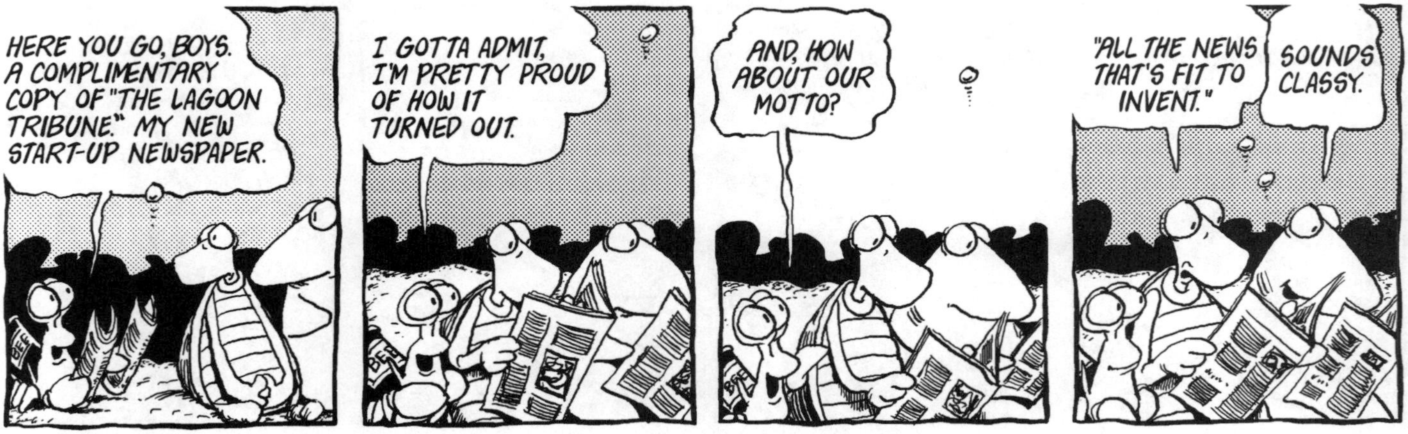
HERE YOU GO, BOYS. A COMPLIMENTARY COPY OF "THE LAGOON TRIBUNE." MY NEW START-UP NEWSPAPER.
I GOTTA ADMIT, I'M PRETTY PROUD OF HOW IT TURNED OUT.
AND, HOW ABOUT OUR MOTTO?
"ALL THE NEWS THAT'S FIT TO INVENT."
SOUNDS CLASSY.

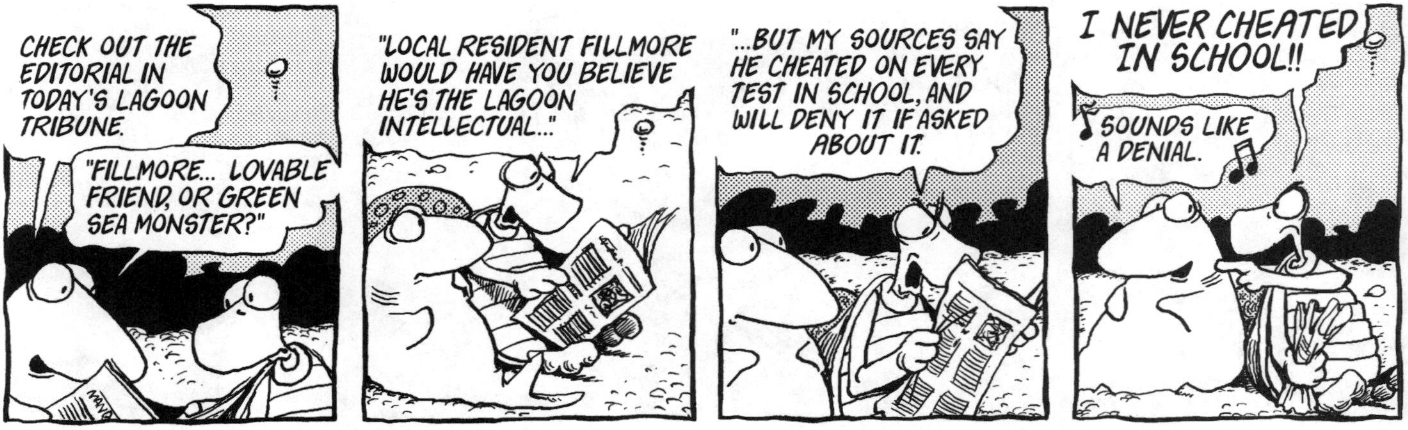
CHECK OUT THE EDITORIAL IN TODAY'S LAGOON TRIBUNE.
"FILLMORE... LOVABLE FRIEND, OR GREEN SEA MONSTER?"
"LOCAL RESIDENT FILLMORE WOULD HAVE YOU BELIEVE HE'S THE LAGOON INTELLECTUAL..."
"...BUT MY SOURCES SAY HE CHEATED ON EVERY TEST IN SCHOOL, AND WILL DENY IT IF ASKED ABOUT IT."
I NEVER CHEATED IN SCHOOL!!
SOUNDS LIKE A DENIAL.

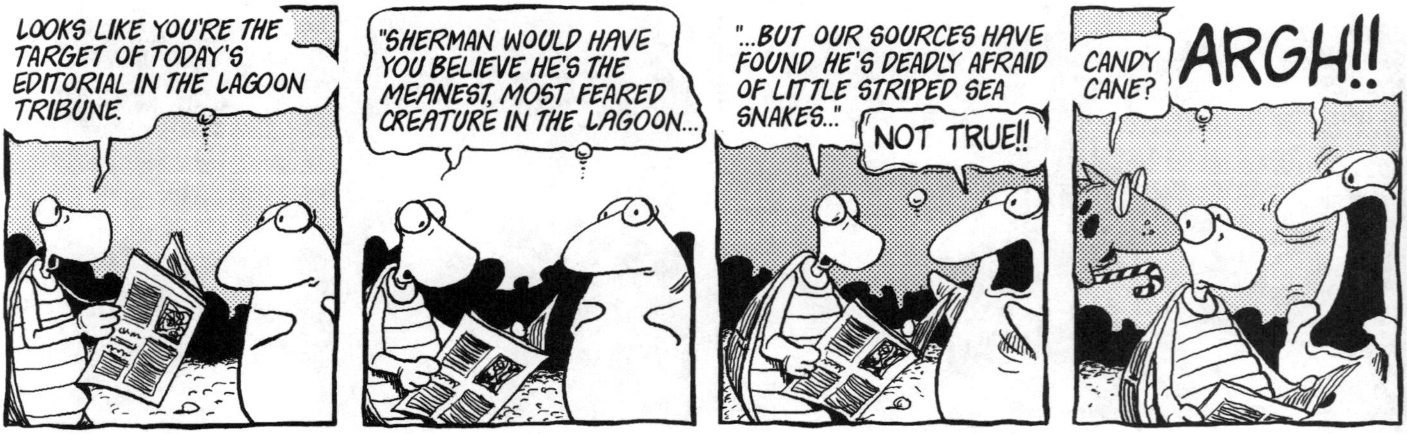
LOOKS LIKE YOU'RE THE TARGET OF TODAY'S EDITORIAL IN THE LAGOON TRIBUNE.
"SHERMAN WOULD HAVE YOU BELIEVE HE'S THE MEANEST, MOST FEARED CREATURE IN THE LAGOON..."
"...BUT OUR SOURCES HAVE FOUND HE'S DEADLY AFRAID OF LITTLE STRIPED SEA SNAKES..."
NOT TRUE!!
CANDY CANE?
ARGH!!

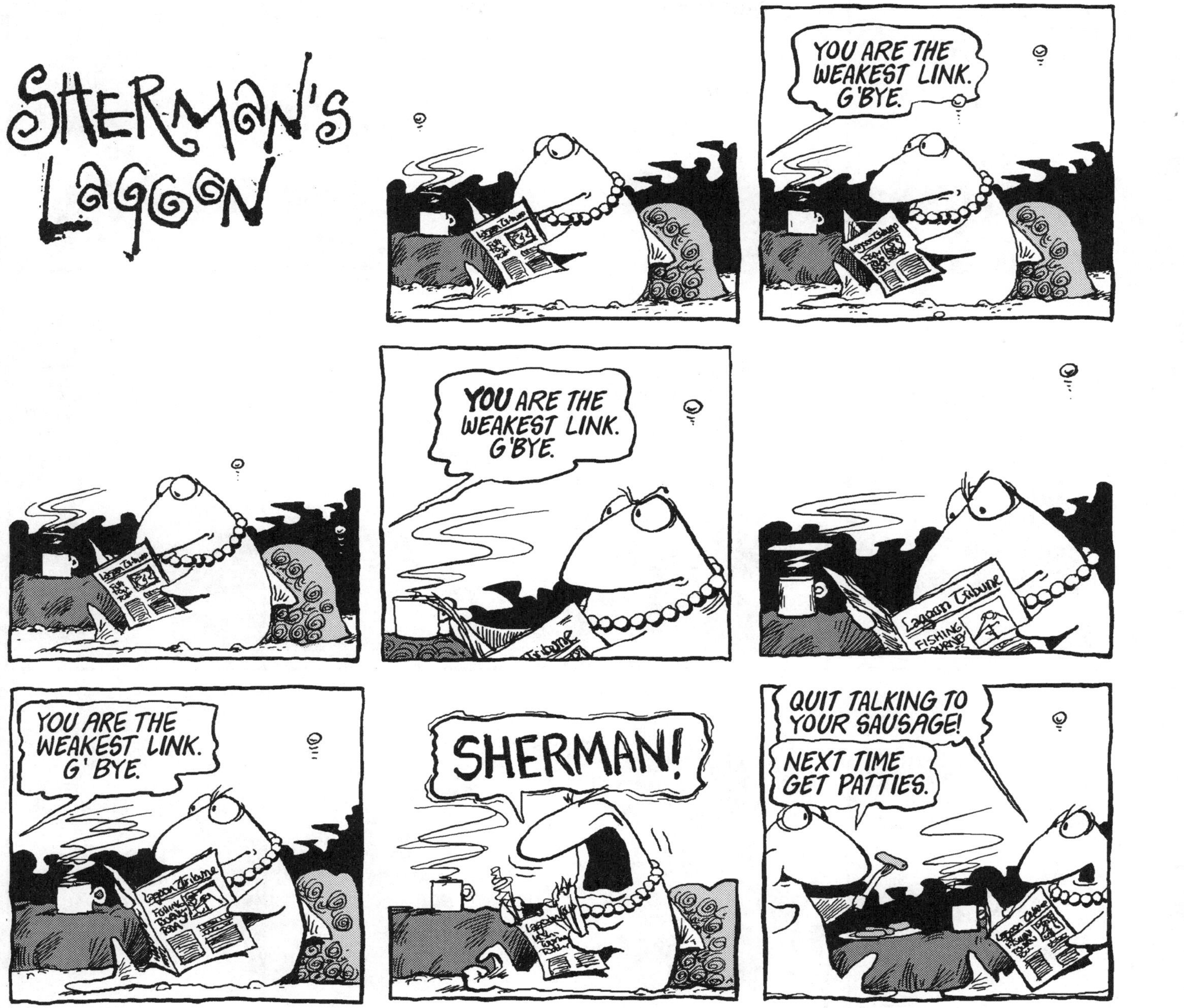
SHERMAN'S LAGOON
YOU ARE THE WEAKEST LINK. G'BYE.
YOU ARE THE WEAKEST LINK. G'BYE.
YOU ARE THE WEAKEST LINK. G' BYE.
SHERMAN!
QUIT TALKING TO YOUR SAUSAGE!
NEXT TIME GET PATTIES.

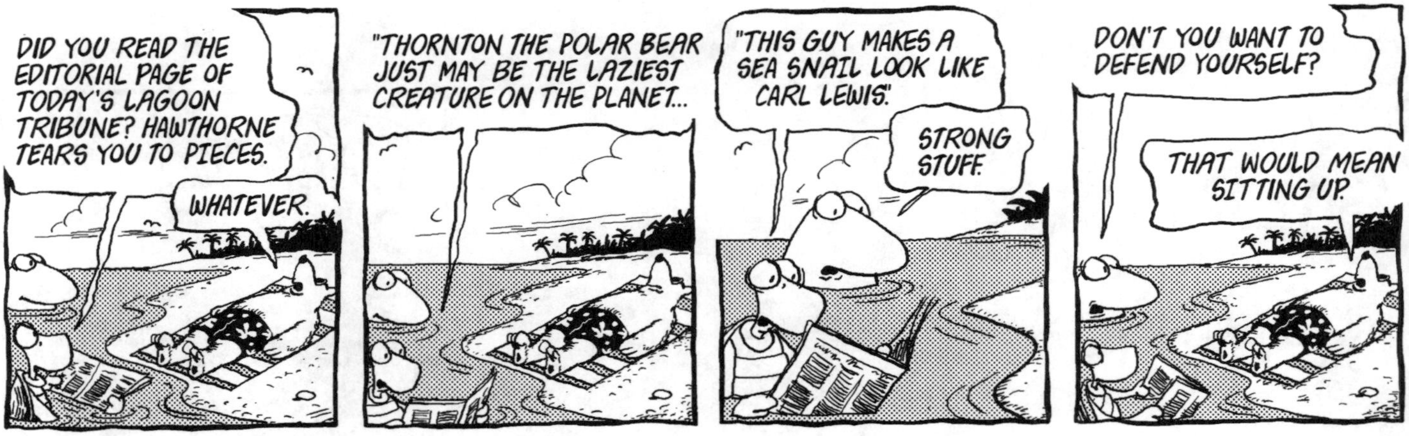
DID YOU READ THE EDITORIAL PAGE OF TODAY'S LAGOON TRIBUNE? HAWTHORNE TEARS YOU TO PIECES.
WHATEVER.
"THORNTON THE POLAR BEAR JUST MAY BE THE LAZIEST CREATURE ON THE PLANET...
"THIS GUY MAKES A SEA SNAIL LOOK LIKE CARL LEWIS."
STRONG STUFF.
DON'T YOU WANT TO DEFEND YOURSELF?
THAT WOULD MEAN SITTING UP.

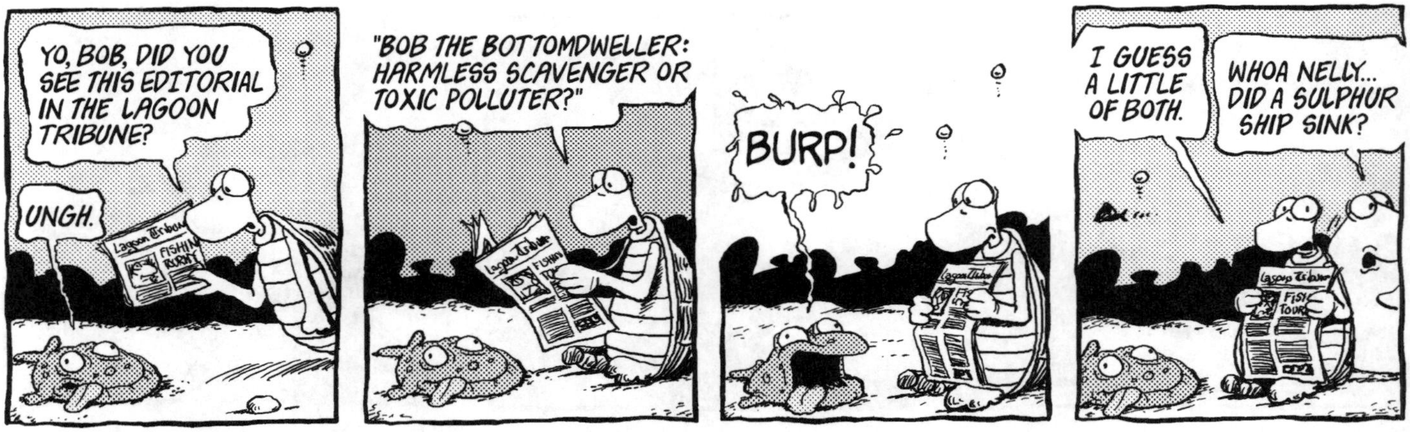
YO, BOB, DID YOU SEE THIS EDITORIAL IN THE LAGOON TRIBUNE?
UNGH.
"BOB THE BOTTOMDWELLER: HARMLESS SCAVENGER OR TOXIC POLLUTER?"
BURP!
I GUESS A LITTLE OF BOTH.
WHOA NELLY... DID A SULPHUR SHIP SINK?

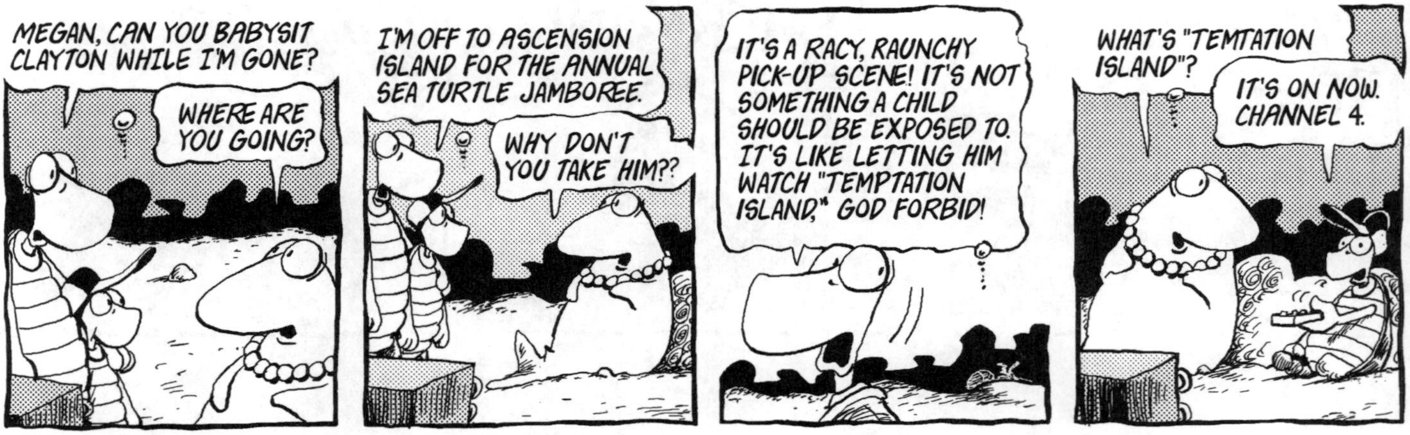
MEGAN, CAN YOU BABYSIT CLAYTON WHILE I'M GONE?
WHERE ARE YOU GOING?
I'M OFF TO ASCENSION ISLAND FOR THE ANNUAL SEA TURTLE JAMBOREE.
WHY DON'T YOU TAKE HIM??
IT'S A RACY, RAUNCHY PICK-UP SCENE! IT'S NOT SOMETHING A CHILD SHOULD BE EXPOSED TO. IT'S LIKE LETTING HIM WATCH "TEMPTATION ISLAND," GOD FORBID!
WHAT'S "TEMTATION ISLAND"?
IT'S ON NOW. CHANNEL 4.

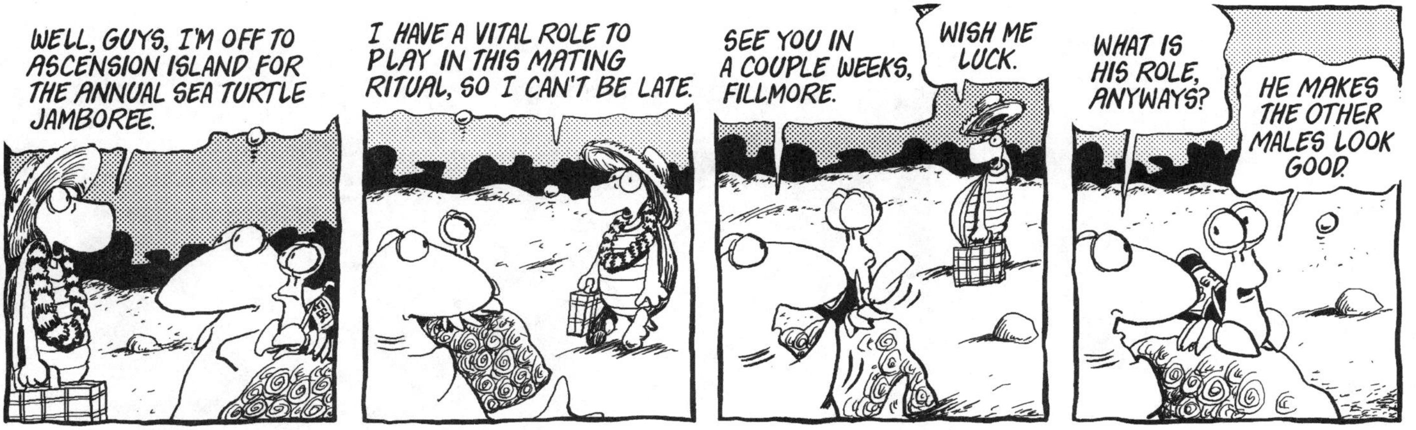
WELL, GUYS, I'M OFF TO ASCENSION ISLAND FOR THE ANNUAL SEA TURTLE JAMBOREE.
I HAVE A VITAL ROLE TO PLAY IN THIS MATING RITUAL, SO I CAN'T BE LATE.
SEE YOU IN A COUPLE WEEKS, FILLMORE.
WISH ME LUCK.
WHAT IS HIS ROLE, ANYWAYS?
HE MAKES THE OTHER MALES LOOK GOOD.

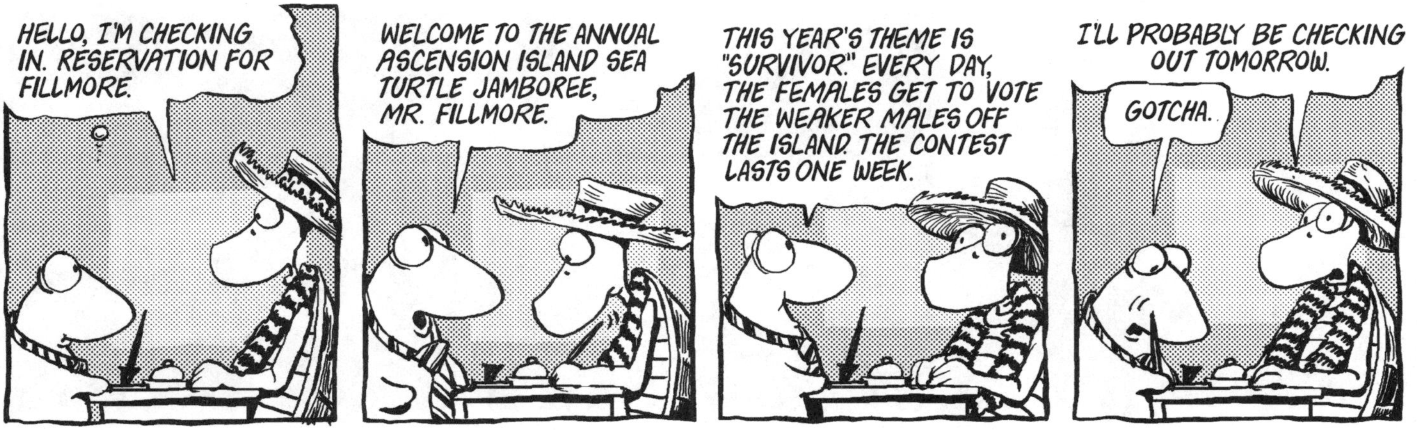
HELLO, I'M CHECKING IN. RESERVATION FOR FILLMORE.
WELCOME TO THE ANNUAL ASCENSION ISLAND SEA TURTLE JAMBOREE, MR. FILLMORE.
THIS YEAR'S THEME IS "SURVIVOR." EVERY DAY, THE FEMALES GET TO VOTE THE WEAKER MALES OFF THE ISLAND. THE CONTEST LASTS ONE WEEK.
I'LL PROBABLY BE CHECKING OUT TOMORROW.
GOTCHA.

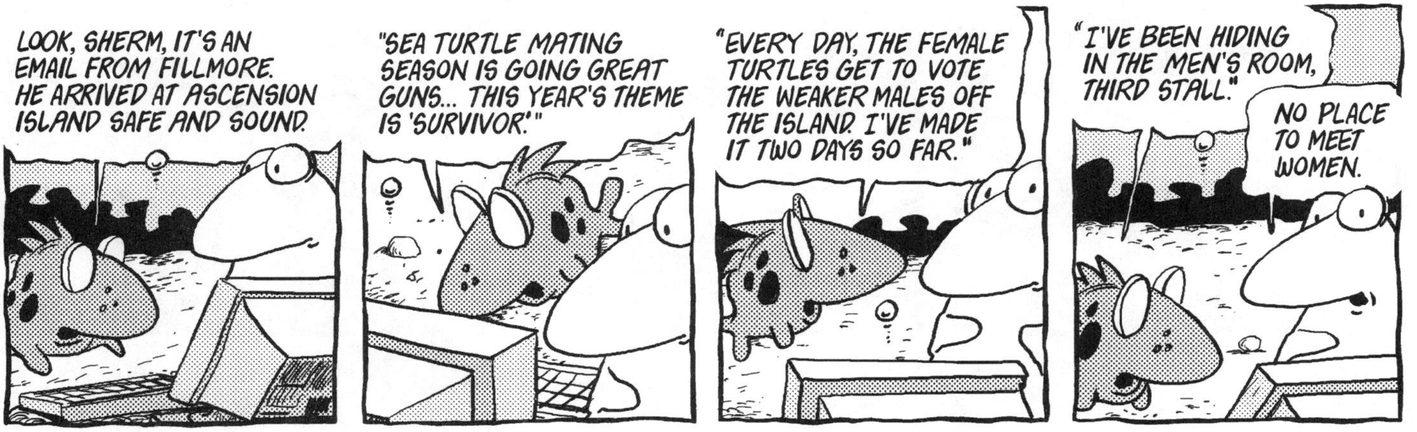
LOOK, SHERM, IT'S AN EMAIL FROM FILLMORE. HE ARRIVED AT ASCENSION ISLAND SAFE AND SOUND.
"SEA TURTLE MATING SEASON IS GOING GREAT GUNS... THIS YEAR'S THEME IS 'SURVIVOR.'"
"EVERY DAY, THE FEMALE TURTLES GET TO VOTE THE WEAKER MALES OFF THE ISLAND. I'VE MADE IT TWO DAYS SO FAR."
"I'VE BEEN HIDING IN THE MEN'S ROOM, THIRD STALL."
NO PLACE TO MEET WOMEN.

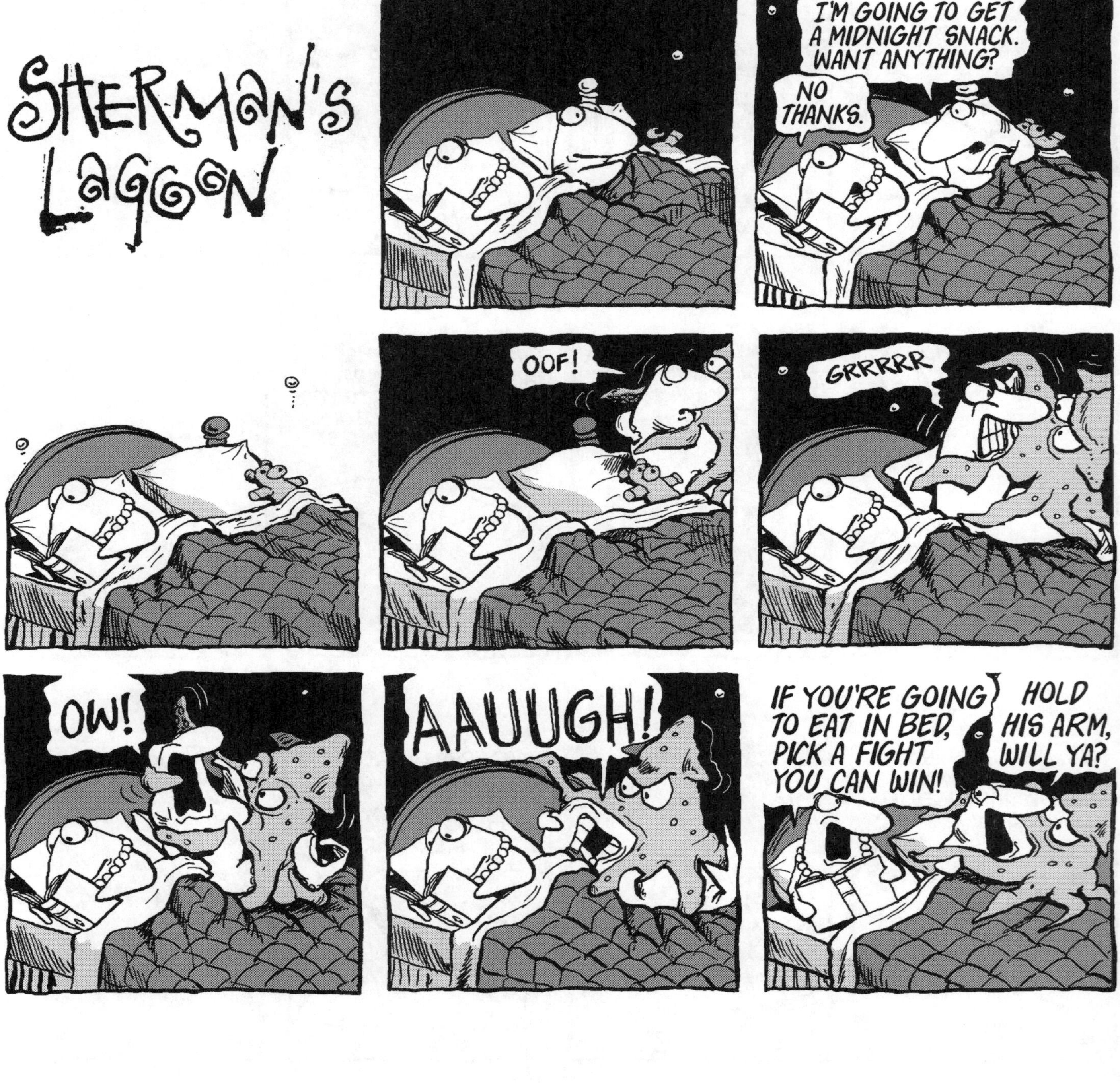
SHERMAN'S LAGOON
I'M GOING TO GET A MIDNIGHT SNACK. WANT ANYTHING?
NO THANKS.
OOF!
GRRRRR
OW!
AAUUGH!
IF YOU'RE GOING TO EAT IN BED, PICK A FIGHT YOU CAN WIN!
HOLD HIS ARM, WILL YA?

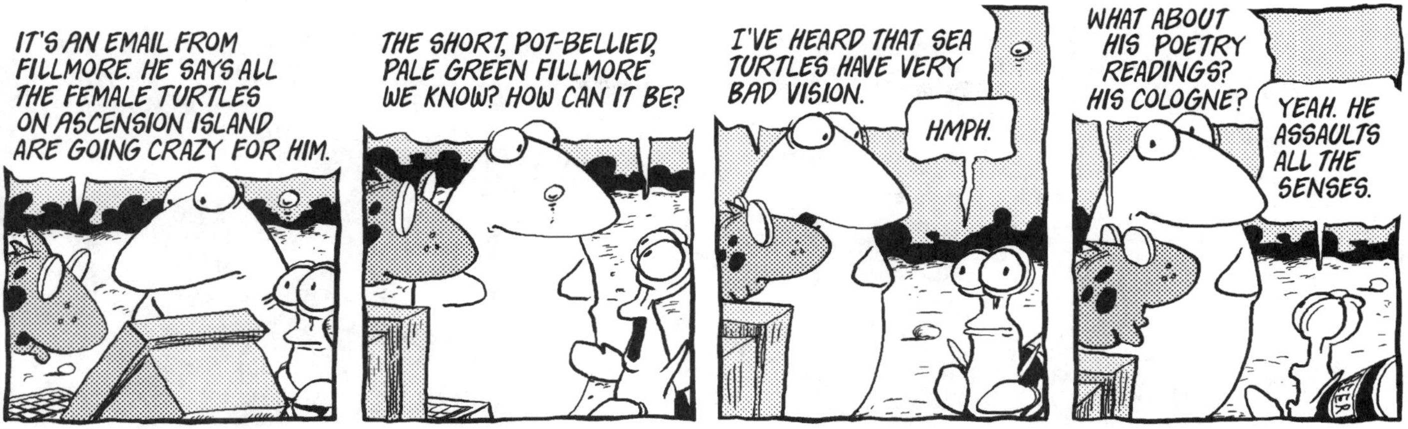
IT'S AN EMAIL FROM FILLMORE. HE SAYS ALL THE FEMALE TURTLES ON ASCENSION ISLAND ARE GOING CRAZY FOR HIM.
THE SHORT, POT-BELLIED, PALE GREEN FILLMORE WE KNOW? HOW CAN IT BE?
I'VE HEARD THAT SEA TURTLES HAVE VERY BAD VISION.
HMPH.
WHAT ABOUT HIS POETRY READINGS? HIS COLOGNE?
YEAH. HE ASSAULTS ALL THE SENSES.

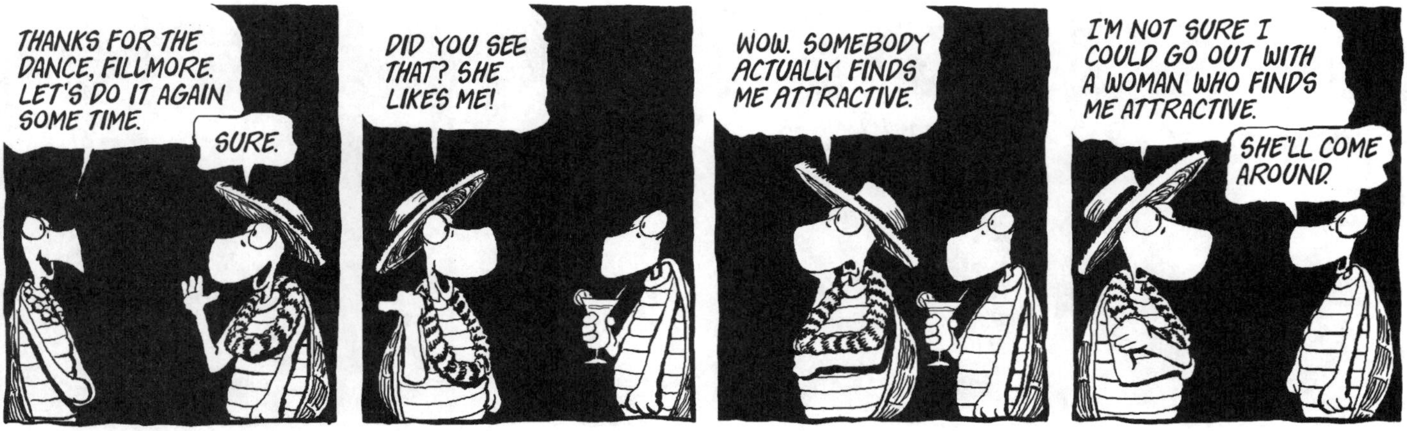
THANKS FOR THE DANCE, FILLMORE. LET'S DO IT AGAIN SOME TIME.
SURE.
DID YOU SEE THAT? SHE LIKES ME!
WOW. SOMEBODY ACTUALLY FINDS ME ATTRACTIVE.
I'M NOT SURE I COULD GO OUT WITH A WOMAN WHO FINDS ME ATTRACTIVE.
SHE'LL COME AROUND.

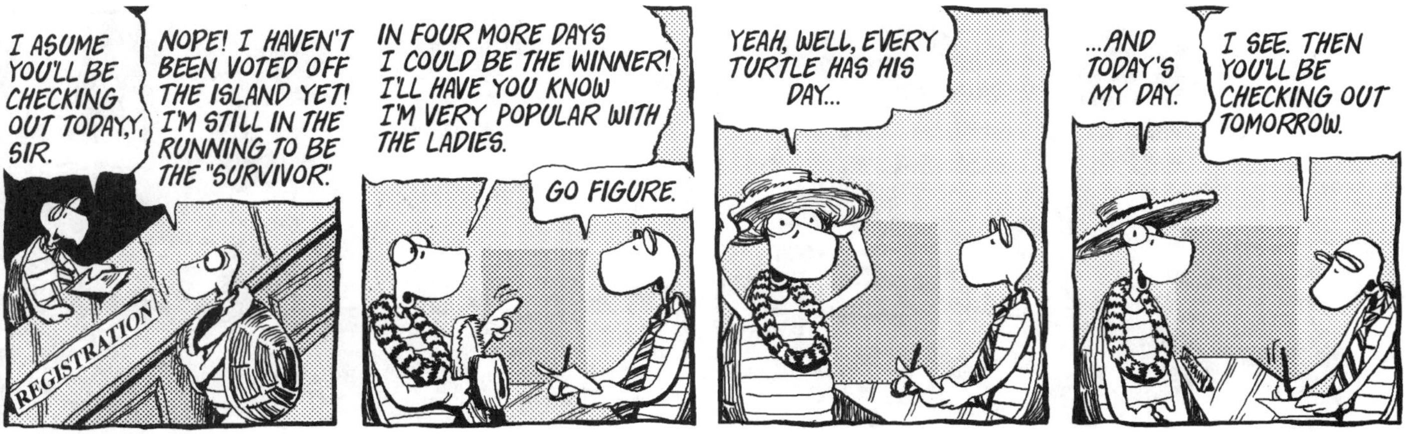
I ASUME YOU'LL BE CHECKING OUT TODAY,Y, SIR.
NOPE! I HAVEN'T BEEN VOTED OFF THE ISLAND YET! I'M STILL IN THE RUNNING TO BE THE "SURVIVOR."
REGISTRATION
IN FOUR MORE DAYS I COULD BE THE WINNER! I'LL HAVE YOU KNOW I'M VERY POPULAR WITH THE LADIES.
GO FIGURE.
YEAH, WELL, EVERY TURTLE HAS HIS DAY...
...AND TODAY'S MY DAY.
I SEE. THEN YOU'LL BE CHECKING OUT TOMORROW.

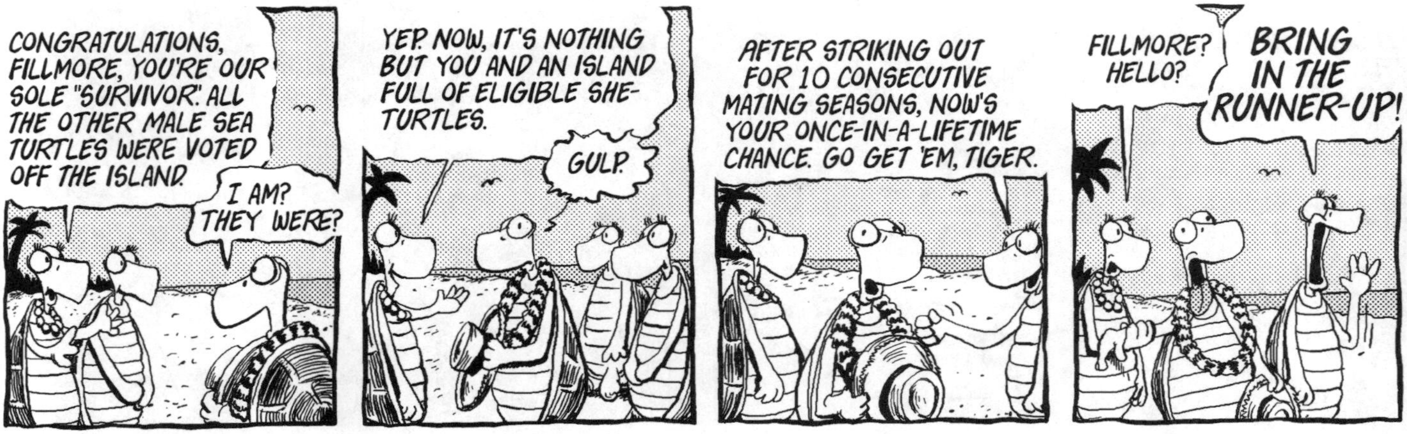
CONGRATULATIONS, FILLMORE, YOU'RE OUR SOLE "SURVIVOR." ALL THE OTHER MALE SEA TURTLES WERE VOTED OFF THE ISLAND.
I AM? THEY WERE?
YEP. NOW, IT'S NOTHING BUT YOU AND AN ISLAND FULL OF ELIGIBLE SHE-TURTLES.
GULP.
AFTER STRIKING OUT FOR 10 CONSECUTIVE MATING SEASONS, NOW'S YOUR ONCE-IN-A-LIFETIME CHANCE. GO GET 'EM, TIGER.
FILLMORE? HELLO?
BRING IN THE RUNNER-UP!

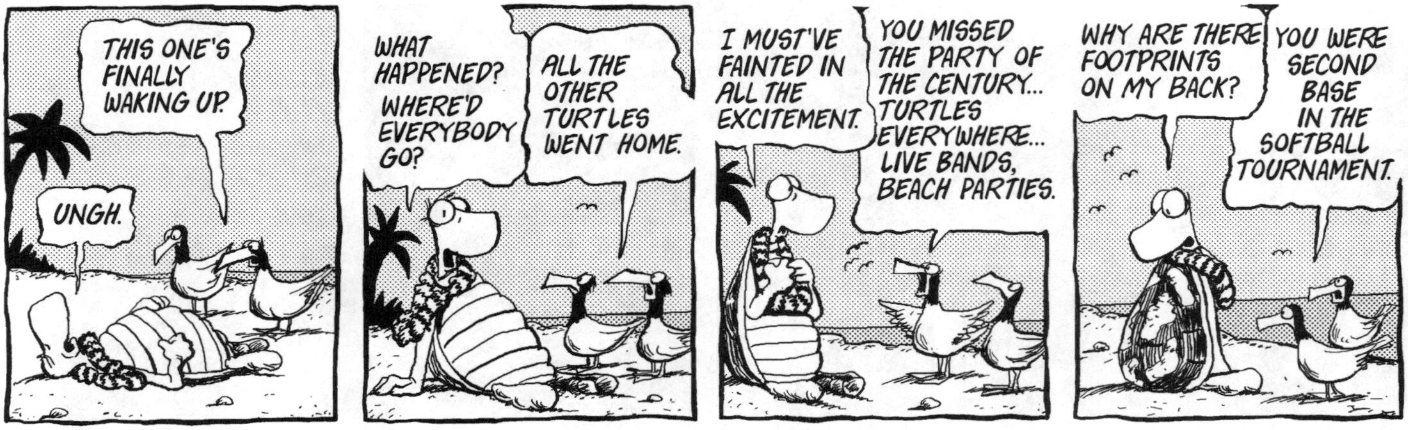
THIS ONE'S FINALLY WAKING UP.
UNGH.
WHAT HAPPENED? WHERE'D EVERYBODY GO?
ALL THE OTHER TURTLES WENT HOME.
I MUST'VE FAINTED IN ALL THE EXCITEMENT.
YOU MISSED THE PARTY OF THE CENTURY... TURTLES EVERYWHERE... LIVE BANDS, BEACH PARTIES.
WHY ARE THERE FOOTPRINTS ON MY BACK?
YOU WERE SECOND BASE IN THE SOFTBALL TOURNAMENT.

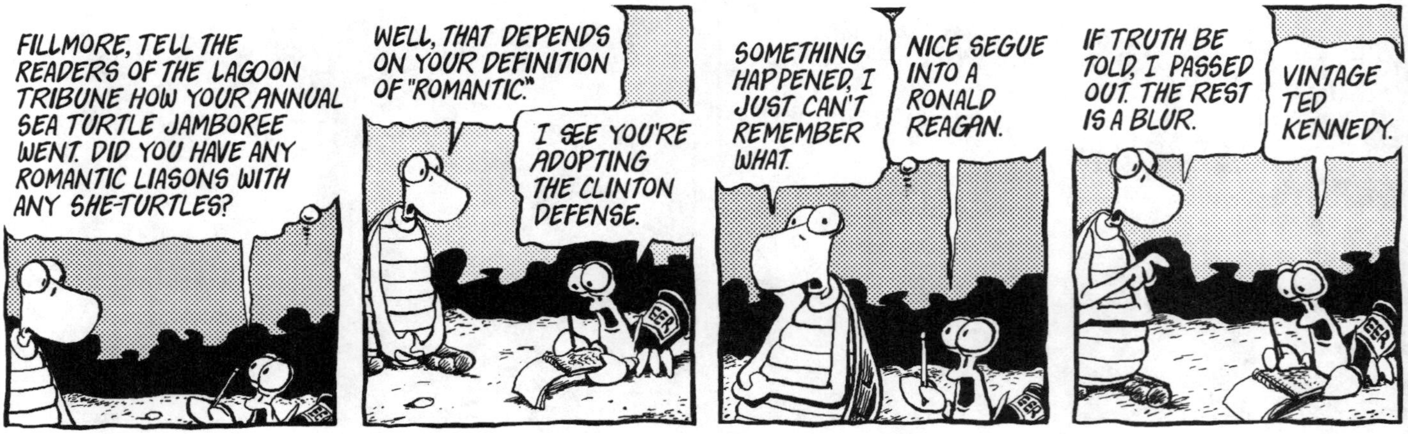
FILLMORE, TELL THE READERS OF THE LAGOON TRIBUNE HOW YOUR ANNUAL SEA TURTLE JAMBOREE WENT. DID YOU HAVE ANY ROMANTIC LIASONS WITH ANY SHE-TURTLES?
WELL, THAT DEPENDS ON YOUR DEFINITION OF "ROMANTIC."
I SEE YOU'RE ADOPTING THE CLINTON DEFENSE.
SOMETHING HAPPENED, I JUST CAN'T REMEMBER WHAT.
NICE SEGUE INTO A RONALD REAGAN.
IF TRUTH BE TOLD, I PASSED OUT. THE REST IS A BLUR.
VINTAGE TED KENNEDY.

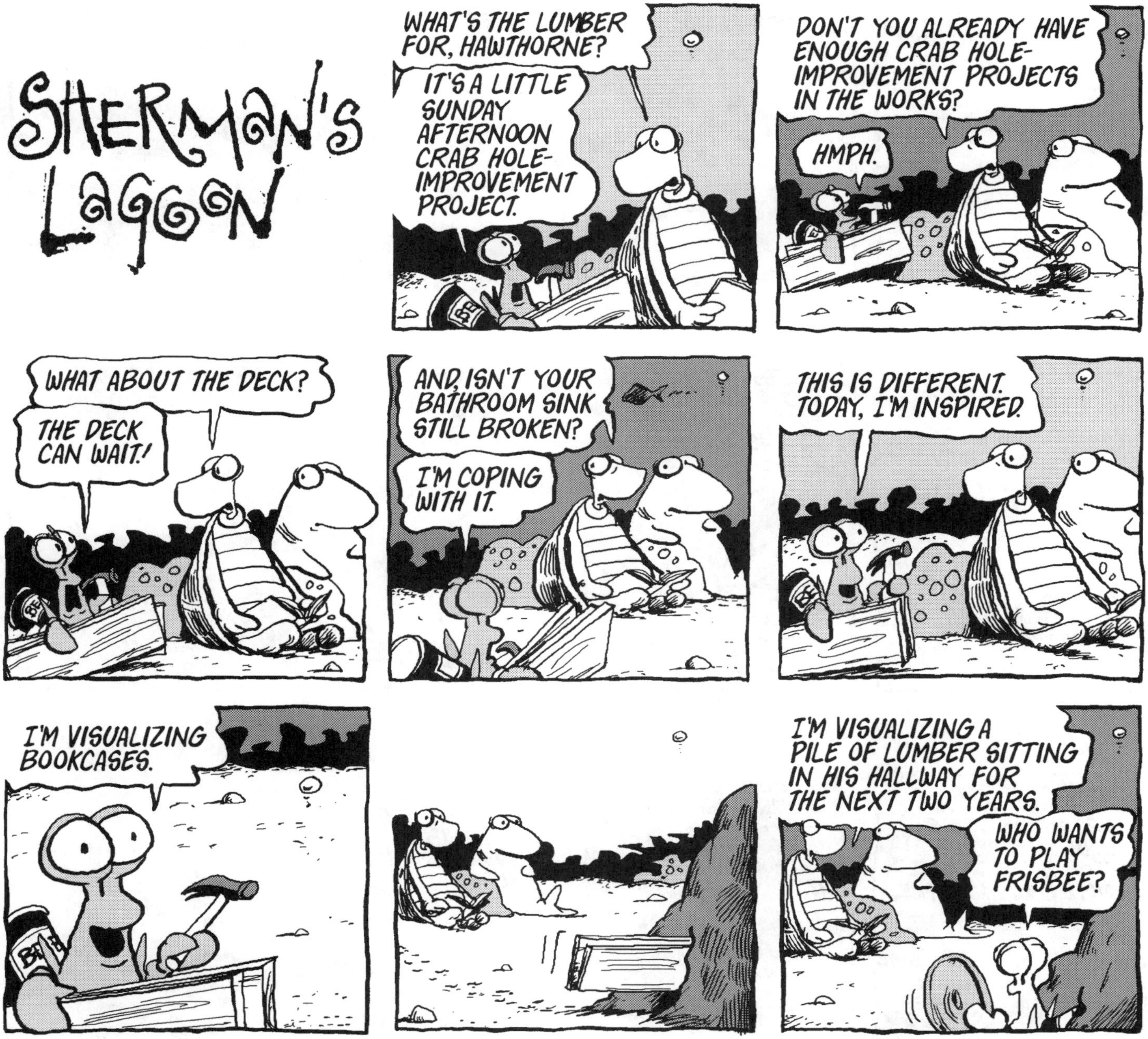
SHERMAN'S LAGOON
WHAT'S THE LUMBER FOR, HAWTHORNE?
IT'S A LITTLE SUNDAY AFTERNOON CRAB HOLE-IMPROVEMENT PROJECT.
DON'T YOU ALREADY HAVE ENOUGH CRAB HOLE-IMPROVEMENT PROJECTS IN THE WORKS?
HMPH.
WHAT ABOUT THE DECK?
THE DECK CAN WAIT!
AND, ISN'T YOUR BATHROOM SINK STILL BROKEN?
I'M COPING WITH IT.
THIS IS DIFFERENT. TODAY, I'M INSPIRED.
I'M VISUALIZING BOOKCASES.
I'M VISUALIZING A PILE OF LUMBER SITTING IN HIS HALLWAY FOR THE NEXT TWO YEARS.
WHO WANTS TO PLAY FRISBEE?

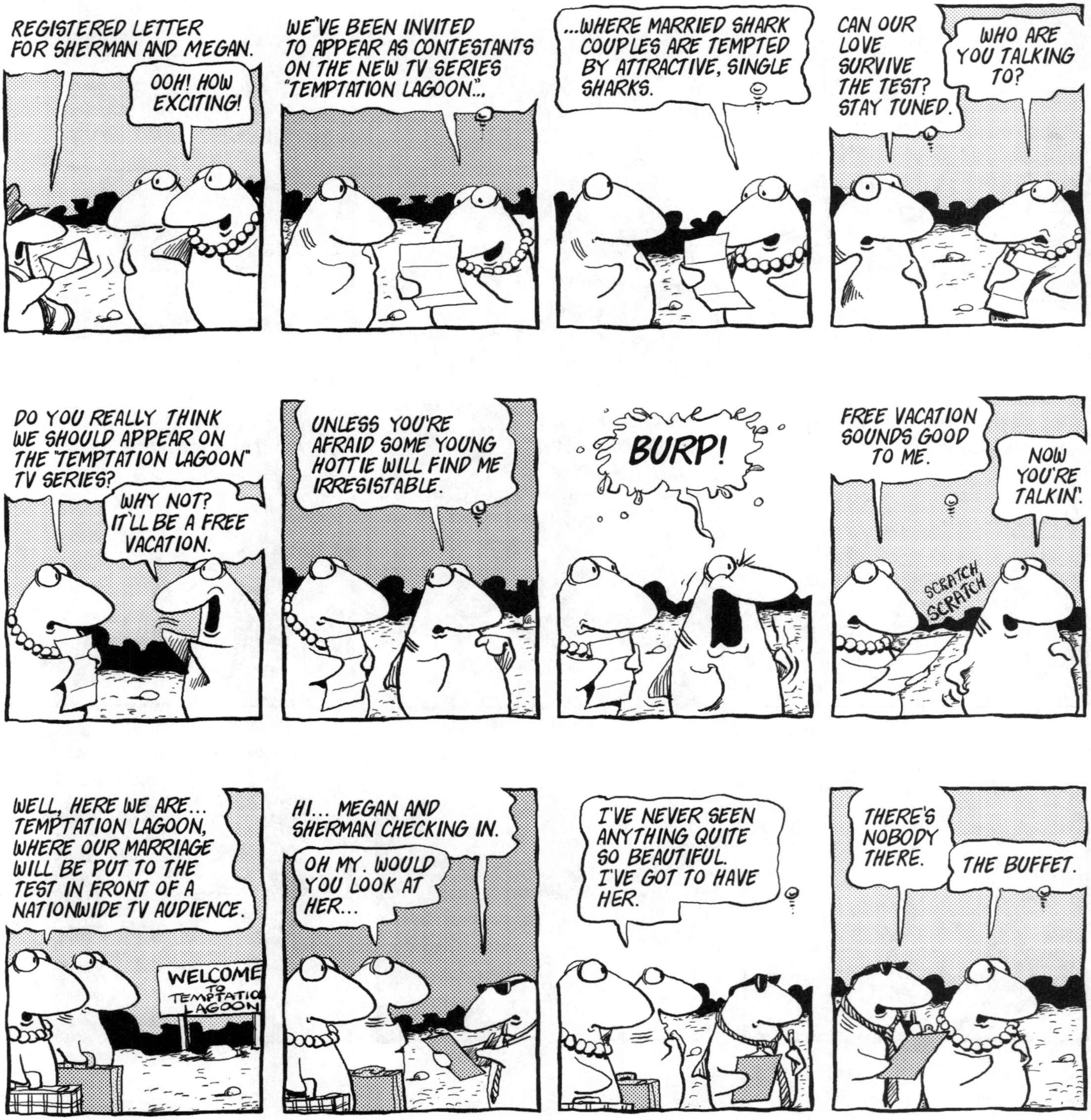
REGISTERED LETTER FOR SHERMAN AND MEGAN.
OOH! HOW EXCITING!
WE'VE BEEN INVITED TO APPEAR AS CONTESTANTS ON THE NEW TV SERIES "TEMPTATION LAGOON"...
...WHERE MARRIED SHARK COUPLES ARE TEMPTED BY ATTRACTIVE, SINGLE SHARKS.
CAN OUR LOVE SURVIVE THE TEST? STAY TUNED.
WHO ARE YOU TALKING TO?
DO YOU REALLY THINK WE SHOULD APPEAR ON THE "TEMPTATION LAGOON" TV SERIES?
WHY NOT? IT'LL BE A FREE VACATION.
UNLESS YOU'RE AFRAID SOME YOUNG HOTTIE WILL FIND ME IRRESISTABLE.
BURP!
FREE VACATION SOUNDS GOOD TO ME.
NOW YOU'RE TALKIN'.
SCRATCH SCRATCH
WELL, HERE WE ARE... TEMPTATION LAGOON, WHERE OUR MARRIAGE WILL BE PUT TO THE TEST IN FRONT OF A NATIONWIDE TV AUDIENCE.
WELCOME TO TEMPTATIO LAGOON
HI... MEGAN AND SHERMAN CHECKING IN.
OH MY. WOULD YOU LOOK AT HER...
I'VE NEVER SEEN ANYTHING QUITE SO BEAUTIFUL. I'VE GOT TO HAVE HER.
THERE'S NOBODY THERE.
THE BUFFET.

OKAY, YOU TWO GET ACQUAINTED WITH THE OTHER "TEMPTATION LAGOON" GUESTS.

MEGAN, LOOK...

THERE'S ALEXIS. SHE WAS FEBRUARY IN THIS YEAR'S SHARK'S ILLUSTRATED SWIMMING SUIT CALENDAR.

I THOUGHT I THREW THAT THING AWAY.

UM... WELL, FILLMORE HAS ONE, TOO.

AND WHY WOULD A SEA TURTLE HAVE A SHARKS ILLUSTRATED BATHING SUIT CALENDAR?

HE'S LONLIER THAN YOU THINK.

ACTUALLY, I'D BUY THAT.

SHERMAN, THIS IS YOUR TEMPTATION LAGOON DATE, TAMMY.

HI.

HELLO.

SAY, YOU'RE A BIG GUY.

THANKS.

SO, ARE YOU LIKE...

AN ATHLETE? YES.

I WAS GONNA SAY "RISK FOR A HEART ATTACK."

HEY, CHECK IT OUT! SHERMAN IS ON TV! THEY'RE TALKING TO HIM ON TEMPTATION LAGOON!

HOW WAS MY DATE? TAMMY WANTED TO GET SERIOUS, BUT I HAD TO PUT THE BRAKES ON.

OUR HIDDEN CAMERAS SHOWED HER FLEEING IN DISGUST, AND ACTUALLY SWEARING OFF MEN ENTIRELY.

CAN I CHANGE MY ANSWER TO "NO COMMENT"?

NOT AND STILL ALLOW US TO MAKE YOU LOOK STUPID.

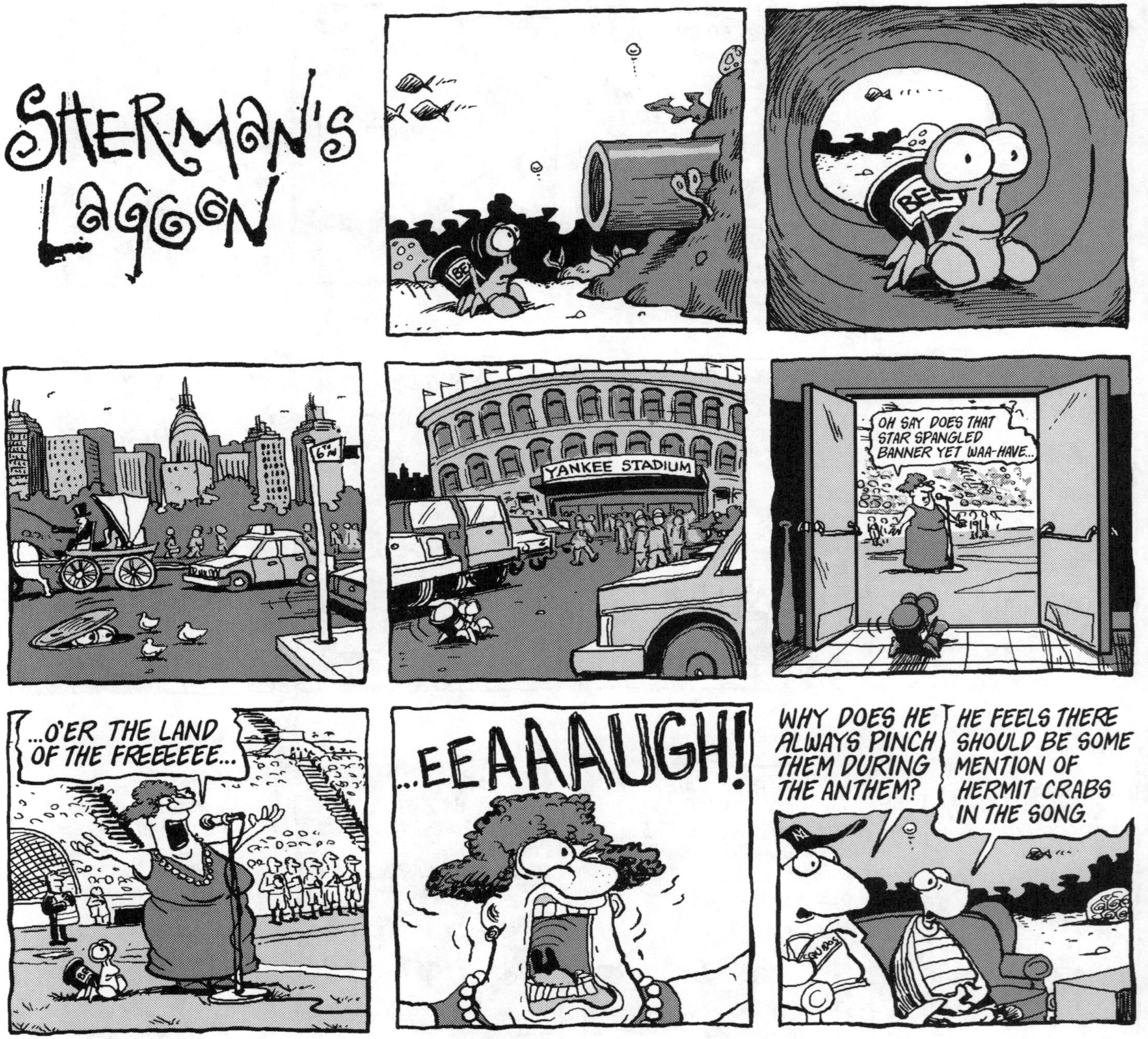
SHERMAN'S LAGOON
BE
BE
6TH AV
YANKEE STADIUM
OH SAY DOES THAT STAR SPANGLED BANNER YET WAA-HAVE...
...O'ER THE LAND OF THE FREEEEEE...
...EEAAAAUGH!
WHY DOES HE ALWAYS PINCH THEM DURING THE ANTHEM?
HE FEELS THERE SHOULD BE SOME MENTION OF HERMIT CRABS IN THE SONG.

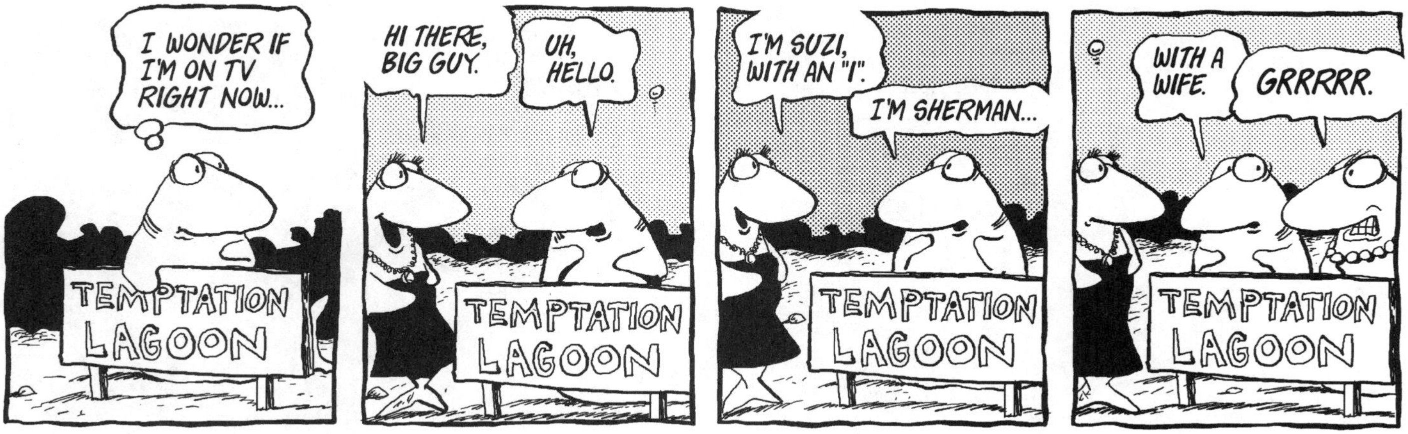
I WONDER IF I'M ON TV RIGHT NOW...
TEMPTATION LAGOON
HI THERE, BIG GUY.
UH, HELLO.
TEMPTATION LAGOON
I'M SUZI, WITH AN "I".
I'M SHERMAN...
TEMPTATION LAGOON
WITH A WIFE.
GRRRRR.
TEMPTATION LAGOON

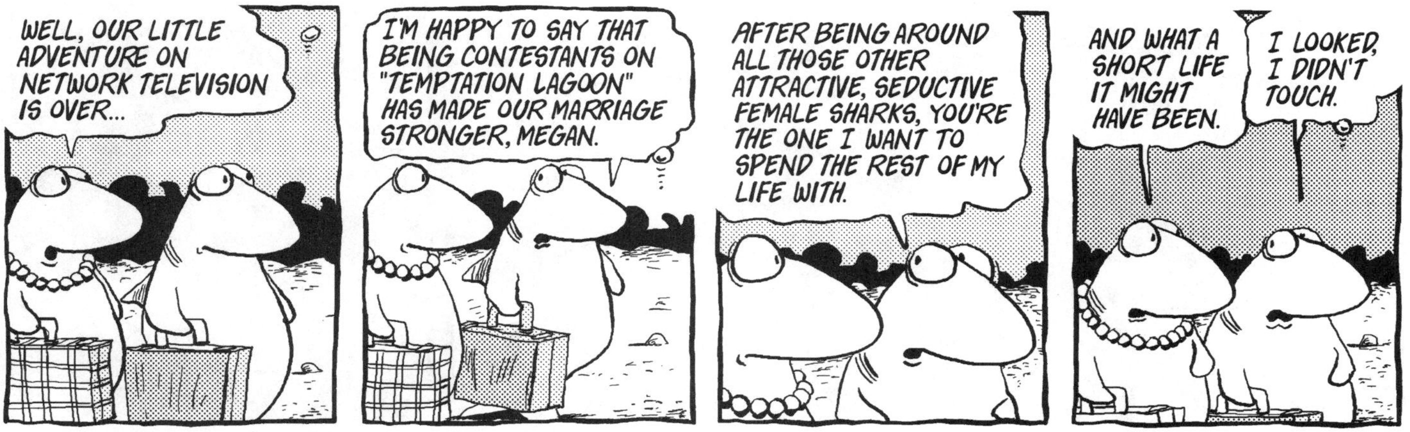
WELL, OUR LITTLE ADVENTURE ON NETWORK TELEVISION IS OVER...
I'M HAPPY TO SAY THAT BEING CONTESTANTS ON "TEMPTATION LAGOON" HAS MADE OUR MARRIAGE STRONGER, MEGAN.
AFTER BEING AROUND ALL THOSE OTHER ATTRACTIVE, SEDUCTIVE FEMALE SHARKS, YOU'RE THE ONE I WANT TO SPEND THE REST OF MY LIFE WITH.
AND WHAT A SHORT LIFE IT MIGHT HAVE BEEN.
I LOOKED, I DIDN'T TOUCH.

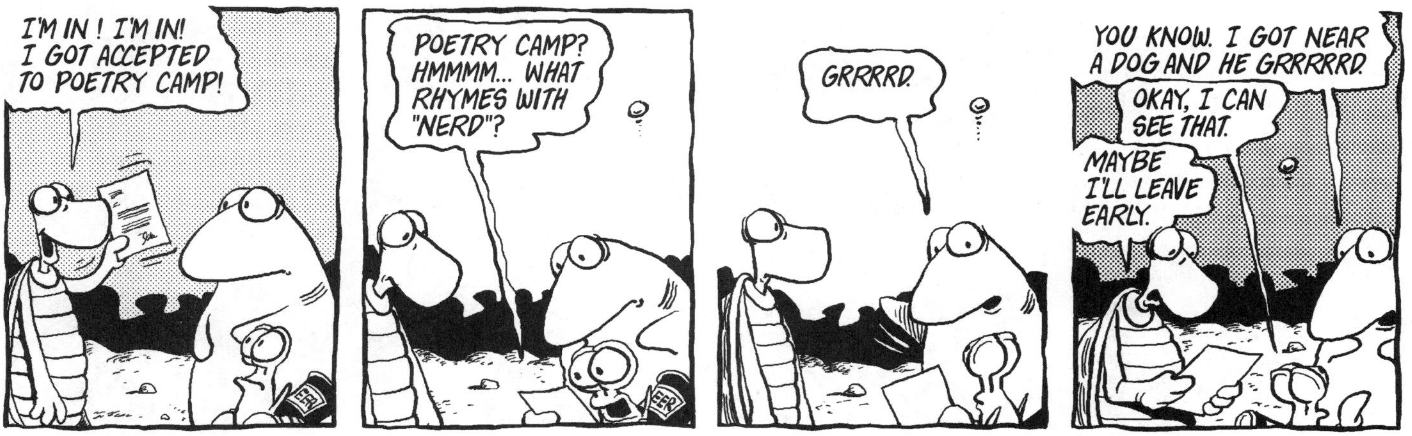
I'M IN ! I'M IN! I GOT ACCEPTED TO POETRY CAMP!
POETRY CAMP? HMMMM... WHAT RHYMES WITH "NERD"?
GRRRRD.
YOU KNOW. I GOT NEAR A DOG AND HE GRRRRRD.
OKAY, I CAN SEE THAT.
MAYBE I'LL LEAVE EARLY.

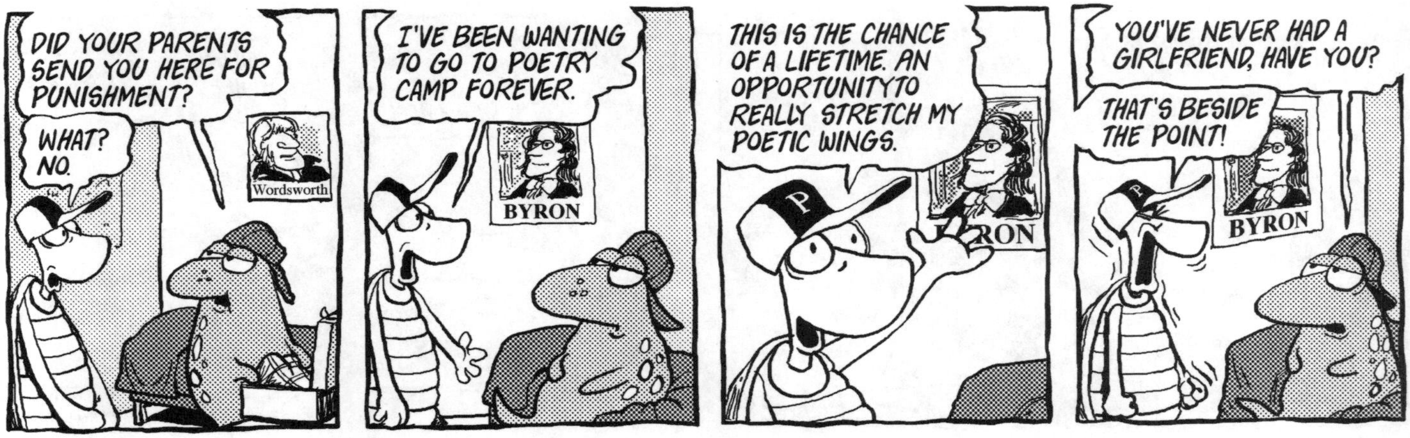
DID YOUR PARENTS SEND YOU HERE FOR PUNISHMENT?
WHAT? NO.
Wordsworth
I'VE BEEN WANTING TO GO TO POETRY CAMP FOREVER.
BYRON
THIS IS THE CHANCE OF A LIFETIME. AN OPPORTUNITY TO REALLY STRETCH MY POETIC WINGS.
YOU'VE NEVER HAD A GIRLFRIEND, HAVE YOU?
THAT'S BESIDE THE POINT!
BYRON

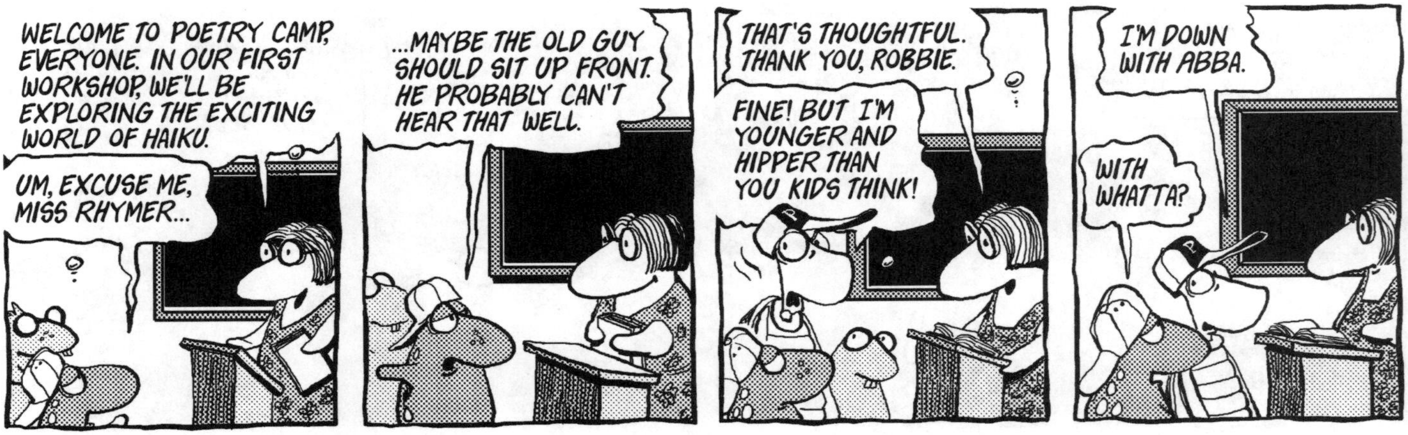
WELCOME TO POETRY CAMP, EVERYONE. IN OUR FIRST WORKSHOP, WE'LL BE EXPLORING THE EXCITING WORLD OF HAIKU.
UM, EXCUSE ME, MISS RHYMER...
...MAYBE THE OLD GUY SHOULD SIT UP FRONT. HE PROBABLY CAN'T HEAR THAT WELL.
THAT'S THOUGHTFUL. THANK YOU, ROBBIE.
FINE! BUT I'M YOUNGER AND HIPPER THAN YOU KIDS THINK!
I'M DOWN WITH ABBA.
WITH WHATTA?

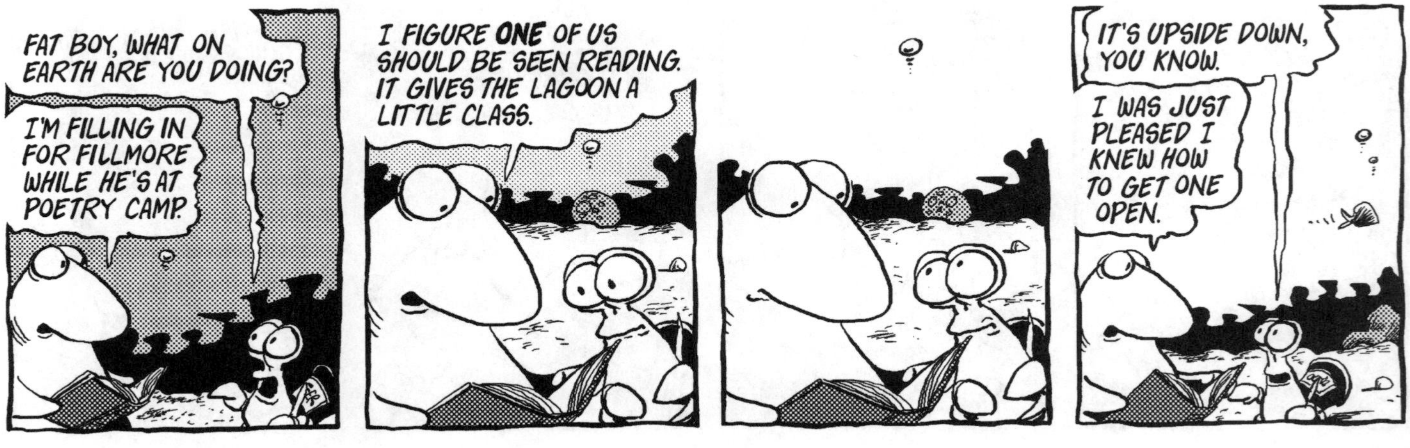
FAT BOY, WHAT ON EARTH ARE YOU DOING?
I'M FILLING IN FOR FILLMORE WHILE HE'S AT POETRY CAMP.
I FIGURE ONE OF US SHOULD BE SEEN READING. IT GIVES THE LAGOON A LITTLE CLASS.
IT'S UPSIDE DOWN, YOU KNOW.
I WAS JUST PLEASED I KNEW HOW TO GET ONE OPEN.

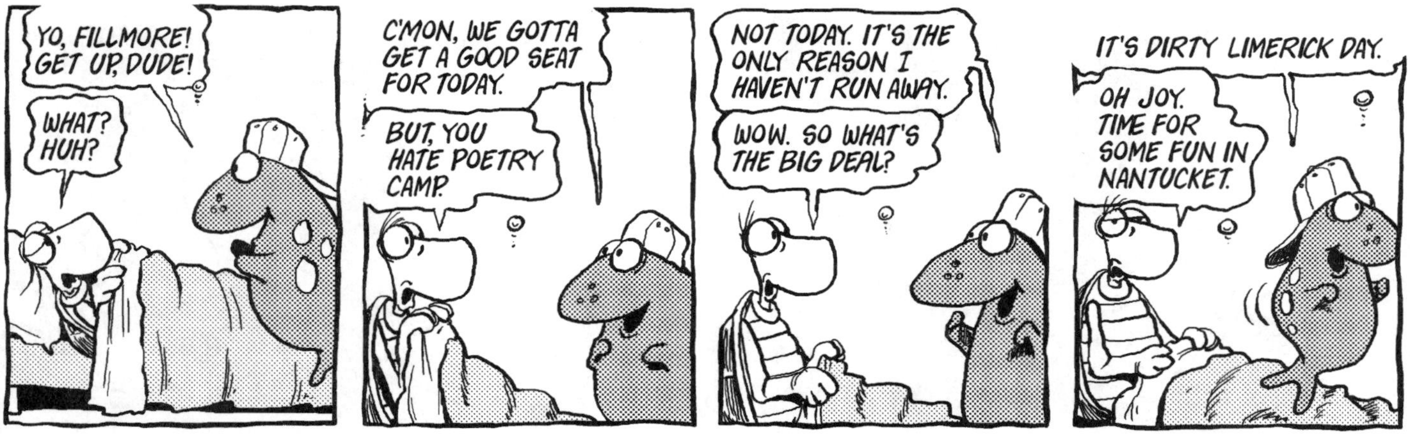
YO, FILLMORE! GET UP, DUDE!
WHAT? HUH?
C'MON, WE GOTTA GET A GOOD SEAT FOR TODAY.
BUT, YOU HATE POETRY CAMP.
NOT TODAY. IT'S THE ONLY REASON I HAVEN'T RUN AWAY.
WOW. SO WHAT'S THE BIG DEAL?
IT'S DIRTY LIMERICK DAY.
OH JOY. TIME FOR SOME FUN IN NANTUCKET.

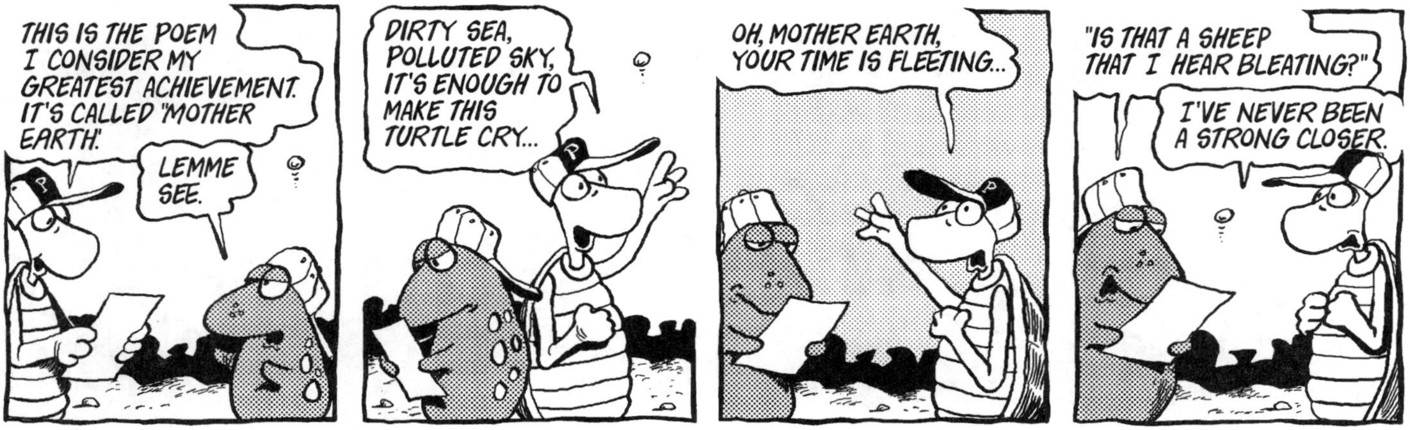
THIS IS THE POEM I CONSIDER MY GREATEST ACHIEVEMENT. IT'S CALLED "MOTHER EARTH."
LEMME SEE.
DIRTY SEA, POLLUTED SKY, IT'S ENOUGH TO MAKE THIS TURTLE CRY...
OH, MOTHER EARTH, YOUR TIME IS FLEETING...
"IS THAT A SHEEP THAT I HEAR BLEATING?"
I'VE NEVER BEEN A STRONG CLOSER.

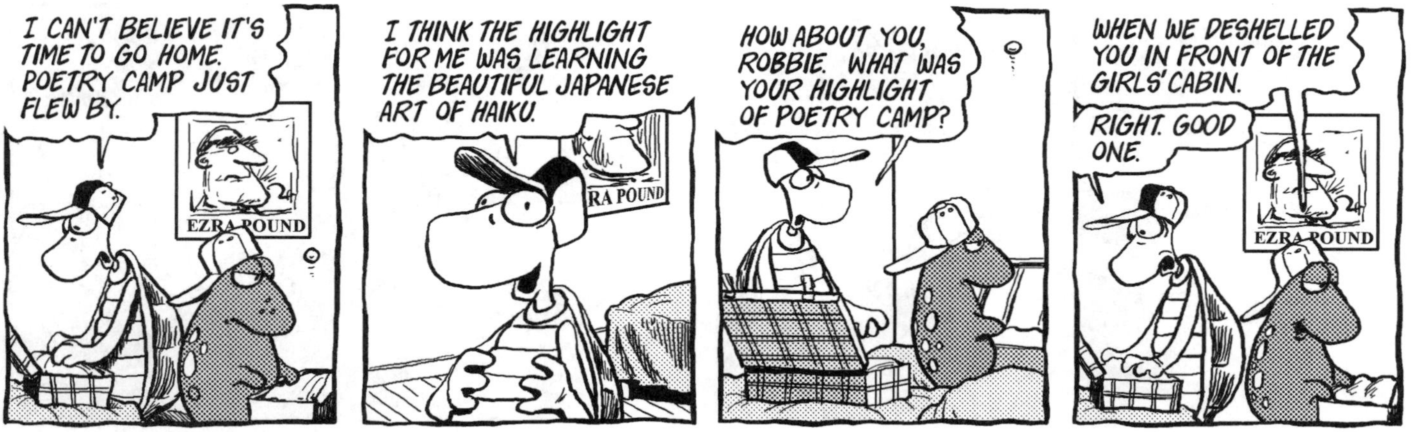
I CAN'T BELIEVE IT'S TIME TO GO HOME. POETRY CAMP JUST FLEW BY.
EZRA POUND
I THINK THE HIGHLIGHT FOR ME WAS LEARNING THE BEAUTIFUL JAPANESE ART OF HAIKU.
HOW ABOUT YOU, ROBBIE. WHAT WAS YOUR HIGHLIGHT OF POETRY CAMP?
WHEN WE DESHELLED YOU IN FRONT OF THE GIRLS' CABIN.
RIGHT. GOOD ONE.
EZRA POUND

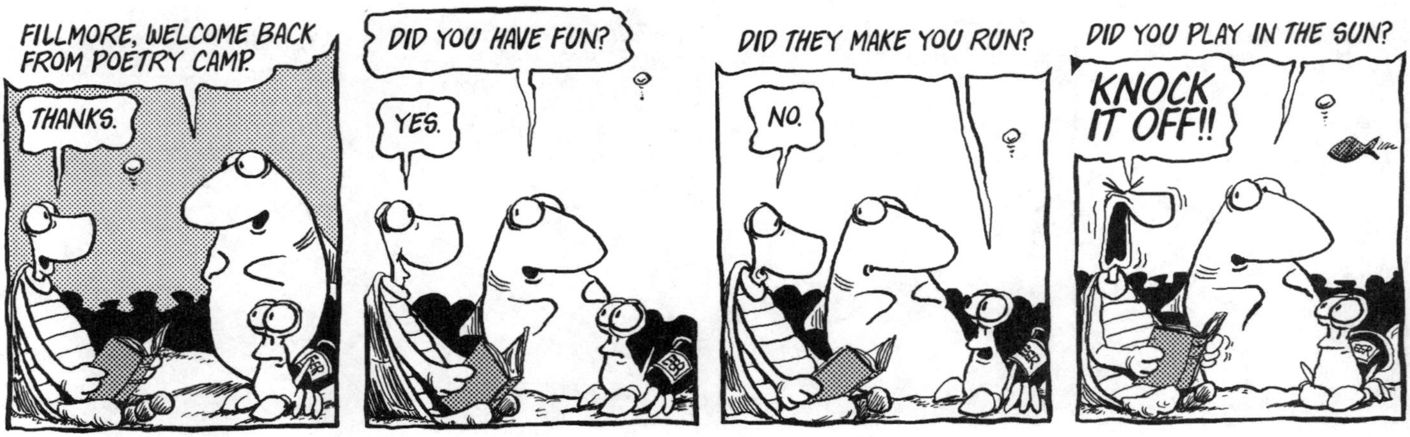
FILLMORE, WELCOME BACK FROM POETRY CAMP.
THANKS.
DID YOU HAVE FUN?
YES.
DID THEY MAKE YOU RUN?
NO.
DID YOU PLAY IN THE SUN?
KNOCK IT OFF!!

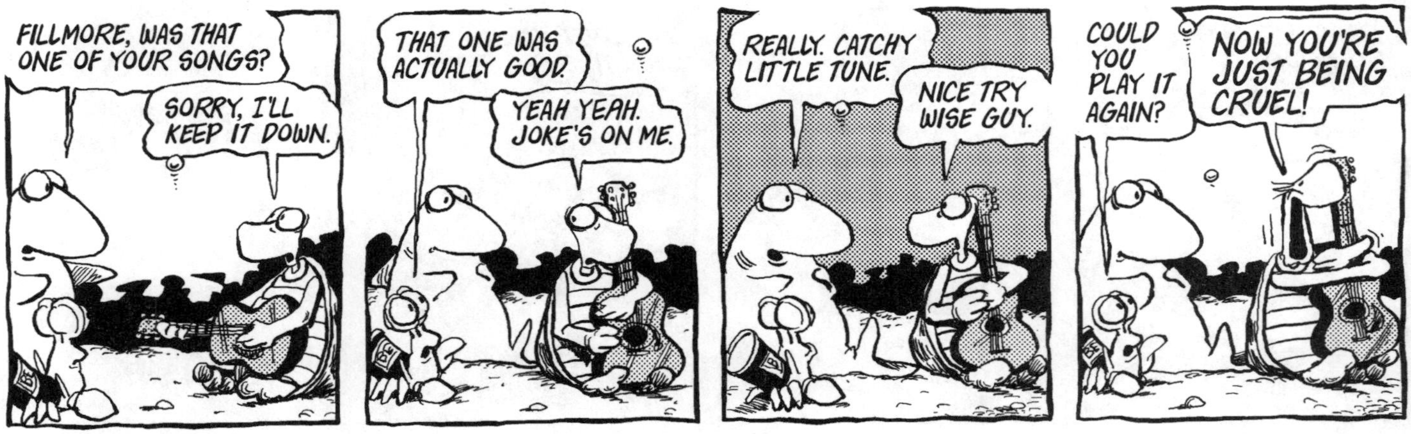
FILLMORE, WAS THAT ONE OF YOUR SONGS?
SORRY, I'LL KEEP IT DOWN.
THAT ONE WAS ACTUALLY GOOD.
YEAH YEAH. JOKE'S ON ME.
REALLY. CATCHY LITTLE TUNE.
NICE TRY WISE GUY.
COULD YOU PLAY IT AGAIN?
NOW YOU'RE JUST BEING CRUEL!

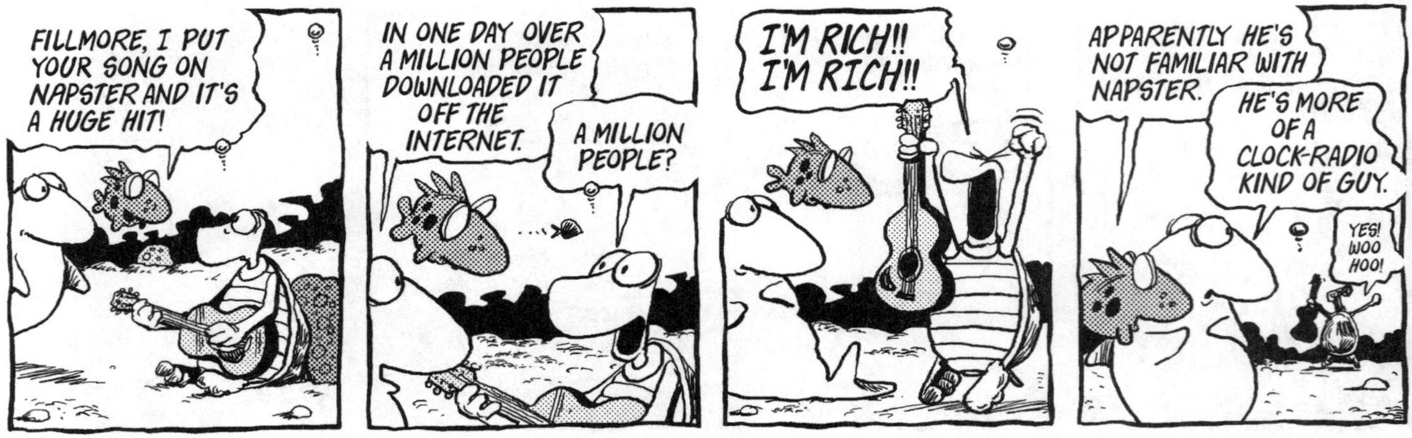
FILLMORE, I PUT YOUR SONG ON NAPSTER AND IT'S A HUGE HIT!
IN ONE DAY OVER A MILLION PEOPLE DOWNLOADED IT OFF THE INTERNET.
A MILLION PEOPLE?
I'M RICH!! I'M RICH!!
APPARENTLY HE'S NOT FAMILIAR WITH NAPSTER.
HE'S MORE OF A CLOCK-RADIO KIND OF GUY.
YES! WOO HOO!

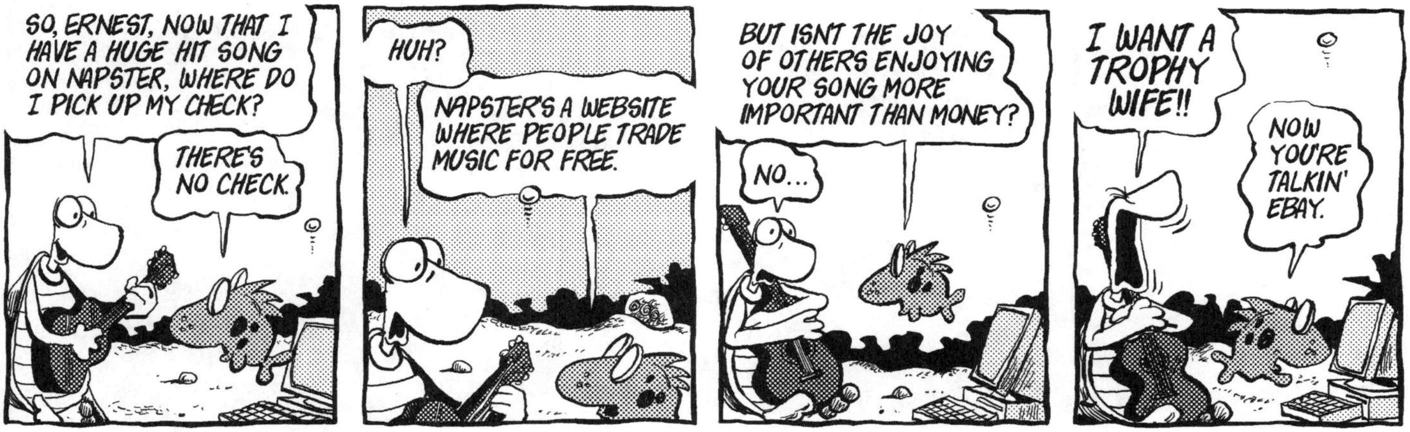
SO, ERNEST, NOW THAT I HAVE A HUGE HIT SONG ON NAPSTER, WHERE DO I PICK UP MY CHECK?
THERE'S NO CHECK.
HUH?
NAPSTER'S A WEBSITE WHERE PEOPLE TRADE MUSIC FOR FREE.
BUT ISNT THE JOY OF OTHERS ENJOYING YOUR SONG MORE IMPORTANT THAN MONEY?
NO...
I WANT A TROPHY WIFE!!
NOW YOU'RE TALKIN' EBAY.

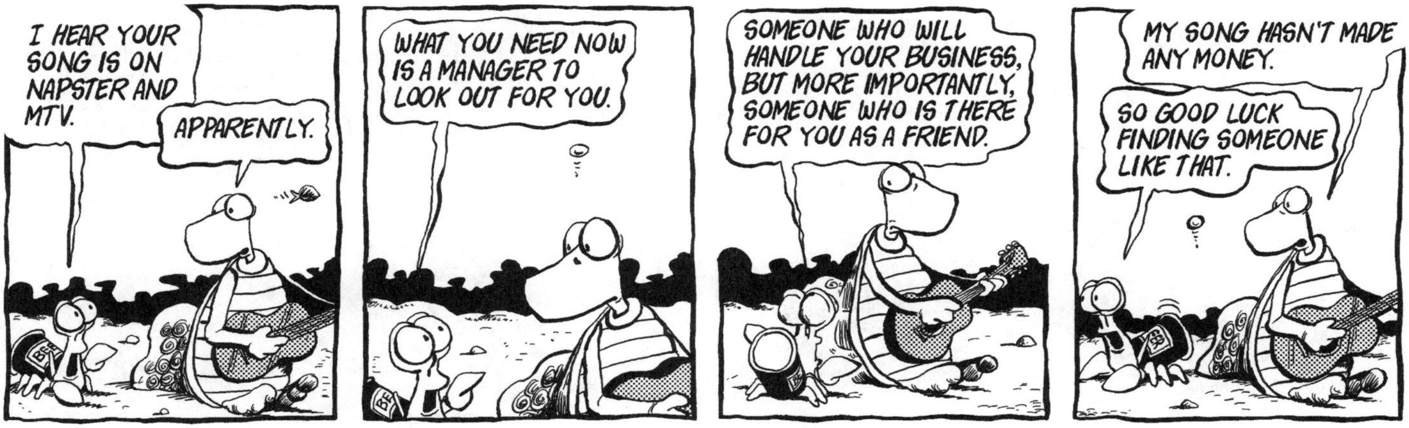
I HEAR YOUR SONG IS ON NAPSTER AND MTV.
APPARENTLY.
WHAT YOU NEED NOW IS A MANAGER TO LOOK OUT FOR YOU.
SOMEONE WHO WILL HANDLE YOUR BUSINESS, BUT MORE IMPORTANTLY, SOMEONE WHO IS THERE FOR YOU AS A FRIEND.
MY SONG HASN'T MADE ANY MONEY.
SO GOOD LUCK FINDING SOMEONE LIKE THAT.

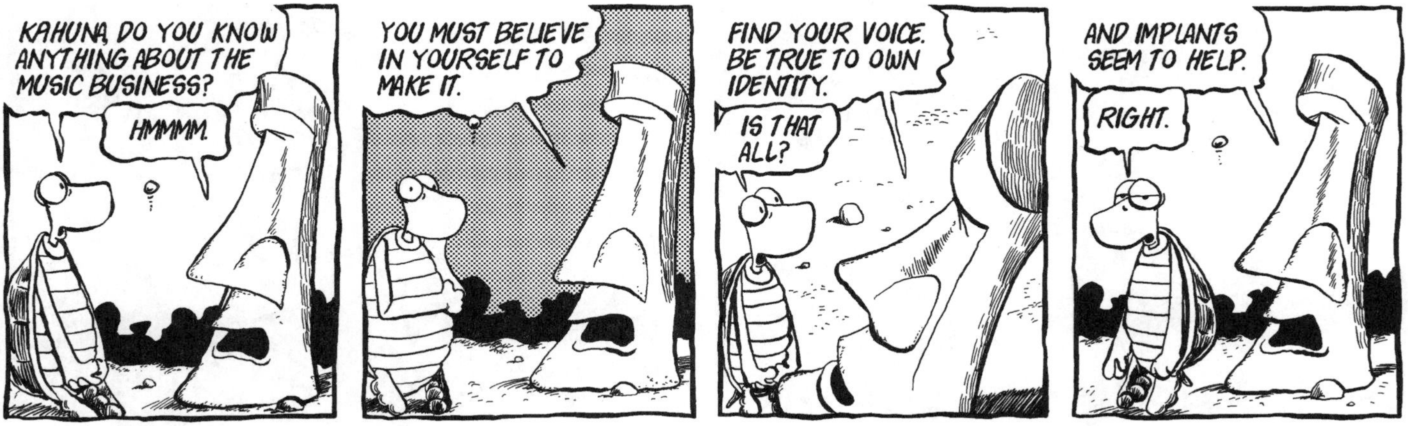
KAHUNA, DO YOU KNOW ANYTHING ABOUT THE MUSIC BUSINESS?
HMMMM.
YOU MUST BELIEVE IN YOURSELF TO MAKE IT.
FIND YOUR VOICE. BE TRUE TO OWN IDENTITY.
IS THAT ALL?
AND IMPLANTS SEEM TO HELP.
RIGHT.

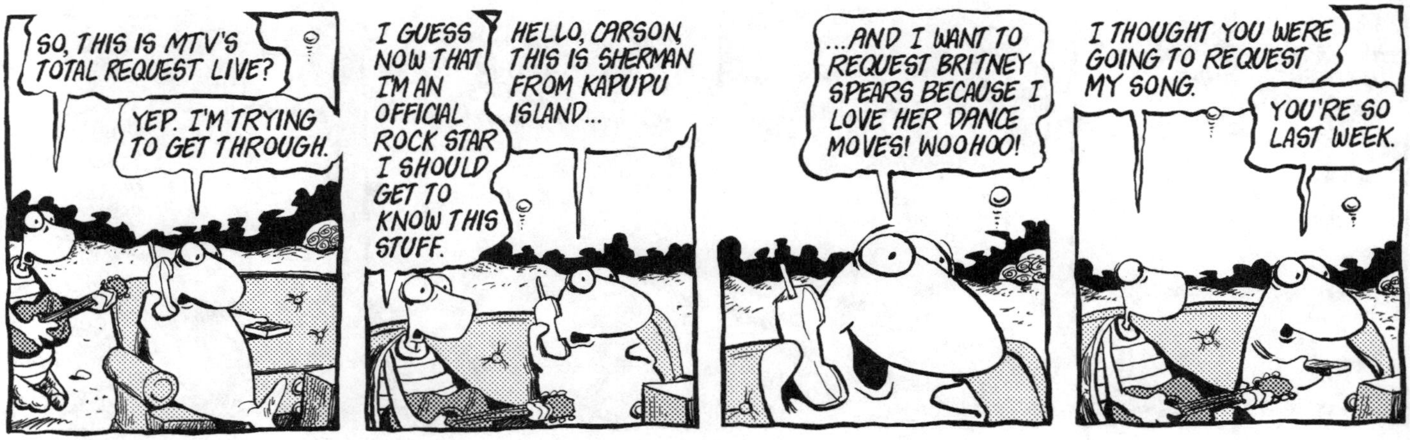
SO, THIS IS MTV'S TOTAL REQUEST LIVE?
YEP. I'M TRYING TO GET THROUGH.
I GUESS NOW THAT I'M AN OFFICIAL ROCK STAR I SHOULD GET TO KNOW THIS STUFF.
HELLO, CARSON, THIS IS SHERMAN FROM KAPUPU ISLAND...
...AND I WANT TO REQUEST BRITNEY SPEARS BECAUSE I LOVE HER DANCE MOVES! WOOHOO!
I THOUGHT YOU WERE GOING TO REQUEST MY SONG.
YOU'RE SO LAST WEEK.

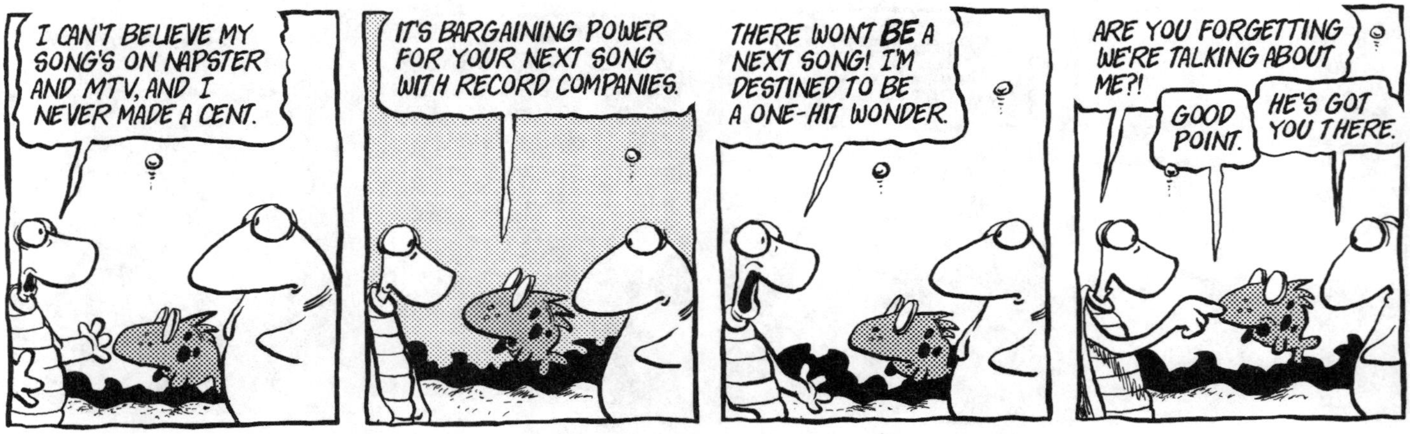
I CAN'T BELIEVE MY SONG'S ON NAPSTER AND MTV, AND I NEVER MADE A CENT.
IT'S BARGAINING POWER FOR YOUR NEXT SONG WITH RECORD COMPANIES.
THERE WON'T BE A NEXT SONG! I'M DESTINED TO BE A ONE-HIT WONDER.
ARE YOU FORGETTING WE'RE TALKING ABOUT ME?!
GOOD POINT.
HE'S GOT YOU THERE.

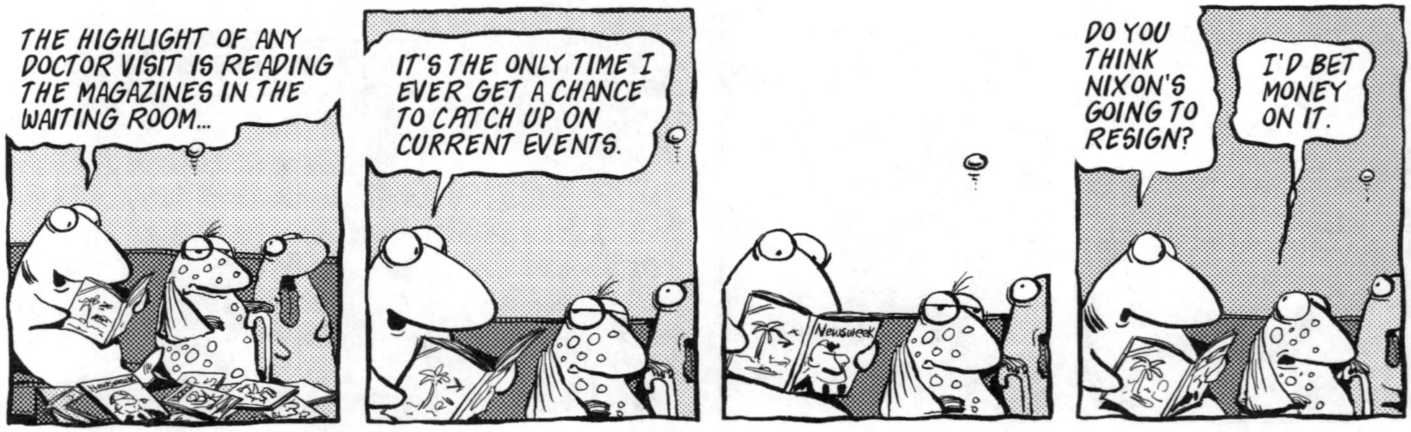
THE HIGHLIGHT OF ANY DOCTOR VISIT IS READING THE MAGAZINES IN THE WAITING ROOM...
IT'S THE ONLY TIME I EVER GET A CHANCE TO CATCH UP ON CURRENT EVENTS.
Newsweek
DO YOU THINK NIXON'S GOING TO RESIGN?
I'D BET MONEY ON IT.

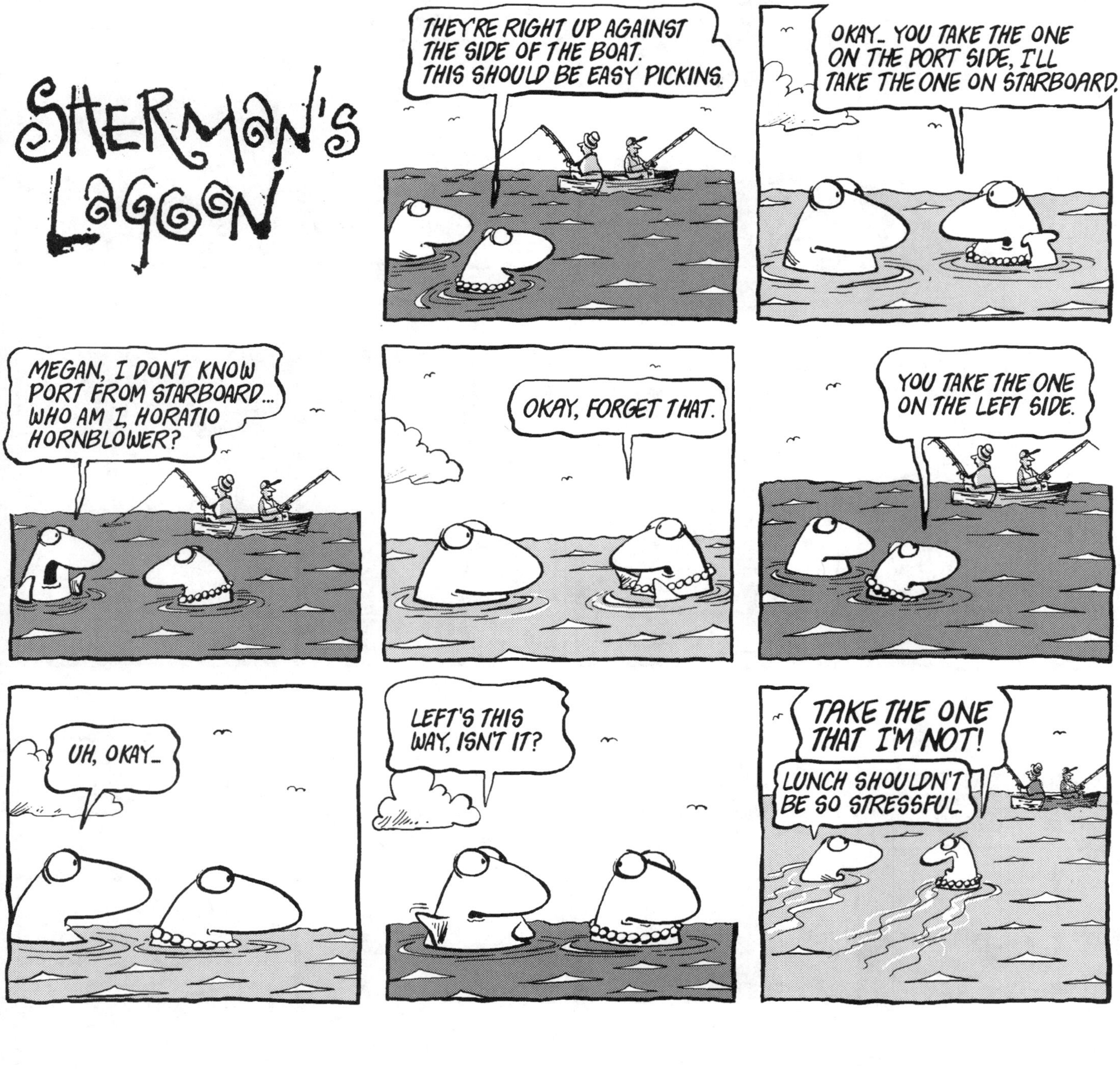
SHERMAN'S LAGOON
THEY'RE RIGHT UP AGAINST THE SIDE OF THE BOAT. THIS SHOULD BE EASY PICKINS.
OKAY... YOU TAKE THE ONE ON THE PORT SIDE, I'LL TAKE THE ONE ON STARBOARD.
MEGAN, I DON'T KNOW PORT FROM STARBOARD... WHO AM I, HORATIO HORNBLOWER?
OKAY, FORGET THAT.
YOU TAKE THE ONE ON THE LEFT SIDE.
UH, OKAY...
LEFT'S THIS WAY, ISN'T IT?
TAKE THE ONE THAT I'M NOT!
LUNCH SHOULDN'T BE SO STRESSFUL.

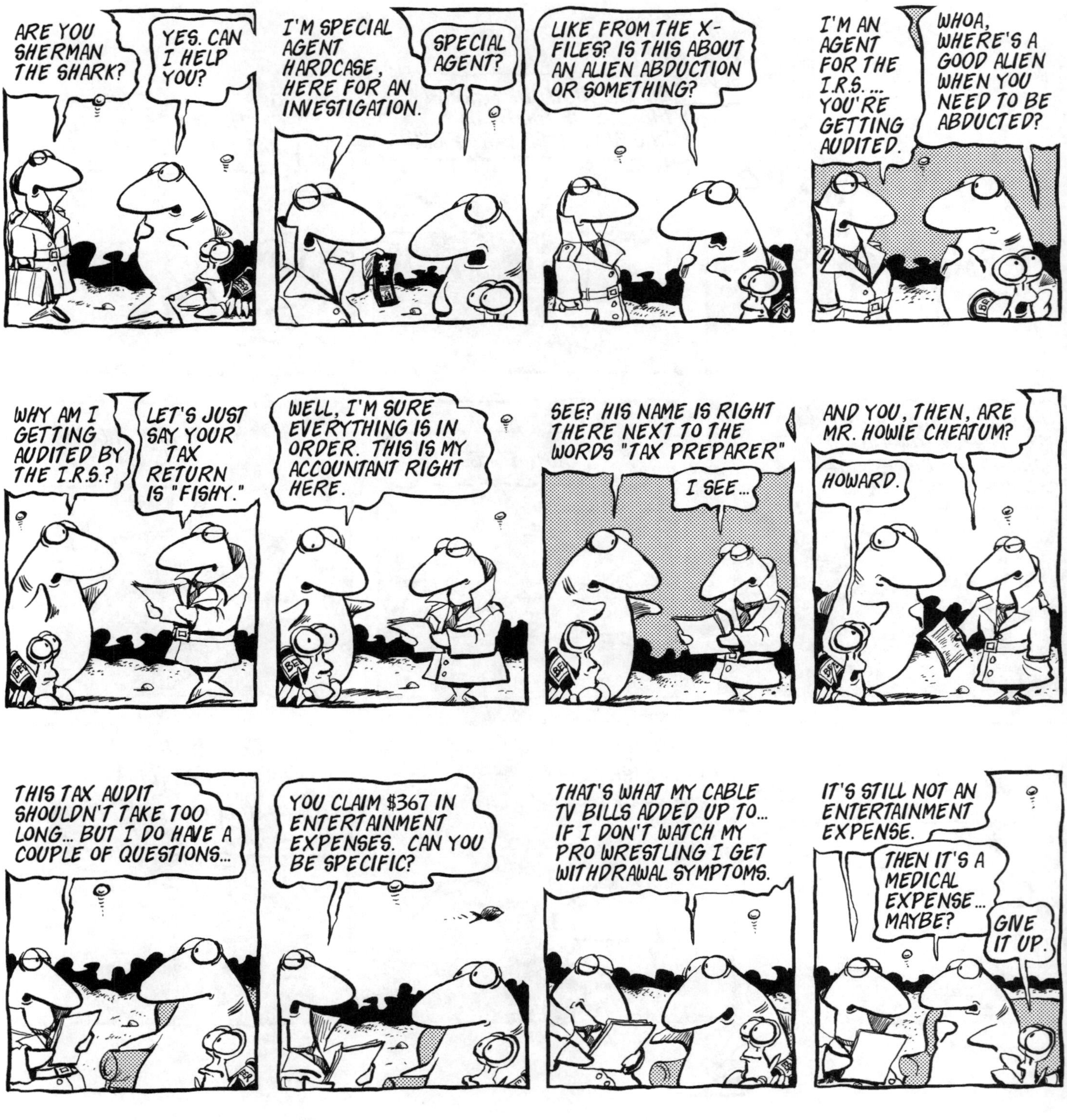
ARE YOU SHERMAN THE SHARK?
YES. CAN I HELP YOU?
I'M SPECIAL AGENT HARDCASE, HERE FOR AN INVESTIGATION.
SPECIAL AGENT?
LIKE FROM THE X-FILES? IS THIS ABOUT AN ALIEN ABDUCTION OR SOMETHING?
I'M AN AGENT FOR THE I.R.S. ... YOU'RE GETTING AUDITED.
WHOA, WHERE'S A GOOD ALIEN WHEN YOU NEED TO BE ABDUCTED?
WHY AM I GETTING AUDITED BY THE I.R.S.?
LET'S JUST SAY YOUR TAX RETURN IS "FISHY."
WELL, I'M SURE EVERYTHING IS IN ORDER. THIS IS MY ACCOUNTANT RIGHT HERE.
SEE? HIS NAME IS RIGHT THERE NEXT TO THE WORDS "TAX PREPARER"
I SEE...
AND YOU, THEN, ARE MR. HOWIE CHEATUM?
HOWARD.
THIS TAX AUDIT SHOULDN'T TAKE TOO LONG... BUT I DO HAVE A COUPLE OF QUESTIONS...
YOU CLAIM $367 IN ENTERTAINMENT EXPENSES. CAN YOU BE SPECIFIC?
THAT'S WHAT MY CABLE TV BILLS ADDED UP TO... IF I DON'T WATCH MY PRO WRESTLING I GET WITHDRAWAL SYMPTOMS.
IT'S STILL NOT AN ENTERTAINMENT EXPENSE.
THEN IT'S A MEDICAL EXPENSE... MAYBE?
GIVE IT UP.

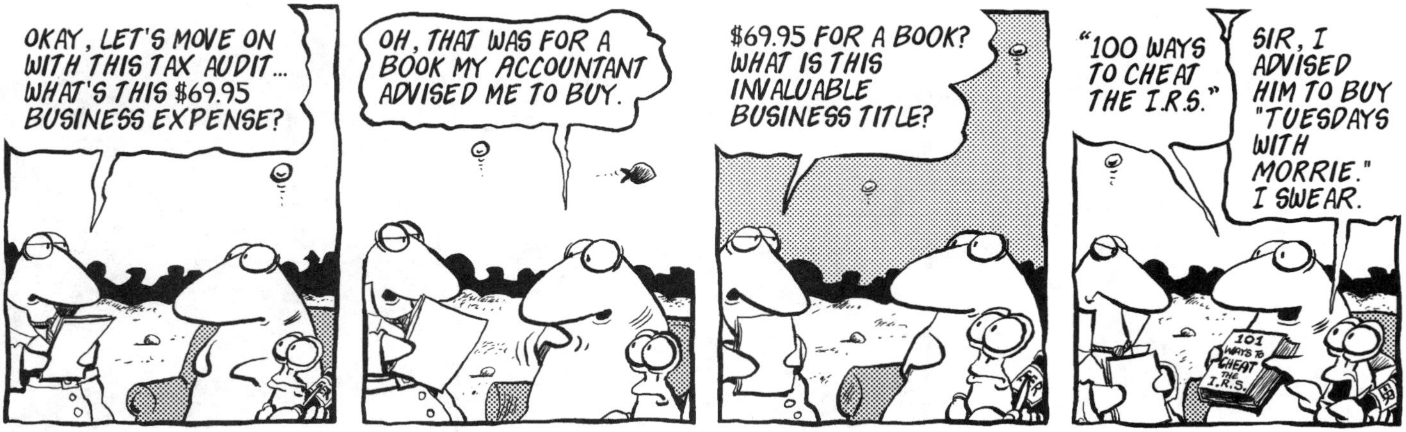
OKAY, LET'S MOVE ON WITH THIS TAX AUDIT... WHAT'S THIS $69.95 BUSINESS EXPENSE?
OH, THAT WAS FOR A BOOK MY ACCOUNTANT ADVISED ME TO BUY.
$69.95 FOR A BOOK? WHAT IS THIS INVALUABLE BUSINESS TITLE?
"100 WAYS TO CHEAT THE I.R.S."
SIR, I ADVISED HIM TO BUY "TUESDAYS WITH MORRIE." I SWEAR.
101 WAYS TO CHEAT THE I.R.S.

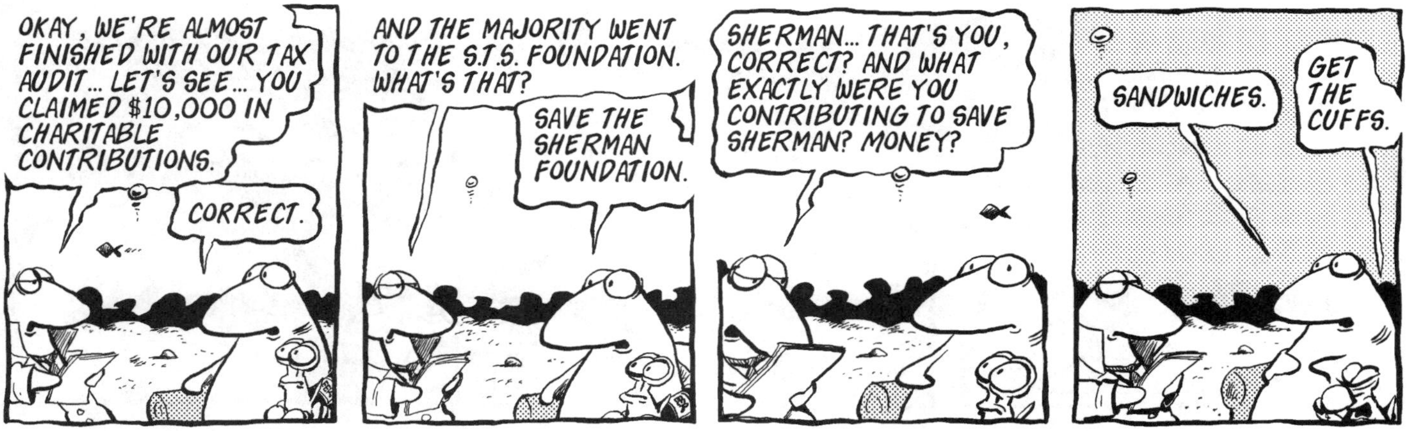
OKAY, WE'RE ALMOST FINISHED WITH OUR TAX AUDIT... LET'S SEE... YOU CLAIMED $10,000 IN CHARITABLE CONTRIBUTIONS.
CORRECT.
AND THE MAJORITY WENT TO THE S.T.S. FOUNDATION. WHAT'S THAT?
SAVE THE SHERMAN FOUNDATION.
SHERMAN... THAT'S YOU, CORRECT? AND WHAT EXACTLY WERE YOU CONTRIBUTING TO SAVE SHERMAN? MONEY?
SANDWICHES.
GET THE CUFFS.

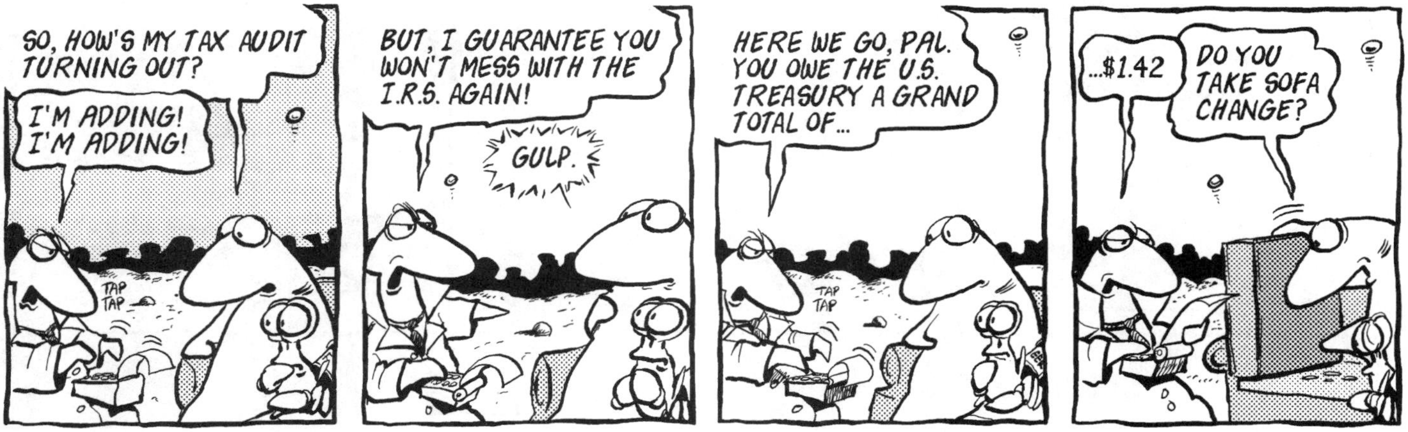
SO, HOW'S MY TAX AUDIT TURNING OUT?
I'M ADDING! I'M ADDING!
TAP TAP
BUT, I GUARANTEE YOU WON'T MESS WITH THE I.R.S. AGAIN!
GULP.
HERE WE GO, PAL. YOU OWE THE U.S. TREASURY A GRAND TOTAL OF...
TAP TAP
...$1.42
DO YOU TAKE SOFA CHANGE?

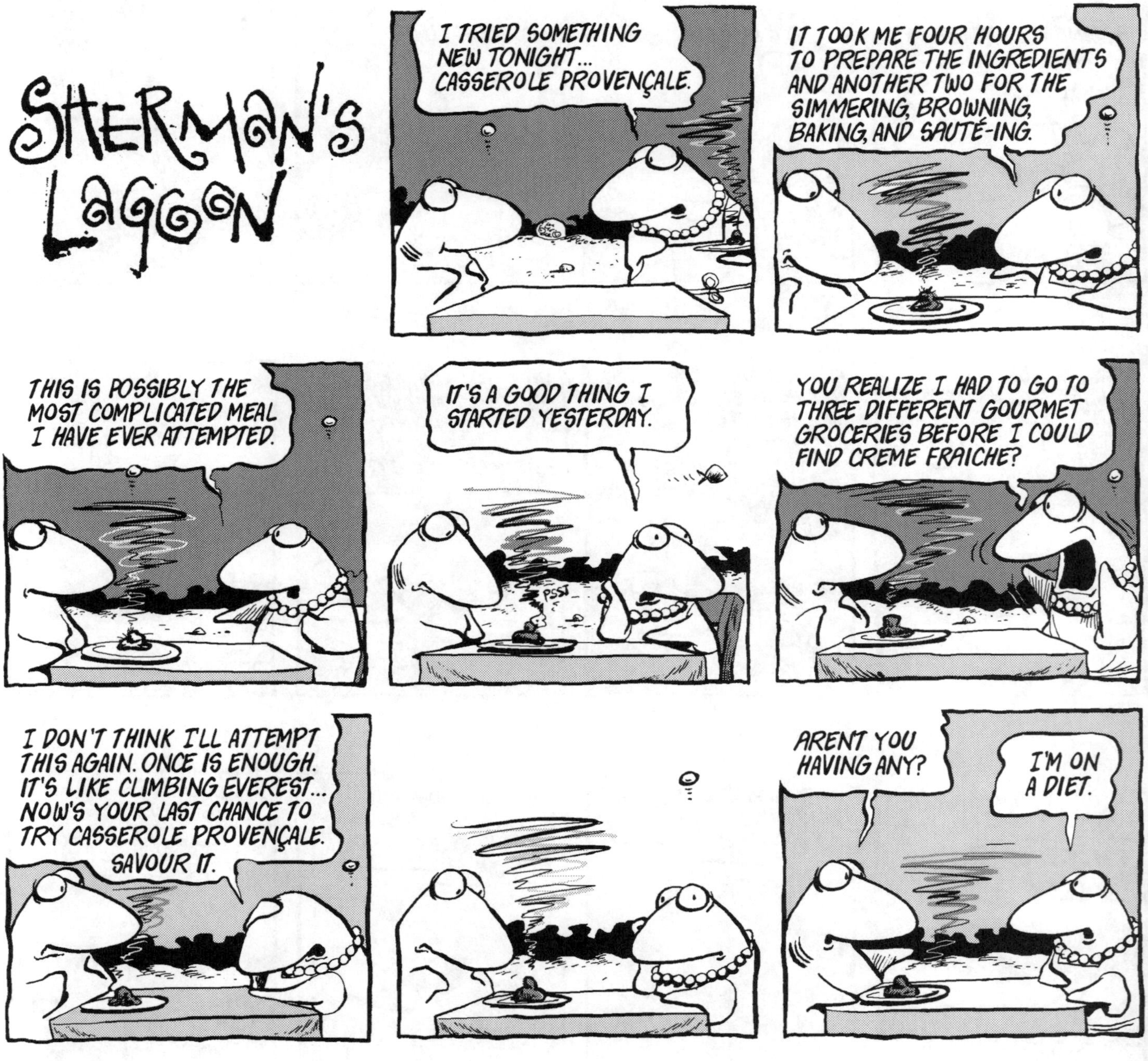
SHERMAN'S LAGOON
I TRIED SOMETHING NEW TONIGHT... CASSEROLE PROVENÇALE.
IT TOOK ME FOUR HOURS TO PREPARE THE INGREDIENTS AND ANOTHER TWO FOR THE SIMMERING, BROWNING, BAKING, AND SAUTÉ-ING.
THIS IS POSSIBLY THE MOST COMPLICATED MEAL I HAVE EVER ATTEMPTED.
IT'S A GOOD THING I STARTED YESTERDAY.
PSST
YOU REALIZE I HAD TO GO TO THREE DIFFERENT GOURMET GROCERIES BEFORE I COULD FIND CREME FRAICHE?
I DON'T THINK I'LL ATTEMPT THIS AGAIN. ONCE IS ENOUGH. IT'S LIKE CLIMBING EVEREST... NOW'S YOUR LAST CHANCE TO TRY CASSEROLE PROVENÇALE. SAVOUR IT.
ARENT YOU HAVING ANY?
I'M ON A DIET.

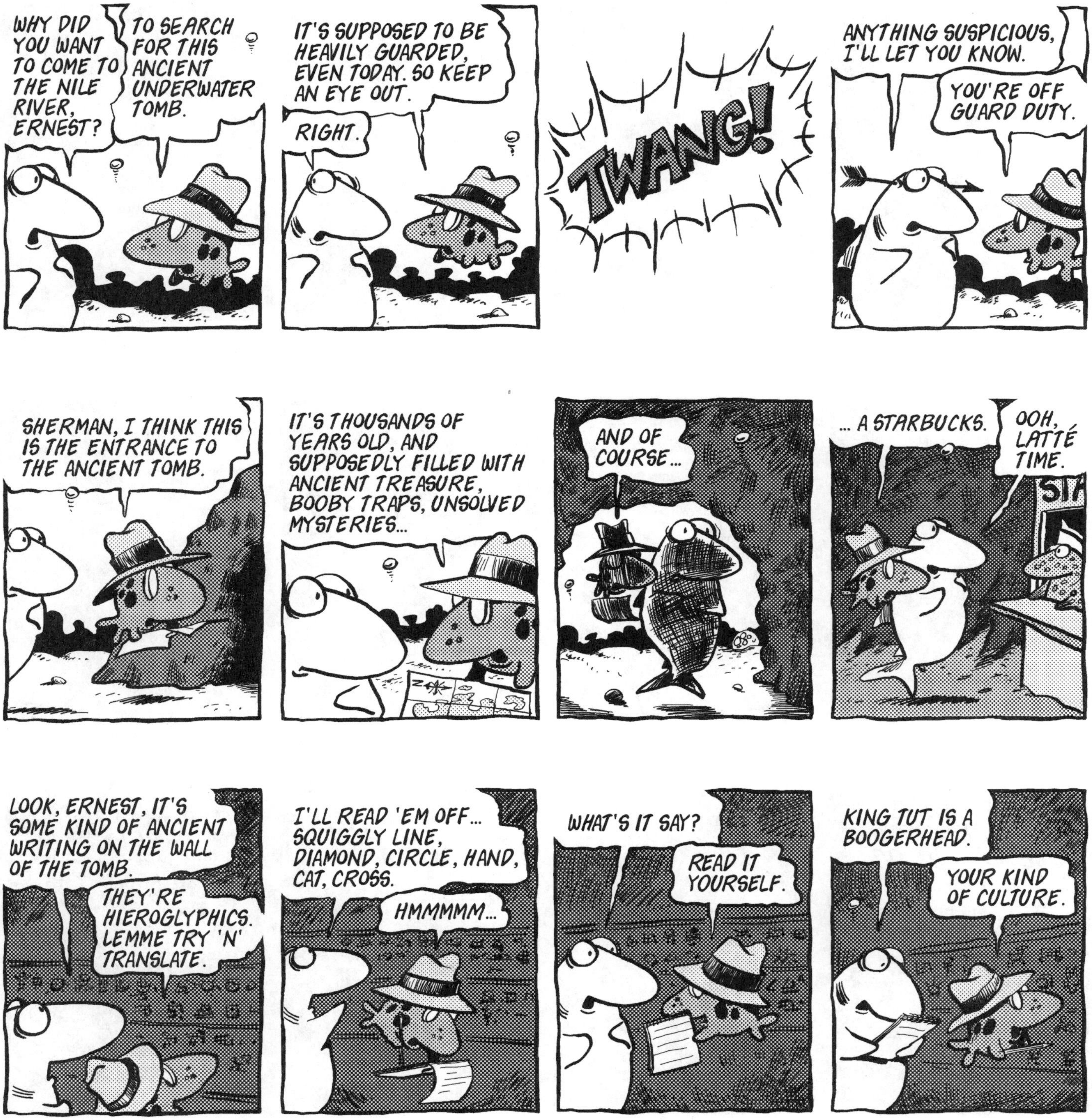

WHY DID YOU WANT TO COME TO THE NILE RIVER, ERNEST?
TO SEARCH FOR THIS ANCIENT UNDERWATER TOMB.
IT'S SUPPOSED TO BE HEAVILY GUARDED, EVEN TODAY. SO KEEP AN EYE OUT.
RIGHT.
TWANG!
ANYTHING SUSPICIOUS, I'LL LET YOU KNOW.
YOU'RE OFF GUARD DUTY.
SHERMAN, I THINK THIS IS THE ENTRANCE TO THE ANCIENT TOMB.
IT'S THOUSANDS OF YEARS OLD, AND SUPPOSEDLY FILLED WITH ANCIENT TREASURE, BOOBY TRAPS, UNSOLVED MYSTERIES...
AND OF COURSE...
... A STARBUCKS.
OOH, LATTÉ TIME.
LOOK, ERNEST, IT'S SOME KIND OF ANCIENT WRITING ON THE WALL OF THE TOMB.
THEY'RE HIEROGLYPHICS. LEMME TRY 'N' TRANSLATE.
I'LL READ 'EM OFF... SQUIGGLY LINE, DIAMOND, CIRCLE, HAND, CAT, CROSS.
HMMMMM...
WHAT'S IT SAY?
READ IT YOURSELF.
KING TUT IS A BOOGERHEAD.
YOUR KIND OF CULTURE.

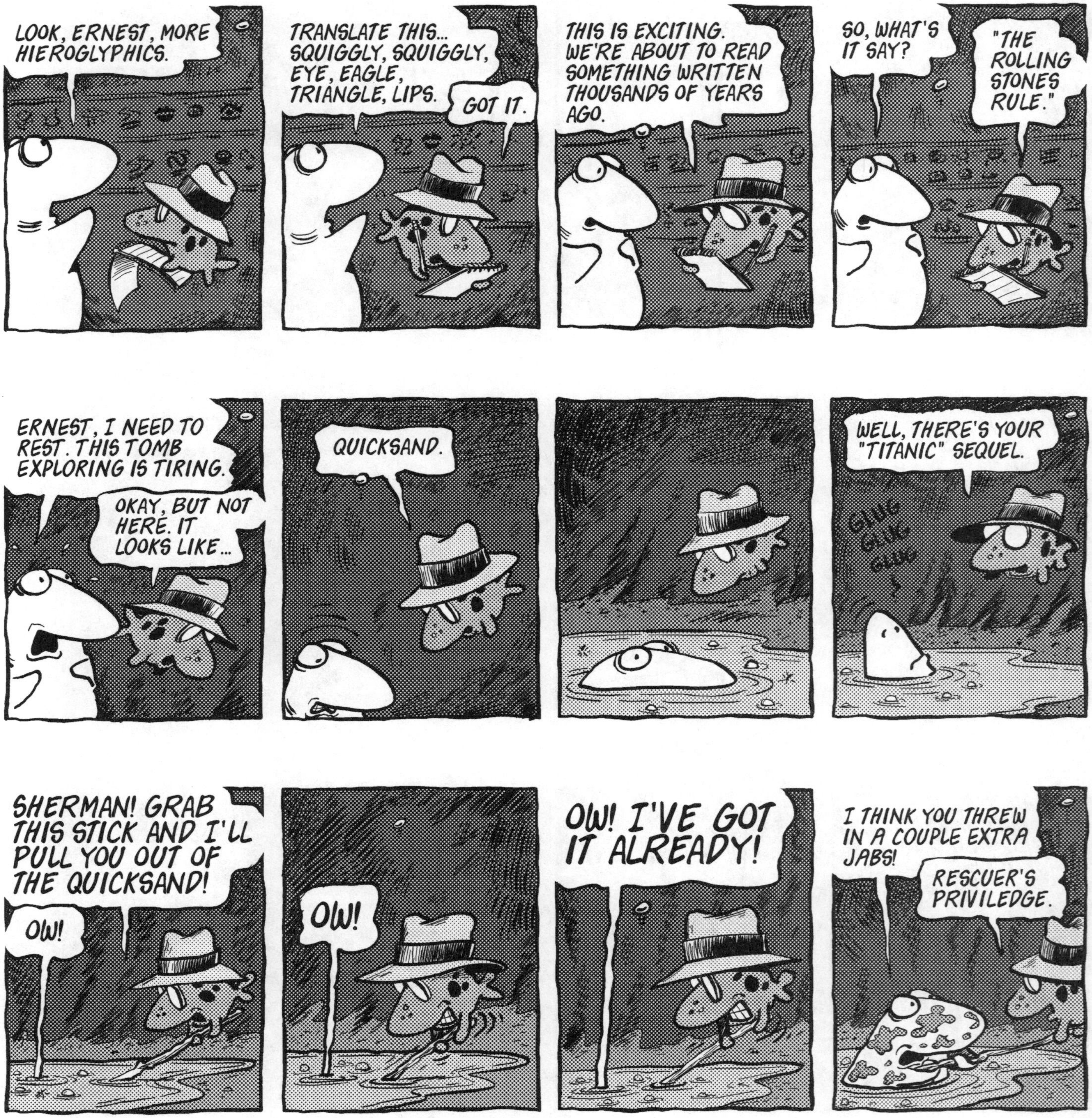
LOOK, ERNEST, MORE HIEROGLYPHICS.
TRANSLATE THIS... SQUIGGLY, SQUIGGLY, EYE, EAGLE, TRIANGLE, LIPS.
GOT IT.
THIS IS EXCITING. WE'RE ABOUT TO READ SOMETHING WRITTEN THOUSANDS OF YEARS AGO.
SO, WHAT'S IT SAY?
"THE ROLLING STONES RULE."
ERNEST, I NEED TO REST. THIS TOMB EXPLORING IS TIRING.
OKAY, BUT NOT HERE. IT LOOKS LIKE...
QUICKSAND.
WELL, THERE'S YOUR "TITANIC" SEQUEL.
GLUG GLUG GLUG
SHERMAN! GRAB THIS STICK AND I'LL PULL YOU OUT OF THE QUICKSAND!
OW!
OW!
OW! I'VE GOT IT ALREADY!
I THINK YOU THREW IN A COUPLE EXTRA JABS!
RESCUER'S PRIVILEDGE.

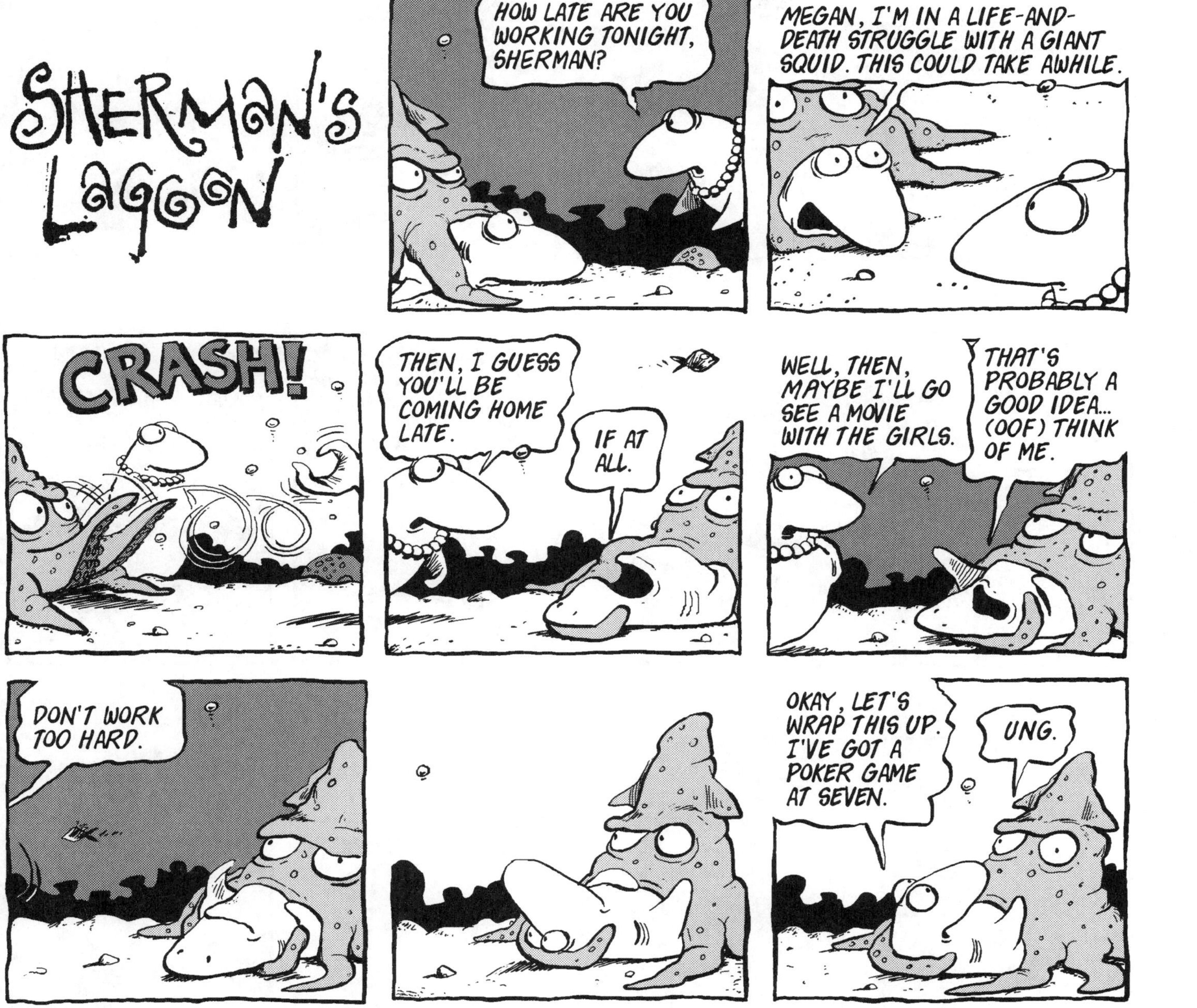
SHERMAN'S LAGOON
HOW LATE ARE YOU WORKING TONIGHT, SHERMAN?
MEGAN, I'M IN A LIFE-AND-DEATH STRUGGLE WITH A GIANT SQUID. THIS COULD TAKE AWHILE.
CRASH!
THEN, I GUESS YOU'LL BE COMING HOME LATE.
IF AT ALL.
WELL, THEN, MAYBE I'LL GO SEE A MOVIE WITH THE GIRLS.
THAT'S PROBABLY A GOOD IDEA... (OOF) THINK OF ME.
DON'T WORK TOO HARD.
OKAY, LET'S WRAP THIS UP. I'VE GOT A POKER GAME AT SEVEN.
UNG.

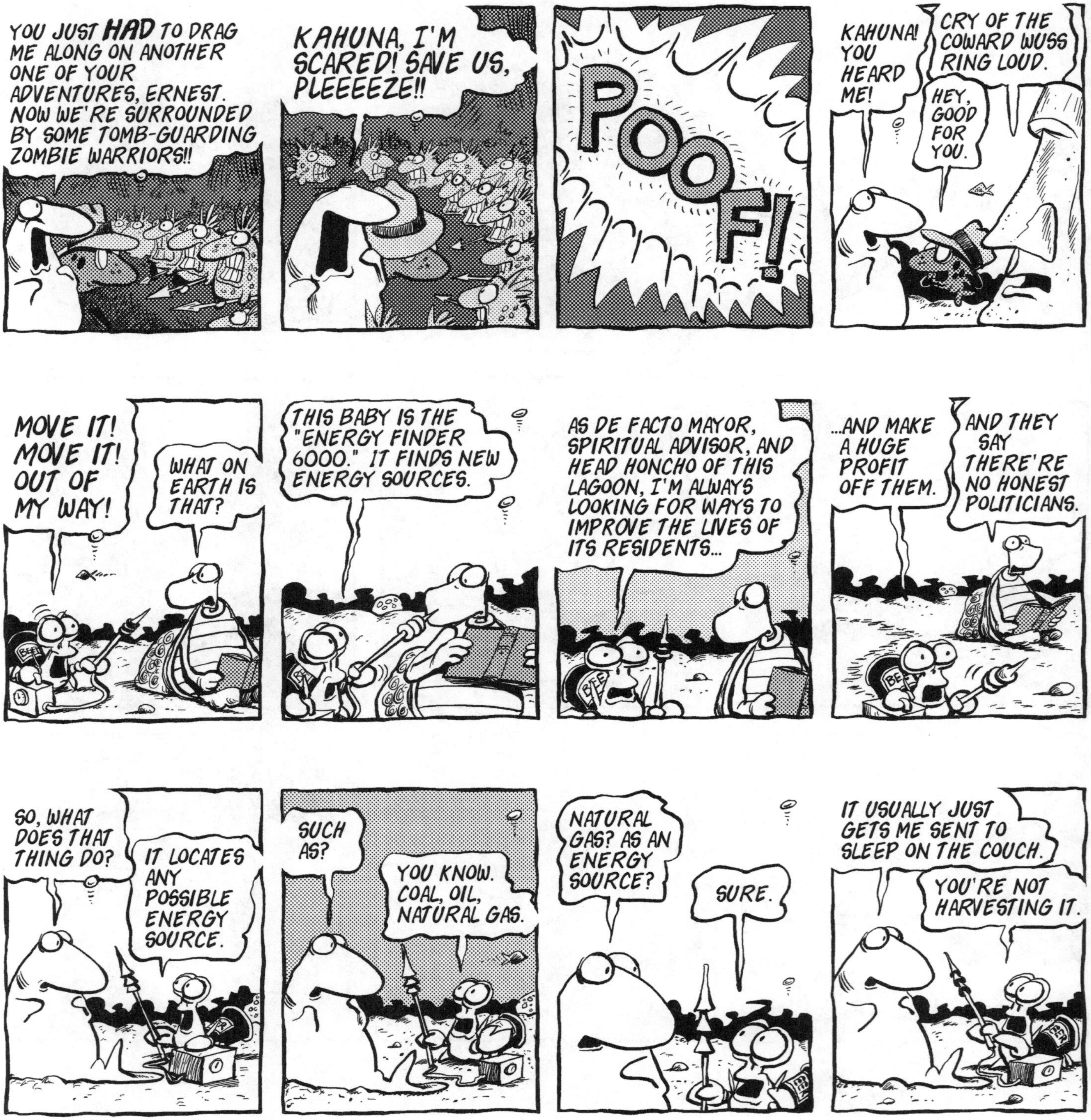
YOU JUST HAD TO DRAG ME ALONG ON ANOTHER ONE OF YOUR ADVENTURES, ERNEST. NOW WE'RE SURROUNDED BY SOME TOMB-GUARDING ZOMBIE WARRIORS!!
KAHUNA, I'M SCARED! SAVE US, PLEEEEZE!!
POOF!
KAHUNA! YOU HEARD ME!
CRY OF THE COWARD WUSS RING LOUD.
HEY, GOOD FOR YOU.
MOVE IT! MOVE IT! OUT OF MY WAY!
WHAT ON EARTH IS THAT?
THIS BABY IS THE "ENERGY FINDER 6000." IT FINDS NEW ENERGY SOURCES.
AS DE FACTO MAYOR, SPIRITUAL ADVISOR, AND HEAD HONCHO OF THIS LAGOON, I'M ALWAYS LOOKING FOR WAYS TO IMPROVE THE LIVES OF ITS RESIDENTS...
...AND MAKE A HUGE PROFIT OFF THEM.
AND THEY SAY THERE'RE NO HONEST POLITICIANS.
SO, WHAT DOES THAT THING DO?
IT LOCATES ANY POSSIBLE ENERGY SOURCE.
SUCH AS?
YOU KNOW. COAL, OIL, NATURAL GAS.
NATURAL GAS? AS AN ENERGY SOURCE?
SURE.
IT USUALLY JUST GETS ME SENT TO SLEEP ON THE COUCH.
YOU'RE NOT HARVESTING IT.

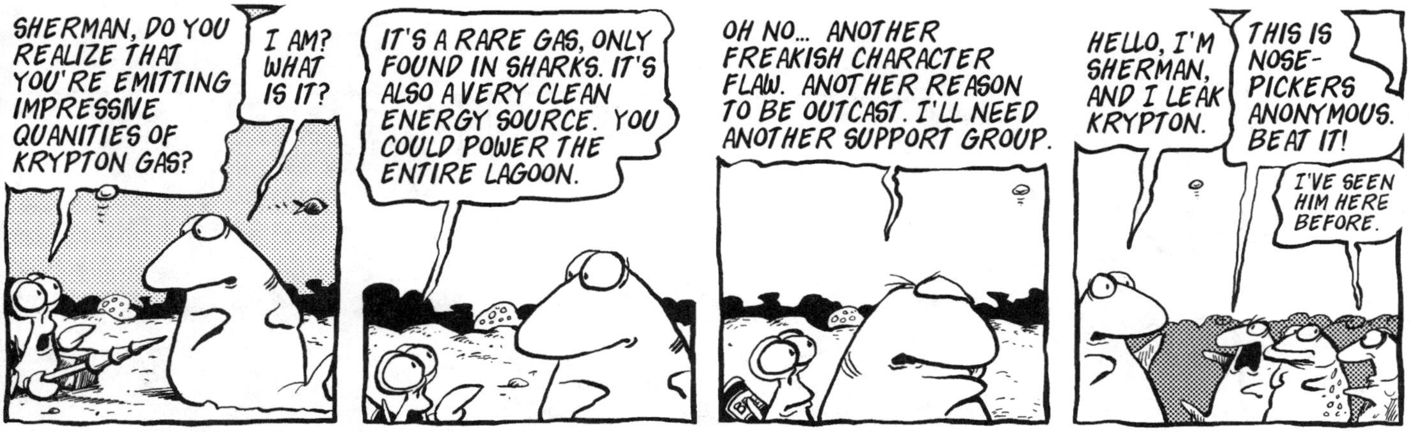
SHERMAN, DO YOU REALIZE THAT YOU'RE EMITTING IMPRESSIVE QUANITIES OF KRYPTON GAS?
I AM? WHAT IS IT?
IT'S A RARE GAS, ONLY FOUND IN SHARKS. IT'S ALSO A VERY CLEAN ENERGY SOURCE. YOU COULD POWER THE ENTIRE LAGOON.
OH NO... ANOTHER FREAKISH CHARACTER FLAW. ANOTHER REASON TO BE OUTCAST. I'LL NEED ANOTHER SUPPORT GROUP.
HELLO, I'M SHERMAN, AND I LEAK KRYPTON.
THIS IS NOSE-PICKERS ANONYMOUS. BEAT IT!
I'VE SEEN HIM HERE BEFORE.

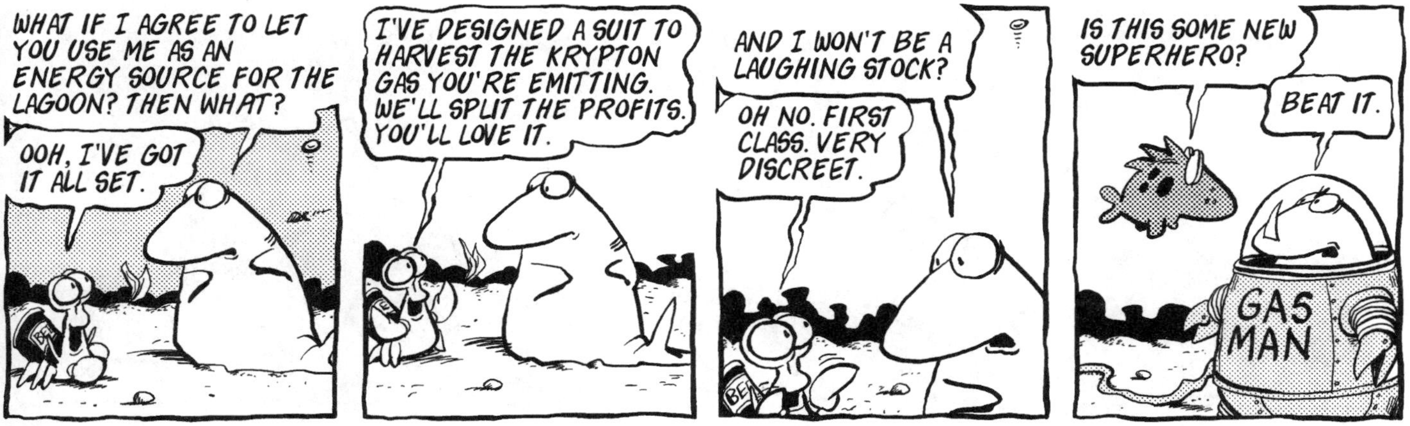
WHAT IF I AGREE TO LET YOU USE ME AS AN ENERGY SOURCE FOR THE LAGOON? THEN WHAT?
OOH, I'VE GOT IT ALL SET.
I'VE DESIGNED A SUIT TO HARVEST THE KRYPTON GAS YOU'RE EMITTING. WE'LL SPLIT THE PROFITS. YOU'LL LOVE IT.
AND I WON'T BE A LAUGHING STOCK?
OH NO. FIRST CLASS. VERY DISCREET.
IS THIS SOME NEW SUPERHERO?
BEAT IT.
GAS MAN

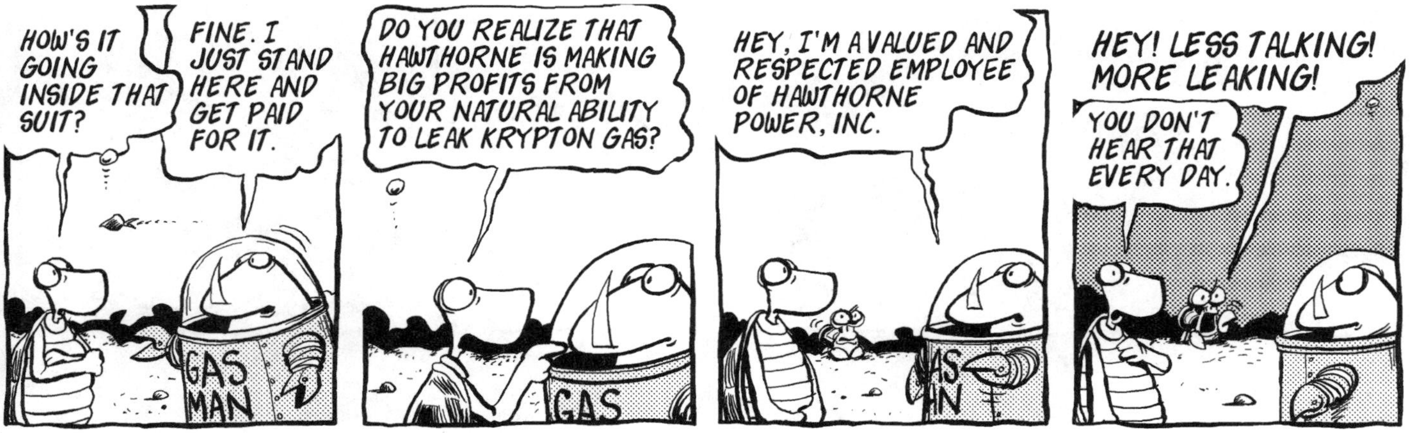
HOW'S IT GOING INSIDE THAT SUIT?
FINE. I JUST STAND HERE AND GET PAID FOR IT.
GAS MAN
DO YOU REALIZE THAT HAWTHORNE IS MAKING BIG PROFITS FROM YOUR NATURAL ABILITY TO LEAK KRYPTON GAS?
HEY, I'M A VALUED AND RESPECTED EMPLOYEE OF HAWTHORNE POWER, INC.
HEY! LESS TALKING! MORE LEAKING!
YOU DON'T HEAR THAT EVERY DAY.

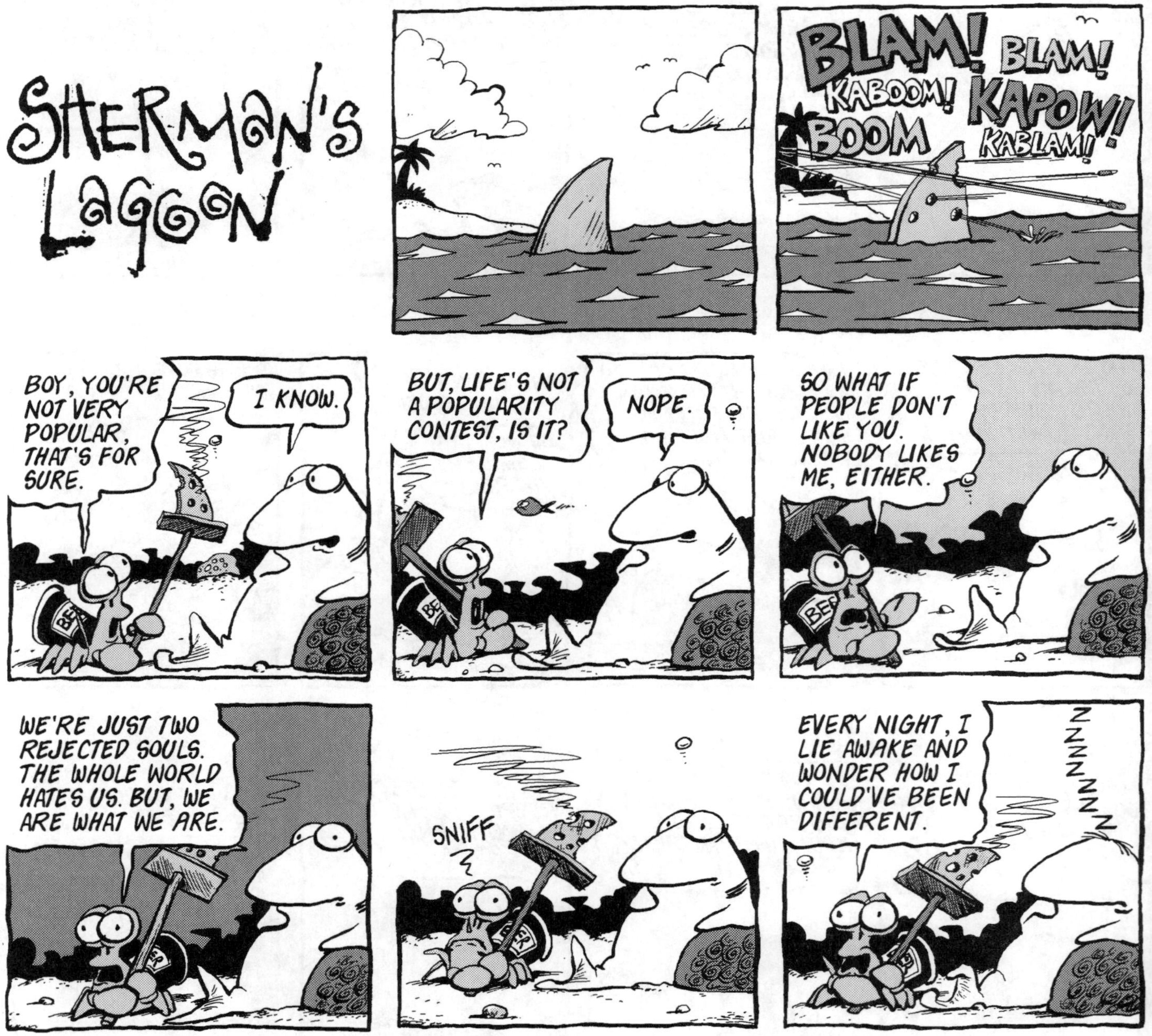
SHERMAN'S LAGOON
BLAM! BLAM! KABOOM! KAPOW! BOOM KABLAM!
BOY, YOU'RE NOT VERY POPULAR, THAT'S FOR SURE.
I KNOW.
BUT, LIFE'S NOT A POPULARITY CONTEST, IS IT?
NOPE.
SO WHAT IF PEOPLE DON'T LIKE YOU. NOBODY LIKES ME, EITHER.
WE'RE JUST TWO REJECTED SOULS. THE WHOLE WORLD HATES US. BUT, WE ARE WHAT WE ARE.
SNIFF
EVERY NIGHT, I LIE AWAKE AND WONDER HOW I COULD'VE BEEN DIFFERENT.
ZZZZZZ

Panel 1: HAWTHORNE POWER, INC. HAS OFFICIALLY STARTED CONSTRUCTION ON ITS POWER PLANT.

Panel 2: I DOWNLOADED THESE DRAWINGS FROM THE INTERNET. WE'VE ALREADY SAVED MILLIONS IN ENGINEERING FEES!

Panel 3: YOU'RE LOOKING AT THEM UPSIDE-DOWN.

I AM? HMPH.

Panel 4: THAT RUSSIAN WRITING LOOKS THE SAME EITHER WAY.

SEE? IT'S SUPPOSED TO READ "CHERNOBYL."

Panel 5: WHAT'S THIS?

I'M PROTESTING THE CONSTRUCTION OF YOUR POWER PLANT. I'M NOT ALLOWING YOUR BULL DOZERS THROUGH.

STOP THE POWER

Panel 6: THIS SIXTIES, HIPPY-DIPPY, FLOWER POWER STUFF DOESN'T FLY ANYMORE, FILLMORE.

Panel 7: IF YOU WANT TO CHANGE SOCIETY, USE THE POWER OF DEMOCRACY!

Panel 8: HERE'S SOME MONEY. GO RUN FOR OFFICE.

ARE YOU TRYING TO GET RID OF ME?

Panel 9: I WANT TO THANK YOU ALL FOR COMING TO THE GRAND OPENING OF HAWTHORNE POWER INC.'S FIRST POWER PLANT.

Panel 10: HERE AT HAWTHORNE POWER, WE BELIEVE THERE ARE NO PROBLEMS, ONLY BUSINESS OPPORTUNITIES...

...I WILL NOW THROW THE SWITCH.

Panel 11: KABOOM!

Panel 12: WHOA NELLY... THE ENTIRE POWER PLANT BLEW SKY HIGH.

I SHOULD'VE SOLD TICKETS TO THIS EVENT.

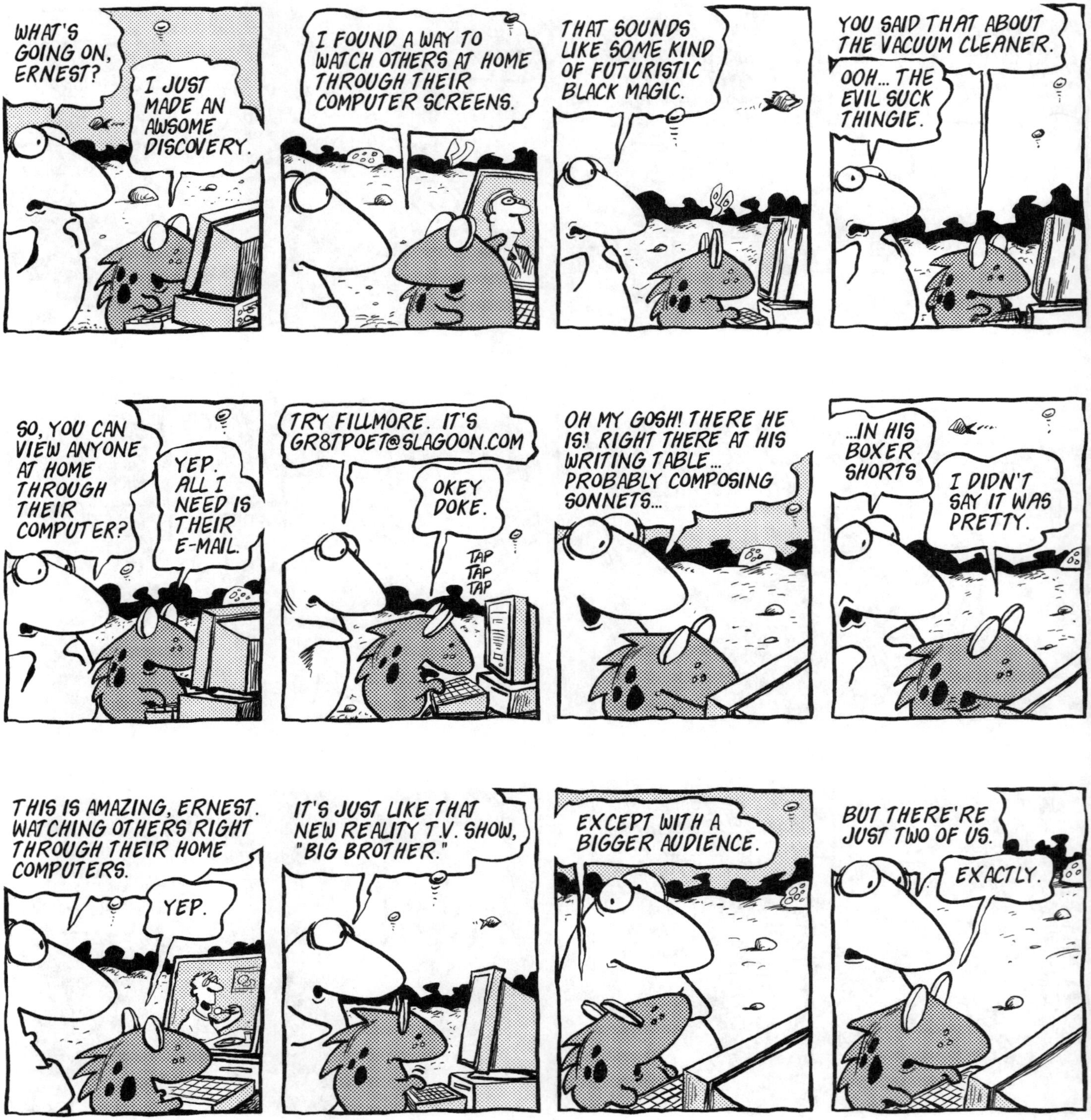
WHAT'S GOING ON, ERNEST?
I JUST MADE AN AWSOME DISCOVERY.
I FOUND A WAY TO WATCH OTHERS AT HOME THROUGH THEIR COMPUTER SCREENS.
THAT SOUNDS LIKE SOME KIND OF FUTURISTIC BLACK MAGIC.
YOU SAID THAT ABOUT THE VACUUM CLEANER.
OOH... THE EVIL SUCK THINGIE.
SO, YOU CAN VIEW ANYONE AT HOME THROUGH THEIR COMPUTER?
YEP. ALL I NEED IS THEIR E-MAIL.
TRY FILLMORE. IT'S GR8TPOET@SLAGOON.COM
OKEY DOKE.
TAP TAP TAP
OH MY GOSH! THERE HE IS! RIGHT THERE AT HIS WRITING TABLE... PROBABLY COMPOSING SONNETS...
...IN HIS BOXER SHORTS
I DIDN'T SAY IT WAS PRETTY.
THIS IS AMAZING, ERNEST. WATCHING OTHERS RIGHT THROUGH THEIR HOME COMPUTERS.
YEP.
IT'S JUST LIKE THAT NEW REALITY T.V. SHOW, "BIG BROTHER."
EXCEPT WITH A BIGGER AUDIENCE.
BUT THERE'RE JUST TWO OF US.
EXACTLY.

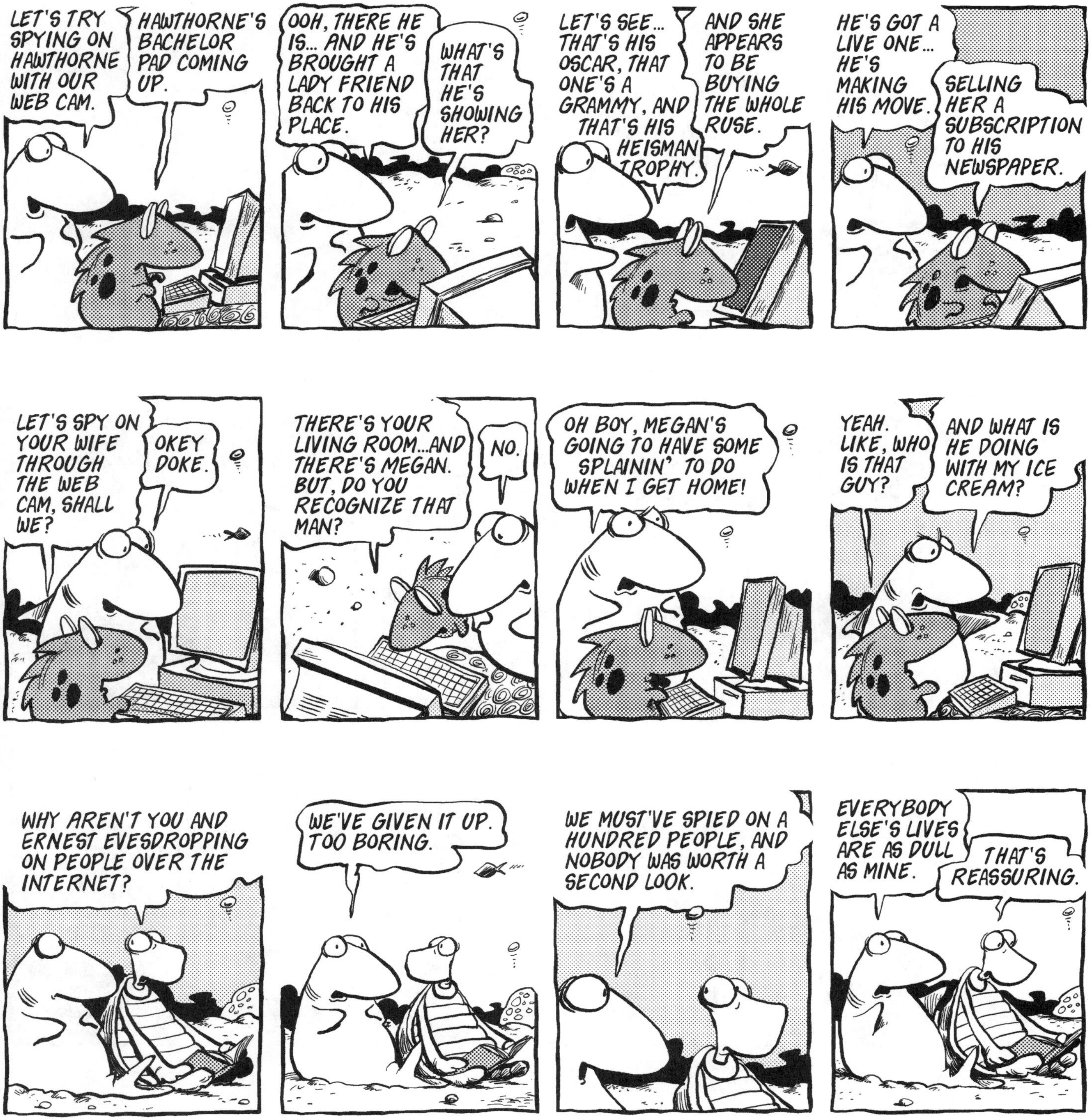
LET'S TRY SPYING ON HAWTHORNE WITH OUR WEB CAM.
HAWTHORNE'S BACHELOR PAD COMING UP.
OOH, THERE HE IS... AND HE'S BROUGHT A LADY FRIEND BACK TO HIS PLACE.
WHAT'S THAT HE'S SHOWING HER?
LET'S SEE... THAT'S HIS OSCAR, THAT ONE'S A GRAMMY, AND THAT'S HIS HEISMAN TROPHY.
AND SHE APPEARS TO BE BUYING THE WHOLE RUSE.
HE'S GOT A LIVE ONE... HE'S MAKING HIS MOVE.
SELLING HER A SUBSCRIPTION TO HIS NEWSPAPER.
LET'S SPY ON YOUR WIFE THROUGH THE WEB CAM, SHALL WE?
OKEY DOKE.
THERE'S YOUR LIVING ROOM...AND THERE'S MEGAN. BUT, DO YOU RECOGNIZE THAT MAN?
NO.
OH BOY, MEGAN'S GOING TO HAVE SOME SPLAININ' TO DO WHEN I GET HOME!
YEAH. LIKE, WHO IS THAT GUY?
AND WHAT IS HE DOING WITH MY ICE CREAM?
WHY AREN'T YOU AND ERNEST EVESDROPPING ON PEOPLE OVER THE INTERNET?
WE'VE GIVEN IT UP. TOO BORING.
WE MUST'VE SPIED ON A HUNDRED PEOPLE, AND NOBODY WAS WORTH A SECOND LOOK.
EVERYBODY ELSE'S LIVES ARE AS DULL AS MINE.
THAT'S REASSURING.

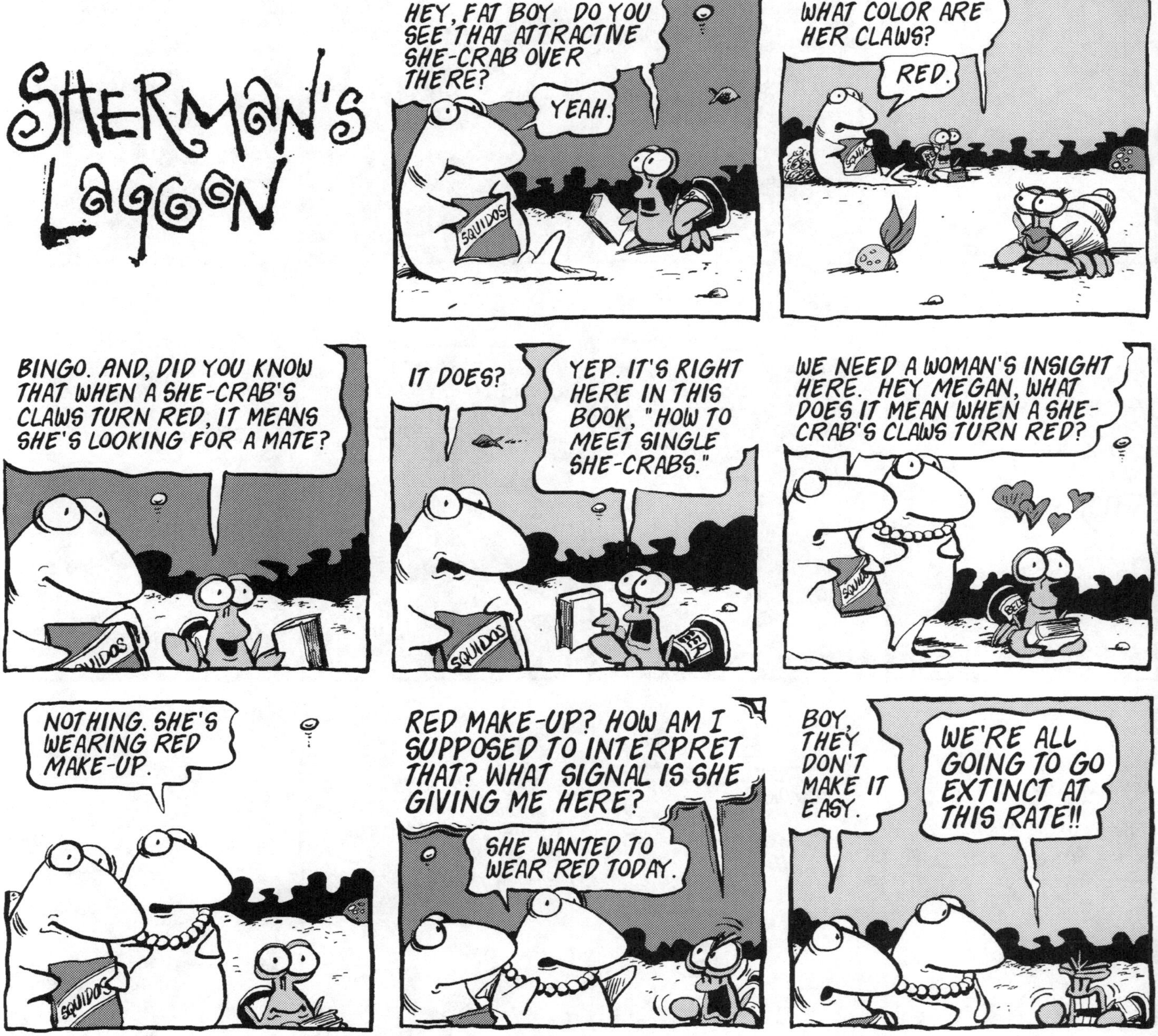
SHERMAN'S LAGOON
HEY, FAT BOY. DO YOU SEE THAT ATTRACTIVE SHE-CRAB OVER THERE?
YEAH.
WHAT COLOR ARE HER CLAWS?
RED.
BINGO. AND, DID YOU KNOW THAT WHEN A SHE-CRAB'S CLAWS TURN RED, IT MEANS SHE'S LOOKING FOR A MATE?
IT DOES?
YEP. IT'S RIGHT HERE IN THIS BOOK, "HOW TO MEET SINGLE SHE-CRABS."
WE NEED A WOMAN'S INSIGHT HERE. HEY MEGAN, WHAT DOES IT MEAN WHEN A SHE-CRAB'S CLAWS TURN RED?
NOTHING. SHE'S WEARING RED MAKE-UP.
RED MAKE-UP? HOW AM I SUPPOSED TO INTERPRET THAT? WHAT SIGNAL IS SHE GIVING ME HERE?
SHE WANTED TO WEAR RED TODAY.
BOY, THEY DON'T MAKE IT EASY.
WE'RE ALL GOING TO GO EXTINCT AT THIS RATE!!
SQUIDOS
BEER

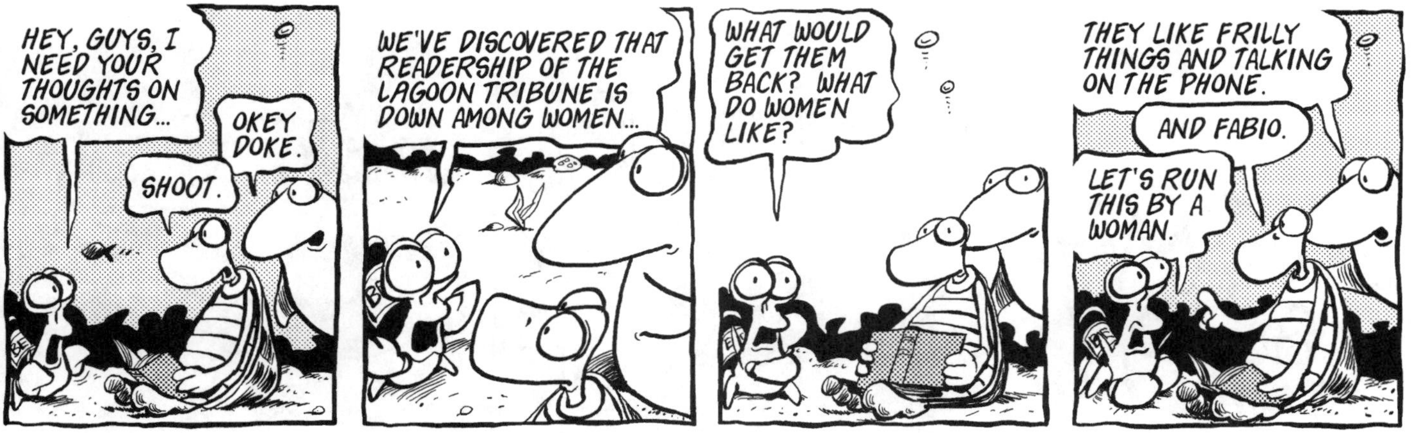
HEY, GUYS, I NEED YOUR THOUGHTS ON SOMETHING...
OKEY DOKE.
SHOOT.
WE'VE DISCOVERED THAT READERSHIP OF THE LAGOON TRIBUNE IS DOWN AMONG WOMEN...
WHAT WOULD GET THEM BACK? WHAT DO WOMEN LIKE?
THEY LIKE FRILLY THINGS AND TALKING ON THE PHONE.
AND FABIO.
LET'S RUN THIS BY A WOMAN.

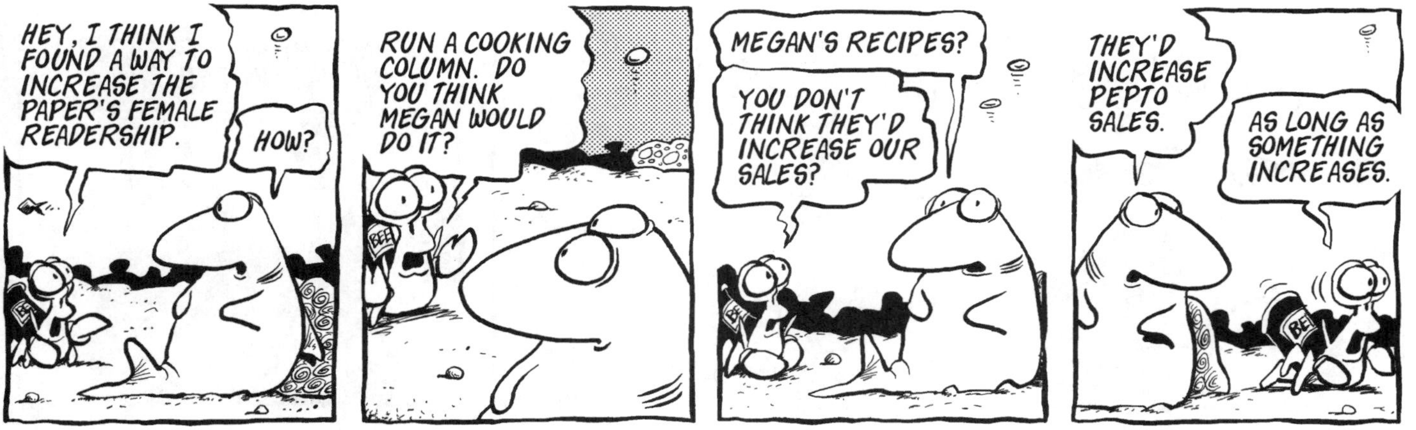
HEY, I THINK I FOUND A WAY TO INCREASE THE PAPER'S FEMALE READERSHIP.
HOW?
RUN A COOKING COLUMN. DO YOU THINK MEGAN WOULD DO IT?
MEGAN'S RECIPES?
YOU DON'T THINK THEY'D INCREASE OUR SALES?
THEY'D INCREASE PEPTO SALES.
AS LONG AS SOMETHING INCREASES.

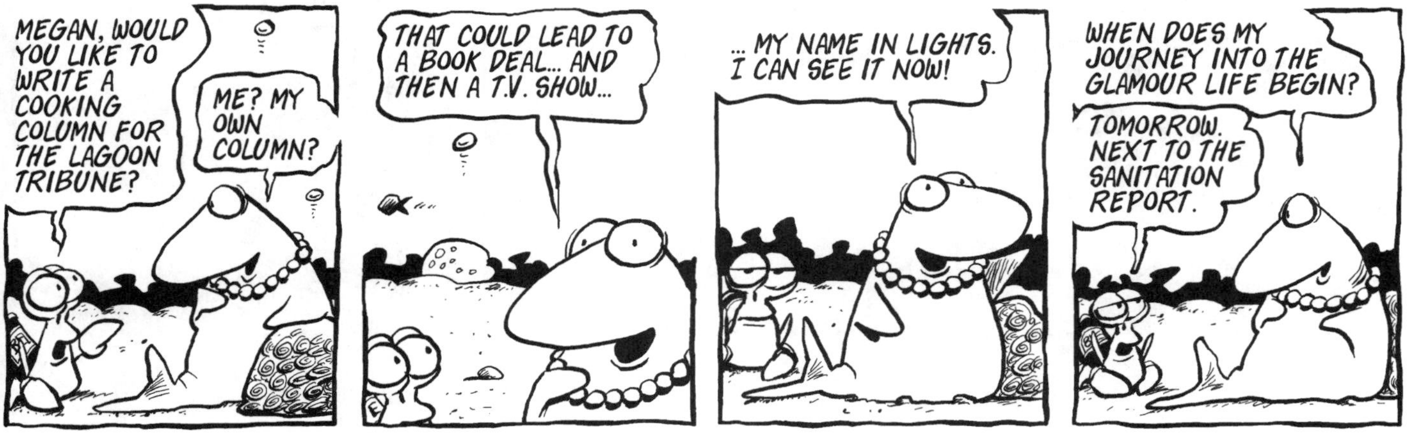
MEGAN, WOULD YOU LIKE TO WRITE A COOKING COLUMN FOR THE LAGOON TRIBUNE?
ME? MY OWN COLUMN?
THAT COULD LEAD TO A BOOK DEAL... AND THEN A T.V. SHOW...
... MY NAME IN LIGHTS. I CAN SEE IT NOW!
WHEN DOES MY JOURNEY INTO THE GLAMOUR LIFE BEGIN?
TOMORROW. NEXT TO THE SANITATION REPORT.

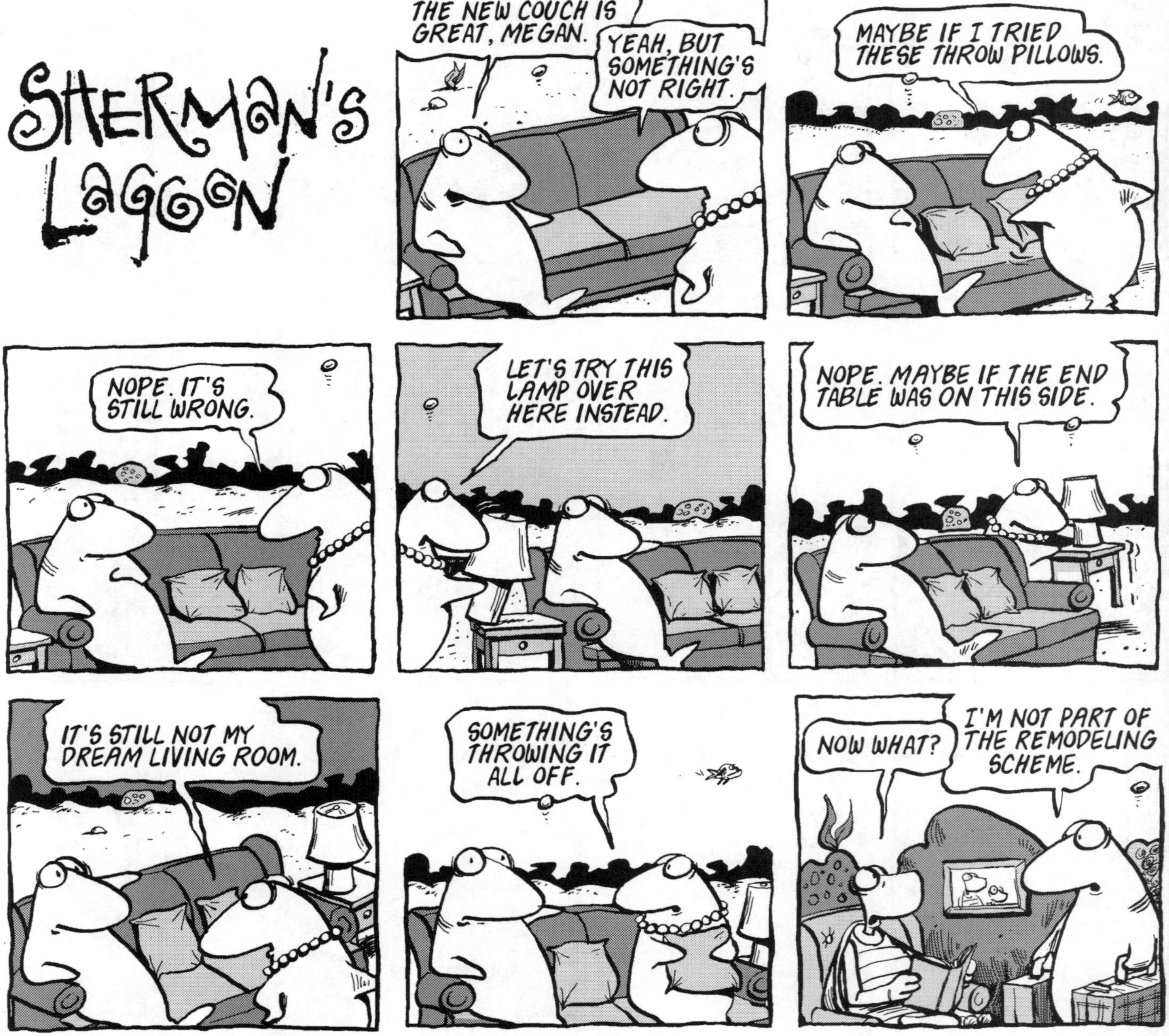
SHERMAN'S LAGOON
THE NEW COUCH IS GREAT, MEGAN.
YEAH, BUT SOMETHING'S NOT RIGHT.
MAYBE IF I TRIED THESE THROW PILLOWS.
NOPE. IT'S STILL WRONG.
LET'S TRY THIS LAMP OVER HERE INSTEAD.
NOPE. MAYBE IF THE END TABLE WAS ON THIS SIDE.
IT'S STILL NOT MY DREAM LIVING ROOM.
SOMETHING'S THROWING IT ALL OFF.
NOW WHAT?
I'M NOT PART OF THE REMODELING SCHEME.

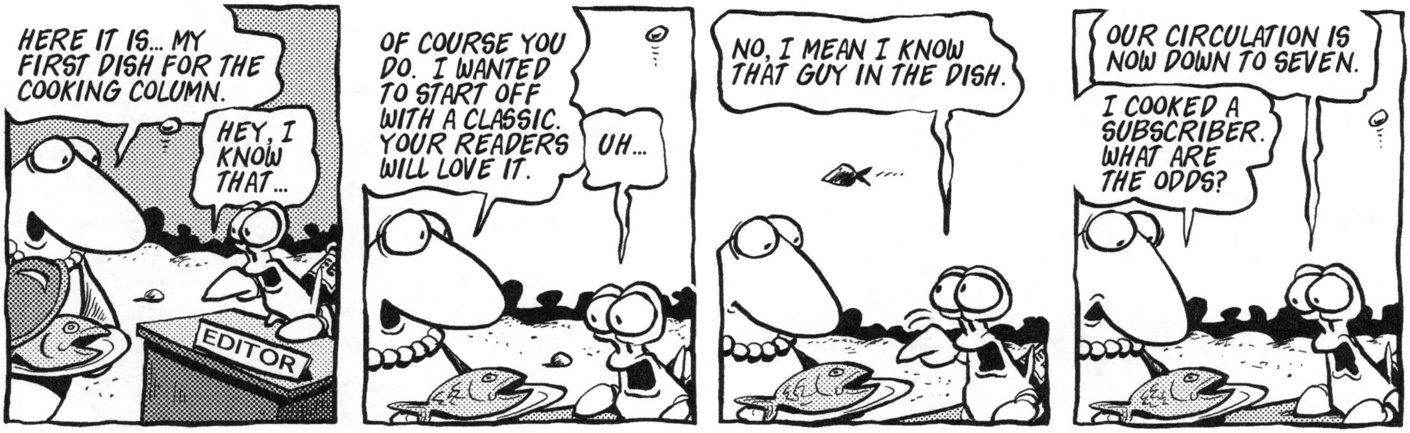
HERE IT IS... MY FIRST DISH FOR THE COOKING COLUMN.
HEY, I KNOW THAT...
EDITOR
OF COURSE YOU DO. I WANTED TO START OFF WITH A CLASSIC. YOUR READERS WILL LOVE IT.
UH...
NO, I MEAN I KNOW THAT GUY IN THE DISH.
OUR CIRCULATION IS NOW DOWN TO SEVEN.
I COOKED A SUBSCRIBER. WHAT ARE THE ODDS?

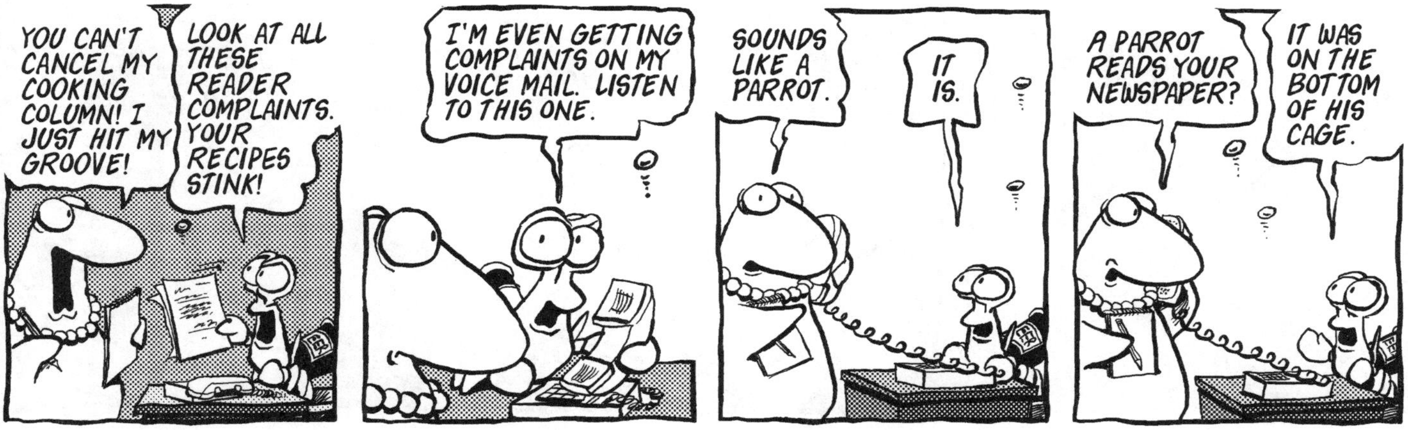
YOU CAN'T CANCEL MY COOKING COLUMN! I JUST HIT MY GROOVE!
LOOK AT ALL THESE READER COMPLAINTS. YOUR RECIPES STINK!
I'M EVEN GETTING COMPLAINTS ON MY VOICE MAIL. LISTEN TO THIS ONE.
SOUNDS LIKE A PARROT.
IT IS.
A PARROT READS YOUR NEWSPAPER?
IT WAS ON THE BOTTOM OF HIS CAGE.

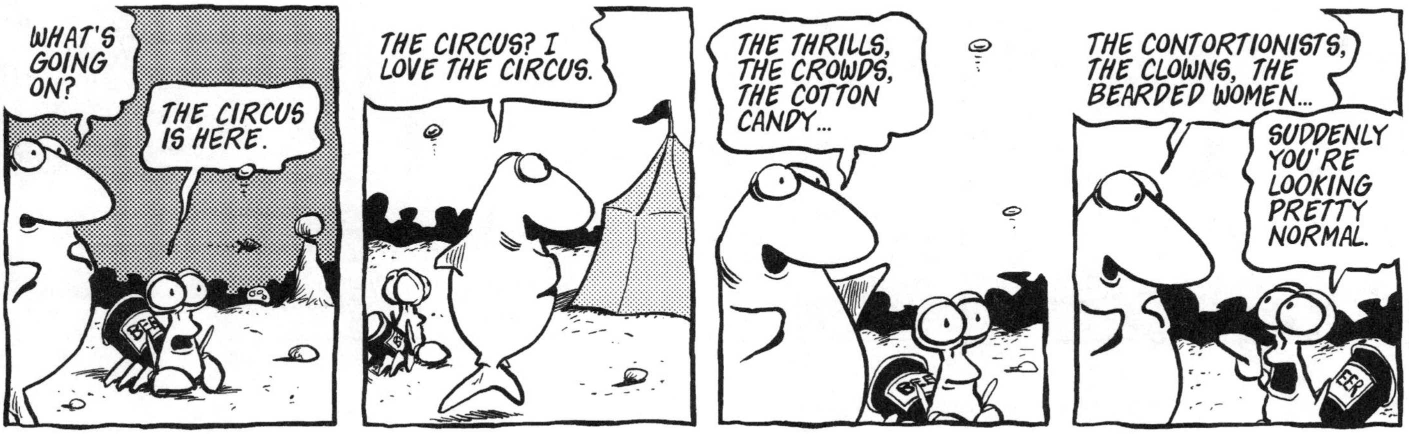
WHAT'S GOING ON?
THE CIRCUS IS HERE.
THE CIRCUS? I LOVE THE CIRCUS.
THE THRILLS, THE CROWDS, THE COTTON CANDY...
THE CONTORTIONISTS, THE CLOWNS, THE BEARDED WOMEN...
SUDDENLY YOU'RE LOOKING PRETTY NORMAL.

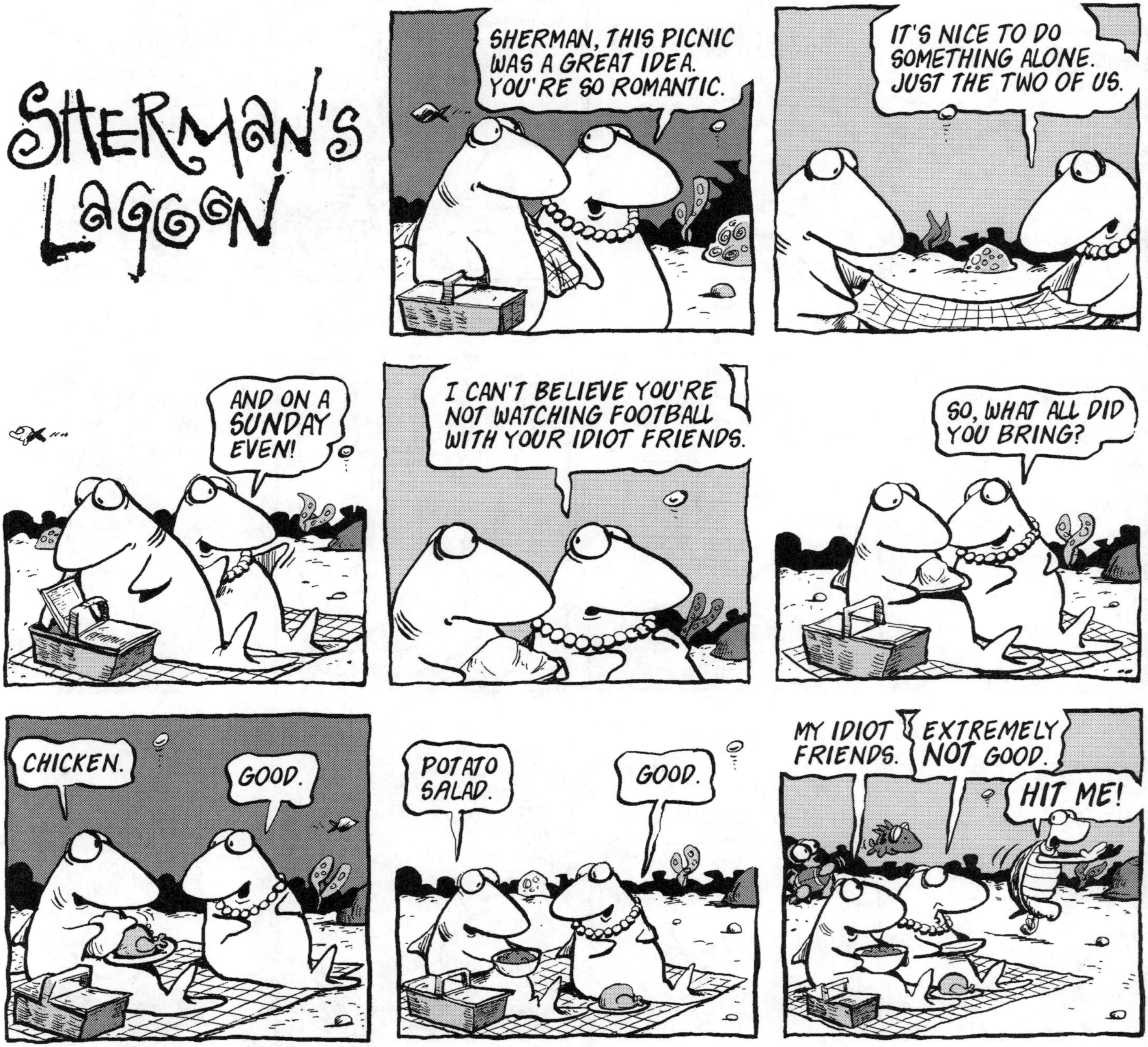
SHERMAN'S LAGOON
SHERMAN, THIS PICNIC WAS A GREAT IDEA. YOU'RE SO ROMANTIC.
IT'S NICE TO DO SOMETHING ALONE. JUST THE TWO OF US.
AND ON A SUNDAY EVEN!
I CAN'T BELIEVE YOU'RE NOT WATCHING FOOTBALL WITH YOUR IDIOT FRIENDS.
SO, WHAT ALL DID YOU BRING?
CHICKEN.
GOOD.
POTATO SALAD.
GOOD.
MY IDIOT FRIENDS.
EXTREMELY NOT GOOD.
HIT ME!

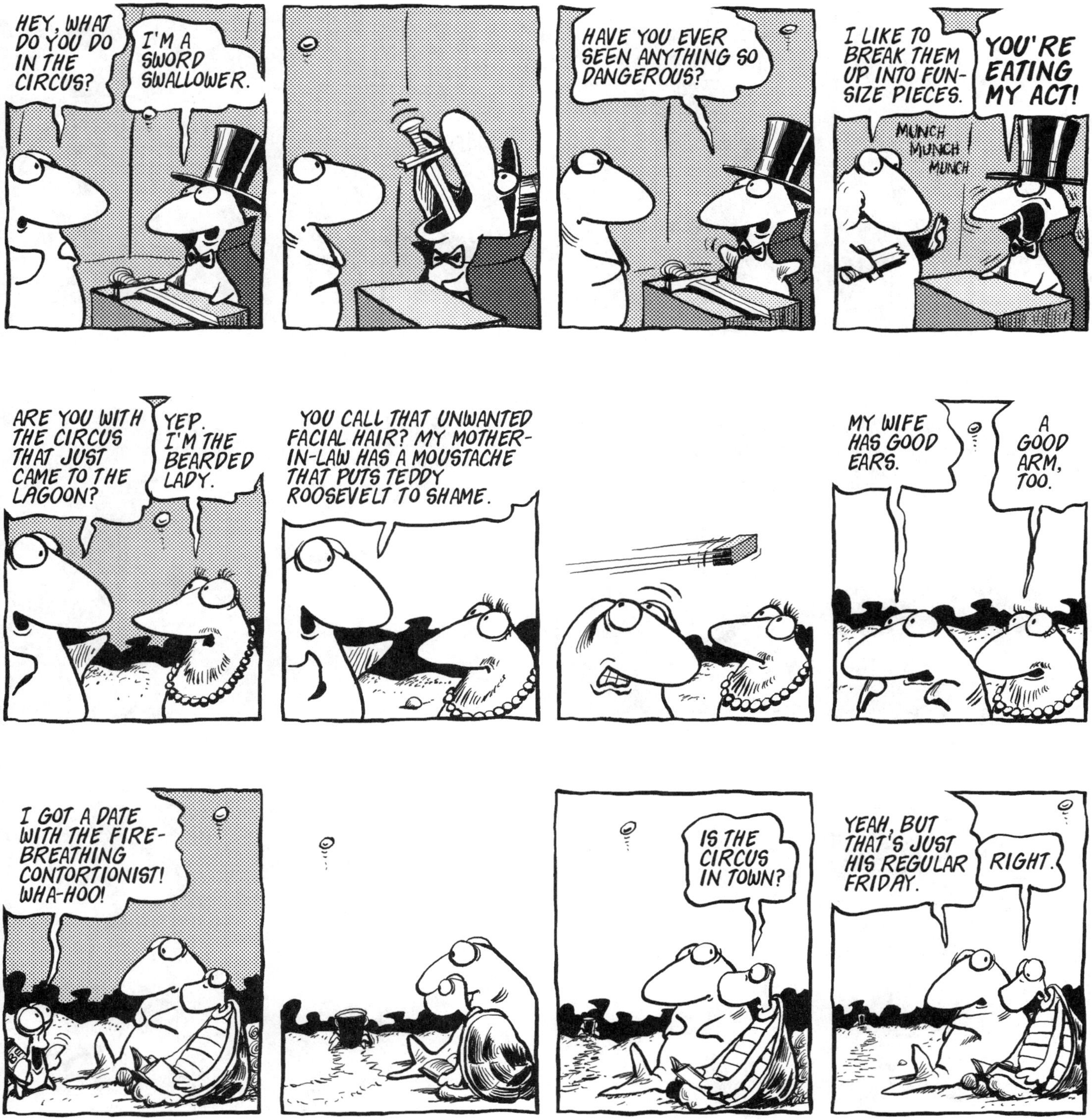
HEY, WHAT DO YOU DO IN THE CIRCUS?
I'M A SWORD SWALLOWER.
HAVE YOU EVER SEEN ANYTHING SO DANGEROUS?
I LIKE TO BREAK THEM UP INTO FUN-SIZE PIECES.
MUNCH MUNCH MUNCH
YOU'RE EATING MY ACT!
ARE YOU WITH THE CIRCUS THAT JUST CAME TO THE LAGOON?
YEP. I'M THE BEARDED LADY.
YOU CALL THAT UNWANTED FACIAL HAIR? MY MOTHER-IN-LAW HAS A MOUSTACHE THAT PUTS TEDDY ROOSEVELT TO SHAME.
MY WIFE HAS GOOD EARS.
A GOOD ARM, TOO.
I GOT A DATE WITH THE FIRE-BREATHING CONTORTIONIST! WHA-HOO!
IS THE CIRCUS IN TOWN?
YEAH, BUT THAT'S JUST HIS REGULAR FRIDAY.
RIGHT.

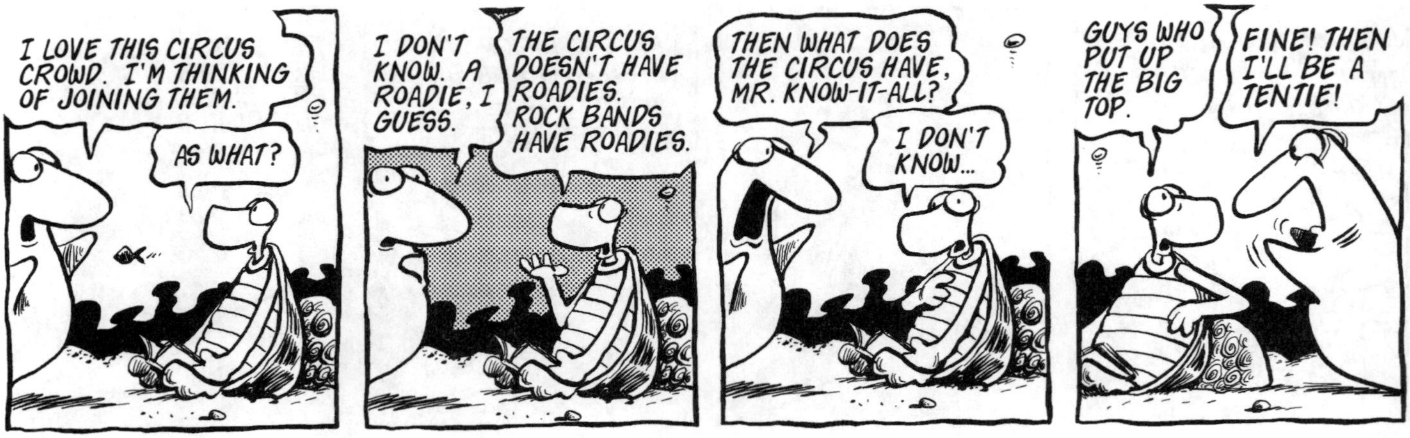
I LOVE THIS CIRCUS CROWD. I'M THINKING OF JOINING THEM.
AS WHAT?
I DON'T KNOW. A ROADIE, I GUESS.
THE CIRCUS DOESN'T HAVE ROADIES. ROCK BANDS HAVE ROADIES.
THEN WHAT DOES THE CIRCUS HAVE, MR. KNOW-IT-ALL?
I DON'T KNOW...
GUYS WHO PUT UP THE BIG TOP.
FINE! THEN I'LL BE A TENTIE!

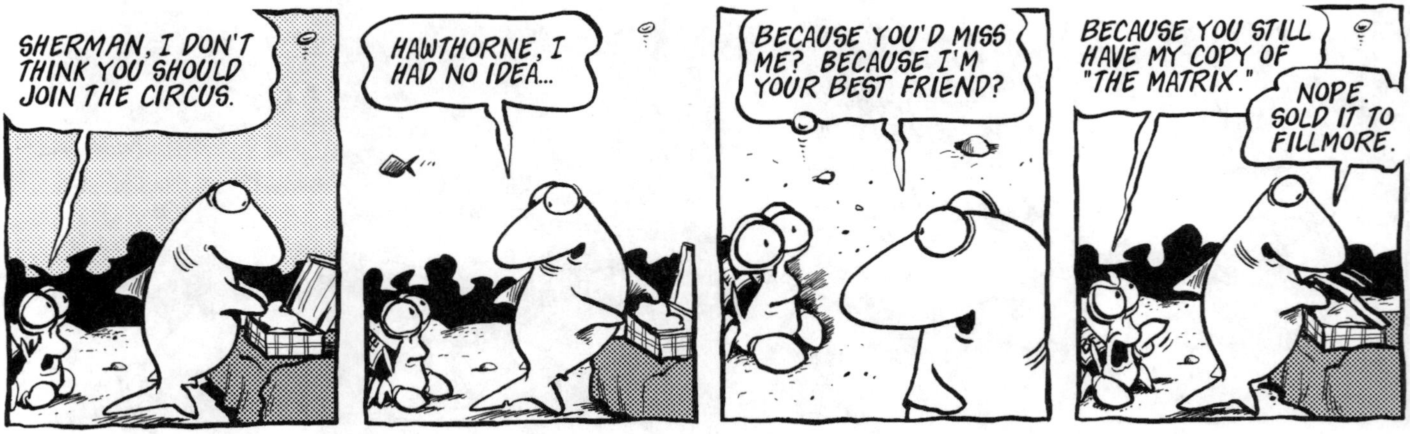
SHERMAN, I DON'T THINK YOU SHOULD JOIN THE CIRCUS.
HAWTHORNE, I HAD NO IDEA...
BECAUSE YOU'D MISS ME? BECAUSE I'M YOUR BEST FRIEND?
BECAUSE YOU STILL HAVE MY COPY OF "THE MATRIX."
NOPE. SOLD IT TO FILLMORE.

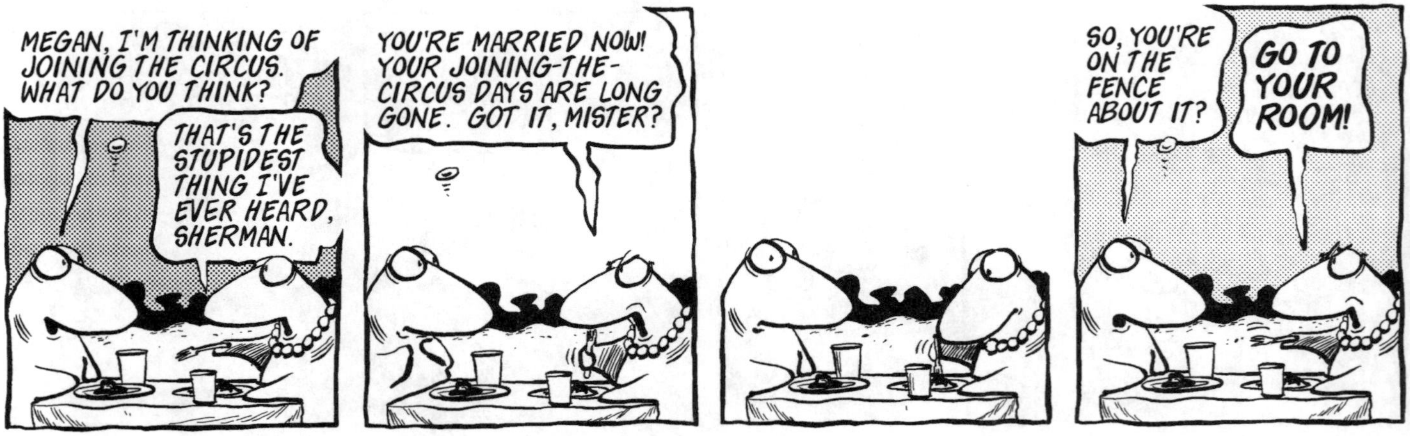
MEGAN, I'M THINKING OF JOINING THE CIRCUS. WHAT DO YOU THINK?
THAT'S THE STUPIDEST THING I'VE EVER HEARD, SHERMAN.
YOU'RE MARRIED NOW! YOUR JOINING-THE-CIRCUS DAYS ARE LONG GONE. GOT IT, MISTER?
SO, YOU'RE ON THE FENCE ABOUT IT?
GO TO YOUR ROOM!

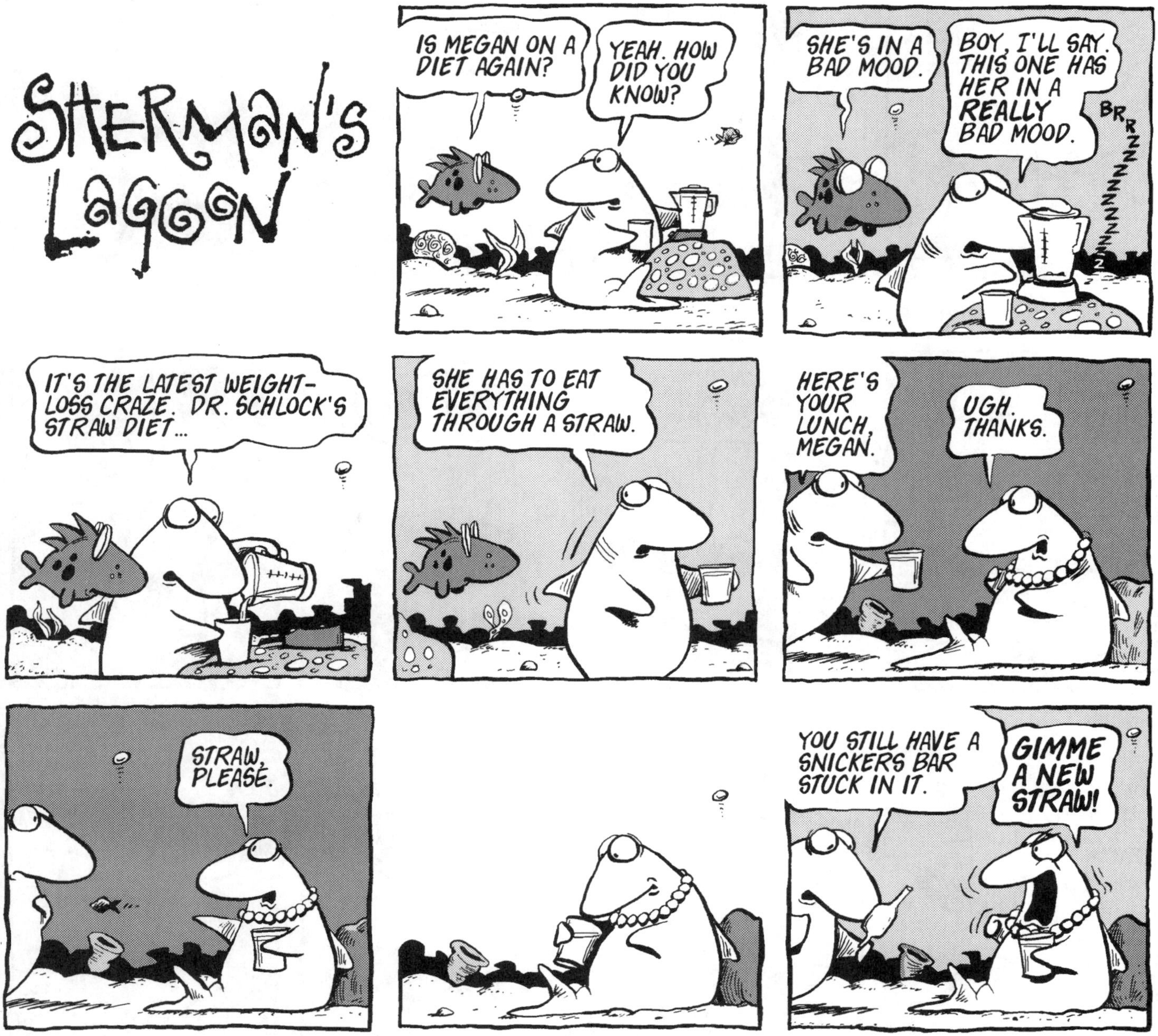
SHERMAN'S LAGOON
IS MEGAN ON A DIET AGAIN?
YEAH. HOW DID YOU KNOW?
SHE'S IN A BAD MOOD.
BOY, I'LL SAY. THIS ONE HAS HER IN A REALLY BAD MOOD.
BRRZZZZZZZZZ
IT'S THE LATEST WEIGHT-LOSS CRAZE. DR. SCHLOCK'S STRAW DIET...
SHE HAS TO EAT EVERYTHING THROUGH A STRAW.
HERE'S YOUR LUNCH, MEGAN.
UGH. THANKS.
STRAW, PLEASE.
YOU STILL HAVE A SNICKERS BAR STUCK IN IT.
GIMME A NEW STRAW!

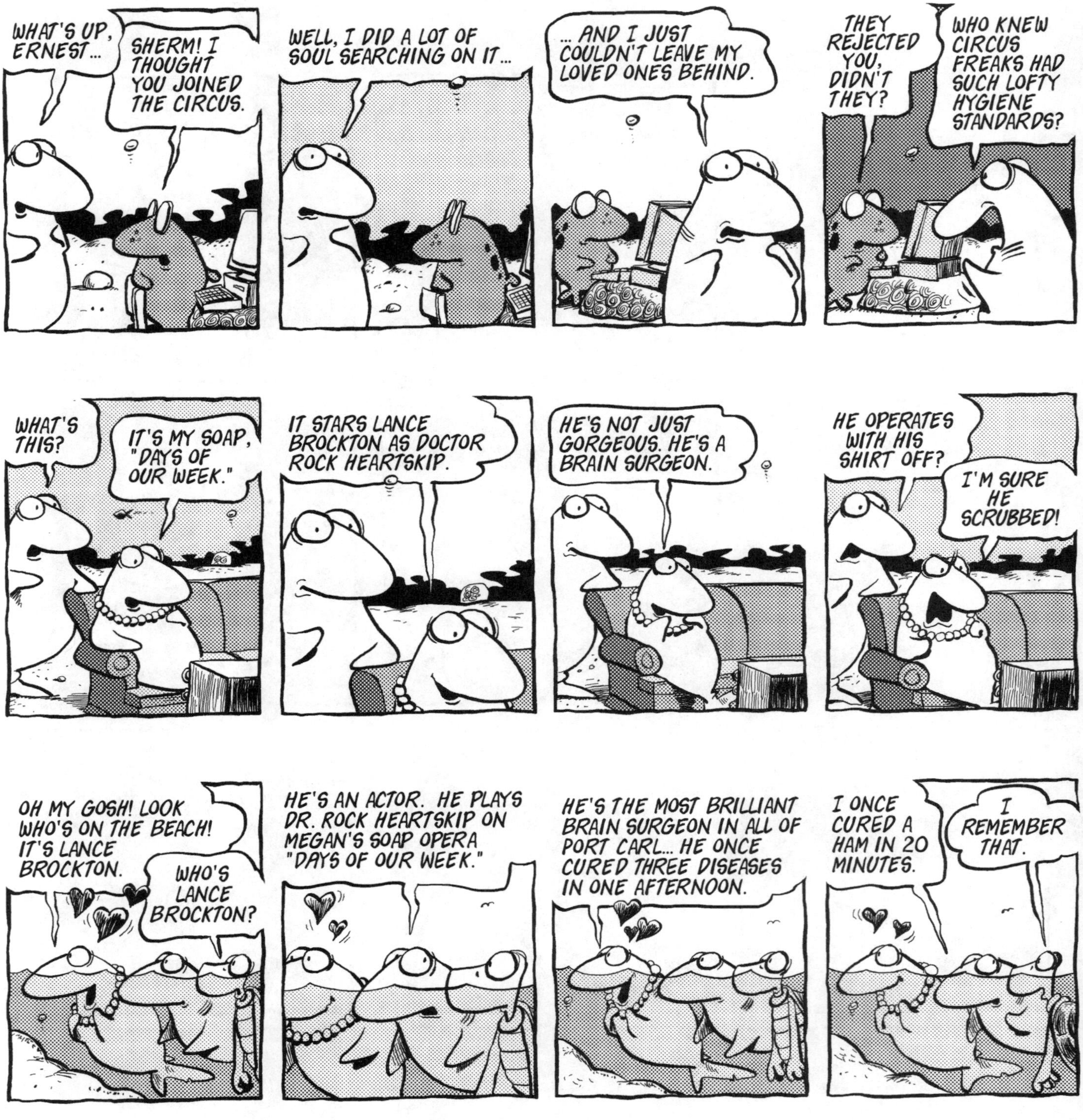
WHAT'S UP, ERNEST...
SHERM! I THOUGHT YOU JOINED THE CIRCUS.
WELL, I DID A LOT OF SOUL SEARCHING ON IT...
... AND I JUST COULDN'T LEAVE MY LOVED ONES BEHIND.
THEY REJECTED YOU, DIDN'T THEY?
WHO KNEW CIRCUS FREAKS HAD SUCH LOFTY HYGIENE STANDARDS?
WHAT'S THIS?
IT'S MY SOAP, "DAYS OF OUR WEEK."
IT STARS LANCE BROCKTON AS DOCTOR ROCK HEARTSKIP.
HE'S NOT JUST GORGEOUS. HE'S A BRAIN SURGEON.
HE OPERATES WITH HIS SHIRT OFF?
I'M SURE HE SCRUBBED!
OH MY GOSH! LOOK WHO'S ON THE BEACH! IT'S LANCE BROCKTON.
WHO'S LANCE BROCKTON?
HE'S AN ACTOR. HE PLAYS DR. ROCK HEARTSKIP ON MEGAN'S SOAP OPERA "DAYS OF OUR WEEK."
HE'S THE MOST BRILLIANT BRAIN SURGEON IN ALL OF PORT CARL... HE ONCE CURED THREE DISEASES IN ONE AFTERNOON.
I ONCE CURED A HAM IN 20 MINUTES.
I REMEMBER THAT.

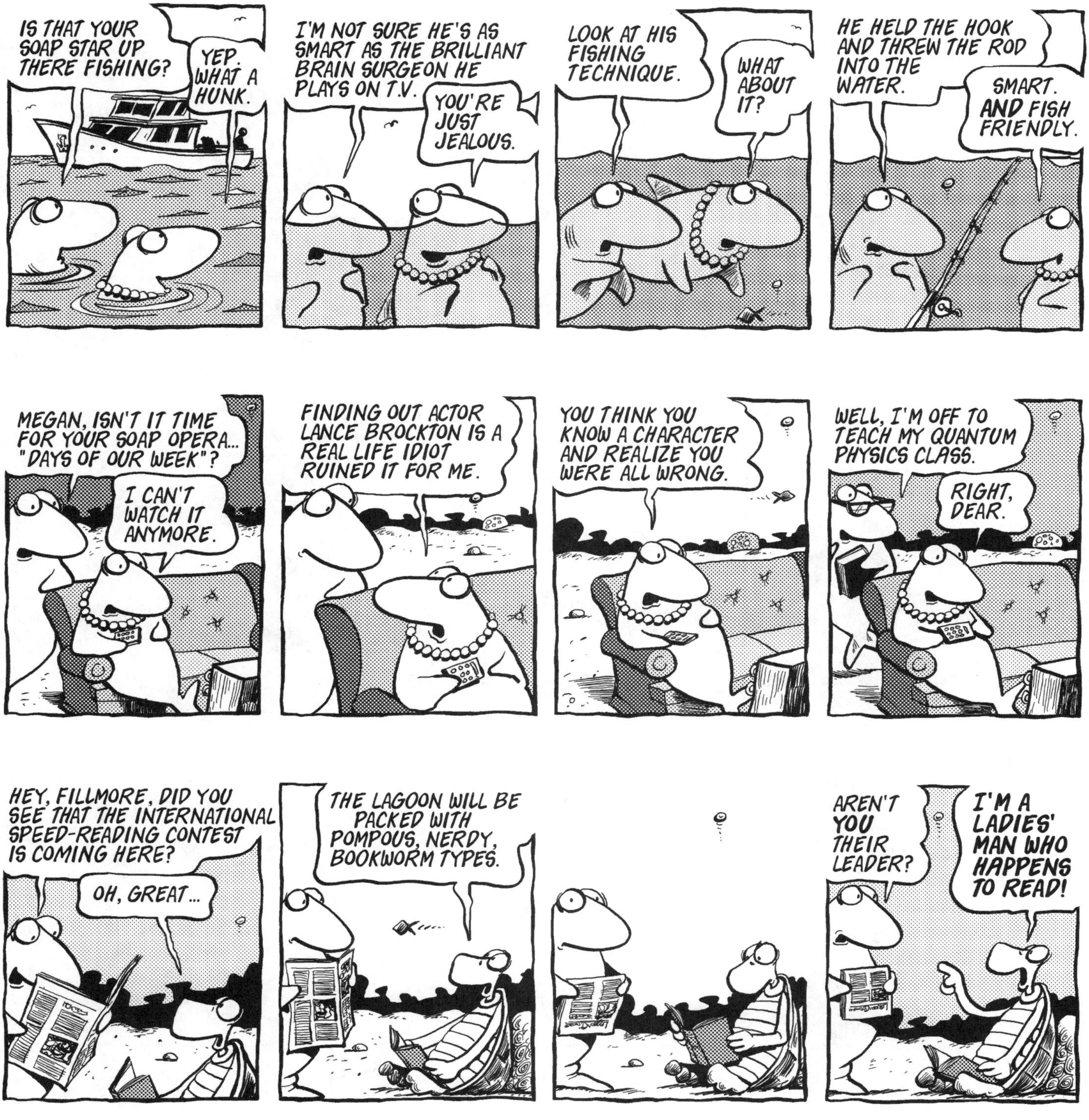
IS THAT YOUR SOAP STAR UP THERE FISHING?
YEP. WHAT A HUNK.
I'M NOT SURE HE'S AS SMART AS THE BRILLIANT BRAIN SURGEON HE PLAYS ON T.V.
YOU'RE JUST JEALOUS.
LOOK AT HIS FISHING TECHNIQUE.
WHAT ABOUT IT?
HE HELD THE HOOK AND THREW THE ROD INTO THE WATER.
SMART. AND FISH FRIENDLY.
MEGAN, ISN'T IT TIME FOR YOUR SOAP OPERA... "DAYS OF OUR WEEK"?
I CAN'T WATCH IT ANYMORE.
FINDING OUT ACTOR LANCE BROCKTON IS A REAL LIFE IDIOT RUINED IT FOR ME.
YOU THINK YOU KNOW A CHARACTER AND REALIZE YOU WERE ALL WRONG.
WELL, I'M OFF TO TEACH MY QUANTUM PHYSICS CLASS.
RIGHT, DEAR.
HEY, FILLMORE, DID YOU SEE THAT THE INTERNATIONAL SPEED-READING CONTEST IS COMING HERE?
OH, GREAT...
THE LAGOON WILL BE PACKED WITH POMPOUS, NERDY, BOOKWORM TYPES.
AREN'T YOU THEIR LEADER?
I'M A LADIES' MAN WHO HAPPENS TO READ!

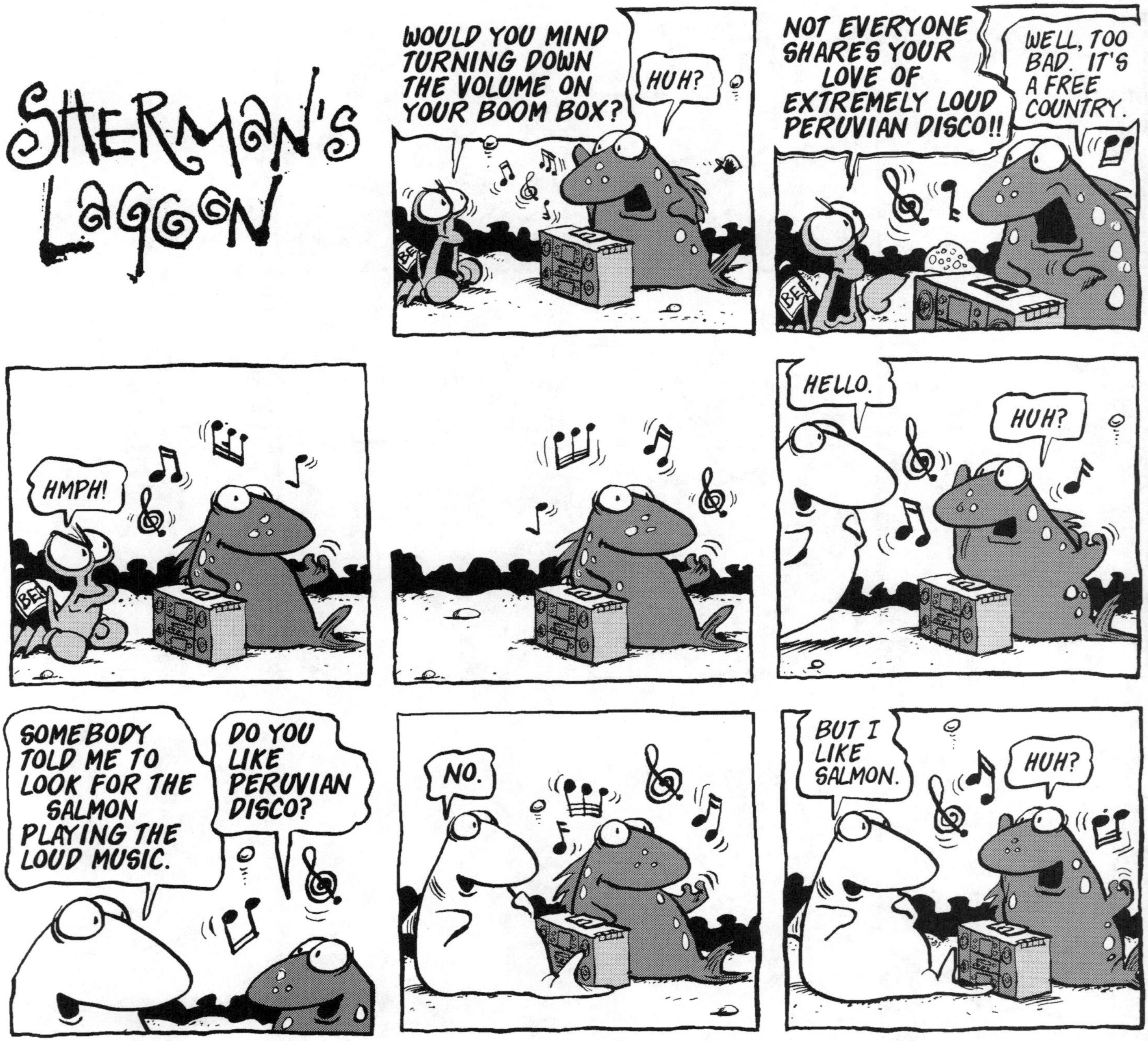
SHERMAN'S LAGOON
WOULD YOU MIND TURNING DOWN THE VOLUME ON YOUR BOOM BOX?
HUH?
NOT EVERYONE SHARES YOUR LOVE OF EXTREMELY LOUD PERUVIAN DISCO!!
WELL, TOO BAD. IT'S A FREE COUNTRY.
HMPH!
HELLO.
HUH?
SOMEBODY TOLD ME TO LOOK FOR THE SALMON PLAYING THE LOUD MUSIC.
DO YOU LIKE PERUVIAN DISCO?
NO.
BUT I LIKE SALMON.
HUH?

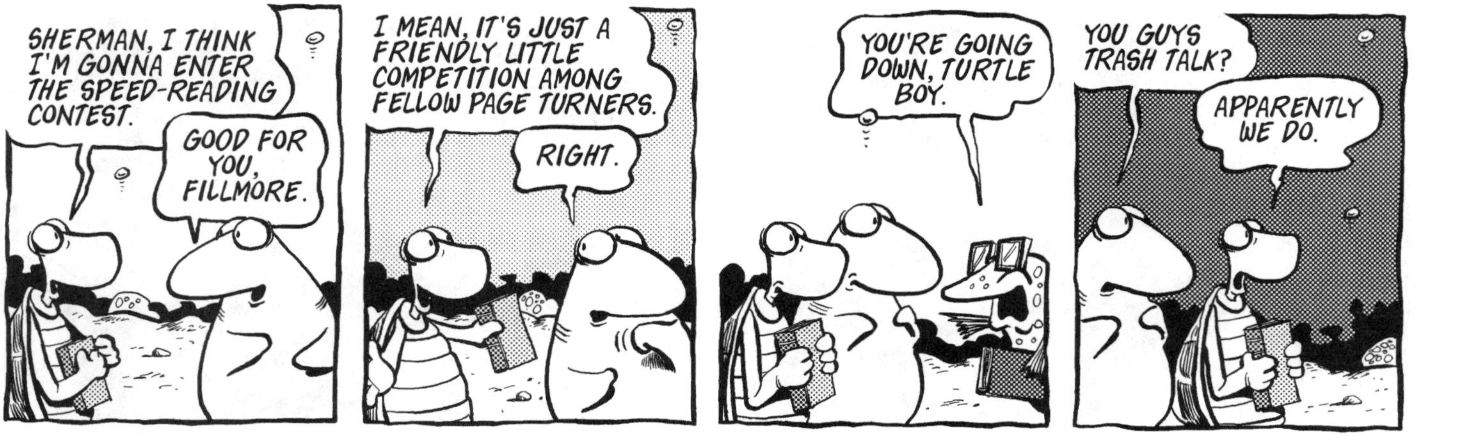
SHERMAN, I THINK I'M GONNA ENTER THE SPEED-READING CONTEST.
GOOD FOR YOU, FILLMORE.
I MEAN, IT'S JUST A FRIENDLY LITTLE COMPETITION AMONG FELLOW PAGE TURNERS.
RIGHT.
YOU'RE GOING DOWN, TURTLE BOY.
YOU GUYS TRASH TALK?
APPARENTLY WE DO.

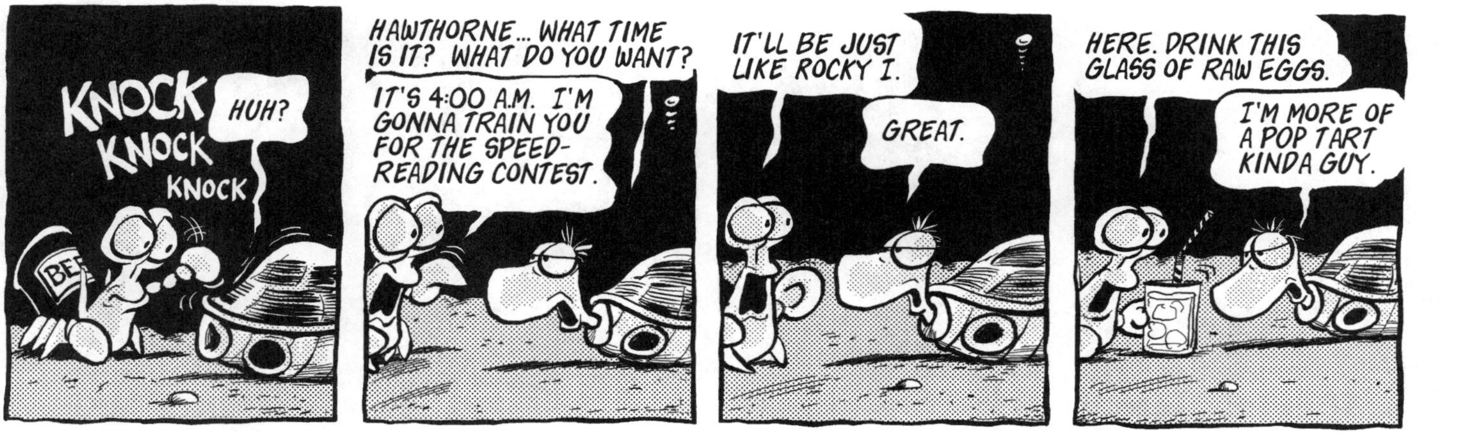
KNOCK
KNOCK
KNOCK
HUH?
BEE
HAWTHORNE... WHAT TIME IS IT? WHAT DO YOU WANT?
IT'S 4:00 A.M. I'M GONNA TRAIN YOU FOR THE SPEED-READING CONTEST.
IT'LL BE JUST LIKE ROCKY I.
GREAT.
HERE. DRINK THIS GLASS OF RAW EGGS.
I'M MORE OF A POP TART KINDA GUY.

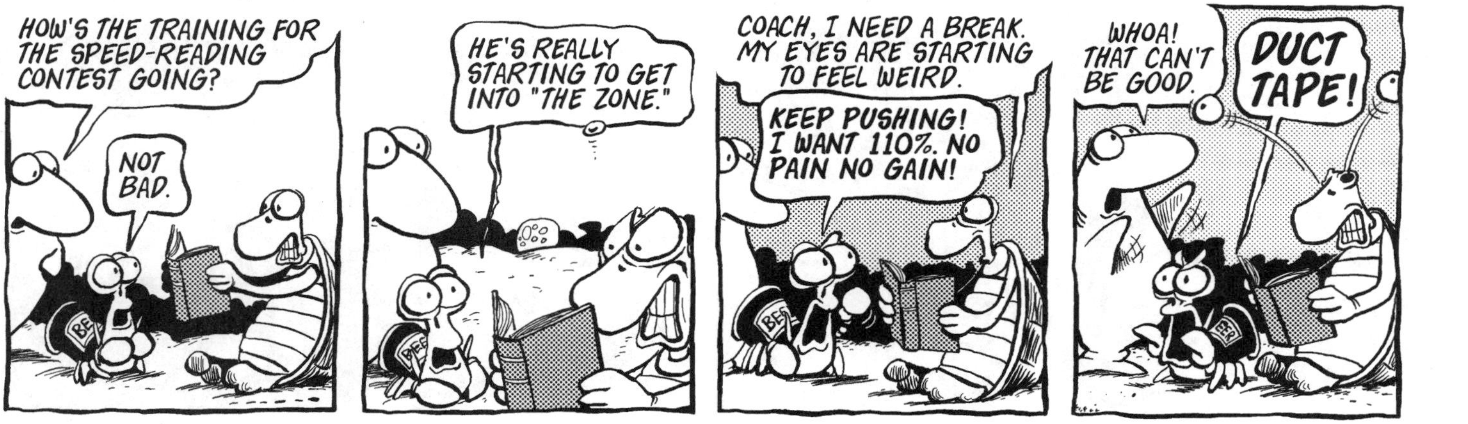
HOW'S THE TRAINING FOR THE SPEED-READING CONTEST GOING?
NOT BAD.
HE'S REALLY STARTING TO GET INTO "THE ZONE."
COACH, I NEED A BREAK. MY EYES ARE STARTING TO FEEL WEIRD.
KEEP PUSHING! I WANT 110%. NO PAIN NO GAIN!
WHOA! THAT CAN'T BE GOOD.
DUCT TAPE!

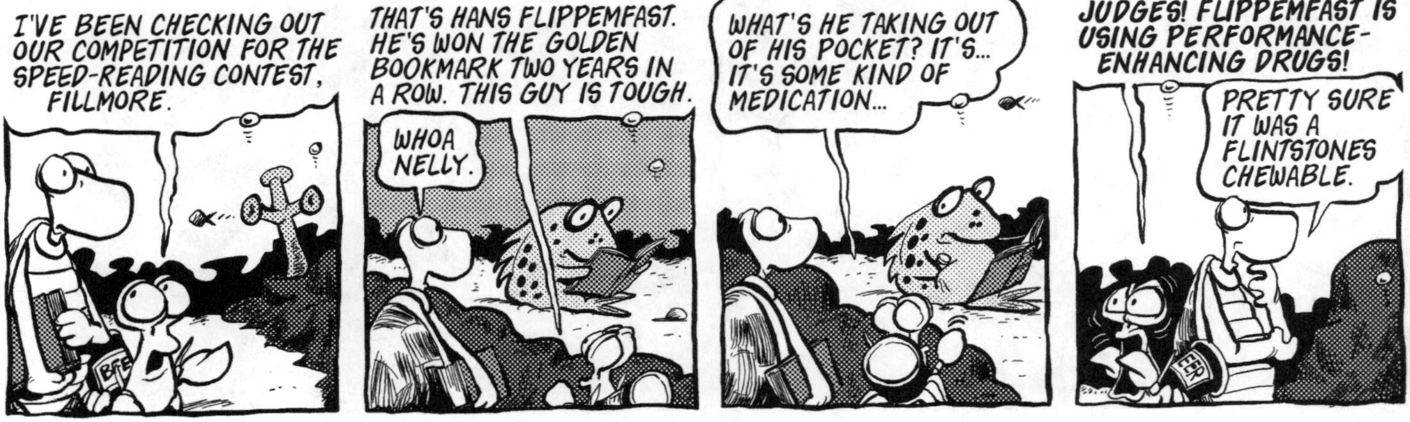
I'VE BEEN CHECKING OUT OUR COMPETITION FOR THE SPEED-READING CONTEST, FILLMORE.
THAT'S HANS FLIPPEMFAST. HE'S WON THE GOLDEN BOOKMARK TWO YEARS IN A ROW. THIS GUY IS TOUGH.
WHOA NELLY.
WHAT'S HE TAKING OUT OF HIS POCKET? IT'S... IT'S SOME KIND OF MEDICATION...
JUDGES! FLIPPEMFAST IS USING PERFORMANCE-ENHANCING DRUGS!
PRETTY SURE IT WAS A FLINTSTONES CHEWABLE.

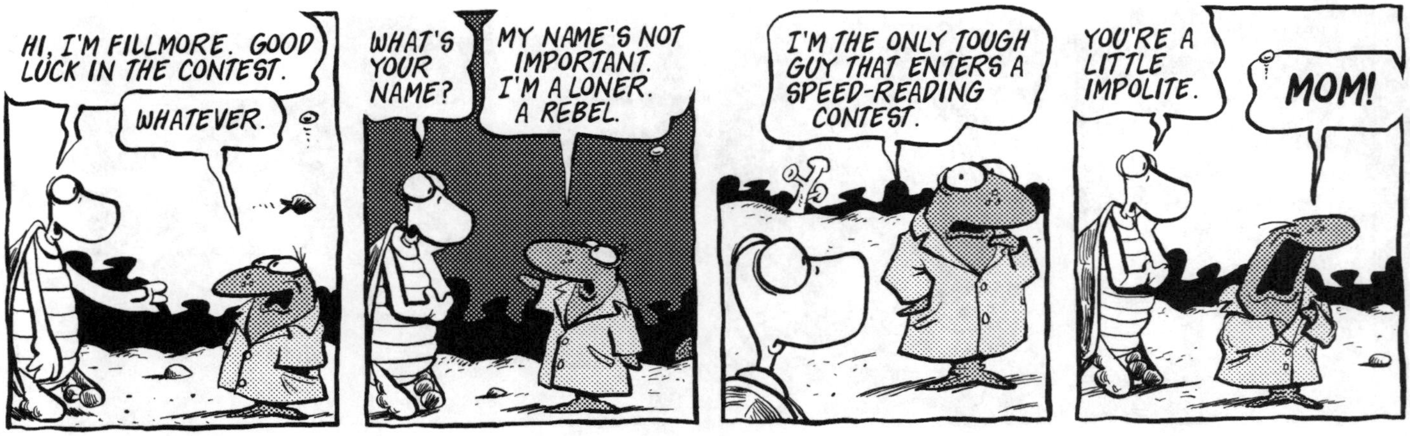
HI, I'M FILLMORE. GOOD LUCK IN THE CONTEST.
WHATEVER.
WHAT'S YOUR NAME?
MY NAME'S NOT IMPORTANT. I'M A LONER. A REBEL.
I'M THE ONLY TOUGH GUY THAT ENTERS A SPEED-READING CONTEST.
YOU'RE A LITTLE IMPOLITE.
MOM!

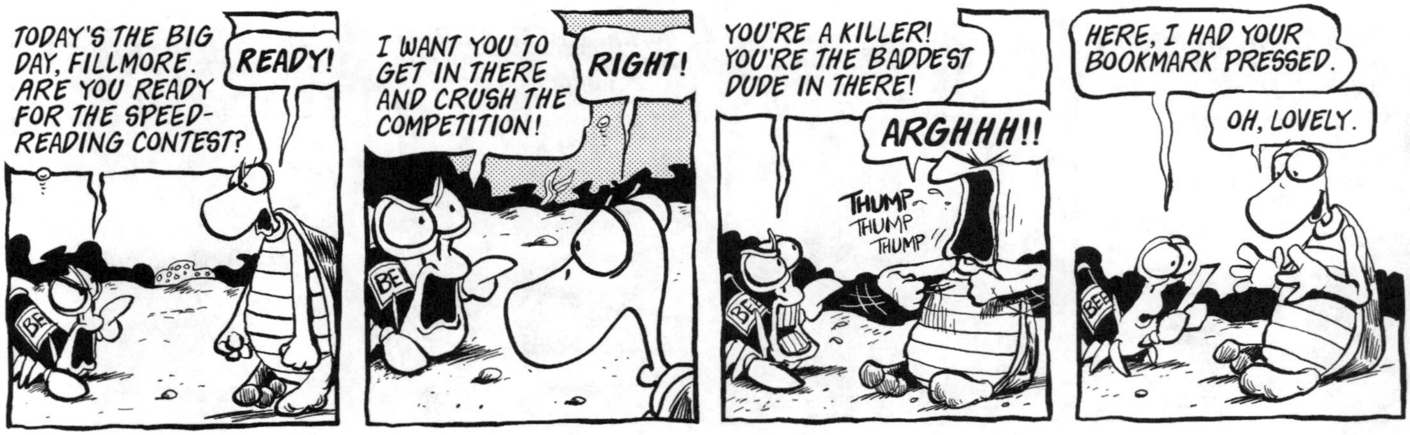
TODAY'S THE BIG DAY, FILLMORE. ARE YOU READY FOR THE SPEED-READING CONTEST?
READY!
I WANT YOU TO GET IN THERE AND CRUSH THE COMPETITION!
RIGHT!
YOU'RE A KILLER! YOU'RE THE BADDEST DUDE IN THERE!
ARGHHH!!
THUMP THUMP THUMP
HERE, I HAD YOUR BOOKMARK PRESSED.
OH, LOVELY.

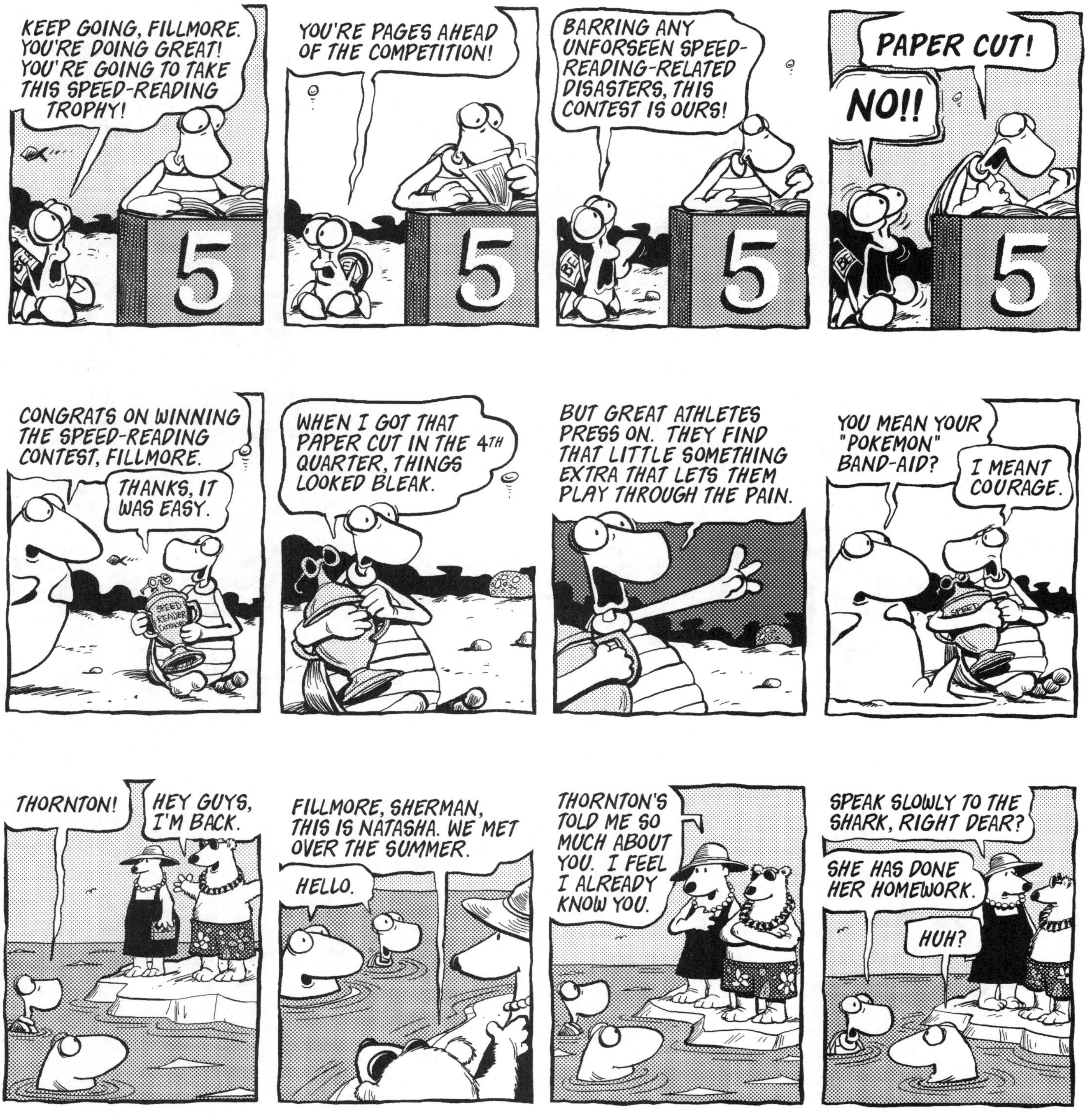
KEEP GOING, FILLMORE. YOU'RE DOING GREAT! YOU'RE GOING TO TAKE THIS SPEED-READING TROPHY!
YOU'RE PAGES AHEAD OF THE COMPETITION!
BARRING ANY UNFORSEEN SPEED-READING-RELATED DISASTERS, THIS CONTEST IS OURS!
PAPER CUT!
NO!!
5
CONGRATS ON WINNING THE SPEED-READING CONTEST, FILLMORE.
THANKS, IT WAS EASY.
WHEN I GOT THAT PAPER CUT IN THE 4TH QUARTER, THINGS LOOKED BLEAK.
BUT GREAT ATHLETES PRESS ON. THEY FIND THAT LITTLE SOMETHING EXTRA THAT LETS THEM PLAY THROUGH THE PAIN.
YOU MEAN YOUR "POKEMON" BAND-AID?
I MEANT COURAGE.
THORNTON!
HEY GUYS, I'M BACK.
FILLMORE, SHERMAN, THIS IS NATASHA. WE MET OVER THE SUMMER.
HELLO.
THORNTON'S TOLD ME SO MUCH ABOUT YOU. I FEEL I ALREADY KNOW YOU.
SPEAK SLOWLY TO THE SHARK, RIGHT DEAR?
SHE HAS DONE HER HOMEWORK.
HUH?

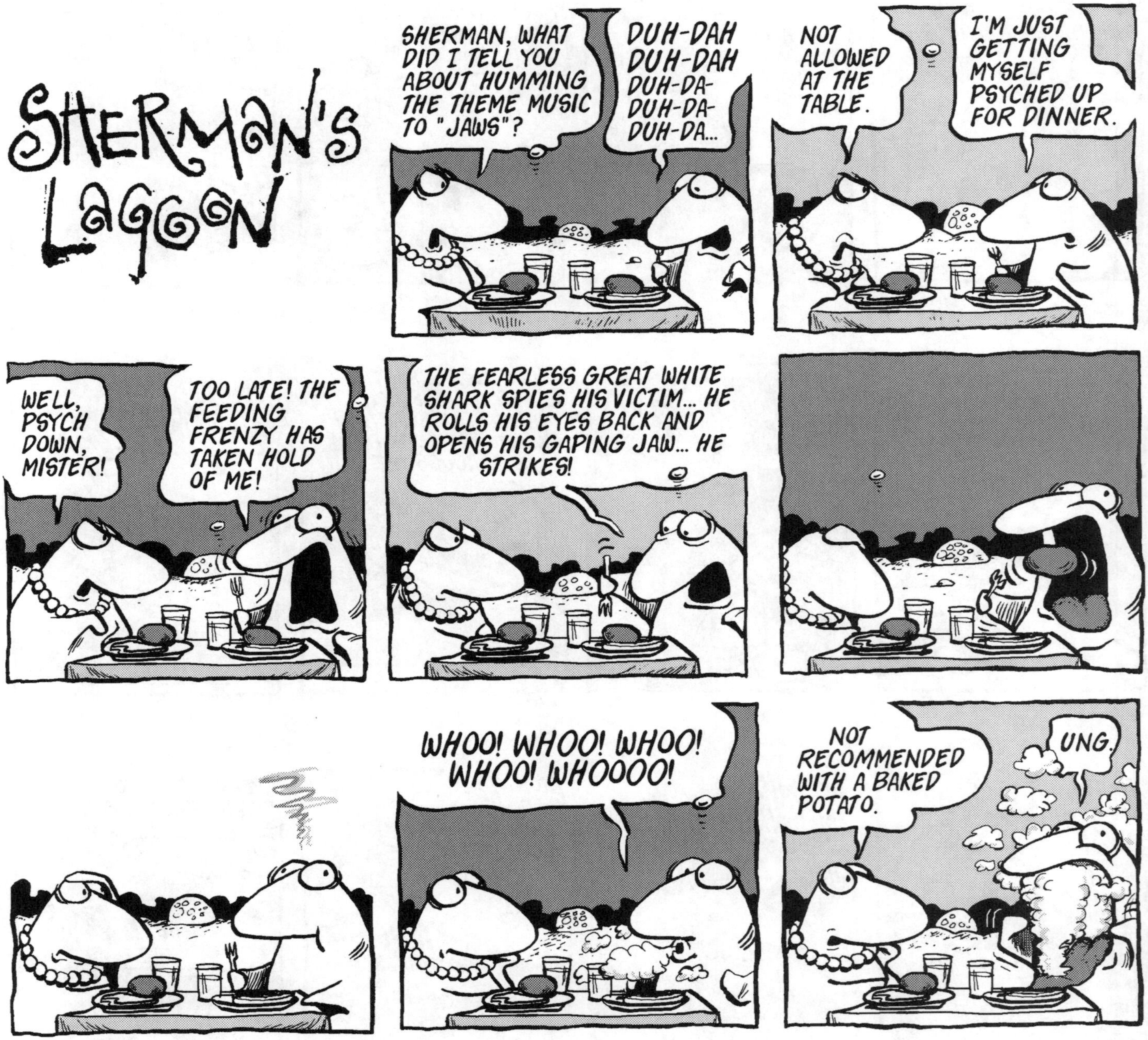
SHERMAN'S LAGOON
SHERMAN, WHAT DID I TELL YOU ABOUT HUMMING THE THEME MUSIC TO "JAWS"?
DUH-DAH DUH-DAH DUH-DA- DUH-DA- DUH-DA...
NOT ALLOWED AT THE TABLE.
I'M JUST GETTING MYSELF PSYCHED UP FOR DINNER.
WELL, PSYCH DOWN, MISTER!
TOO LATE! THE FEEDING FRENZY HAS TAKEN HOLD OF ME!
THE FEARLESS GREAT WHITE SHARK SPIES HIS VICTIM... HE ROLLS HIS EYES BACK AND OPENS HIS GAPING JAW... HE STRIKES!
WHOO! WHOO! WHOO! WHOO! WHOOOO!
NOT RECOMMENDED WITH A BAKED POTATO.
UNG.

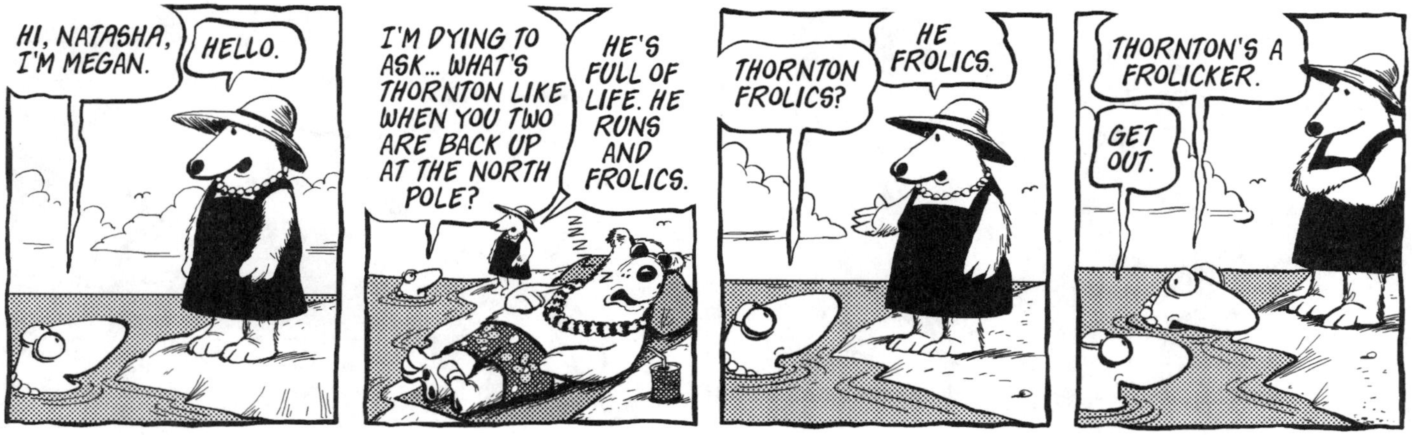
HI, NATASHA, I'M MEGAN.
HELLO.
I'M DYING TO ASK... WHAT'S THORNTON LIKE WHEN YOU TWO ARE BACK UP AT THE NORTH POLE?
HE'S FULL OF LIFE. HE RUNS AND FROLICS.
THORNTON FROLICS?
HE FROLICS.
THORNTON'S A FROLICKER.
GET OUT.

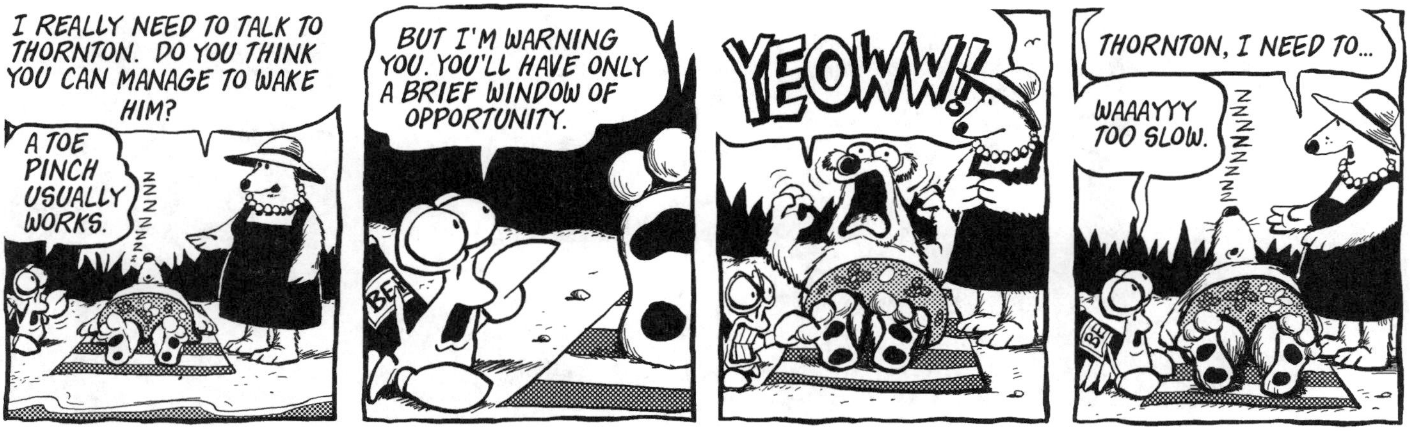
I REALLY NEED TO TALK TO THORNTON. DO YOU THINK YOU CAN MANAGE TO WAKE HIM?
A TOE PINCH USUALLY WORKS.
BUT I'M WARNING YOU. YOU'LL HAVE ONLY A BRIEF WINDOW OF OPPORTUNITY.
YEOWW!
THORNTON, I NEED TO...
WAAAYYY TOO SLOW.

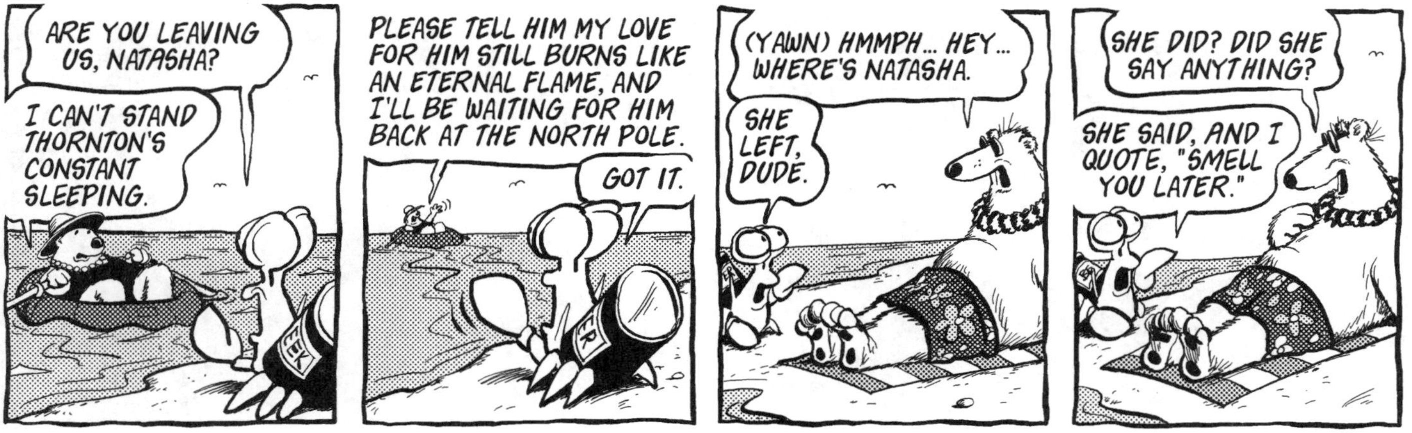
ARE YOU LEAVING US, NATASHA?
I CAN'T STAND THORNTON'S CONSTANT SLEEPING.
PLEASE TELL HIM MY LOVE FOR HIM STILL BURNS LIKE AN ETERNAL FLAME, AND I'LL BE WAITING FOR HIM BACK AT THE NORTH POLE.
GOT IT.
(YAWN) HMMPH... HEY... WHERE'S NATASHA.
SHE LEFT, DUDE.
SHE DID? DID SHE SAY ANYTHING?
SHE SAID, AND I QUOTE, "SMELL YOU LATER."

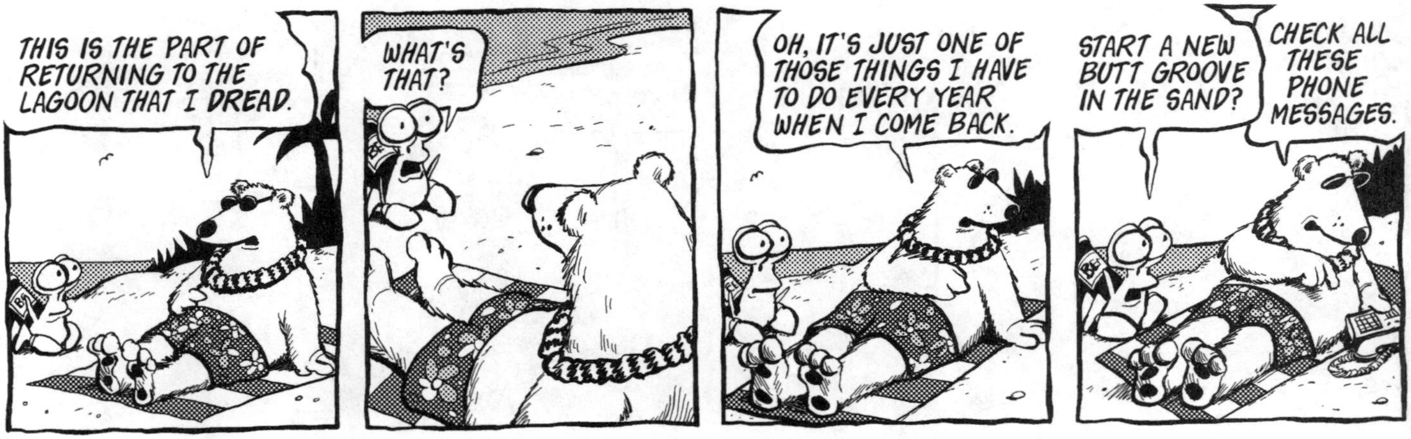
THIS IS THE PART OF RETURNING TO THE LAGOON THAT I DREAD.
WHAT'S THAT?
OH, IT'S JUST ONE OF THOSE THINGS I HAVE TO DO EVERY YEAR WHEN I COME BACK.
START A NEW BUTT GROOVE IN THE SAND?
CHECK ALL THESE PHONE MESSAGES.

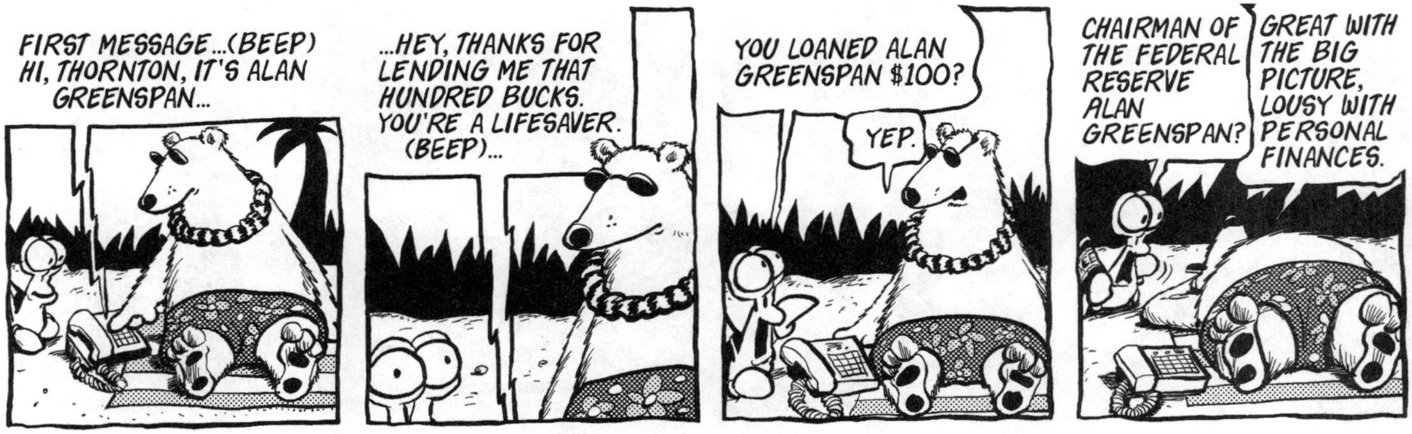
FIRST MESSAGE...(BEEP) HI, THORNTON, IT'S ALAN GREENSPAN...
...HEY, THANKS FOR LENDING ME THAT HUNDRED BUCKS. YOU'RE A LIFESAVER. (BEEP)...
YOU LOANED ALAN GREENSPAN $100?
YEP.
CHAIRMAN OF THE FEDERAL RESERVE ALAN GREENSPAN?
GREAT WITH THE BIG PICTURE, LOUSY WITH PERSONAL FINANCES.

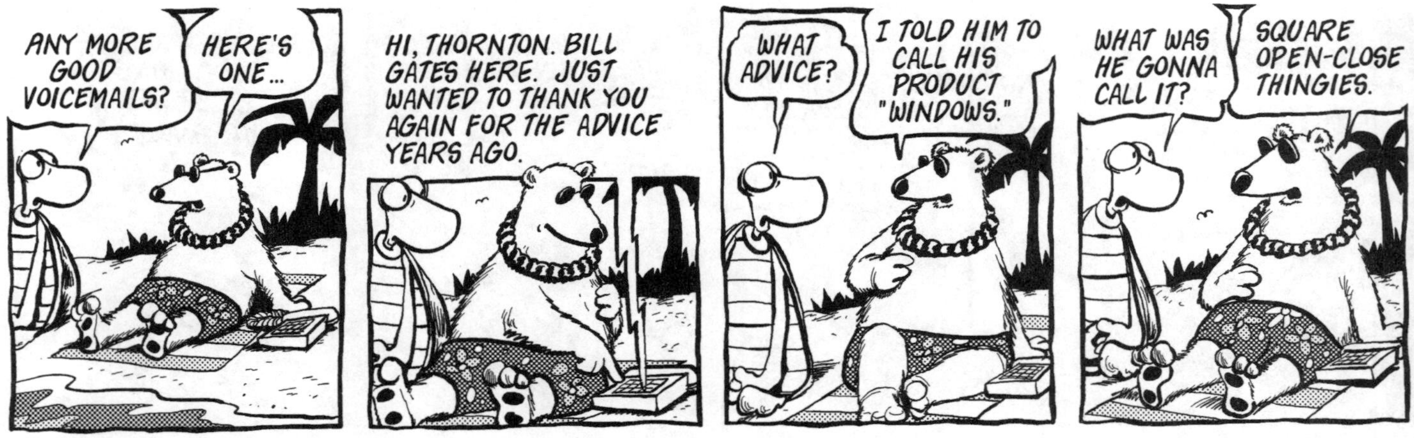
ANY MORE GOOD VOICEMAILS?
HERE'S ONE...
HI, THORNTON. BILL GATES HERE. JUST WANTED TO THANK YOU AGAIN FOR THE ADVICE YEARS AGO.
WHAT ADVICE?
I TOLD HIM TO CALL HIS PRODUCT "WINDOWS."
WHAT WAS HE GONNA CALL IT?
SQUARE OPEN-CLOSE THINGIES.

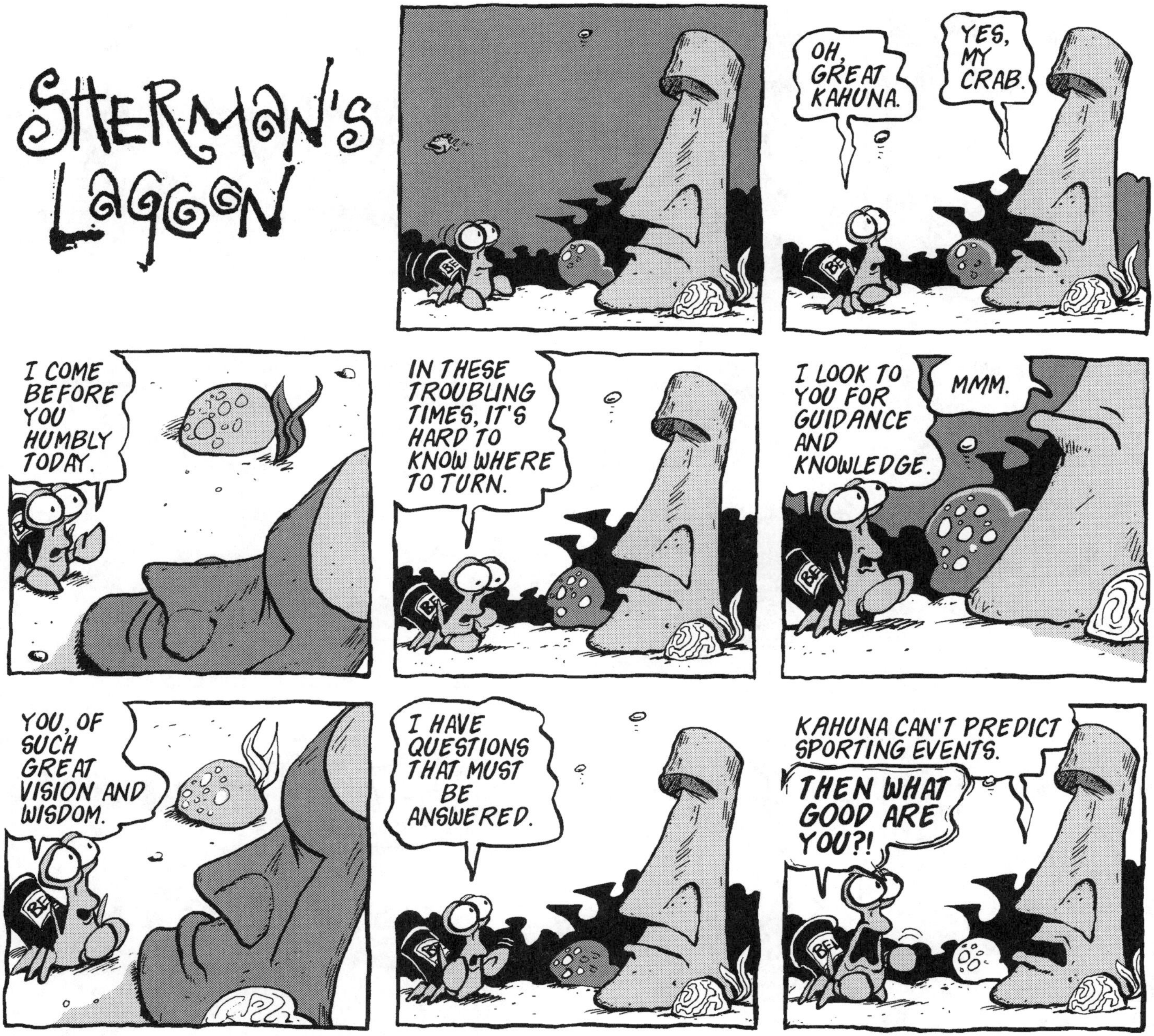
SHERMAN'S LAGOON
OH, GREAT KAHUNA.
YES, MY CRAB.
I COME BEFORE YOU HUMBLY TODAY.
IN THESE TROUBLING TIMES, IT'S HARD TO KNOW WHERE TO TURN.
I LOOK TO YOU FOR GUIDANCE AND KNOWLEDGE.
MMM.
YOU, OF SUCH GREAT VISION AND WISDOM.
I HAVE QUESTIONS THAT MUST BE ANSWERED.
KAHUNA CAN'T PREDICT SPORTING EVENTS.
THEN WHAT GOOD ARE YOU?!

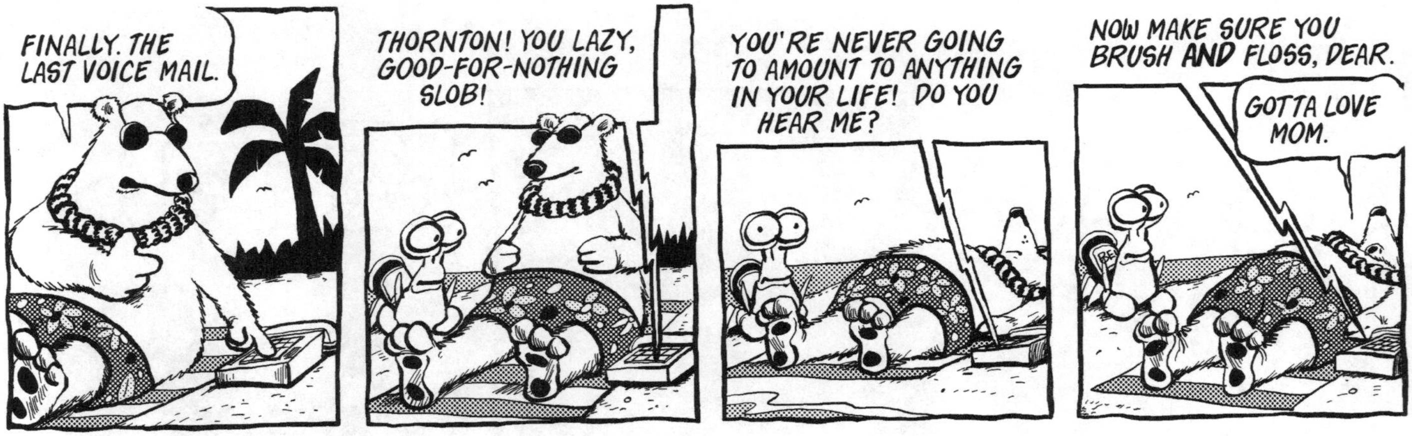
FINALLY. THE LAST VOICE MAIL.
THORNTON! YOU LAZY, GOOD-FOR-NOTHING SLOB!
YOU'RE NEVER GOING TO AMOUNT TO ANYTHING IN YOUR LIFE! DO YOU HEAR ME?
NOW MAKE SURE YOU BRUSH **AND** FLOSS, DEAR.
GOTTA LOVE MOM.

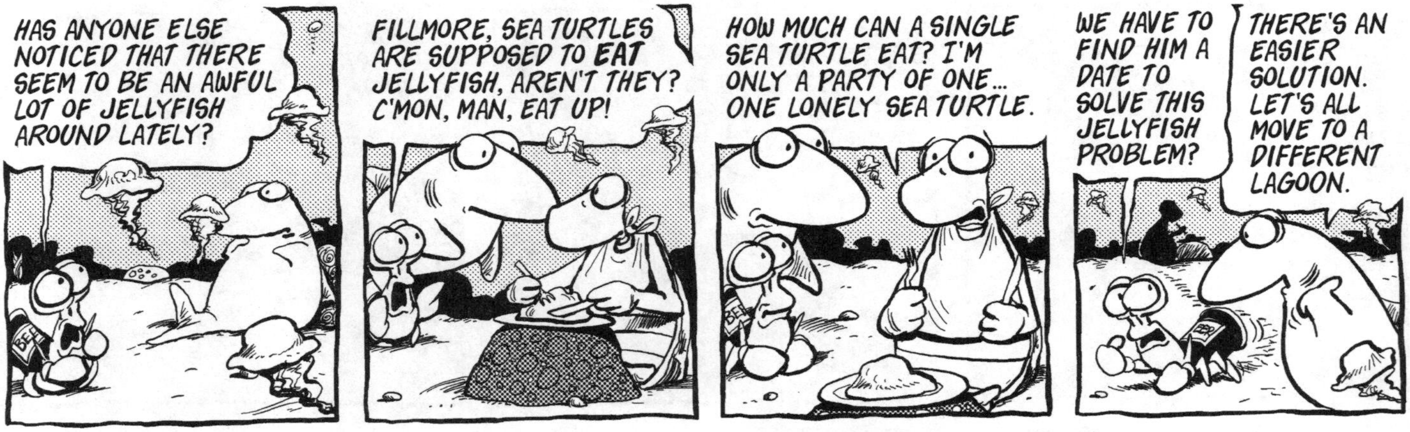
HAS ANYONE ELSE NOTICED THAT THERE SEEM TO BE AN AWFUL LOT OF JELLYFISH AROUND LATELY?
FILLMORE, SEA TURTLES ARE SUPPOSED TO **EAT** JELLYFISH, AREN'T THEY? C'MON, MAN, EAT UP!
HOW MUCH CAN A SINGLE SEA TURTLE EAT? I'M ONLY A PARTY OF ONE... ONE LONELY SEA TURTLE.
WE HAVE TO FIND HIM A DATE TO SOLVE THIS JELLYFISH PROBLEM?
THERE'S AN EASIER SOLUTION. LET'S ALL MOVE TO A DIFFERENT LAGOON.

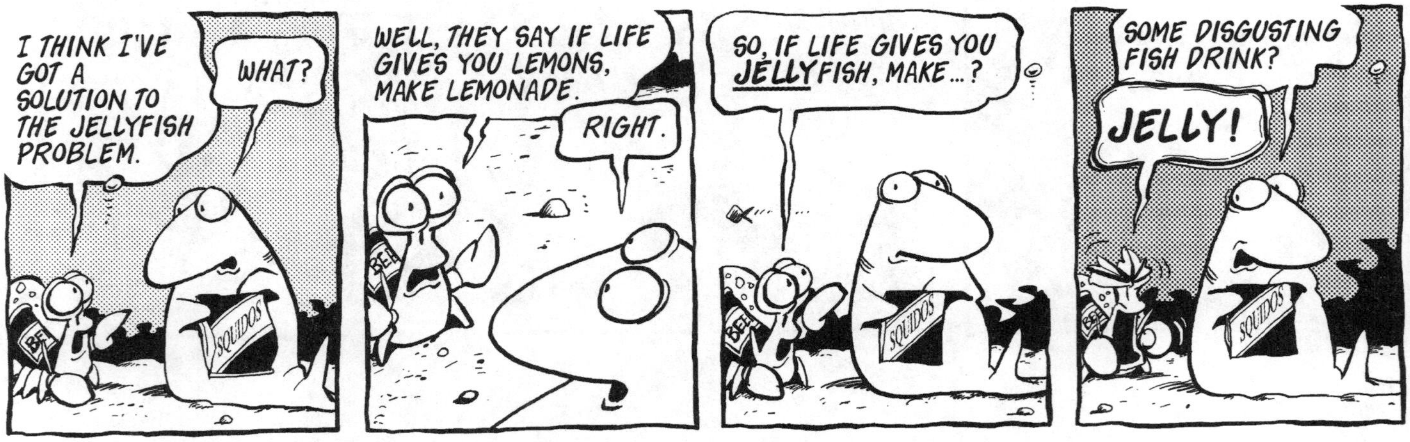
I THINK I'VE GOT A SOLUTION TO THE JELLYFISH PROBLEM.
WHAT?
WELL, THEY SAY IF LIFE GIVES YOU LEMONS, MAKE LEMONADE.
RIGHT.
SO, IF LIFE GIVES YOU JELLYFISH, MAKE...?
SOME DISGUSTING FISH DRINK?
JELLY!

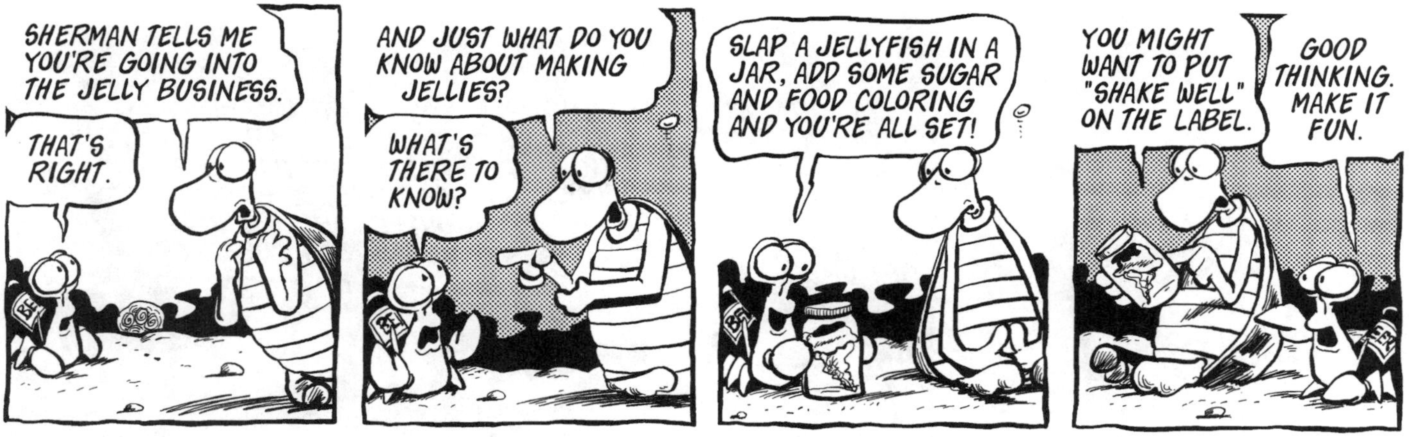
SHERMAN TELLS ME YOU'RE GOING INTO THE JELLY BUSINESS.
THAT'S RIGHT.
AND JUST WHAT DO YOU KNOW ABOUT MAKING JELLIES?
WHAT'S THERE TO KNOW?
SLAP A JELLYFISH IN A JAR, ADD SOME SUGAR AND FOOD COLORING AND YOU'RE ALL SET!
YOU MIGHT WANT TO PUT "SHAKE WELL" ON THE LABEL.
GOOD THINKING. MAKE IT FUN.

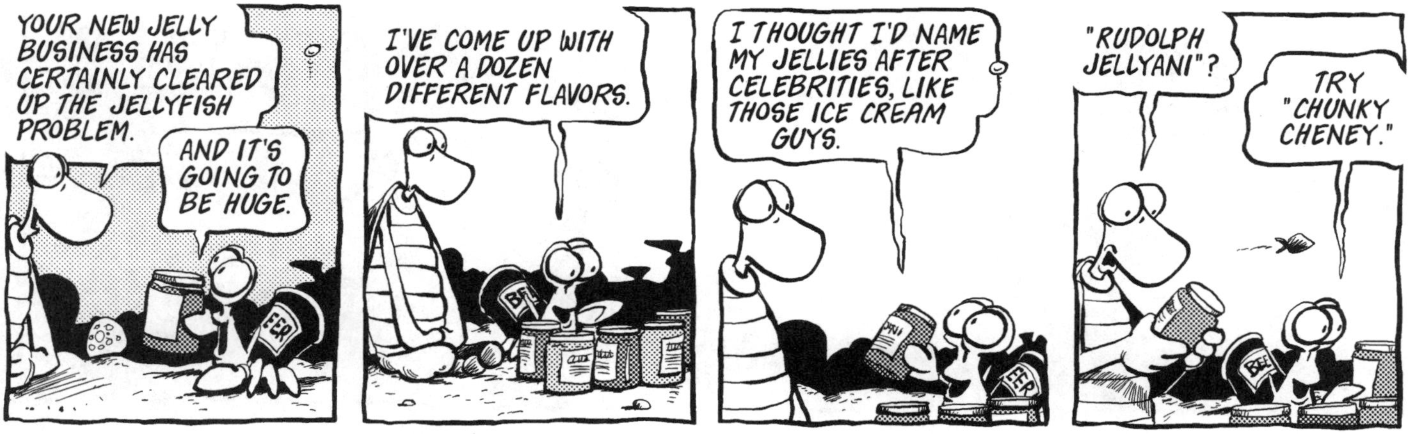
YOUR NEW JELLY BUSINESS HAS CERTAINLY CLEARED UP THE JELLYFISH PROBLEM.
AND IT'S GOING TO BE HUGE.
I'VE COME UP WITH OVER A DOZEN DIFFERENT FLAVORS.
I THOUGHT I'D NAME MY JELLIES AFTER CELEBRITIES, LIKE THOSE ICE CREAM GUYS.
"RUDOLPH JELLYANI"?
TRY "CHUNKY CHENEY."

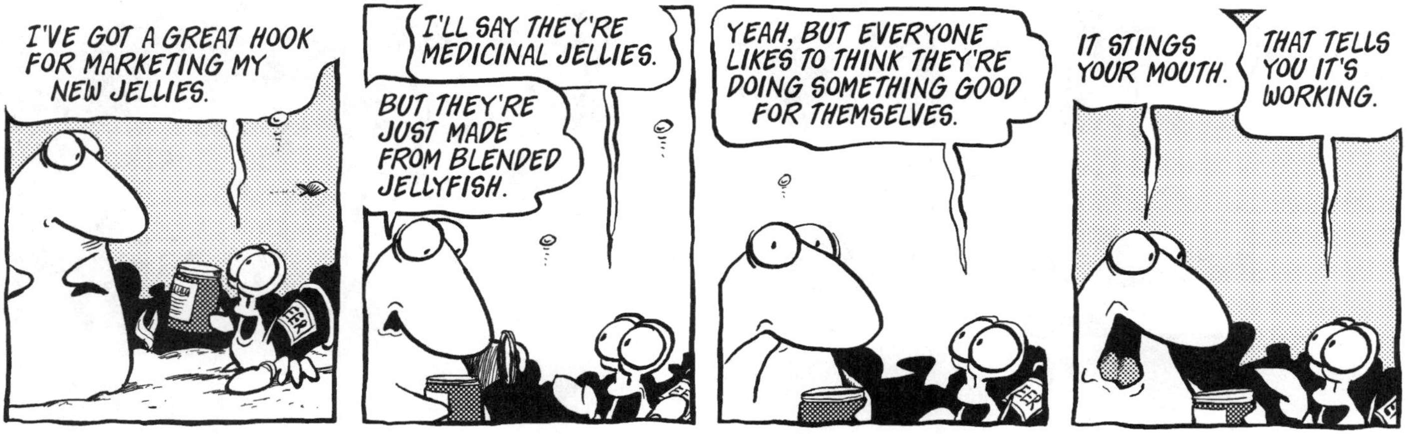
I'VE GOT A GREAT HOOK FOR MARKETING MY NEW JELLIES.
I'LL SAY THEY'RE MEDICINAL JELLIES.
BUT THEY'RE JUST MADE FROM BLENDED JELLYFISH.
YEAH, BUT EVERYONE LIKES TO THINK THEY'RE DOING SOMETHING GOOD FOR THEMSELVES.
IT STINGS YOUR MOUTH.
THAT TELLS YOU IT'S WORKING.

SHERMAN'S LAGOON

SHERMAN, WE'RE LEAVING FOR THE COSTUME PARTY IN 15 MINUTES. HURRY UP AND GET INTO YOUR COSTUME.

I DIDN'T GET ONE.

YOU DON'T HAVE A COSTUME? I SPENT DAYS MAKING MY HANGING GARDENS OF BABYLON OUTFIT, AND YOU DIDN'T EVEN GET A COSTUME?

I AM THE HANGING GARDENS OF BABYLON! I WILL NOT BE ACCOMPANIED BY A COSTUME-LESS DATE!

OH, ALL RIGHT.

THAT'S NOT A COSTUME, THAT'S A BASEBALL HAT.

I'M A BASEBALL PLAYER.

LAME! PUT SOME IMAGINATION INTO IT, MISTER!

I'M A PSYCHO BASEBALL PLAYER. WATCH OUT OR I'LL STAPLE YOU.

LET'S GO.

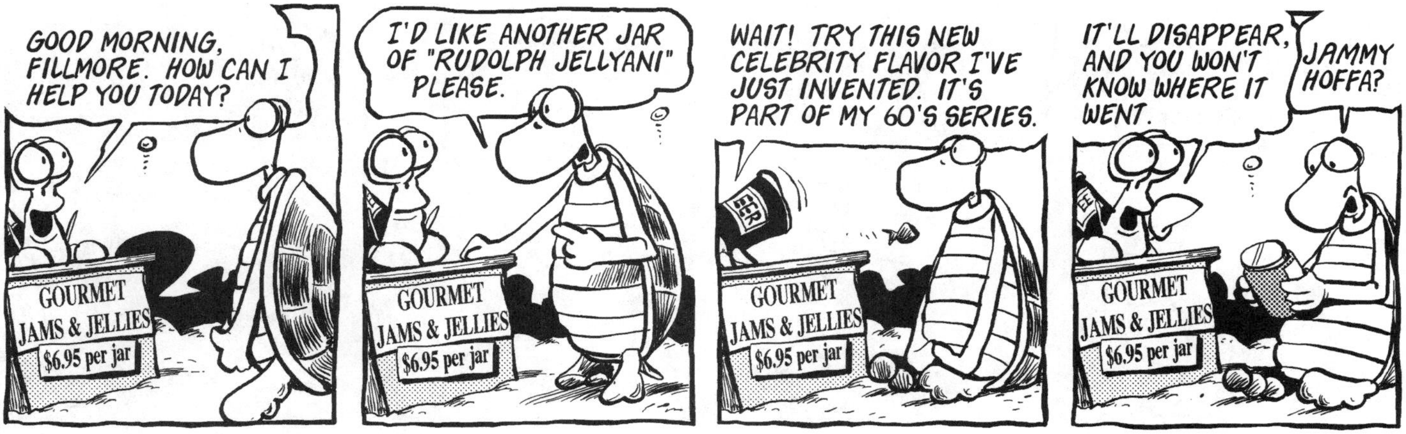
GOOD MORNING, FILLMORE. HOW CAN I HELP YOU TODAY?
GOURMET JAMS & JELLIES
$6.95 per jar
I'D LIKE ANOTHER JAR OF "RUDOLPH JELLYANI" PLEASE.
GOURMET JAMS & JELLIES
$6.95 per jar
WAIT! TRY THIS NEW CELEBRITY FLAVOR I'VE JUST INVENTED. IT'S PART OF MY 60'S SERIES.
GOURMET JAMS & JELLIES
$6.95 per jar
IT'LL DISAPPEAR, AND YOU WON'T KNOW WHERE IT WENT.
JAMMY HOFFA?
GOURMET JAMS & JELLIES
$6.95 per jar

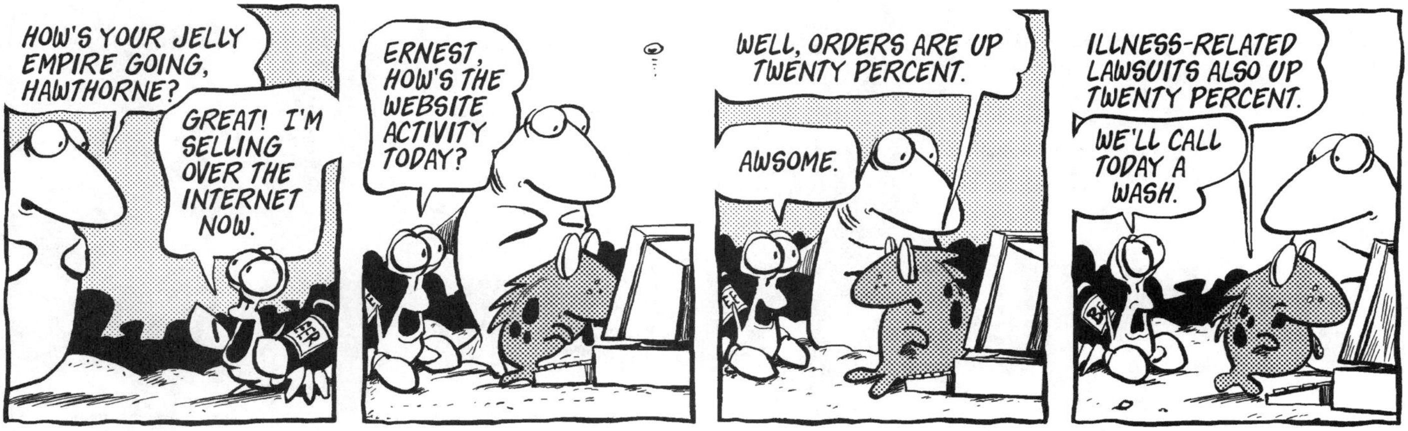
HOW'S YOUR JELLY EMPIRE GOING, HAWTHORNE?
GREAT! I'M SELLING OVER THE INTERNET NOW.
ERNEST, HOW'S THE WEBSITE ACTIVITY TODAY?
WELL, ORDERS ARE UP TWENTY PERCENT.
AWSOME.
ILLNESS-RELATED LAWSUITS ALSO UP TWENTY PERCENT.
WE'LL CALL TODAY A WASH.

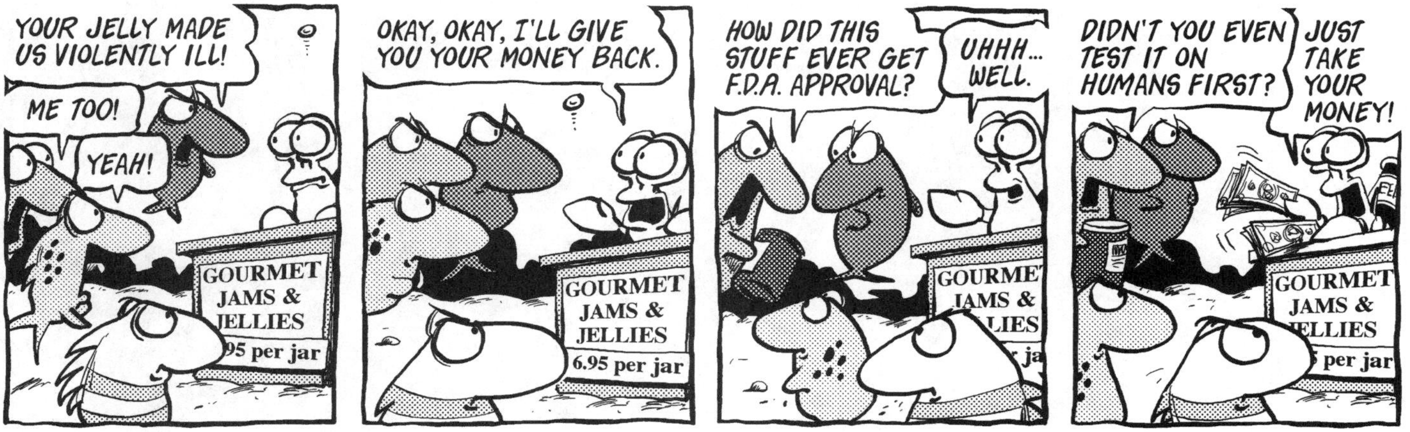
YOUR JELLY MADE US VIOLENTLY ILL!
ME TOO!
YEAH!
GOURMET JAMS & JELLIES
95 per jar
OKAY, OKAY, I'LL GIVE YOU YOUR MONEY BACK.
GOURMET JAMS & JELLIES
6.95 per jar
HOW DID THIS STUFF EVER GET F.D.A. APPROVAL?
UHHH... WELL.
DIDN'T YOU EVEN TEST IT ON HUMANS FIRST?
JUST TAKE YOUR MONEY!
GOURMET JAMS &
per jar

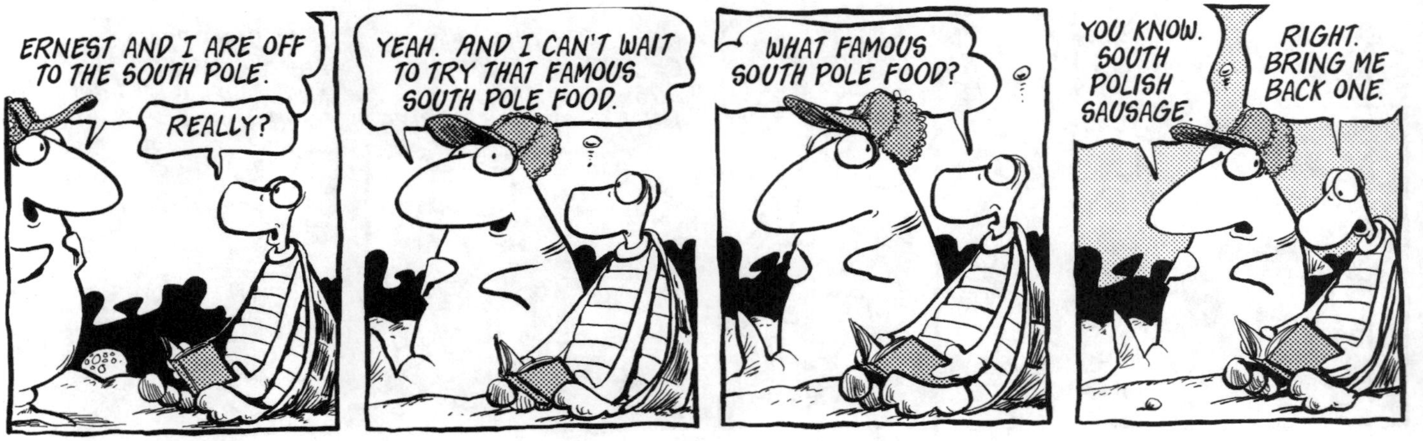
ERNEST AND I ARE OFF TO THE SOUTH POLE.
REALLY?
YEAH. AND I CAN'T WAIT TO TRY THAT FAMOUS SOUTH POLE FOOD.
WHAT FAMOUS SOUTH POLE FOOD?
YOU KNOW. SOUTH POLISH SAUSAGE.
RIGHT. BRING ME BACK ONE.

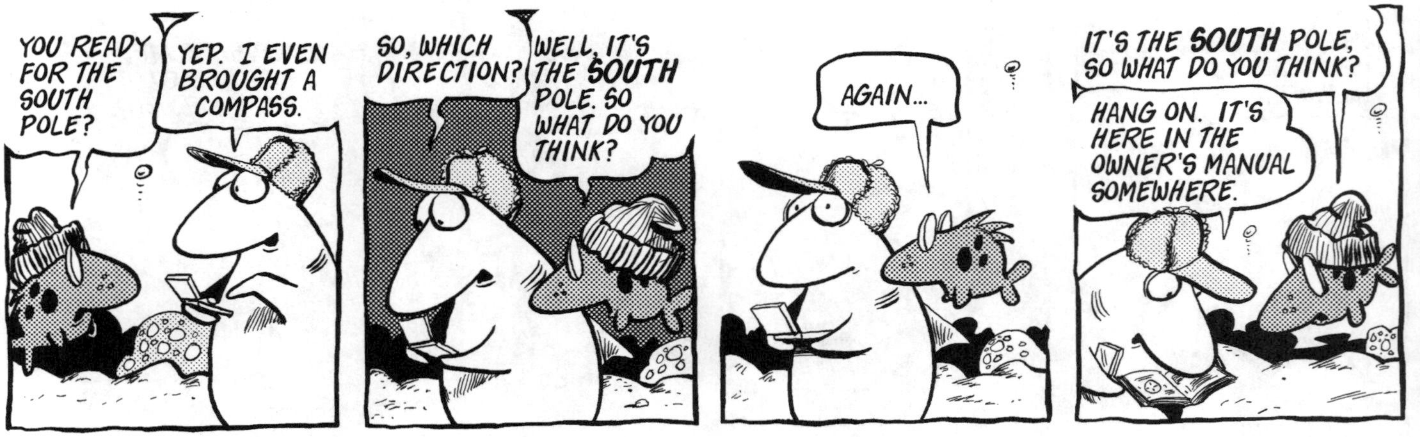
YOU READY FOR THE SOUTH POLE?
YEP. I EVEN BROUGHT A COMPASS.
SO, WHICH DIRECTION?
WELL, IT'S THE SOUTH POLE. SO WHAT DO YOU THINK?
AGAIN...
IT'S THE SOUTH POLE, SO WHAT DO YOU THINK?
HANG ON. IT'S HERE IN THE OWNER'S MANUAL SOMEWHERE.

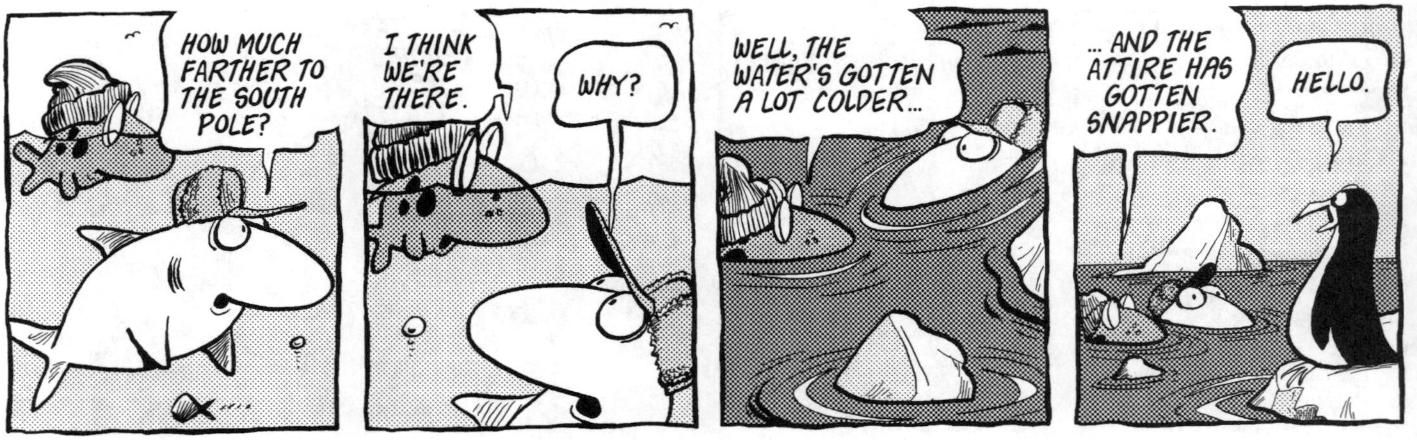
HOW MUCH FARTHER TO THE SOUTH POLE?
I THINK WE'RE THERE.
WHY?
WELL, THE WATER'S GOTTEN A LOT COLDER...
... AND THE ATTIRE HAS GOTTEN SNAPPIER.
HELLO.

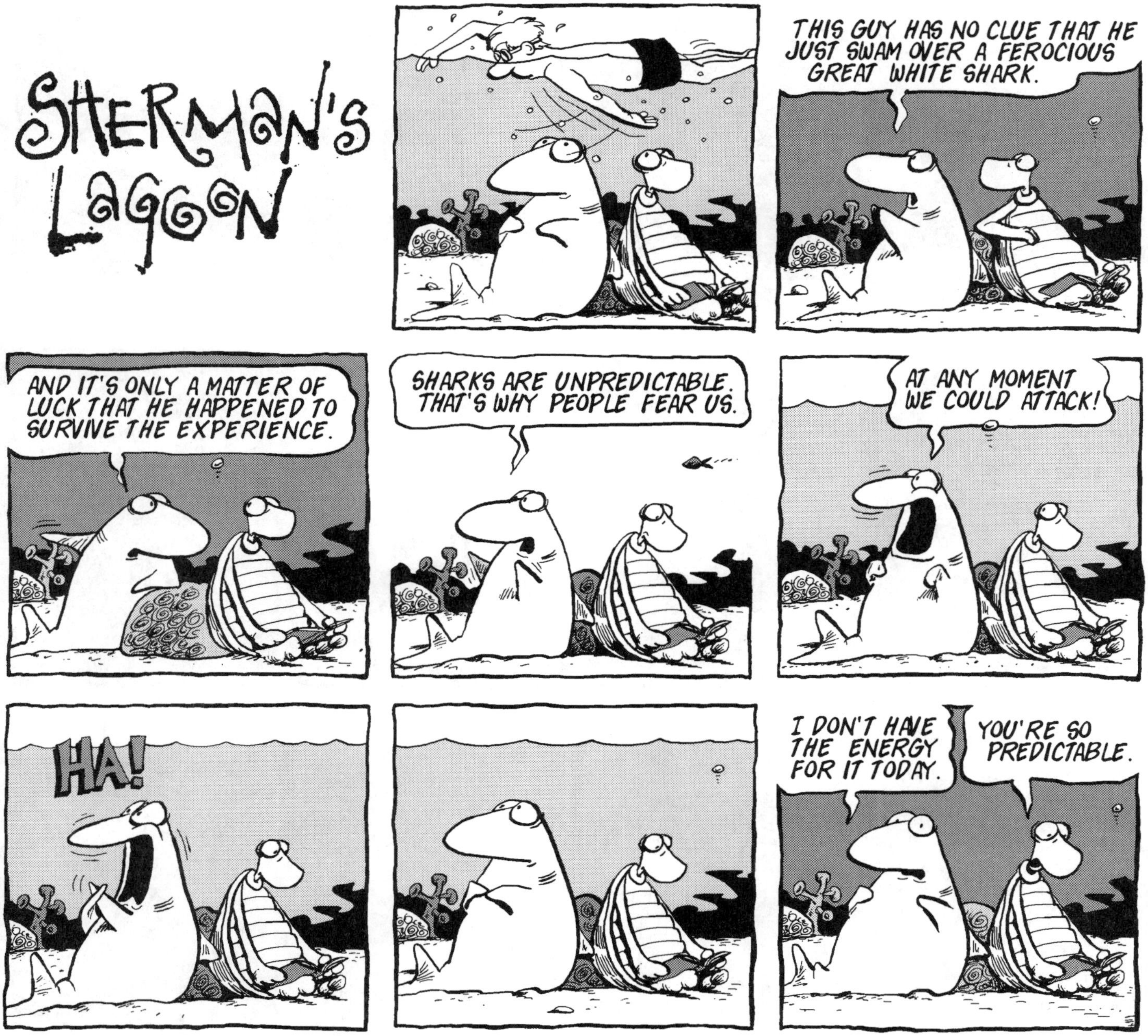
SHERMAN'S LAGOON
THIS GUY HAS NO CLUE THAT HE JUST SWAM OVER A FEROCIOUS GREAT WHITE SHARK.
AND IT'S ONLY A MATTER OF LUCK THAT HE HAPPENED TO SURVIVE THE EXPERIENCE.
SHARKS ARE UNPREDICTABLE. THAT'S WHY PEOPLE FEAR US.
AT ANY MOMENT WE COULD ATTACK!
HA!
I DON'T HAVE THE ENERGY FOR IT TODAY.
YOU'RE SO PREDICTABLE.

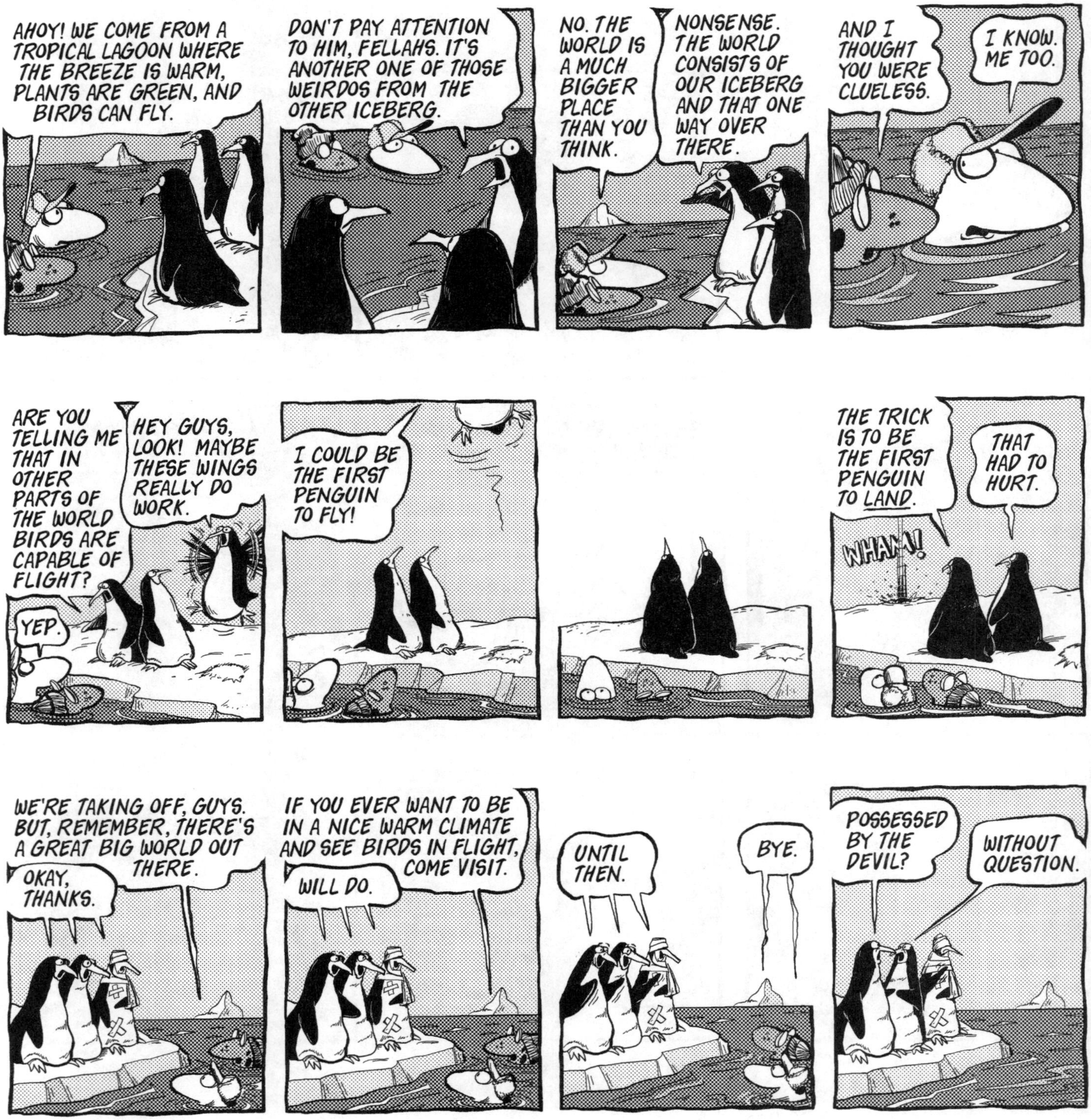
AHOY! WE COME FROM A TROPICAL LAGOON WHERE THE BREEZE IS WARM, PLANTS ARE GREEN, AND BIRDS CAN FLY.
DON'T PAY ATTENTION TO HIM, FELLAHS. IT'S ANOTHER ONE OF THOSE WEIRDOS FROM THE OTHER ICEBERG.
NO. THE WORLD IS A MUCH BIGGER PLACE THAN YOU THINK.
NONSENSE. THE WORLD CONSISTS OF OUR ICEBERG AND THAT ONE WAY OVER THERE.
AND I THOUGHT YOU WERE CLUELESS.
I KNOW. ME TOO.
ARE YOU TELLING ME THAT IN OTHER PARTS OF THE WORLD BIRDS ARE CAPABLE OF FLIGHT?
HEY GUYS, LOOK! MAYBE THESE WINGS REALLY DO WORK.
YEP.
I COULD BE THE FIRST PENGUIN TO FLY!
THE TRICK IS TO BE THE FIRST PENGUIN TO LAND.
THAT HAD TO HURT.
WHAM!
WE'RE TAKING OFF, GUYS. BUT, REMEMBER, THERE'S A GREAT BIG WORLD OUT THERE.
OKAY, THANKS.
IF YOU EVER WANT TO BE IN A NICE WARM CLIMATE AND SEE BIRDS IN FLIGHT, COME VISIT.
WILL DO.
UNTIL THEN.
BYE.
POSSESSED BY THE DEVIL?
WITHOUT QUESTION.

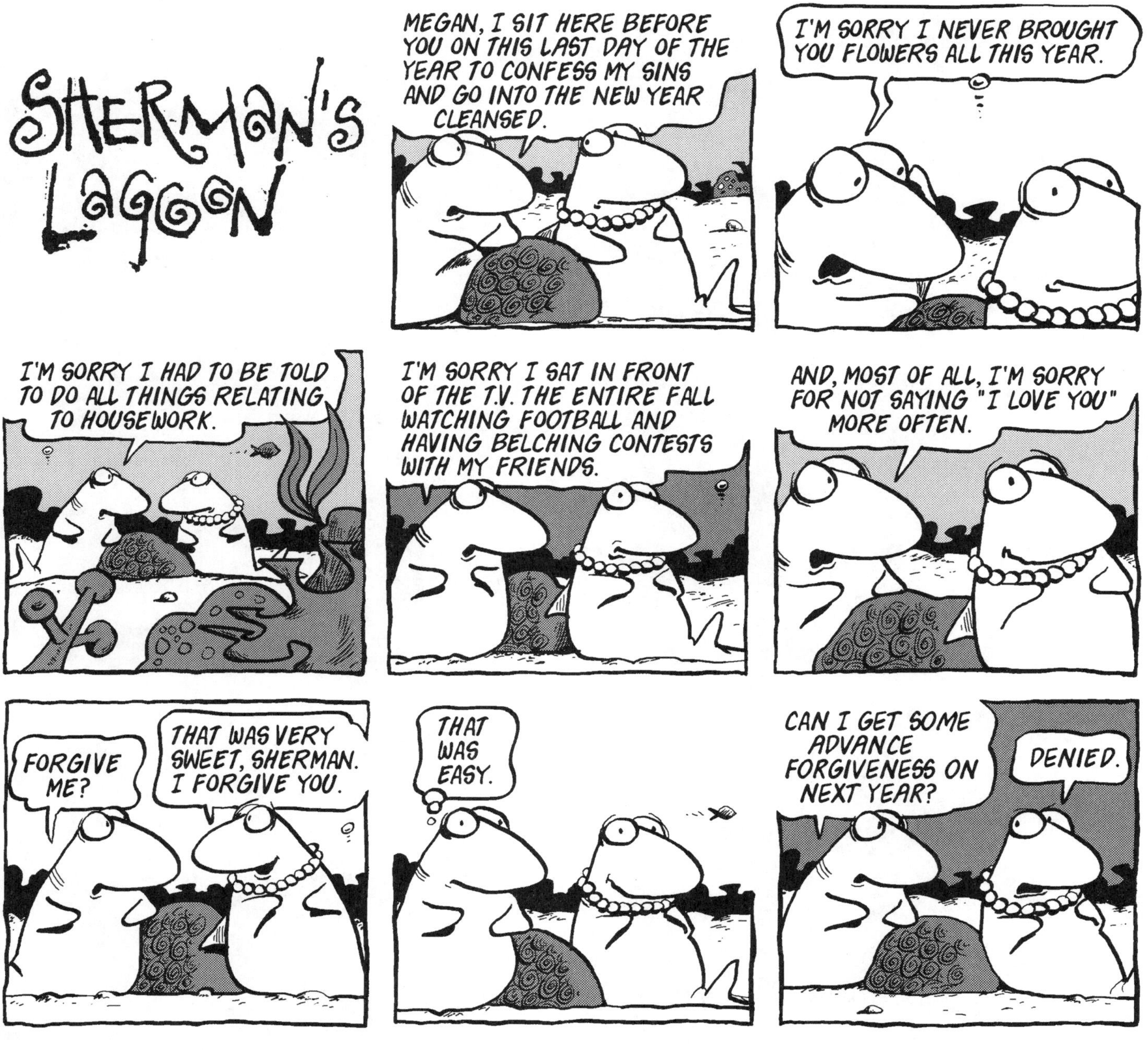
SHERMAN'S LAGOON
MEGAN, I SIT HERE BEFORE YOU ON THIS LAST DAY OF THE YEAR TO CONFESS MY SINS AND GO INTO THE NEW YEAR CLEANSED.
I'M SORRY I NEVER BROUGHT YOU FLOWERS ALL THIS YEAR.
I'M SORRY I HAD TO BE TOLD TO DO ALL THINGS RELATING TO HOUSEWORK.
I'M SORRY I SAT IN FRONT OF THE T.V. THE ENTIRE FALL WATCHING FOOTBALL AND HAVING BELCHING CONTESTS WITH MY FRIENDS.
AND, MOST OF ALL, I'M SORRY FOR NOT SAYING "I LOVE YOU" MORE OFTEN.
FORGIVE ME?
THAT WAS VERY SWEET, SHERMAN. I FORGIVE YOU.
THAT WAS EASY.
CAN I GET SOME ADVANCE FORGIVENESS ON NEXT YEAR?
DENIED.